EDIE

E D I E

An American Biography

by Jean Stein

edited with George Plimpton

Alfred A. Knopf New York 1982

Picture credits appear on pages 454–455.

LIBRARY OF CONGRESS CATALOGING IN PUBLICATION DATA
Stein, Jean.
Edie, an American biography.
1. Sedgwick, Edie.   2. Moving-picture actors and
actresses—United States—Biography.
I. Plimpton, George.   II. Title.
PN2887.S83   791.43′028′0924   [B]   81-48118
ISBN 0-394-48819-9   AACR2

At the back of the book, among the Addenda, are a Sedgwick family tree, an afterword, acknowledgments, and biographical notes.

EDIE

1

JOHN P. MARQUAND, JR.   Have you ever seen the old graveyard up there in Stockbridge? In one corner is the family's burial place; it's called the Sedgwick Pie. The Pie is rather handsome. In the center Judge Theodore Sedgwick, the first of the Stockbridge Sedgwicks and a great-great-great-grandfather of Edie's and of mine, is buried under his tombstone, a high rising obelisk, and his wife Pamela is beside him. They are like the king and queen on a chessboard, and all around them like a pie are more modest stones, put in layers, back and round in a circle. The descendants of Judge Sedgwick, from generation unto generation, are all buried with their heads facing out and their feet pointing in toward their ancestor. The legend is that on Judgment Day when they arise and face the Judge, they will have to see no one but Sedgwicks.

Judge Sedgwick moved to Stockbridge right after the Revolution. I'm afraid he is going to smite me down if I go on talking this way, but he certainly did ingratiate himself with the movers and shakers of his day. He was a political ally of Alexander Hamilton and George Washington, and he became Speaker of the House of Representatives. He wasn't a signer of the Declaration of Independence but he was in with all those people. There's a picture in the old Sedgwick house of Martha Washington's first reception and Judge Sedgwick and Pamela are in this picture. Poor woman, halfway through her life she went mad.

As a child I heard that her condition was due to having been left alone in Stockbridge through many winters while the Judge was politicking in New York and Philadelphia and Washington. Pamela Sedgwick may have been one of the first American wives to be the martyr of her husband's political ambitions. The epitaph on her grave is sad testimony:

SHE LONG ENDURED AND WITH PATIENCE SUPPORTED
UNPARALLELED SUFFERINGS:
A BRIGHT EXAMPLE
OF
CHRISTIAN PATIENCE AND RESIGNATION

Anybody who is a descendant of the Judge may be buried in the Pie. But at the Judge's feet lies a woman named Elizabeth Freeman, known to the family as Mumbet. She is supposed to have been the first freed slave in the Commonwealth of Massachusetts. The story goes that she happened to hear the Declaration of Independence read aloud at a town meeting. I recall reports that Mumbet's owner treated her cruelly, that he beat her up with a warming pan, that sort of thing. She ran away and sought out Judge Sedgwick and said, "Sir, I heard that we are all born equal and every one of us has the right to be free" and Judge Sedgwick was so impressed that he argued for her freedom. Mumbet stayed with him in gratitude for the rest of her life. An odd detail is that close by Mumbet's grave another grave is marked with the bronze figure of a dog that lies beneath it. I never learned precisely who owned that dog or whether the Judge had not also set it free.

Lying next to Mumbet is Judge Sedgwick's daughter, Catharine. She was a spinster and a novelist in the early 1800s and the author of *A New England Tale* which was widely read at the time. Catharine used to give literary parties in the Old House—I've heard that Hawthorne and Melville came to tea. Despite her literary propensities, Catharine Sedgwick remained intensely loyal to her many brothers and sisters and to Stockbridge. Someone is supposed to have told her that she spoke of Stockbridge as if it were Heaven, to which Catharine replied, "I expect no very violent transition."

Catharine's brother Charles lies next to her in the Pie. He was an addled man who wandered about giving speeches to his livestock, especially to a favorite cow. One of his servants is thought to have said: "Ah, I'd rather be Mr. Sedgwick than anybody else in the wide world, and next to that I'd rather be Mr. Sedgwick's cow!"

The Sedgwick Pie, Stockbridge, Massachusetts

SAUCIE SEDGWICK   Although Judge Sedgwick lived in Boston toward the end of his life when he was Chief Justice of the Supreme Judicial Court of Massachusetts, the family was always based in Stockbridge, where the Judge had built the Sedgwick mansion just after the Revolution. It has always been the Old House to the family, and a real haven and home. They lived rather quietly, always well educated and fairly well off, brought up to think of themselves as neither rich nor poor.

JOHN P. MARQUAND, JR.   It's important to think of the Sedgwicks not as Bostonians but as from Western Massachusetts—what the Kennedys call "the Western *paht* of the state"—Berkshire County about fifteen miles below Pittsfield, which is the main metropolis in that area. The only Sedgwicks who could even remotely be called Bostonian were those who married into Bostonian families. Historically, this part of the state was once heavily populated with the Stockbridge Indians, who were much more interesting than anybody else, including the Sedgwicks. Jonathan Edwards, the great Calvinist divine and hellfire-and-brimstone preacher, was sent up there to establish a mission when he fell into disgrace with the Hartford establishment of the church. He was sent to Stockbridge to do penance, and it may be that the Indians were the first to hear his famous sermon about man's soul . . . the one where he says that the grace of God is the strand of web which keeps a man suspended above the fires of hell. Robert Lowell wrote a beautiful poem about that—"Jonathan Edwards in Western Massachusetts."

The irony is that today on the site of Jonathan Edwards' residence is the Riggs Center, a very fancy nut house for young people. Some of the Sedgwicks passed through there. It's right across the street from the Old House.

Stockbridge and the Sedgwick tradition can be somewhat intimidating. One year I took Norman Podhoretz, the editor of *Commentary,* up to see Stockbridge and the Sedgwick Pie and the rest of the Sedgwick world . . . a sort of cultural exchange in which I was going to take him on a tour of Waspland. I told Norman that it was going to be like taking a trip to the other side of the moon. To give him a bit of a foretaste of what he might be running into, I had him read *In Praise of Gentlemen,* written by my great-uncle Henry Dwight Sedgwick, who was called Babbo in his family. It produced quite a reaction. As Norman and his wife, Midge Decter, were putting their suitcase in the

trunk of our car, he said, "Look, I've got to tell you before we go anywhere that I *hated* that book by your uncle. I don't think I'm going to
like any of those people or anything else if it's like that book. There's
no excuse for such views." I tried to calm him by saying that the old
gentleman was from another era, and besides he was dead. Norman
kept saying, "That doesn't matter, there's just absolutely nothing to be
said in defense of a book like that. He's taking the view that the only
people who have made it are God's gentlemen and that *they* don't have
to try any more—that's a tremendous insult."

As we drove along, Norman wouldn't even help with the directions.
I'd say, "Ask this guy which way to turn," and he'd say, "*You* better do
it, these are your people." He began to get more and more apprehen-
sive the closer we got to Stockbridge, as if we were going into some
sort of enemy world. In fact, I heard afterwards he told somebody that
he and Midge felt like—it was some Russian reference—yes, that they
were like little people hiding in the snowdrifts from the Cossacks. The
Cossacks were going to pour out of the Sedgwick house and just beat
up on everyone.

The weekend turned out to be a collision of cultures. I remember at
one point Norman asked me where all the Sedgwick money came
from—a question he never would have asked if he had read Babbo's
book carefully: you're not supposed to ask things like that. And that's
what I told him—that I didn't really know, it's just *there*, and that he
shouldn't ask, which made him furious at my implicit arrogance. But
it's a question which would occur to anyone, particularly a very intelligent man like Norman and a journalist to boot. Anyone would want
to know where all that loot came from. No, it wasn't at all easy for
Norman.

I took them to see the Sedgwick Pie. It was winter with a heavy snow
on the ground so that the Pie became rather more impressive or op-
pressive, depending on what you thought of it, with evergreens all
around and this great drooping snow everywhere. Norman was trying
to suppress a great deal of hostility and handle it nicely because we
were friends. I pointed out a cousin of mine named Kate Delafield
who was buried there, saying, "And that's my cousin Kate." Upon
which Norman began to sing . . . he did a strange little dance . . .
snapping his fingers to the rhythm of "I wish I could shimmy like my
sister Kate!" Lillian Hellman, who had come along for the fun, wasn't
interested in the Sedgwick Pie. She wanted to get to the Ritz in Boston.
She kept asking: "When are we going to get to the Ritz?"

Even family feeling is not unanimous about the Pie. I've heard of a quarrel which took place on the main street of Stockbridge. A Cabot shouted across the street at her Sedgwick sister-in-law, "At least *my* family's graveyard isn't the *laughingstock* of the entire Eastern seaboard." But most of the Sedgwicks take it very seriously. In 1971 my cousin Minturn Sedgwick, Edie's uncle, wrote a letter to the town Selectmen asking the town to return some property next to the Pie which the family had donated to the community. By the year 2101, he prophesied, the Pie would be overcrowded with Sedgwicks, and if more land was not made available, the Sedgwicks would have nowhere to go. The Selectmen considered all this carefully and replied to Minturn that since the Doomsday date for the family was well over a century away, his anxiety seemed premature.

Minturn had always been very much involved in the traditions of the Pie. For a long time, I remember, he'd been looking for the family pall, a deep purple cloth that's put over the casket. Apparently it was missing. The tradition was that the casket, with the pall over it, was taken about Stockbridge not in a hearse but in an open cart, like a gun carriage, drawn by a black horse and hung with hemlock and a few white lilacs. An elderly mailman, Thomas Carey, led the horse on foot. They'd leave the funeral services in the small Episcopalian stone church, St. Paul's, and the family and friends would walk along behind the cortege. When the procession passed the Sedgwick house, it stopped for a moment of silence, and then everyone continued on up the main street to the graveyard and the Pie.

Three or four days after John F. Kennedy's funeral I received a letter from Minturn which I gave to my aunt, who took one look at it and said, "Oh, no, no, no . . . it's got to be *burned!*" Minturn's letter reported that he had heard from a cousin, Charles Sedgwick, who for a brief period had done some interpreting in French for President Kennedy, that Kennedy knew all about the Sedgwick Pie, and Minturn wondered after having watched the sad but impressive events of the Kennedy funeral on television—the casket on the horse-drawn cart, the widow and the mourners walking along behind, and so forth—if perhaps Mrs. Kennedy hadn't "borrowed" the idea from us. That was the way he put it: "borrowed"—with quotes around it. Such was Minturn's curiosity that he sent a self-addressed stamped postcard on which I was to inform him whether it was indeed true that Mrs. Kennedy had "borrowed" our funeral procedures.

As I say, that would have been just like Minturn. The Pie meant a great deal to him. He stocked up on simple coffins—ornate mahogany coffins with gold handles just aren't used by the Sedgwicks. But it's very difficult to buy a simple coffin: if you ask for just a plain Puritan pine box, the undertakers look at you with disgust and they say, "Oh, we have those for the potter's field, Mac—for paupers, city cases." Minturn persisted, apparently. He got a whole stack of simple pine boxes up in Pittsfield somewhere—certainly enough for his immediate family. A Stockbridge woman friend of mine who plays the organ at the church and is hired to perform at funerals told me that the local undertaker simply couldn't understand this man, Minturn Sedgwick, who not only insisted on these plain boxes but got into them and "tested" them. He was a big man, a famous Harvard football player, and he got into his box to make sure it was long enough and would accommodate his shoulders.

ALEXANDER SEDGWICK   There's a General William Bond in the Sedgwick Pie who may be somewhat surprised to find himself rising and facing Judge Sedgwick on the Day of Resurrection. He was one of the few field generals killed in the Vietnam War—he was picked off by a sniper as he was climbing out of a helicopter to take over his command—and he probably would have ended up in the Arlington cemetery if it hadn't been for his Sedgwick wife, Theodora, who felt that since the General was married to a Sedgwick he ought to be buried up in Stockbridge. Theodora was a very staunch Sedgwick. She was once overheard saying to a companion at the bar in the Red Lion Inn in Stockbridge: "I was a Sedgwick; therefore I *am* a Sedgwick." So it wasn't surprising that her husband would end up in the Pie. Actually, there were *two* funerals—the first at the military cemetery at Arlington, a service full of pageantry—a riderless horse with the stirrups up, and General Westmoreland there—and suddenly, just at the point when the coffin would normally be lowered into the ground, a hearse drove up and the coffin was transferred into it . . . almost as if the Sedgwicks were plucking the General from his sleep among the military heroes and hauling him back to the bosom of the family. The Army didn't let go of him easily. It sent a detachment of Green Berets to Stockbridge as part of the honor escort. They caused quite a stir. The troops—almost a company of them—marched up and down the village streets and scared the life out of the hippies who were thronging the place in the 1960s, a lot of them draft-dodgers who must have assumed the Berets had been sent to get *them*.

So General Bond was seen to his hero's funeral in the Sedgwick Pie. He's buried right behind Ellery Sedgwick, his wife's father.

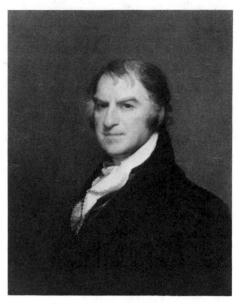

Elizabeth Freeman
(Mumbet, 1742?–1829)
by Susan Sedgwick

Judge Theodore Sedgwick
(1746–1813)
by Gilbert Stuart

The three Sedgwick brothers (*left to right*):
Theodore, Henry Dwight (Babbo), and Ellery

JOHN P. MARQUAND, JR.   My great-uncle Ellery Sedgwick is one of
the best-known members of the Sedgwick clan. He became the editor
of the *Atlantic Monthly* in about 1905 and maintained its influence
and status during the Twenties and Thirties. I always thought him a
pretentious, rather arrogant man with an enormous ego. He was born
in New York in a house where Radio City Music Hall now stands,
about which he says in his memoirs, *The Happy Profession*—one hopes
jokingly—"What an appropriate memorial to me!" Toward the end of
his life he became very reactionary—a friend of Generalissimo Franco
and so forth. He was quite a snob, which was not surprising for a
Sedgwick. The Sedgwicks always looked down on my father when he
married into the family—they just didn't like the idea of their darling
daughter Christina throwing herself away on a penniless nobody they
must have thought of as a beatnik—but when my father made it as
an author, Ellery began to suck up to him. I always felt my father
never should have given in to this sort of behavior, but at the end of
his life he was always delighted to lunch with Ellery in Boston at the
Somerset Club. When my father was young he was very insecure
among them—so he must have found it comforting when they accepted him.

The Sedgwick my father was most impressed by was Minturn Sedgwick, and that for his athletic prowess—he was a Harvard legend. He
was on the team that won the Rose Bowl against Oregon. When I was
a little boy running around between people's legs at a cocktail party,
I remember my father calling out, "Minturn, show us how you did it"—
really terribly interested—and he'd go on, "Minturn, how did you get
down there and *crouch* in the line, I mean when you were playing
against Princeton, what position did you assume? How did you
charge?" . . . and they'd get Minturn down in his football stance at
that party, charging up and down among the guests standing there
drinking cocktails.

Of course, my father wasn't above getting some mileage out of the
Sedgwicks for his books—the Sedgwick Pie, for example. In *The Late
George Apley* there's an old-maid cousin, a distant family connection
named Hattie, who gets buried in the wrong place in the family plot,
indeed in what George Apley considers his *own* segment, and there's
quite a lot of correspondence about whether Cousin Hattie shouldn't
be dug up and moved to where she might more properly belong. I
don't know what the Sedgwicks made of this fun at their expense—it
didn't keep Ellery from asking father to those Somerset lunches. But
Ellery was a very smart man.

HARRY SEDGWICK Ellery was a dominating, difficult, and exciting man, lacking none of that outstanding Sedgwick male quality, charm. He was very different from his older brother, Babbo, who was Edie's and my grandfather: Babbo the dandy, the scholar, epicurean, lover of beautiful countries—France, Spain, and Greece—beautiful literature, and, last but by no means least, beautiful women. Ellery was the hard-headed, tough businessman. Though his business was literature, he always knew how to get things done, understood the workings of power, and always had his eye on the "bottom line." Ellery's second wife, Marjorie, put it very well: "Your grandfather Babbo was the most charming man that ever lived, but your uncle Ellery has more solid virtues."

Babbo lived until he was ninety-five. He could remember people shouting in the streets of Stockbridge that Abraham Lincoln had been shot. He was especially anxious to outlive his Harvard classmate Godfrey Cabot—known to his Cabot nephews and nieces as Uncle God—who was a teetotaler. Babbo always referred to him as a "disgrace to the class of '82," and worried that if Cabot outlived his classmates he would credit abstinence from alcohol as the reason. I remember hearing about a class dinner at which five of them turned up. There they were, these wonderful old Harvard men in their nineties gathering for a reunion supper, and Cabot, who was the secretary of the class, had, of course, ordered no wine. This was more than Babbo could bear. He stood up on a chair and called out, "Champagne!" He reported afterwards that one of his elderly classmates, a man he could not recall having ever met before, looked over and said, "I'm *so* glad you came."

There was a family rumor that Babbo had been offered the editorship of the *Atlantic* before his younger brother, Ellery. True or not, the *Atlantic* got the right man. Babbo was not a man of affairs, at least of a business nature. He practiced law in New York for nearly fifteen years and gave it up. He wrote about it: "I was mentally and morally uncomfortable, as if I were swimming in glue. I did not understand the law. It seemed to me to create most of the difficulties it professed to settle."

Life must not have been easy for Babbo then. His courtship of my grandmother was not going well. She had declined his offer of marriage. He said, "I can't take it any longer." He bought ammunition, went back to his law offices, wrote farewell letters, and started to load the gun. The ammunition wouldn't fit. He never knew if the clerk in the gun shop had made a mistake, or whether he thought my grandfather looked too high-strung and had slipped him the wrong ammunition on purpose.

He kept trying different jobs. He was the headmaster at the Brearley School in New York for a year. The demands of headmastering escaped him completely, and neither he nor the trustees were sorry to see him move on after the year. He wrote almost thirty books—histories and biographies. But his real career was his life: the people, places, and literature that filled it. He closed one of his letters to me, "Squeeze the flask of life to the dregs."

FAN SEDGWICK Babbo was widowed in 1919, and he moved to Cambridge. My father, Minturn, a Harvard undergraduate, went to live with him. Then in 1924 my father married Helen Peabody, the daughter of Endicott Peabody, the founder and headmaster of Groton School, and she invited Babbo to live with them. My mother and Babbo were wonderful company for each other. They had lunch together every day. At dinnertime theirs was *the* conversation—often quite glittering and literate—with Daddy the quiet, benevolent brown bear at the end of the table. He didn't seem to mind, and we children listened with some wonderment. Babbo and Mummy had a good time and loved to laugh, and we all laughed with them. One exceptional moment was when a conversation drifted (with Babbo's guidance) into "Free Love." Mummy's face froze, and that was the end of *that* conversation. She had a superb sense of humor but her archetypal New England heritage imposed limits. Babbo really loved her. There had been troops of women in his life, but his daughter-in-law held a special place. She came down to Stockbridge from Murray Bay for young Tina Marquand's wedding not feeling especially well and she died during the night. I've heard that Babbo stood at her grave at the Pie and he called out, "Oh, Helen, Helen, it should be I."

SAUCIE SEDGWICK Aunt Helen loved Murray Bay, and so did Babbo. It was the family's summer place on the St. Lawrence River in Quebec. It was the place where Babbo and my grandmother had always spent their summers. For Babbo it must really have been home. He would say, "I am very eager for another summer in that dear place," and "Beyond Murray Bay there is only heaven."

HELEN BURROUGHS STERN The first time I went to Murray Bay was with Harry Sedgwick, my new husband. Edie's first cousin. I was just married—a young farm girl from New Hampshire, thrust suddenly into this incredible Sedgwick family as a young bride. Perhaps they were as puzzled by me as I was by them. People from Boston used to say, "Where are you from?" And I'd say, "Manchester, New Hampshire," and they'd say, "Oh, way up north?" as if they thought I came from Alaska.

The Murray Bay house was large, with porches, and an enormous green lawn leading down to the water. The water was just freezing cold. The days were like the water—shining and scintillating. Everything smelled like summer cedar. The house contained the strangest combination: beautiful braided rugs were everywhere, made in the local abbeys up there . . . glowing rooms with satiny walls and lovely lamps . . . and yet the lampshades were bought down at J. C. Penney's and they had Mickey Mouses on them. Suddenly you found things that were totally tasteless. The Sedgwicks just didn't care about that sort of thing. I did, passionately. It just killed me. I wanted it *all* to look wonderful.

The picnics, for instance, were *such* a tradition. Someone would announce in the morning, "Now it's the time of year when we must go to the . . ." and off we would go on these expeditions—pilgrimages, really—always to the same place year after year. The wicker picnic baskets had to be brought down. The thermoses had to be filled with syllabub, which was a kind of drink made out of claret and milk. The Sedgwicks would say, "Syllabub is like Claret Cup, only it's far better." This was apparently because it had cinnamon in it. Eugène, the Canadian who worked for the Sedgwicks, would launch these two Old Town canoes. I always imagined they had been hewn out of the trees by the Indians. Babbo would somehow get himself down the hill with his two sticks and get into one of them. He wore stockings that came up to his knickerbockers and folded over once, and what he always called his Cinderella slippers. He had a special seat for himself, and the women sat in some sort of raffia wicker seats placed in the bottom of the canoe. The men paddled like mad. I always remember they *feathered* their paddles—Minturn and Harry, my husband—after all, they had been Harvard crew men. Eugène would go ahead of us in the little rowboat to clear the ground where we were to picnic. He was always dressed in a striped waistcoat, a white shirt, a black tie over a celluloid collar.

When we got to the island we'd spread blankets—lap-robes from cars, big plaid blankets from the football games—and the things would be brought off the canoes: the supplies, the thermoses, the syllabub. The food was really marvelous . . . thin sandwiches with cucumbers in them, and watercress, and almost no mayonnaise and a lot of butter and no crusts. They were cut in half, and each half was carefully and perfectly wrapped in wax paper. Everything was just so. Even the Sedgwick lemonade had to be made in a certain way. But it was all taken for granted. It was that way because it always had been. Always Minturn would make scrambled eggs. It was the tradition— scrambled eggs *Minturn*. He would say: "I am going to make some scrambled eggs . . . I don't hear many huzzahs." This was supposed to produce a great cheer.

After the picnic Babbo would always read aloud—usually whatever was interesting him at the moment. P. G. Wodehouse was his absolute favorite, but if he found something in the *Letters of Marcus Aurelius* that really turned him on, he would read *that* to us, and he would say, "This is superbly couched, and you must listen, and you must remember it." One was never allowed to say "memorize." I used to say "memorize" and Babbo would correct me. "Commit to memory" was how it was supposed to be said. He would read for about half an hour, and of course it was dark by then and everyone took turns holding the *torch*, my dear, not a flashlight, so that Babbo could see the pages. And that was quite a privilege, right?

Tradition, that was all the Sedgwicks thought about. They were so involved with the past that the present was not real-seeming. If you could couch some phrase in a way that harked back to Herodotus, then they loved you . . . because they loved history. They would spend hours talking about Cromwell, but as if he were their uncle! The best, dearest relative!

SAUCIE SEDGWICK Babbo, being a gentle scholarly person and a widower without a bean, was totally dependent upon his sons to support him—a most undignified position for a heavenly old gentleman. When he wasn't with the children he lived terribly frugally. A friend of the family described staying with him when he was a widower in Cambridge and getting nothing to eat but boiled eggs. Obviously he preferred to stay with his sons, and it was while he was staying with our family on the ranch near Santa Barbara that he fell in love with Gabriella Ladd. My parents introduced them. She was staying nearby with friends of theirs and they invited her to come riding. Later she told me that my father made a pass at her that first day, and she was horrified.

Gabriella was in her early forties then, never married, and Babbo was almost ninety. Her father was quite a well-known Boston pediatrician; her mother was a sculptress. Gabriella had been a champion high jumper at Vassar. At one point she decided to be a nun, and she might even have embarked on this course but when she met Babbo, they fell in love that first night. In the middle of dinner, Babbo was quoting some Greek verse—I think it was Anacreon—and when he hesitated over a line, Gabriella picked up where he left off and completed the passage—in Greek. She had the most musical voice— Babbo's heart must have turned right over. Their courtship lasted five years, during which they wrote each other every day, sometimes several letters a day. I came across one of his recently which began, "I have a new name for you, it is Great Heart."

MINTURN SEDGWICK Babbo made no bones about the fact that he was in love with Gabriella, but he said, "It's ridiculous at my age getting married. We have this perfect relationship, and why spoil it?" But the lady had other ideas. She was determined. In Bermuda in the spring of '53 she wrote Babbo saying that there was a very attractive young man she was considering marrying. It worked. He flew to Bermuda, and within a day or two we had a cable saying, ALL IS WELL. SHE ACCEPTS.

HELEN BURROUGHS STERN I was in love with the idea of the two of them marrying. Babbo! I was infatuated with him. What was remarkable about him was what a romantic he was—especially for an older person. He called me "the barefoot angel," and he always had strawberries on the breakfast table when I came down. He was an absolute fiend about how English should be spoken. He did not wear a tie; he wore a *cravat*. It was "knickerbockers," not "knickers," and he wore them, too, with long woolen socks. Once I said something was ex*quis*ite, and he said, "How vile! I can't believe that's my granddaughter-in-law *speaking!*" He said, "Ex*quis*ite doesn't exist. *Exquisite* or nothing!" He had his way. At his wedding to Gabriella he came down the aisle alone, walking along with his two canes, wearing a lily of the valley in his buttonhole, a soft white shirt, a rose-pink cravat, and shiny shoes—I think he had the same pair of shoes for about thirty-five years and he shined them every day: they were what old leather was meant to look like, mellow, you know, mellow things encasing what he always referred to as his Cinderella feet, though they were *enormous*—and in this ensemble he came down the aisle with the music blaring, and your heart just melted at

Henry Dwight Sedgwick (Babbo) and Gabriella May Ladd,
on their wedding day, May 18, 1953

the sight of this old, old man moving down the aisle alone, with his two canes, toward his bride, who was waiting at the altar in an unusual reversal of the normal procedure—quite a show! As the vows were being said, the minister, who was a spry young thing of about sixty-five, asked the bride and groom to repeat after him, "Thereto I plight thee my troth." He pronounced it "trawth," whereupon Babbo in a loud and insistent voice, projecting it in this way he had, boomed forth: "*Troth*, young man! *Troth!*" He banged his stick, brandishing the other, and then banged *it* down. He meant business! At the wedding dinner afterwards he got up to offer some toasts, but he wouldn't allow anyone to stand up to join in them. He would not permit it. He said, "You only stand to drink someone's health if they're dead. It's only for the dead that you rise. You must *sit* to the living." He yelled: "Sit down! Sit down!" in this quite frantic way while guests sort of half stood up, glasses half raised, everyone looking at each other quite dazed. He kept banging his spoon on the table and insisting: "Sit *down!*" He must have been a fiend when he was younger. Can you imagine? Gabriella was not one to be overshadowed by anyone, but that was Babbo's day.

JOHN P. MARQUAND, JR.   My great-uncle Harry, whose descendants call him Babbo, and Gabriella had three very happy years together until he died peacefully in 1957 at the age of ninety-five. His funeral was in the winter. The Sedgwick Pie was covered with fresh snow. Gabriella stood there at the grave. She seemed to have envisioned her husband as having been transmogrified into some celestial lamb of God. Gabriella was a pious woman and free of the wry agnosticism of Uncle Harry, for all that he assiduously studied the Bible . . . and in Greek at that. Gabriella believed in heaven and transcendence over evil. As you know, she was really striking-looking . . . eternal youth in her face, those black eyes and that radiant smile. She had on widow's weeds, which made her look even more ethereal, particularly with the white snowdrifts in the background. I remember she turned to my wife and me: "I was saying to Babbo just the other day"—I would imagine when he was expiring—" 'When you get to Paradise, you're going to *leap* and *leap* and *leap*.' "

SAUCIE SEDGWICK   Gabriella is in the Pie, too. She was cremated, so it's not so easy imagining her rising up and facing the Judge on the Day of Resurrection. I persuaded my sister Kate to help me do something with Gabriella's ashes, which made her very nervous when she thought about it. We took half of the ashes and scattered them in the ocean at Singing Beach on the North Shore of Boston. Do you know the beach? It's called Singing Beach because the sand sings in this strange way under your bare feet when you run across it. Gabriella loved the place. But Kate thought: "What if we really *are* reassembled on the Judgment Day, and part of Gabriella is in the ocean off Singing Beach, and the rest in the ground at Stockbridge?"

JOHN P. MARQUAND, JR.   There's still a little room on the exterior of the Pie for the new generation of the Judge's descendants. Edie was entitled to be buried there; so is Saucie and so am I. But being only collaterally a Sedgwick, I've chosen to be buried in Newburyport. . . . I don't know what my Sedgwick cousins will do. Edie's grandfather, my grandfather, and most all the Sedgwicks of that generation were of an old and vanished school—Stockbridge was their Mecca. They had this place and all the myths and traditions about it which had been cultivated over the years, and the Pie was the greatest of the Sedgwick illusions. Greater even than the illusion that on a summer's night in Stockbridge the crickets sing Sēdg-wick, Sēdg-wick.

The four Minturn sisters (*left to right*): Mildred, Edith,
Gertrude, and Sarah May (Edie's grandmother)

2

SAUCIE SEDGWICK   Stockbridge has always been linked with New York rather than Boston . . . all the connections were up and down the Hudson, by boat or stagecoach or horseback. In comparison, the trip to Boston was long and arduous. So although the men of my family went to Harvard, it was usually New York after college. They went there to work, and many of them married there. Babbo had gone to New York to practice law, and it was there that he met our grandmother, May Minturn.

MINTURN SEDGWICK   The Minturns were very rich, successful shipping merchants. The swallowtail company flag was seen everywhere—most noticeably on the famous clipper ship the *Flying Cloud*, which my grandfather Robert Bowne Minturn had purchased for $90,000, a colossal sum in those days. The family's quite proud of the *Flying Cloud*. There's usually a framed picture of her hanging around somewhere in a Minturn house.

Then, just the year my mother was to have come out in New York with great fanfare, a dishonest agent for the family sugar plantations in Cuba got away with three quarters of a million dollars, which is worth at least three million today. It crippled the firm for a long time. So, as my mother used to say, instead of coming out in satin and pearls, she came out in cotton. I doubt it bothered her. She was an idealistic person, very interested in good works and education.

The clipper ship *Flying Cloud,* 1851

Saint-Gaudens' memorial on Boston Common honoring Robert Gould Shaw (Edie's great-great paternal uncle) and his black regiment that fought in the Civil War

The family lived near Gramercy Park. My widowed grandmother owned four brownstone houses on Twenty-third Street, forming a sort of Minturn compound in the heart of Manhattan. She was a very domineering lady, a kind of a Queen Bee dowager.

HELEN STOKES MERRILL   Granny Minturn loved the children. She took such great interest and pride. She pulled out my tooth for me by tying floss silk to the handle and then slamming the door. I suppose I screamed. Well, they were much fiercer then, they really were. I remember my grandmother's Gramercy Park house, but, curiously, I don't remember the furnishings except for the white druggets that were put over everything when we went away for the summer to Murray Bay in Canada. They were made of plain cotton or linen, and there was one which fitted the rug perfectly, so that the floor was suddenly white, and there was one for both these sofas, so that the room in the summer, the windows barred shut, was shrouded in white. In winter I remember how dark the rooms were—gas-lit, and when you left the room, you pulled the little chain and that cut the gas down so that there was just a little glow inside the lamp. It didn't quite go out. When you came in, you pulled the other chain and the light blazed up. It was the latest thing—like what we have now with the rheostat.

Granny Minturn kept a carriage, a coupé, a horrible thing. It was enclosed, lined with leather, and you rode backwards if you were little. I got seasick in it. Finally, at the end of her life, she took to hiring a car. She went for drives, always wearing—in such contrast to those widow's weeds she wore at home—a white, heavily starched muslin cap with little flutings down the side. It surprised me because she had such lovely silver hair. I remember the maid brushing it—the old maid who couldn't do anything else coming in to brush her hair. It took her half an hour to do it. Her name was Crocksey, just a tiny, wrinkled woman about four feet tall, and we loved her as children because she was about our size.

Granny Minturn's children—my uncles and aunts—just dropped like flies. A doctor once told me that the corsets of that time had a lot to do with it—they squeezed the vital organs. Granny seemed to be in mourning all the time. She was quite old when I remember her, but she carried herself beautifully and held her head up. By then she had become very tyrannical and high-strung. She had outlived her husband and all but two of her seven children. She stayed in the house and dwelt on the past and her passionate devotion to the dead. She was such a figure of sorrow. She kept a linen-covered table in the corner

Susanna Shaw Minturn, Murray Bay, Canada

of her upstairs sitting room with the portraits of her family—so many of them gone—lined up in silver frames. I secretly called it "the dead table."

Three of her children died within four years. The terrible tragedy of Granny Minturn's life was the death of her fourth child, Francis, who died of diphtheria at the age of six. She wrote about him in a book she had privately printed afterwards. The doctors had asked permission to perform a tracheotomy.

> His father and I said we were willing; and they took our darling, laid him on a table, and lit gas-lights and candles all about him. He looked like a beautiful marble image as he lay there. Four doctors held him; they wanted us to leave the room, but we could not. As soon as the incision was made, he whispered in a frightened, hurried way: "Mamma, mamma, mamma, mamma!" And I ran to him and taking his dear hand, I said, "Frankie, darling, mamma is here, she will not leave you." Then he said to the doctors, "Please don't, please don't." Those were the last words we ever heard him say, for after this operation the voice was gone. . . .

MINTURN SEDGWICK   My brother Francis, Edie's father, was named after that Francis Minturn. There were four of us. The eldest was Henry Dwight Sedgwick, Jr., whom we called Halla. I was the second. Then my mother had a daughter, Edith, who only lived for a half a day or a day. I can remember picking flowers for her grave in the rain. Then two and a half years later came Francis. He was the last.

Francis was a very delicate child. They said he was born with an umbilical hernia, which is a hole in the abdominal muscles, but he screamed so much I have since thought the strain of his yelling was perhaps what caused the hernia. I remember as a baby he always had a big piece of adhesive tape covering his tummy with a little hole in it for his belly button, sort of pulling him together. My mother told me years later that when Francis was about two, he wanted to stand up and run around, but he didn't have the strength. He'd just collapse. My mother could see that Francis was sort of fading away and she was terribly concerned. Then Halla developed pneumonia for the second time so our father, Babbo, decided for the sake of the whole family to go to a warm climate; he chose Santa Barbara in California.

My parents rented a small house up in Mission Canyon with the Sierra Mountains behind them and the Pacific Ocean in front. The house had a little decklike veranda covered with morning glories. My father's letters from that time express the kind of reservations about

John Singer Sargent's portrait of Edith Minturn Stokes (for whom Edie was named) and her husband, Isaac Newton Phelps Stokes

California one might expect of a New Englander on his first visit to the Coast. He said he felt he was in exile. One of his letters complained that California lacked the marks of man's labor; it needed ruins and castles.

My parents brought along an Irish maid and a trained nurse for Francis called Miss Thompson, who told the maid, "I'm going to stay here until the little fellow is put in his grave." It was true that Francis seemed to be losing ground, and I think my mother should get credit for bringing him through, because she made up her mind that he was going to get well. She dismissed the first nurse and asked a remarkable Christian Scientist nurse to come out. *She* made all the difference. She was gay and always sang to Francis. The whole atmosphere changed, and he survived.

SAUCIE SEDGWICK My grandmother May must have been magnificent when she was young: large and dark, with an austere kind of beauty. But she could be fierce. Uncle Minturn told me she once hit Halla in the face with the bristle side of her hairbrush. He said she was terribly embarrassed because when the family gathered at Grandmother Minturn's for Sunday lunch, there was this little boy with angry marks on his face. And I know she was severe with my father. Having already lost her infant daughter, Edith, she must have focused an enormous amount of anxiety and rage on him. She hit him, and he was scared to death of her. In photographs he has a sad but gallant look on his face . . . poor little man. He never said a word against her and spoke of her as if she were a saint. She *willed* him to survive. As for Babbo, he read stories to his sons and did plays and charades with them, but he cannot have been a strong figure as a father. He told me once that he tried to intercede for my father, but, as he said, "I never had any influence with her." My grandmother was the dominant force in the family.

HELEN STOKES MERRILL It irritated May Sedgwick that Francis wasn't strong. She felt that he must take hold of himself and rise above it. She was anxious for him to outgrow his weaknesses and his delicacy. Auntie May was quite fierce. She wanted to teach Francis what "hot" was, so she put his finger in the candle flame and said, "Now, that's hot, that's bad. You mustn't get burned."

She had a great many theories about bringing up children. Minturn told me years later that he was brought by his mother to see me in the tub when I was about three so that he'd know what little girls looked

Francis Minturn (1871–1878)

Francis Minturn Sedgwick
(Edie's father)

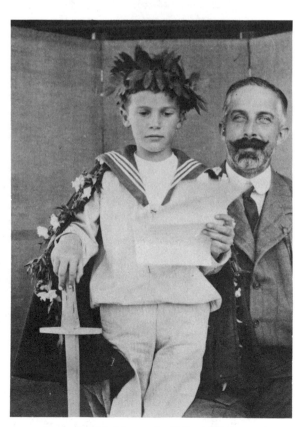

Francis with his uncle, Robert Minturn

Rosamond Pinchot

like. They had no girls in their family—they had lost their daughter, Edith, who only lived for a day—so Auntie May thought it was important for the boys to know how girls were put together.

The Sedgwicks used to come and stay, always a jump behind us as we moved from one house to a larger one on our Greenwich estate. My father—he was a recognized young architect and the author of the *Iconography of Manhattan Island*—had bought a Tudor mansion he'd seen in an advertisement and brought it over from Ipswich, England, in wooden crates. Next to the mansion he built a walled garden—it was a little kingdom, all protected—which was called the Pleasaunce. It was designed by Frederick Law Olmsted, the architect of New York's Central Park.

I remember Francis' mother with her feet up a lot, lying on a chaise longue in the little cottage on the estate which she and Babbo rented from my parents. She seemed withdrawn and concerned about her health.

At that time Francis—he was about nine—was very tense, always on the move, just a little dynamo with dancing brown eyes. We were always on a very competitive basis. He lived a life of fantasy in which I, his devoted follower, would do whatever he dreamed up. Once he told me to jump off the wall of the Pleasaunce. It was about six feet high, and he said, "Go first!" I jumped off, and for a couple of days I could hardly walk. He just slid down the wall when he saw how low I had been laid.

We fought wars against the neighborhood children. Indoors he had enormous sets of toy soldiers. He had whole battle plans. He was always planning wars. His brothers began calling him the General, and I think he liked that nickname. He wanted to grow up and be a general. He played the commanding officer on both sides of his war games—a type of military solitaire.

I was Francis' closest friend, and Rosamond Pinchot, another cousin of ours, often played with us. She was very tempestuous, Rosamond was. In fact, in later years Francis worried that his daughter Edie might turn out like her. Rosamond once took a carving knife to her older brother, Gifford. I actually saw it happen. The two had an argument of some sort at lunch, and she just grabbed up the knife and went for Gifford until her mother, Aunt Gertrude, intervened. Rosamond was a lovely-looking child—great blue eyes, shining blond hair, and a very full mouth. She grew up to be quite a beauty. On an ocean crossing with her mother in the mid-Twenties, Max Reinhardt, the theatrical producer, became infatuated with her and offered her the role of the nun in *The Miracle*. Lady Diana Manners was the Virgin. Anyway, Aunt Gertrude accepted, or let Rosamond accept. And it was her debutante year, too. The part was nothing, no acting involved at *all*. Rosamond was just required to *run* (I think she was escaping from a nunnery) up one aisle of the theater, around the back, and down the other, in her habit and with her hair flying. Everybody was just fascinated. The play had a tremendous success—it ran for three hundred performances or so on Broadway—and all of it went to Rosamond's head. She went into something else, and she was a total flop: she couldn't act at all.

She committed suicide finally, years later. She asphyxiated herself in the front seat of her car in the closed garage on a rented estate. Mother's chauffeur told me that just before, she had gone back to our house in Greenwich, where she spent a long time sitting in the Pleasaunce. I can understand why. It was an island for all of us—a serene, secure place. But it was all torn down after the Second World War. When Francis went to boarding school, we drifted apart. I felt hurt at first, because we'd done everything together.

HARRY SEDGWICK   Childhood for Sedgwick boys ended when we were sent to Groton. It was founded by my maternal grandfather, Endicott Peabody, who was always called the Rector. "Just a great slab of New England granite," as Alice Roosevelt Longworth once described him. What he liked was muscular Christianity, and though he was the head of this remarkably prestigious school, he was rather suspicious of too much intellectual learning. He once said, "I am not sure I like boys to think too much. A lot of people think a lot of things we could do without." His aim was to turn out "perfect Christian gentlemen" and "enlightened public servants."

MINTURN SEDGWICK   Franklin Roosevelt, who was a Groton graduate, wrote to Mrs. Peabody when the Rector died that no one except his parents had affected him so much all his life as Mr. Peabody. FDR revived the custom of having the incoming Cabinet at Holy Communion before the inauguration. The Rector took it the first time. He went to Washington for similar occasions a number of times. Of course he always stayed at the White House. On one occasion, so the story goes, he came into the Oval Office to say goodbye, and as the Rector went out the door, the President said to a friend, "You know, I'm still scared of him." And I'll bet he was. Fortunately, I was a pet of the Rector's, so we got on splendidly.

My older brother, Halla, and I were there at the same time. Francis was still at school elsewhere. Before Groton, Halla and I had been to school in England, and we had come back with these charming accents. The Groton boys nicknamed him the Duke, and they tried various nicknames on me like Viscount, but none of them stuck except Duke. So I became Duke, too, and then when I got to be a well-known athlete, it really stuck.

My brother and I rowed on the second crew at Groton. For me it was quite an honor because I was only a third-former. One Saturday, about a month before Halla was to graduate, we rowed in the hour and a half between classes and lunch. When we came in, it looked as if we might be late. We ran up from the river. My brother had a ravenous appetite and bolted his food; it disagreed with him. He went in the infirmary the next morning with a bad stomach upset. He wrote a letter about how he'd raced under a hot sun and how exhausted he'd become. Then he developed pneumonia. The last night of his life my parents were both up there. Babbo's privately printed book, *In Memoriam*, was written about Halla—Babbo always called him Harry—and describes what happened:

> That night we gathered about his bed, Minturn on one side kneeling and holding his hand, their heads near together, May and I on the other side, Ellery and Mr. Peabody at the foot. Mr. Peabody read from the prayer book and we repeated the daily prayers we had always said with the boys. It was a bitter cold night, and the windows were wide open to give Harry air. Toward morning a bird sang on the little tree close beside the window, and then, as the day was dawning, his spirit left us.
>
> He looked very handsome as he lay there in his white linen, with sprigs of many coloured snapdragon about him. . . . The coffin was covered with a deep red pall, and lay in the chapel. A dim light was burning as Minturn and I went in to bid good night. Ellery was there. The chapel looked solemn and beautiful, full of traditional feeling, and of Harry's sentiment for it. Horatio's words burned themselves into me:
>
> > *Good night, Sweet Prince;*
> > *And flights of Angels sing thee to thy rest.*

On Sunday afternoon the funeral service was held in the chapel. Mr. Peabody delivered the eulogy, in which he compared Halla to a description from Chaucer:

> *He was a verray parfit gentil knyght . . .*

My parents and I had breakfast in the Groton infirmary the morning after Halla's death. My mother was in tears. I have a vivid recollection of blood oozing out of the pores of my father's nose. An official came that day to ask my father for the "vital statistics"—to confirm Halla's age. He was seventeen years, seven months, twenty-six days.

Francis was still a little boy at home. He came up from New York the day after our brother died. I introduced him to one of the masters at Groton since he would soon be coming to the school, and I told the master: "We're filling up the ranks."

My mother went into a decline right off. It was she who persuaded Babbo to write his book about Halla, just as her mother had written the little volume about Francis Minturn. Now she expressed her grief in a letter to her mother:

Darling, darling, Mamma—All that last night, I thought of you so often, and after the end, all the first day, I kept saying, "Poor, poor Mamma, I don't wonder she nearly went crazy." Every year, I felt more and more I understood but it is not until our own hearts are pierced that we can begin to know the suffering.

Within a year the blood vessels broke in my mother's eyes and it seemed as if she'd become totally blind, but something arrested it. I remember she was very touching. She said, "You're practically grown up, so I don't worry. All I wanted was to see how Francis looks when he grows up."

Francis was a terribly ambitious fellow, but he was very delicate when he was at Groton. He complained of severe pains. The doctors tried to tell him it was his imagination. His football coach took me aside once and said, "I hate to ask this, but is Francis sandless?" What do you call that now?—no guts, afraid of contact. Finally, a great doctor diagnosed that he had osteomyelitis. Do you know what that is? It's a dangerous infection of the bone; it could have led within a few weeks to death or come to a head and had to be operated on. With Francis it just sort of whistled around his body. He had to use crutches at times. But there were other problems. He was high-strung, too. He told me: "I have these faraway feelings that are not part of me." He was full of phobias. He was afraid of darkness—he *saw* things in the dark. He was so scared of water that he didn't learn to swim until he was fourteen. He was afraid of horses for a long time, and dark woods.

Babbo at Harvard, 1879

SAUCIE SEDGWICK   It didn't help that at the time my grandmother May had a series of strokes. Each time, my father was taken out of Groton and hurried down to be with her. But she didn't die. He would return to school in a state of terrible anguish.

MINTURN SEDGWICK   Our mother didn't recognize us any more. Her mind was gone. She had aged terribly, her nose was red from a drug she had to take, and I remember Babbo telling Francis and me, "How I wish you had known your mother when she was young and beautiful."

When she finally died, all the color was drained out of her face and I remember being startled that she looked young again and extraordinarily handsome lying there. That first night I offered to sleep in the same room as Francis, but he said it wasn't necessary.

My mother's body was cremated and there was a big, fancy funeral at Calvary Church in New York. Afterwards we all went up to Stockbridge. Babbo walked down the village street to the Sedgwick Pie carrying my mother's ashes in a green student's bag. He chose two quotations for her tombstone: "Some lives bend over other lives as the heavens bend over the earth." The other was from Dante: *"Beatrice in suso, ed io in lei, guardava,"* which translates: "Beatrice was gazing upward, and I on her."

SAUCIE SEDGWICK   My grandmother's death was an unbelievable strain on my father. He finally had a nervous breakdown and it was recommended that he leave Groton. Babbo sent him out to Santa Barbara to the Cate School, which was run by a remarkable pair, Curtis Cate and his wife, Katherine Thayer. Bostonians often sent their children to the Cate School. Katherine Cate was what you would call a character. My father used to tell a story about her when she was a younger woman living in Boston. She had gone to a dinner party, and when the ladies were alone having their coffee, she grew bored. She was wearing a long dress with a fishtail in the fashion of the day, and she tucked that fishtail between her ankles and stood on her head!

By the time I knew Mrs. Cate she was a tiny, erect lady whose most remarkable feature was her voice, a kind of *basso profundo* bark. My father said she used to have to insist over the phone that she was not *Mr.* Cate.

Curtis Cate was a scholarly man who believed in Spartan discipline, tempered by a sense of humor. The atmosphere of the school was much less formal and competitive than Groton's. There was a lot of riding rather than team sports. It was perfect for my father. He was the *only* Duke. According to Uncle Minturn, my father put on twenty pounds in the first six months; he was so happy he stayed there for two and a half years, working summers on a ranch nearby.

HARRY SEDGWICK   But then, after the Cate School, Uncle Francis went to Harvard. He was back in the competitive furnace. Babbo always said that the two essential things to do at Harvard were to play football and to join the Porcellian Club. He himself had played on one of the earliest football teams, in 1878. My father, Minturn, was always a great athlete—at his birth the family doctor said, "This boy doesn't need a nanny, he needs a trainer." He made quite a record at Harvard. He had played for a team that never lost a game. In his senior year, after the Princeton-Harvard game, the sports page of the Boston *Globe* read SEDGWICK TURNS TIDE. Babbo was proud of being introduced as "the father of Duke Sedgwick."

So Uncle Francis had quite a name to live up to at Harvard. He hated the name Francis, and clung to "Duke" for the rest of his life. In fact, thirty-odd years later at his twenty-fifth Harvard reunion, he and Dad actually quarreled over who was the *real* Duke. Dad told him, "You will always be 'Little Duke.'"

In his freshman year Uncle Francis went out for football and crew, and while he made the football team, he got ill that spring and was dropped from the crew. He took six courses that first year and got A's in all of them. In his sophomore year he was awarded the Jacob Wendell Scholarship, and Babbo took him to Europe as a reward. But in all his years at Harvard he never won a single H. He kept trying, forcing himself, building up his body to such a degree that some of his Porcellian Club classmates referred to him as "Physical Francis."

It was a tradition in the Sedgwick family to belong to the Porcellian Club. Babbo had been a member, and even Judge Theodore Sedgwick, the one at the center of the family graveyard, had been elected an honorary member just before he died, one of the very few Yale men so chosen. Uncle Francis was invited to join, and he accepted. But although I've heard that he later considered the club an important part of his life, another member told me that he rarely went there and that when he did, nobody seemed to notice him. He was sort of a vacant spot in the room.

Francis with his parents

The Sedgwicks *(left to right)*: Halla, Babbo, Francis, May, and Minturn

MINTURN SEDGWICK Francis was concentrating on Fine Arts at Harvard, but what he really wanted to be was a tycoon. When he won a Clarence Dillon scholarship, Babbo, who was not in the least worldly-wise, told his son, "Now that you've won this scholarship, why don't you go down to New York and call on the great man? I'm sure none of his other scholars will ever come near him." So Francis went to see Mr. Dillon and made a great hit with him. Dillon asked him what he was concentrating on. "Fine Arts and Finance," said Francis. Dillon apparently said, "Splendid. That's just what *I* did in college." Then Dillon asked him what he expected to do when he'd graduated. Francis told him that he planned to study at Trinity College in Cambridge for a year. Then he said, "After that I'd like a year of banking experience in Europe."

Clarence Dillon wrote several letters of introduction for Francis. So for the summer of 1927 he was a sort of an honored aide representing the powerful and brilliant Clarence Dillon throughout European banking circles, starting in Berlin with the Diskont Gesellschaft. In Paris that year Francis received a cable from Dillon saying, "I'm taking a few friends on a Mediterranean trip. Will you join us in Gibraltar?" There I was working away at a little branch bank in Boston, while Francis seemed already well on his way to becoming an international tycoon.

LILY MAYNARD The cruise ship was called the *Baltic*. I was about nineteen or twenty, and my family thought I was up to no good in New York. I was idle, like most of my generation. And they didn't like the young man I was seeing. I was to be chaperoned on the trip by Mrs. Rogers Winthrop, who had her eighteen-year-old daughter, Alice, along with her. Also on the trip were Charles Dana Gibson, the celebrated illustrator, and his wife, who was the original Gibson Girl. I remember the older ladies on the trip saying to Mr. Dillon about Francis: "Let's see the Adonis."

I had a bit of a flirt with Francis—a modest, chaste kiss in the moonlight. He was a very handsome man, quite vain, a rather faddish person who drank two glasses of milk a day—a kind of a health maniac. He was enormously clean; he smelt good.

Mr. Dillon had expected to like Francis, but I had a feeling that he did not take to him. He was being tried out as an assistant, a courier, a private secretary; he would get tickets, pick up baggage.

After the trip I saw Francis in Paris and then in Cambridge. He was very intense with his emotions. He fantasized quite a bit. I think he was a man who saw himself in pictures of his imagination and dreams. He got rather intense about marriage. I found him a very attractive beau . . . a very pleasant Cicerone . . . but I was not prepared to get married. I told him in Cambridge it was all over, and he looked sad punting on the Cam River.

MINTURN SEDGWICK   Soon after the cruise Francis went to London to work in the investment banking firm of Lazard Frères. Again he played and worked very hard until one morning he suddenly collapsed to the floor. We knew nothing about it until about two or three weeks later, when a cable arrived from Francis saying: "The reason I haven't written was they thought I was going to die, and there was no sense in telling you that. But what they thought was a heart attack was a nervous breakdown." Of course, that was the end as far as his financial possibilities with the Dillon empire were concerned.

After he'd been in a nursing home in England, his doctor said: "Is there some pleasant place near here where you can stay quietly for a month before going home?" Francis remembered a close friend and classmate from Groton, Charles de Forest, whose father had taken a summer place called Tilney, a manor house in the English countryside. The de Forests said they would be glad to have him. So he went, and that's where he met Charlie's younger sister, Alice.

4

SAUCIE SEDGWICK   My parents actually met for the first time years earlier, when my father was at the Cate School. My mother had gone out to Santa Barbara on a trip with her parents, and my uncle Charlie de Forest had suggested they look up my father. My father was about sixteen years old and very handsome, my mother was twelve. When my mother saw him, she fell in love with him then and there for life. She had to wait about eight years. My grandmother told me that my mother knew what she wanted and no one could talk her out of it.

My mother grew up on Long Island on an enormous place called Nethermuir, which had been in the family since 1866. It was a hundred and fifty acres of wild laurel, woods, and lawns that went to the edge of the water, with a view of Long Island Sound. My grandfather Henry de Forest was an amateur landscape gardener, and I remember as a child walking around the grounds with him. He wore dark gray or brown tweed suits with a waistcoat, and he always had a hat on and carried a walking stick. I'd see the gardeners tipping their hats to him.

GEORGE PLIMPTON   When I was a boy I used to see the de Forest estate across Cold Spring Harbor from the Beach Club. There was a boathouse with a dock on the water, and the big white house up the hill, with lawns and formal gardens.

I used to wonder what went on up there—very grand doings, I always supposed. One thing I knew about them was that they once had a private railway car. The old man must have cut quite a figure—he came from a distinguished New York family. He was a director of the Southern Pacific Railway, which put him at the right hand of E. H. Harriman, the railroad tycoon, who was one of the most powerful men around. So the de Forests in their heyday could have lived like princes, but apparently they never did.

In a way, the community is characterized by the Cold Spring Harbor Beach Club. It's quite an institution. To begin with, it has no beach. The clubhouse is a simple, shacklike structure. No liquor is served. My father told me that it used to have a rule that if you were a man, you had to wear a top to your bathing suit, which was due largely to Colonel Henry L. Stimson, the onetime Secretary of War and one of the great figures of Cold Spring Harbor, who had a slightly hairy chest which he didn't want to display. A number of distinguished figures turned up there—John Foster Dulles, Marshall Field, Allan Dulles (I can remember him playing tennis invariably under a wide-brimmed straw hat), Arthur Ballantine, and, of course, the de Forests. My father used to say that the general ambience of Cold Spring Harbor was one of a restrained Presbyterianism marked by austerity, virtually no excesses of any sort, with nobody throwing his weight around, a very simple community which attracted the best because it made a point of not being at all flamboyant or like a Gold Coast.

SAUCIE SEDGWICK   My grandfather de Forest must have been a man of strong opinions, but I heard of them only through my grandmother. She told me once that she and Grandpa had voted for Franklin Roosevelt because "Grandpa said that any child of Sarah and Jimmy's was bound to be a good governor." But then, she said, "Franklin was very impolite to your grandfather. There was an anti-trust hearing, and not only was Franklin on the other side, but he didn't even take off his hat to your grandfather when he came into court! Grandpa never voted for him again."

My grandfather didn't marry until he was forty-two. Then he chose a young woman from St. Paul, Minnesota, named Julia Gilman Noyes. She was staying near Cold Spring Harbor, visiting her friend May Tiffany, the daughter of Louis Tiffany, whose family lived in Laurel Hollow next to the de Forests. My grandmother was twenty-three then, and while she belonged to what she would have called a "respectable" Connecticut family, I think she felt at a disadvantage coming from

Henry de Forest
(Edie's maternal grandfather)

Julia Noyes, Edie's maternal grandmother, with her mother

St. Paul. Her father had moved there for reasons of health in the 1860s, and I suppose he prospered, because Grandma was told as a young girl that she could afford a cook even if she married a clergyman—she would have a dowry of a quarter of a million dollars. So perhaps when she landed Henry de Forest she may have been a bit provincial. But she soon learned. She loved expensive clothes; she loved respectability, but mainly she must have loved being grand. She told me once that her bare feet never touched the floor because her French maid always left a pair of slippers at her bedside.

No question, my grandmother became a great lady in everybody's eyes. You cannot imagine the stately progression of her day: interviewing the cook in the bedroom in the morning, reading the mail at her desk before lunch, followed by sherry, followed by lunch, then a little walk around the garden, changing to a long dress in the afternoon, pouring tea at five even if she was by herself. And no day varied from the day before or from the day after. She did exquisite needlework and embroidery; she read a lot of history and kept charts of European royalty in big notebooks.

My grandparents had four children. My mother, Alice Delano de Forest, was the youngest, born in 1908 when her father was fifty-three. There were two older brothers and an older sister. In 1913 the eldest son died suddenly of a brain tumor just before he was thirteen years old. My grandmother went into mourning and put away the wardrobe she had bought each year on trips abroad. My mother was only five at the time, but the message of terror and suffering must have gotten through to her. She remained closest to her other brother, Uncle Charlie, who she felt was the most important person in her life, and she worshiped her father—she called him Fuzzy because of his beard.

My mother was the darling of her father—there was a strong bond between them. She was very much a tomboy. And her relationship with him was very close—lots of hugging and sitting in his lap. There was definitely competition between my mother and grandmother for Grandfather de Forest.

I've seen pictures of my mother taken that summer of 1928 at Tilney when she and my father met again. She wore tweed skirts, wool sweaters, and brogues—shoes that look as if she was about to set off on a round of golf. She has a shy, happy look in those pictures—they show her warm nature. Although I have never known whether my father shared his mental horrors with her, I'm sure he confided in her and that he trusted her utterly. I imagine that she may have felt that only she understood him, and that her faith would restore him.

OLD FAMILIES SEE MISS DE FOREST WED

Younger Daughter of Mr. and Mrs. Henry W. de Forest Marries Francis M. Sedgwick

CEREMONY IN GRACE CHURCH

Rev. Dr. Peabody Officiates— Bridal Party Passes Through a Lane of White and Green

There was a representative gathering of old New York families yesterday afternoon in Grace Church, Broadway and Tenth Street, for the marriage of Miss Alice de Forest, younger daughter of Mr. and Mrs. Henry W. de Forest of this city and Nethermuir, Cold Spring Harbor, L.I., to Francis Minturn Sedgwick, son of Henry Dwight Sedgwick, author, and the late Mrs. Sedgwick, who was a member of the Minturn family of this city. . . .

The Rev. Dr. Endicott Peabody, headmaster of Groton School, where the bridegroom prepared for college, performed the ceremony. He was assisted by the Rev. Dr. W. Russell Bowle, rector of Grace Church. There was a full choral service, the vested choir singing "Ancient of Days" as it made its way from the vestry room to the choir stalls. As the bride entered the church escorted by her father, the choir sang the Lohengrin wedding march. . . .

. . . At the chancel steps she was joined by the bridegroom and his brother, Robert Minturn Sedgwick, the best man. . . . She wore a princess costume of ivory colored satin, the skirt shorter in front and ending in a long train in the back. She wore two veils, one of old family lace over another of tulle edged with godet ruffles of tulle. The veils extended to the end of the long train and were arranged with a cap of lace caught across the back of the head with a narrow bandeau of tiny orange blossoms. Her bouquet was of lilies of the valley.

The costumes of the bridesmaids were of primrose yellow chiffon, that of the matron of honor being of a darker shade of yellow. All the attendants wore large picture hats of yellow straw trimmed with apple green moiré ribbon. Their bouquets were of pink and yellow Spring flowers and blue iris.

. . . Owing to the recent illness of the bride's mother, there was no reception.

. . . Mr. Sedgwick and his bride after their wedding trip to California will live in Cambridge, Mass., while he continues his studies at the business school of Harvard.

. . . As the bride and bridegroom left the chancel Mendelssohn's wedding march was played on the organ by Ernest Mitchell, organist of Grace Church, and as they left the church the chimes were rung. For the recessional the choir sang "Rejoice the Lord Is King."

. . . During the service the choir sang "Oh Perfect Love."

My parents had a great deal in common. They both liked being out-doors—riding, swimming, playing tennis. They shared a certain scorn for social phoniness. They adored dogs and horses. They were both talented artistically. And on the other hand they had a shadow side in common—each had lost an idolized elder brother. Both had implacable grieving mothers and must have lived with a terrible sense of jeopardy.

My mother must have seemed a strong, compassionate figure to my father, and her family offered the sense of security and power he was looking for. He was drawn to my grandfather de Forest as a father figure—he was always looking for a powerful, rich, well-born person in the mainstream of things rather than a scholarly dreamer like his own father. My mother seemed to have everything—no wonder he fell in love with her. For her part she was painfully shy and must have felt secure marrying someone so dashing who would yet be totally de-pendent upon her and on her father. When my father proposed, she had no reservations about marrying him. My grandparents insisted on a medical opinion before giving their permission. But my mother's commitment was—and remained—total.

MINTURN SEDGWICK   The de Forests were crazy about Francis. I mean, so it appeared. Francis claimed he overheard Mr. de Forest say-ing, "I hope young Sedgwick wins the race." Anyway, they were en-gaged. Francis came back from England and I met him at the dock. He looked the picture of health, but suddenly he said, "Gubby"—that's what he called me—"you've got to pass my baggage out. I'll collapse if I stand around here." He was in trouble. He went around to various doctors who did him no good, and then he asked if I could get him into the Austen Riggs Center in Stockbridge.

JEAN STEIN   Dr. John Millet was assigned as Francis Sedgwick's psychiatrist at Riggs. His father was a painter—Mark Twain had been his father's best man. Mr. Sedgwick spent three months at Riggs under his care. He had a large private room with a chaise longue by the fire-place. The patients were called "guests." Mr. Sedgwick's bed was turned down by a maid, who left him a pitcher of milk by his bedside table.

Alice de Forest visited Francis Sedgwick regularly. It must have been very difficult for her. Dr. Riggs, the head of the Riggs Center, and Dr. Millet told them that Mr. Sedgwick was recovering from a phase of manic-depressive psychosis. Dr. Millet suggested that Mr. Sedgwick rest for a few months and then have a quiet wedding and honeymoon.

MINTURN SEDGWICK   Mr. de Forest went to see Dr. Riggs and Dr. Millet, and the reports were not very encouraging. He telephoned me and said, "The next time you're in New York I'd appreciate it if you'd come and call on me." So I said I'd be delighted, and I saw the great man in his office. The first thing he said was: "We're advised that Francis and Alice shouldn't have any children." Well, to me that meant: Don't get married. But there was nothing I could do about it.

The service was held in Grace Church in New York. Like most Groton boys, Francis was a tremendous admirer of the Rector, Mr. Peabody, and he had him at the wedding to perform the service. But Francis didn't realize that under church protocol it's the clergyman of the church who has to declare you man and wife. I was Francis' best man; we met there early to run over the high points before the service. When he overheard the Rector say that the other fellow would make the final pronouncement, Francis told me in such a loud voice that the clergyman must have heard, "If I'd known *that*, we wouldn't be married in this church!" There was never a moment when Francis didn't want to have his way.

5

SAUCIE SEDGWICK   I was the first child—born Alice on August 29, 1931, a little more than two years after my parents were married. I was nicknamed Saucie—short for sausage, which is what my father thought I looked like at birth. Edie was the seventh child. Between Edie and me, the children came along every two years or so—Bobby, Pamela, Minty, Jonathan, and Kate—and then the eighth, Suky, was born in 1945. Our lives as we grew up were divided between winters in Cold Spring Harbor on Long Island and summers at a house in Santa Barbara that my parents had bought on their honeymoon.

The year after their marriage my parents lived in Cambridge while my father attended classes at the Harvard Business School. He was bored by learning the nuts and bolts of business, and by 1930 the prospects for future tycoons must have been pretty dismal. Even brilliant businessmen like my grandfather de Forest were losing millions in the Depression. Also my father was having asthma attacks and other nervous symptoms, so his doctors advised him to develop his artistic side.

My parents moved to Long Island, where they spent winters first in a house called Airslie on my grandfather de Forest's place, and eventually in a house of their own nearby. My father became a sculptor. I think he was ashamed not to be a banker like everyone else who took the Long Island Railroad into town, so he commuted into New York wearing a bowler hat and carrying an umbrella. He looked as if he was going to spend the day at Number One Wall Street. Our butler, William Kennedy, would drive him to the train, and often he'd finish his breakfast in the car, his eggs on a plate in his lap, because he was always late. He'd go to classes at the National Academy of Fine Arts and then spend the day at his studio on East Fifty-seventh Street. His cousin Gifford Pinchot told me he went there once and discovered my father in a G-string strapped to a huge cross, staring at himself in a full-length mirror. He explained that he was doing a crucifixion scene and didn't want to be bothered to pay a model.

Typical of my father to see himself as a combination of Messiah, victim, and great male nude. Oh, he worked very hard on himself. It was an obsession with him to be strong and fit. At Cold Spring Harbor he rowed a single scull out on the pond, and he ran five miles in his little running shorts at night when he came home from New York. One of the major memories of my childhood is the punching bag and the sound of it being hit: *pocketa, tocketa, pocketa, tocketa.* He was scornful of people who were not physically fit. He told me once he would never vote for Adlai Stevenson, whom he used to see at the Francis Plimptons', because "he looked like a woman—breasts and a flabby stomach—and besides he was bald."

GEORGE PLIMPTON   I can remember very well when the Sedgwicks came to our house to play mixed doubles against my parents. Francis Sedgwick was a very romantic figure to my young eyes . . . close-cropped hair—it sort of shone like a beaver's pelt—and his bare chest, of course. He never wore a tennis shirt. He drove over from Cold Spring Harbor in his convertible with the top down and his chest bare. He was very tan. I remember a sort of soldier's stance and his walk, very cocky. He had a habit of slapping at the back of his calves with the edge of his racquet as he walked down the slope toward the tennis court. Very lively man. A smile that blazed out of that dark tan. There was always a lot of banter and jollity on the court. It was fun to watch the Sedgwicks play. They made everyone else around feel a little rumpled and dowdy. I envied the children their parents.

SAUCIE SEDGWICK   My father hadn't really wanted to have children. My mother told me once that it used to break her heart that he just wasn't interested in the little things she told him about us. She would say, "Aren't they sweet?" and he wouldn't respond. He didn't want to be called Daddy; he wanted us to call him Fuzzy, the name my mother had given her own father.

MINTURN SEDGWICK   I described my brother Francis to a friend of mine after he'd had his eighth child, and how surprised I was, considering the increasing difficulties Alice had in childbirth, and she said, "I'll bet he had those children just to show he could have more than anyone else." It might well have been. I know he was pleased that no one else in his Harvard class had produced eight children, or anything close. After the eighth, Susanna, was born, I sent him one of those canned telegram messages, "Good work, keep it up"—a slightly sardonic message, considering the circumstances. He never acknowledged it.

SAUCIE SEDGWICK   Little children get sick a lot, of course, and by the time there were three or four of us, colds and measles and all those things would just go bouncing from one of us to another. There were always doctors and nurses around. Minty, I remember, had to wear a horrible sort of wire helmet on his head to flatten his ears. He came down with scarlet fever when he was quite small and had to be watched for a heart condition. Bobby used to rock in his bed and bang his head. Twice he ran through the glass of the French doors leading to the terrace of our house in Cold Spring Harbor, and cut his wrists horribly. The second time, we were all being driven into New York by Grandpa de Forest's old steward, Dancer, to see the Lionel train exhibit. Bobby was dressed up in his little gray flannel suit with short pants and no lapels, and the blood began to seep through his sleeves. He hadn't said a word.

My mother took care of us on the nurse's day off and gave us baths. She would take Bobby into her bed and comfort him when he had nightmares. Nurses were let go if they were unable to cope with disciplining us. The only time I ever saw my mother cry then was when she had to discharge a nurse. It upset her terribly.

Our house in Cold Spring Harbor was dark and gloomy, although it had a rather pretty situation on a pond. My parents built a long, high cinderblock wall to shut out the noise of the road, which gave the place an ominous look. I suppose we lived there to be near my grandparents, although there was a lot of tension under the surface between my parents and my grandmother. My father told me that when my mother's brother Charlie died—he died of typhoid fever in Rome right after my parents married—Grandma had actually said to my mother, "Oh, why couldn't it have been you?" I have no idea if that's true or not. You don't know what people will say under stress.

Francis Sedgwick

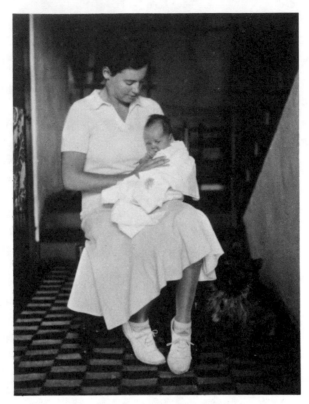

Alice Sedgwick and Saucie, 1931

A sampler showing the de Forest home, Cold Spring Harbor.
Alice's mother embroidered it as an engagement gift for Alice.

My mother and grandmother were very different. Grandma was very devout and very generous, active in charities and clubs. My mother thought all that was for the birds. Grandma grieved that my mother no longer went to church. She was very strict about manners. I heard her ask people not to smoke at table, very nicely, but that was it. She did everything quietly and calmly, though I know from stories that she was strong-willed. Her French maid told me that Grandma had once forgotten an ivory-handled hairbrush in a Santa Barbara hotel, and she made my grandfather stop the train and go back for it.

From the time I was born, my parents literally grafted me onto my grandmother. I was sent to Grandma's with a trained nurse when I got sick, and for long holidays when I grew older. She had a special cupboard of toys with a real microscope and specimens, a set of Chinese fingernail guards in heavy gold filigree, and seashells from the Bahamas. She played games with me endlessly, and she was affection itself. But as much as I loved to be with my grandmother, I never liked life on Long Island. It always seemed basically dreary. And I had an unaccountable sense of danger: I was afraid to close my eyes when I was around adults. I didn't want anybody looking at me that I couldn't keep my eyes on. I had to watch out. Our months in the East were like Persephone's six months in Hades—dark, winter, death. My parents dressed like Easterners, very buttoned up, in dark colors and evening clothes. Their friends were quiet and well spoken, and the women kissed each other on the cheek by turning their faces away from each other. My father seemed incredibly vivid and boisterous among them.

California! That was the ideal world—it was Arcadia. Eternal sunlight, endless blue sky, just seamless harmony and perfection. In 1943 we moved there for good—that's where Edie and Suky were born. We first lived on a fruit ranch in Goleta, fifty acres or so in the foothills near Santa Barbara. The house stood halfway up a slope beside a grove of eucalyptus trees, which gave a great soughing sound in the wind, especially at night. The view seemed to stretch away infinitely—a vast sweep of orchards as far as the sea. Off in the distance you could see the Santa Barbara Islands. Just below the house was a small wild garden, with steppingstones down to a grotto where huge ferns grew under live-oak trees. Beyond were lemon orchards—twenty acres or so—and a creek, barns and corrals for the horses, the greenhouse, and walnut orchards. On the hill behind the house there were avocado and persimmon trees and a steep, narrow path that went up to the pool and the tennis court. The house itself was white stucco covered in vines: plumbago, lantana, trumpet vine, a glorious magenta bougainvillea, and ivy. It was Spanish in style, built around a patio. There was marvelous furniture, and paintings—Ruysdaels and a Carpaccio. We children lived with our nurse in bedrooms at the back which gave onto the patio. My mother and father's room was at the front, toward the view, but they often slept outdoors on a porch over the terrace. There was a ladder and a trapdoor and a double bed up there.

When we were little, we thought that our parents lived the life of Greek gods. Don't forget that there was a strong classical tradition in our family. We knew the myths from early on, and my parents and their life seemed somehow suffused with the same light and feeling as gods. Their physical beauty was very apparent to us. They seemed golden and dressed in white—in fact, they *were,* since they played tennis every day. They led their own life, and it seemed to be full of light and joy. But we had very little access to them . . . none to my father except as a sort of Olympian figure who would punish us. Of course, they *had* to be gods if they were to avoid what happens to humans.

There was a tremendous feeling of happiness in that place—so incredible in light of what happened later. I remember my parents singing all the time. My father was hopelessly tone-deaf, but he had a beautiful voice. He sang "Penny Serenade" . . . "Si, si, si, you can hear it for a penny. Si, si, si, just a penny serenade." My mother sang, too, in a low, rather windy voice, without words. They called each other "darling" all the time. And the air was fragrant—on hot days you could smell the orange orchard in the house. It was just paradise. In fact, that was Babbo's name for it—Paradise Ranch—and he always said he half expected to find St. Peter standing at the gate. My parents gave us the feeling that life was sensational and you couldn't get enough of it. And their friends enjoyed it with them—I remember the place literally ringing with laughter and conversation. You can't fool children: that was real, absolutely real.

Both my parents came from the world in which "connections" and schools and clubs were fantastically important. Like everyone else they knew, they were class conscious, though my mother—perhaps because she was more secure—never showed it. My father would often refer to people as being or not being "out of the top drawer." But in California, even though most of their friends had come from the East, it was a more varied and vivid group. I remember an old lady whom we called Mrs. Fithy, who always came wearing a floppy hat and carrying a wicker market basket full of presents; Kate and Curtis Cate of the Cate School; the Baring-Goulds, who were Scottish; Jane Wyatt, the actress, and her husband, Eddie Ward; Chris and Maddie Rand; Alex Tonetti—gloriously beautiful—with her husband, B. C. White, who taught tennis at the Montecito Club; lots of Hoyts, Rogers, and MacVeaghs, especially Jack MacVeagh, who came every week to play tennis; Lockwood de Forest, my mother's cousin, who was responsible for all the planting at Goleta; and Mary Joyce, who had red hair and blue eyes and a very droll lisp. I can still hear her squeaking with laughter at some outrageous remark of my father's: "Franthith, you are a detethtable man."

From very early on, one of the family's closest friends was Dr. Horace Gray, a Jungian analyst, who came every Sunday for lunch. My mother and father used to boast that he had tested them and found them to be the most extreme examples of introvert and extrovert of his experience. I think my parents liked to define themselves this way: my mother was the feeler, my father was the thinker. Horace Gray didn't play tennis, he didn't come up to the pool, I doubt if he came to parties—he was the wise man, the seer, Merlin.

In a way, my parents were really Renaissance people, but they were more cultivated than intellectual. They read aloud every evening— Dickens, Macaulay, Turgenev. And my mother always knew a lot about music. Even after my father made her stop playing the piano because he said she should devote more time to the children, she still found time every day to listen systematically to records and read and learn. The tragedy was that along with their happiness and their incredible appetite for life, the forces of darkness were always there, although you would never have known it: the surface looked so good. So it was a life of extremes—paradise and paradise lost.

6

The Twentieth Reunion Book, Harvard University, 1946:

FRANCIS MINTURN SEDGWICK

Occupation: Rancher
Married: Alice de Forest, May 8, 1929, New York, N.Y.
Children: Alice; Robert Minturn, 2d; Pamela; Francis Minturn, Jr.;
          Jonathan Minturn; Katherine; Edith; Susanna.

My endeavors to enlist in the armed forces having been thwarted by asthma, I settled on my ranch and devoted myself to raising a few cattle and quite a lot of children.

Ranching has the undoubted advantage of providing beef and pork, chickens and rabbits, and milk and eggs as well as vegetables; and also the doubtful advantage of spare time for indifferent sculpture, worse painting, and a novel, "The Rim," worst of all, the latter published in April, 1945, since four hours a day in the saddle sufficed for the cattle work.

In these peaceful pursuits I have been bucked off three times, thrown twice, had a horse fall on me three times, and, for real excitement, bid in the Grand Champion and Reserve Champion Pens of Bulls at the Great Western Livestock Show at prices below average for the show—very dangerous for blood pressure. Strange uses for a Harvard degree!

I am a trustee of the Cate-Vosting School.

SAUCIE SEDGWICK   During the war my parents bought another place in California, a ranch called Corral de Quati. We children heard about it first from the cook, Nancy Kennedy. Later I remember hearing my father tell some people, "I've decided to raise cattle for the war effort. That's the one thing I can do, since I can't get into the service."

Corral de Quati was a real working cattle ranch, not romantic like Goleta, but glorious because of the land. It was in the Santa Ynez Valley, about fifty miles inland from Santa Barbara—three thousand acres of dry yellow tableland, with sagebrush and live-oak trees. The buildings were strung out around a big open circle, including a nice big cottage where Jonathan, Kate, Edie, and Suky eventually lived. Everything was painted yellow and brown. Near the back door of the main house there was a huge pepper tree, and a bell which was rung fifteen minutes before meals and again at mealtime. Out of earshot of the main house my parents built three little bunkhouses. Bobby and Pamela and I each had one. There was a bed, a desk and a chair, and hooks screwed into the wall for clothes, simple Indian bedspreads, and one single light bulb in the ceiling with a long string. The main house had a big living room with a polar-bear rug in front of the fireplace. The furniture was all very simple—unpainted, or covered in plain cotton. Everything was plain—no sybaritic pleasures, no tennis court, no pool, no parties to speak of.

DR. JOHN MILLET   When the Second World War came, Francis Sedgwick tried very hard to get into the military. His brother, Minturn, was on his way to establishing an excellent and glamorous record with the intelligence branch of the Eighth Air Force in Europe. But though Francis tried very hard, he was turned down—I'm almost sure for the bronchial asthma he had suffered since his early twenties, and very likely because of that large brood of his—six children by then. I wrote to the U.S. Medical Corps that he was a man of exceptional ability and superior intelligence who had learned how to manage his extremely dynamic make-up, both emotional and physical, and that in my opinion he could be of great value in the service. The letter didn't work.

SAUCIE SEDGWICK   I think my father was ashamed and disappointed not to be in the service. He felt that people would look at this glorious physical specimen and think of him as a shirker. I'm sure that's one of the reasons we moved to California. If anyone thought we were trying to avoid the war, it was ironic, because the only attack on continental American soil took place when a Japanese sub lobbed a few shells into an orchard not far from where we were living.

My father took it very hard when two of his best friends were killed in the war: Richard Scott, who was in the Porcellian Club at Harvard with my father, and who was killed on flight duty in North Africa; and Rex Fink, who was killed on Iwo Jima. Both men were incredibly handsome, and admirable in every way. Certainly their dying heroically added to the effect on my father. He did a painting of Rex, and a bas-relief of Dick Scott, which is at Cambridge University, where they were both at Trinity College. He also dedicated his first novel, *The Rim,* to Dick Scott. Here is the dedication: "To the friend of my boyhood, youth, and manhood," with a quote, "And the elements / So mix'd in him that Nature might stand up / And say to all the world, 'This was a man!'" and another: "Though they fell, they fell like stars, / Streaming splendour through the sky." My father was quite self-effacing about his book and it did not get good reviews. The best was in the *Atlantic.* One reviewer said that art and adultery had got a good workout.

JOHN P. MARQUAND, JR. I never read *The Rim,* but I remember hearing that he wrote a horrible description of his poor wife brushing her teeth. She is fat and standing in front of the bathroom mirror; her flesh is jiggling and she is spattering herself with toothpaste. It's a rather sadistic novel about his wife and children. He had a really brutal kind of hold on all of them and brought his children up on this huge ranch in the Groton–Harvard–Porcellian Club myth that he lived in.

SAUCIE SEDGWICK My father never told my mother anything about the book while he was working on it. She was in the East when she read it for the first time—I think she had the chicken pox, which she had caught from us, and she was stuck at my grandmother's on Long Island. I found the letter she wrote him about it in a desk drawer in the study, and even though I was only thirteen at the time, I had the feeling that my father had shut my mother out.

It was an unhappy time. My mother's looks had changed. She'd had a mastoid operation in her late twenties, and in the course of it the doctor cut a nerve. At first the right half of her face was paralyzed. It sagged and her smile was very lopsided. Her eye rolled uncontrollably and she had muscle spasms. I remember trying to imitate it, to the horror of my governess. I didn't think it was ugly, but it was pro-

Francis and Alice Sedgwick at Corral de Quati

nounced, and it must have driven her in on herself terrifically. I never once heard her complain or saw her give in to it.

The symptoms abated eventually, but my mother wasn't beautiful any more. She always looked nice, but she was heavy from so many pregnancies, and she wore her hair in a tight little permanent.

Then there was a feeling at this stage of being pinched for money, of cutting corners. We children were dressed in hand-me-downs from our Eastern cousins, and we got very little for Christmas or birthdays.

The only reason my parents had been able to buy Corral de Quati was because my grandfather had died. They couldn't have bought it before; now they invested so much of my mother's inheritance in land that they were land poor. Before my grandfather died, he had lost fifty or sixty million dollars in the Wall Street crash. He willed half of his remaining money—several million dollars—to my grandmother, the other half to be divided equally between my mother and her older sister, Molly. My grandmother changed the will so that she, my mother, and Aunt Molly got equal amounts. But my father always complained to Uncle Minturn that his father-in-law had died penniless, which is ridiculous but shows how disappointed my father was that there were no longer private railroad cars or rented castles in England.

Owning a three-thousand-acre ranch was very important to my father. Because Babbo was a historian and never made much money, his family had always lived in borrowed houses, rented houses, little houses on big places. They had always been one step behind—always the poor relations. And my father wanted to live in the *big* house. He tried to buy the Old House in Stockbridge but the Sedgwick family wouldn't sell it to him because they wanted to make a trust and have the house belong to the entire family. My father wanted the big house to himself.

After my grandfather de Forest's death, particularly after we moved to Corral de Quati, my father began to behave differently: he was only boisterous with guests. Around the family he was icy and remote. My mother became cautious and reserved. At the same time, they began opening up to different types of friends—ranchers from around the Santa Ynez Valley, artists from Santa Barbara, people here and there that they took a fancy to. They began adopting young couples. Often my father would have an affair with the wife. So by the time my youngest sisters, Edie and Suky, were born, my father was definitely fooling around.

7

SAUCIE SEDGWICK My mother had a difficult time with the births of her last children, but she kept getting pregnant anyway. I know my parents expected to have another boy. My mother turned out to be allergic to anesthetics, and when Edie was born she nearly died. It was very close. It affected everyone. Babbo used to say that he had told the Lord in words of one syllable what he thought of his "baby system." My father was afraid when my mother was having those last babies that she was going to die, but on the other hand he had begun to like the idea of producing a spectacular number of children. As for my mother, I have no idea why she went on having children when it was so dangerous for her.

Edie was born at the Cottage Hospital in Santa Barbara, April 20, 1943, the first child after my parents moved permanently to California. She was the seventh of the eight of us, and named for our father's favorite aunt, Edith Minturn Stokes.

Edie was very little when Jane Wilson became her nurse. She was a strong, kind, straightforward person—she was strict, but you knew where you stood with her; nothing was devious. She loved those children in her way, and she interceded for them and invested quite a lot in them, I think.

The Sedgwick family at home, Corral de Quati *(clockwise):*
Suky with Francis, Edie, Alice, Jonathan, Kate, and Minty

JANE WILSON   Edie was six months old when I took over. I had
Kate and Edie and then Suky. I started to toilet-train Edie right away.
She did everything in her diapers, and I wouldn't have that. She had
to sit until she did it. That's the one thing I was always fussy about
with all my children. Suky was only two weeks old when she came
home, and I started *her* on the potty. You hold them up, the little potty
on your lap, and then patiently wait. It doesn't take them long to know
what they're there for. I never spanked Edie or any of them. Jonathan
used to claim he had nightmares. He was about seven. I told him, "Is
this what you want?" and I showed him a hairbrush. He never had
another nightmare.

I'd take Edie over to the main house from the cottage we lived in
to say good morning to her parents. She'd refuse. Edie knew she'd
have to sit until she'd said good morning, but she was determined
not to give in and she would just stare at you. She never cried, that
was the last thing she'd ever do.

Edie had a will of her own. It was born in her. The parents spoilt
her. Anything Edie wanted to do was fine with her parents, but not
with me. She had to mind and she had to eat everything on her plate,
and I wouldn't allow her to push Suky around.

SAUCIE SEDGWICK   I was almost twelve when Edie was born, and
most of the time when she was growing up I was away at school. So
were Bobby and Pamela. Even when we were home we didn't see much
of the younger children in those early years.

Right after the war, "the three little girls," as Kate, Edie, and Suky
were always called, lived like poor kids, dressed in hand-me-down
pale green overalls and jackets and scuffed brown shoes. They looked
like little Maoists playing in the sandpit.

JONATHAN SEDGWICK   Birthdays were really strange. The joy was
out of the presents that you might get and the ice cream and the cake,
because you'd get a pinch from my father, which really hurt, to grow
an inch. After the pinch you got a swat for each year since your birth.
I never liked that. Seemed weird. You'd have to spend most of the day
trying not to get caught.

SAUCIE SEDGWICK   When Edie was five, a new nurse came along
called Addie. She was different from the earlier nurses in that she was
utterly loving and gentle. She was a pudding of a person, white

whiskers, buck teeth, a small skull, and a big, fat face. There was just not one mean thing about that woman—she was something out of a fairy tale, but she was incapable of maintaining any kind of authority. Edie was unbelievably cruel to her and kicked her, but she loved her very much.

Some of the games Edie and Suky played seemed a little sadistic at times. Edie turned Suky into a horse, herself into a wolf, and she chased Suky, whimpering and whinnying, out into the fields. That game terrified Suky and gave her nightmares. She even began to see wolves in the scrapbasket. Edie also made a whole series of animal heads to go on a broomstick, and she'd ride around on them. But the heads had to be perfect.

JONATHAN SEDGWICK   When it came to real horses, Edie would always get the best-looking one. She could get anything she wanted. Spoiled. Even if I had the best-looking horse, it became *her* horse because she convinced everyone that I was too heavy for him and that he'd get tired under my weight. That was cool; it didn't bother me.

We were on top of horses at fourteen months. They'd prop us up on them for a picture to be taken, and then you'd keep wanting a horse. Everybody rode, and you just started riding the first thing you could. The big game was Cowboys and Indians. One would be a cowboy and the other an Indian and we'd chase each other through the trees. Edie and Suky rode at night, through the moonlight. I didn't ever go with them. I don't know what they talked about. They'd get up really early and watch the sun come up—things like that.

I remember this picture of us being lined up on our horses. Weird trip. Bobby didn't like it at all. Saucie thought it was strange. Pamela tried to play it super cool. Minty was just bashful, and Kate was smily. But Edie . . . she seemed French to me when this one was taken. The picture was for an article in *Life* magazine which never appeared, called "The Working American" or something like that, and it was supposed to show how we worked the ranch with horses and eight children. Edie is on Zorillo, which means Skunk in certain derivations of the word in Spanish. Otherwise it means Little Fox. She really knew how to get it on. Look at her, man. Little French lady. Already her hands are in place; nobody else has their hands that way. She already has her little thing going.

SAUCIE SEDGWICK   I remember thinking how phony the *Life* pictures were—the family wasn't united like that at all. The main thing

I resented was the image of everyone sitting together devotedly reading after dinner. We read after dinner only because nobody could *talk* about anything. It was a form imposed, like a cookie cutter, from outside.

There isn't much in common between these cosmetic pictures and the old photos of the earlier Sedgwicks with their amusing, knobbly faces . . . they all looked like a bunch of Jerusalem artichokes. The "Sedgwick Nose" is large and curves downward like a beak. None of us got it, though my parents kept an eye on Minty. I told you my father thought I looked like a sausage when I was born. "Sausie" is what's in the early photograph albums and on my christening pin. My father used to say, "Sauce, pauce, puddin' and pie, kissed the boys and made them cry." He also called me Puddin'. He had nice nicknames for us. Kate was Miss Rincus, Kate-a-rinks-Kate-a-rincus. Minty was Squints, Squinterino. Pamela was Pamelelagraph, Giraffe. Edie was Weedles, sometimes Weasel. At dinner he would carve, and he would say, "Well, what are you going to have, Miss Weedles?" He would sometimes refer to the whole lot of us as "monkeyshines."

My parents also named animals very well. My mother had a mare named Lady Murasaki, and Flying Cloud was my father's horse—so beautiful, a pale strawberry roan. Gazette was also my father's horse, even though he was too heavy for her. She was a lovely dappled gray, small and slight and narrow in the chest, and my father was a big man and he had all this macho stuff on his saddle. He kept a rope, though he didn't rope. His saddle must have weighed 50 or 60 pounds, and he weighed 180. He was so heavy for her that she would "cross feet" when she was tired in order to support his weight. She was the most beautiful, affectionate, intelligent creature . . . absolutely responsive. My father practically didn't have to use the reins at all. He loved her very much, but he didn't reduce the weight of his tack. It reminded me of the scenes where Vronsky breaks his mare's back in *Anna Karenina*. My father looked terrific on a horse, but my mother was "with" her horse when she rode, though she didn't look like much. She never braced like a cowboy; she rode forward as an English rider might who was sitting to the trot, so she jiggled a lot. But the cowboys said she was really the good rider. She had wonderful hands and a real feeling for her horse. The animals loved her very much. When we would go riding, the dogs would come tumbling after. Lord, there were the dogs. My parents had two Airedales named Gog and Mig. There was Queechy, an English bull terrier who was very fierce . . . a fiend . . . my father's dog. When Edie was little, they had a St. Bernard named

The Sedgwick family outside the tack room, Corral de Quati, 1946 (*left to right*):
Kate, Francis, Bobby, Alice, Jonathan, Edie, Minty, Pamela, Suky, and Saucie

Pougachev for the leader of the people's rebellion in the time of Catherine the Great. They had Great Danes—a dog named Woof who was half Great Dane and half greyhound.

HARRY SEDGWICK I remember that dog Woof. It was so fast and powerful, it would go for whatever was in its way—pigs, deer. Once, we were riding off in the West Mesa and suddenly this horrible scream came from a clump of bushes. My uncle Fuzzy jumped off his horse and went in there and pulled out the dog attached to a deer! The dog had the deer by the hindquarters, and the animal was really screaming . . . it was almost human. Fuzzy kept clubbing the dog with his quirt, or whatever they call a horsewhip out in the West, until he finally let go, and we all bounced back into the ranch. Well, this old cowboy who worked on the place heard about it, and he said he was going to get the authorities after Fuzzy and his dog. I happened to mention that to Fuzzy, foolishly, and I'll tell you, he just hit the ceiling. He thought of it as a threat to himself! The dog, the horse, the house, the mistress—they were all *his*. Expressions of himself. They couldn't be tampered with. With the kids . . . well, the dogs and the horses made out a lot better. Somehow the kids were a threat to him.

SAUCIE SEDGWICK My parents owned the land from horizon to horizon in every direction. Imagine a situation like that where nobody entered who wasn't invited or hired! In this landscape my mother and father rooted out any influence that they could not dominate. You weren't even told where you were going to ride that day. "Wait and see," they'd say. "Can we go to Santa Barbara tomorrow?" "Wait and see." As far as I know, the three little girls never went off the ranch except to go to Santa Barbara to the doctor.

Edie had so little to work with. How small the furniture of her life was! She grew up with a total lack of boundaries, a total lack of a sense of scale about herself. She was stuck in there. When I was small and growing up, I had a very distinct feeling of background and tradition—what lay back of my parents' way of life—which was a very strong sense of being connected to my grandmother and to Uncle Ellery and my grandfather Babbo and all those older people with linen suits and silk dresses and Bostonian voices. The impression when you're little is powerful, and it made it possible for me to reach beyond my parents to a feeling of being connected. That possibility had vanished by the time Edie came along. For her there was no sense of anything except the ranch: the world had shrunk to that.

WENDY WILDER The Sedgwicks lived in their own world. We went over sometimes, but they were hard to know. They even had their own schoolhouse. I don't think Edie had a good friend—horses maybe.

SAUCIE SEDGWICK The schoolroom was very small—just a shack in the corner of the ranch where one of the cowboys had lived until my parents decided to make it into a school. My parents had kept track of a couple named Bryant they knew from New York—he had been a music student at Juilliard and she had earned money by modeling, for my father among other people. My father sent them a telegram—they were living in Oregon—proposing that they come down and run the school. In those days you could send a telegram up to ten words for a fixed amount. The Bryants sent back a telegram which read, YES, YES, YES, YES, YES, YES, YES, YES, YES, YES! They brought a couple of their own children with them, who were also in the school. So were the Luton children from the ranch next door. From our family were Jonathan, Kate, Edie, and Suky.

JONATHAN SEDGWICK The Bryants arrived at the ranch in this broken-up little old car with one of those trailers behind it that fold out into a tent. He looked . . . like he'd been siphoned, you know . . . there was nothing in him . . . almost dead . . . skinny, sad, and weak. She was much stronger—tall, with a Roman nose. They taught us the Calvert System. Each kid was working at his own level. The Bryants went around the schoolroom to check up on us. I took exams for Groton and failed miserably on the writing. So I had to write essays all summer long. We weren't allowed to go to the local public schools. Weren't good enough for us. "We are aristocracy. We have to be educated." We were taught in a weird way, so that when we got out into the world we didn't fit anywhere; nobody could understand us. We learned English the way the English do, not Americans.

JOHN P. MARQUAND, JR. They spoke in a sort of language in which the grandparents would have talked. It was always straight Grotonian all the way through and it obviously was preserved in their consciousness by the father, who just laid it onto them that they were Sedgwicks. The way you pronounced words implied a certain attitude that you took toward life and to other people in society. It would be too superficial to say that it was snobbish or arrogant, it was sort of supernatural . . . surreal.

Edie, age three

Babbo with Edie and Kate

SAUCIE SEDGWICK We really lived in two worlds—indoors and outdoors. Outdoors, that vast physical world of the ranch, was just pure freedom and elation, especially if you were out riding alone. Indoors meant inside the main house with the family. That was the world of form—very strict rules of conduct, all repressive, all belonging to that other world in the East that my parents were from.

For me, life at Corral de Quati was one long degradation. In front of anyone—guests, cowboys—my father would say I was fat, or stupid, or a liar. I remember once he introduced me to a new choreman, a guy named Lee who looked like a turkey gobbler, "This is my daughter Alice and she's fat." Lee said, "I got a daughter Alice and she's fat, too," and they both had a good laugh.

Meals were especially tense. I can remember sitting in that dining room, just waiting for the axe to fall, and being grateful when it fell on somebody else. My brother Minty told me years later that he always used to ask William, our butler, if there were going to be guests, because it would be so much easier then.

SUKY SEDGWICK Under the bed was a refuge. I remember an earthquake. Edie came into my room. It was early in the morning because I remember my teeth chattered I was so scared. And the first thing we did was to get under my bed because that was the safest place. We clung to each other, and then somebody came in and sort of looked after us. My parents were miles away.

SAUCIE SEDGWICK One saving grace at Corral de Quati was our grandfather Babbo, although he was so old that my mother was afraid he might die on the ranch and one of the children would find him. At Uncle Minturn's in the East he was the life of the party, quick-witted, well read, amusing, very much a part of the scene. But in the West, when he came out to stay at our ranch, he spent much of his time alone.

I remember Babbo stumping off every afternoon down toward the pig barns, with a gray fedora hat with a feather in it and his Harvard letter sweater tied round his neck, and a raggle-taggle of dogs behind him. He often had his supper early with the children, and we would all clamor for an installment of his tales of the Baron Münchhausen. Although he lived in a bunkhouse, he used the study in the main house: there he'd read Cicero, or Ovid, or Virgil, and laugh away as if it were some modern novel. His favorite author was Saint-Exupéry. He used to read Caesar's *Gallic Wars* and shout with laughter. He went out into the fields and communed with the cattle. He had pet names for those huge Hereford bulls, like Paul Potter, after the Dutch painter. The Herefords were his candidates for president of the United States. He told me once that if men were to be succeeded by another race, he hoped it would not be ants, or bees, or mosquitoes, or cockroaches, but Hereford cattle. Actually, I don't think he could be lonely anywhere. You could set him down on the desert.

Everyone had their own separate lives on the ranch and Babbo had his. He loved to go to Santa Barbara when my mother went in to do errands or take us to the doctor. We'd leave him off at the library, and what with all the children, and everything she had to remember, sometimes my mother would forget him. One time we got all the way back to the top of the San Marcos Pass, twenty miles away, and my mother suddenly realized we'd left him behind. We went back. Babbo didn't say a word. He was sitting outside on the bench where the buses go by and waiting for my mother to come.

Babbo also used to ride to Santa Barbara with my mother to go to the movies. He was the only one interested in them. He was much more "modern" in a sense than anyone else. He was the only person on the ranch who was interested in the news during the war. He'd sit with his hands cupped over his ears, crouched over and listening to the nurse's radio. I remember the day Roosevelt died, Babbo said, "I feel as though the world has fallen off Atlas' shoulders."

Babbo had a passion for mail-order houses. Once, he ordered himself a whole lot of shirts with zippers rather than buttons, and my father made him send them back because they were "too disgraceful." It didn't matter that he was an old man for whom zippers were much easier than buttons. He used to say that he longed for a beautiful, silent Japanese lady with delicate fingers to do up just that *one* collar button. My father felt that the zippered shirts "shamed" us. He spoke to Babbo as if he were a child: "That won't do, Father, I'm sorry." Babbo accepted it. He'd say, "That's all right, Sonny."

MINTURN SEDGWICK   Francis was the only person who seemed to disapprove when Babbo married Gabriella, whom he'd met right there on his ranch. Francis made this frightful fuss about it. He went right on refusing to see them. Saucie told me that at one point she tried to reason with him. "You must see Babbo. He's unbelievably happy with Gabriella and your attitude causes him such sorrow." He said, "No, I can't help it. It's emotional."

SAUCIE SEDGWICK My father went bananas. Perhaps he simply couldn't stand the idea of Gabriella in his mother's place. He wrote to Uncle Minturn: "It ain't no good no how . . . the idea of having that horror as my stepmother makes my hair wiggle like a serpent's." He was even afraid they would have a baby. He wrote to a number of Babbo's contemporaries to persuade them to intervene. And he wrote desperate letters to Babbo himself: "No one has ever come between you and me—and at the end of life in pops a total stranger. I need no psychiatrist to comprehend my distaste." I think my father's rage had an effect on all of us. He'd lost his father, so he thought, and he tightened his grip on the children.

JONATHAN SEDGWICK   In the early Fifties oil was discovered on
the ranch. I remember seeing a derrick at Corral de Quati, coming
across it on a horse when I was very young, or seeing it from a truck,
but there was no oil, it was a dry well. Then Flying A came in and by
the fall of 1952 there was a lot of activity—trucks, and men everywhere. They had redrilled one of the old wells and went thirteen or
fourteen feet further down and there was the oil. It had taken time for
things to generate because it was low-grade oil which wouldn't have
been pumped in the Valley if it weren't for the war, when Getty
pumped it, and he did pretty well.

SAUCIE SEDGWICK   My parents were neurotic about the oil. We
weren't allowed to drive or ride anywhere near the pumps. When I
took these Italian boys—there weren't any oil wells in Italy and I
thought they'd be interested—why, you'd think I'd taken off my clothes,
turned upside down, and displayed my bottom. That's how obscene
and shocking my parents thought it was. They always said it was the
lowest grade of oil and practically worthless. So they must have felt
fishy about the money. Before the oil, the money was my mother's.
My grandfather de Forest earned his fortune and so did *his* father.
Nobody in our branch of the Sedgwick family made any money
except that my father happened with the de Forest family money to

Suky and Edie at Rancho La Laguna

buy a ranch which had oil on it. It must have made my father feel freer not to have to rely so much on my mother's money.

JONATHAN SEDGWICK   I think there were seventeen wells by the time we left. They were coming in the back door, literally. The last well went in fifty feet from the back door of the house, so the stench was getting pretty bad. Of course, the money coming in meant that my parents could move on. In July, 1952, my father bought Rancho La Laguna de San Francisco—the third of their California ranches— about six miles away from Corral de Quati as the crow flies. I remember when we first saw it. We all got saddled up and rode off with my father, the feudal lord, leading us, and suddenly we were riding up a hill called the Ventura Field with pine trees on top, moving through the wild oats which were so tall, six or seven feet high, that on our small ponies it was like swimming through them. Edie flowed through the grass on her pony. She couldn't see where she was going. Really exciting. I read somewhere that the prairies were like that without the cattle to browse the grass down to two or three feet, and that the Prairie Indians rode through tall grass all the time.

Then my father paused at the top of the hill and looked down over the land like an emperor, just beaming with joy and pride, and announced: "Look at this! Since I came to this valley, I've always wanted this ranch. Isn't this magnificent . . . as far as I can see it's beautiful!" He was really talking about himself . . . really admiring himself. That was the first time we realized we were moving to Rancho Laguna. He was looking over his duchy, and we were part of it, too.

SUKY SEDGWICK   The new ranch was gloriously beautiful. It was a natural balance that anything short of nature would have had a difficult time sculpting. The old ranch was less aesthetically beautiful and not as clean-cut. . . . I mean sharp like a blade that shines in the sun. Our human world was something very different from our natural world, deeply different but equally as intense. I'd call it something like a peaceful refuge from the pains of various types we experienced in our intensified play-works. Play-works, play and work. Little play but intense. All intensity . . . horse games.

Edie made us stick horses, and if one stick horse's ear hung a little bit that way, she'd get what she called her "icky feelings." Oh, they were awful! I mean, a detail would become an absolute torture. I'd want to get away from whatever she was feeling and go play, and she would be turmoiling over some useless and absolutely nonsensical detail. I began to realize that Edie had times when she wasn't totally herself. She couldn't escape from it either. I knew it wasn't her fault but I didn't know what the hell it was.

Edie and I had a secret world that belonged just to us two. Only us two in the whole family. And in that sense we were twins. She made up a family called the Chieftains, and that was really something. There was a father, who was an Indian chief. He had red skin. I imagined him as being a big Indian Buddha with red skin. He was nothing but kindness and understanding. Absolutely no punishments or anything like that. *Ever, ever.* There was no mother, isn't that curious? There were about eight or ten children. There was one just like Edie. And there was a horse! And a dog. Twinkleberry was the name of the horse. Edie used to be all these things; I mean in this imaginary world Edie would act them out. She would *be* each one of the family. This world was a pure world for both of us—pure in the sense that there could be nothing wrong in it—no evils or no injustices and no unhappiness . . . a family which was an absolute paradigm of joy! Everything was wonderful when we played that game. It was just a very kind, soft world, as far as I can remember.

Another game we had was playing horse. You had to look at a picture and you would choose what you wanted to look like. Edie used to make me stare at the picture of a goddam horse's face for hours, it seemed to me, so that I'd remember what she looked like. She inevitably chose something that was very delicate and very Arab, and I inevitably chose the opposite: something very strong and not so beautiful. Sort of solid workhorse type . . . but not quite a workhorse. And Edie was always a beautiful prancing princess-type horse.

At Corral de Quati, Edie and I had lived in a cottage with my sister Kate and the nurse, Addie. We were little savages, but we were independent little characters, both of us. And when the chips were down we were by ourselves.

We were brought up in one family, in absolute, total isolation, with people coming in the summer to visit us, and then as soon as you got fond of them, they never came back again, it seemed. A lot of people disappeared, a lot of people were sent away, a lot of people didn't want to come back, I guess. We rarely left the ranch, but when Edie and I had to go to the doctor in the Valley, Minty would come and put on puppet shows for us with our stuffed animals. He'd make us laugh and distract us, and then somebody would get us dressed. We used to get vitamin B shots. They *hurt!* We got them every day. *Every* day. Edie and I both had allergy tests, too. Powders. With what seemed to me something along the lines of a thumbtack, up and down our backs. Powder. Poke. Powder. Poke. Powder. Poke. Until you could throw up on the floor. With a lady doctor who lived in the Santa Ynez Valley near Ballard. We used to be taken over in the car as if we were going to the vet.

I saw the doctor bend a needle in Edie's *bee*-hind and I felt like screaming because I was the one who was watching and I got mine next. You don't give people shots in front of other little people who are going to get it next. That was a vitamin B shot . . . all shots in the rear end. "Pull down your pants and let's have it over with." Oh, shit! "And don't you dare cry, or even whimper."

Summer was the time when all of the children were home, and we rambled around and had games after dinner, and it was light until nine o'clock at night. And that was freedom for us! I'd compare it to a Shakespearean play—I mean Shakespearean tragedy takes intervals for comic relief. Well, that's exactly the way our kind of playing was. It was extremely intense. Absolute bliss.

We *lived* the seasons! It was living in an absolute. If you have the galaxies above you and the changing seasons below you, you live in another dimension. And the only thing that we had besides that were a few skimpy little actors on our stage, and that's all.

Each new season brought new feelings. Fall brought deep sadness. Winter—Christmas pageantry and other rituals. It was exciting; it was the time when you gave presents. We didn't have stockings, we had boots, and they were sort of rigid things. I would have preferred stockings. Isn't that funny? Cowboy boots. And they were lined up in front of the fireplace in their various sizes. Then the heaps of presents around the room. We usually made presents for Mummy and Fuzzy. They made us understand that anything we could buy was off the point. We didn't have the money, anyway. Edie made some beautiful things. She made stamp holders—Mummy still has them—with a horse head on them. Kate made pictures. Minty made comics. All of us made things, usually useful things.

My memories of Corral de Quati are very splattered . . . something along the lines of a color in Pollock's paintings, one of the underneath ones, I'd say. We used to have parties with all the people at the ranch. And that was really fun! The night before Christmas. All of the children and all the adults had a big party together and we all played games. Together. Just pure unadulterated fun, no strings attached.

There were also seasons of fire. And there were fires, big fires when we first got to the new ranch at Laguna. I mean that's fire! Edie and I used to sit by our window, which happened to look out over the mountains. The *whole* rim of the mountains was outlined in fire. The pass—that's a trap, too—the pass road was cut off; that was the way to get to Santa Barbara. Behind us was real wilderness. We'd watch the sky get BLACK, the sky is filled with cinders. Hell is not too far away. When the two forest fires mount to the top, there's an explosion, instantaneous combustion—BOOM! What blows up then rolls down and starts new fires and winds are created. We lived through that kind of thing happening next door.

When nature was just calm and comfortable, it couldn't have been more beautiful to us. The ranch has so many different places to go and different atmospheres to partake of. There's Pine Needle Canyon, with big, lofty pine trees. You can actually hear the wind in the pines, which is a completely different sound than oak trees or just no trees at all. It's a beautiful sound. I love it. And I know that there were only two places on the ranch that you could go and really listen to it. It was music. And what else was there? Oh, there was the Uplands, and that's where Edie wanted to stay. That was dangerous in a storm. So much violence. The ranch was potential violence—both human and natural.

Do you know Coleridge? "Kubla Khan"? "In Xanadu did Kubla Khan / A stately pleasure dome decree: / Where Alph, the sacred river, ran / Through caverns measureless to man / Down to a sunless sea." The ranch was all those things and, boy oh boy, does Coleridge know what he's talking about. It was the pleasure dome. It was a sunless sea. And that's funny, but it's one of the few poems I've always remembered by heart.

9

SAUCIE SEDGWICK Laguna, the new ranch, was twice as big as Corral de Quati—six thousand acres—and the land, even the approach, was much more dramatic—a long, flat valley between hills and the mountains at the end. At Corral de Quati, there were dairy cows and pigs, and the chickens wandered around loose. At Laguna there was no dairy or pigs, and the chickens were shut in these terrible dark hen sheds; they just stood on nets and dropped their eggs. Their feet got so misshapen they couldn't have walked on the ground. My mother wouldn't go out there to see them; she said it was too upsetting. The barns and the houses for the men working on the ranch were grouped together in a grove of live oaks. The main house was set apart, out in the Valley, and it was white. In between, my father built a tennis court, a big swimming pool with changing rooms, a guesthouse, and a large studio for himself, identical to the one at Goleta, our first ranch.

The house itself always seemed somehow banal to me—it had none of the magic of Goleta or the wonderful plain quality of Corral de Quati. The good furniture from Goleta was there, eighteenth century English mostly, and there were leather sofas in the living room. My mother put Fortuny curtains everywhere. My father bought his uncle Robert Minturn's family collection of fifteenth- and sixteenth-century Italian and Flemish pictures, had them restored, and hung them in the house. I remember also two T'ang horses, very beautiful, but my father said one was a fake, he could tell by this feeling he had. The food became suddenly much fancier. William, our butler on Long Island, who had milked cows at Corral de Quati, began wearing a white coat again and waiting at table. At Corral de Quati, I don't remember my parents drinking or offering anything before meals except Dubonnet shaken up with lemon peel and ice in a cocktail shaker. They rather disapproved of people who drank. At Corral de Quati the normal drink had been milk, but at Laguna there was wine at meals, and I remember my father having a great tub of Scotch and soda at the table. And afterwards there were liqueurs—Tia Maria, of all things, or Brandy and Benedictine, sweet things, but strong. My brother Minty became an alcoholic at Laguna when he was about fifteen. He told me later it was because everything was so tense and the booze was so available. Maybe Edie got addicted to pills the same way because my parents took so many for their allergies and whatever problems they had.

Suddenly my father broke out in Mercedes sports cars and he got a big Mercedes sedan for my mother. A foreign car was a big step in those days; it was ostentatious. My father gave my mother a solitaire diamond and a mink coat. Something had really happened. I think a certain resignation set in on my father's part, and he abandoned puritanical attitudes that they had shared before.

Another big change was that the three little girls moved into the main house. They had had their own house with their nurse, Addie, most of their lives, but now Edie and Suky and Addie moved right next to my parents' room, and Kate lived at the other end, near the kitchen. Later Kate moved in with Pamela in the girls' bunkhouse, which had been brought over from the old ranch. I seldom came home, but when I did I was struck by how close and jolly the rest of the family seemed. Bobby and Pamela always had friends staying and there was lots of joking and teasing. I noticed that my mother had suddenly drawn Edie and Suky very close to her. They were like little stamping, whinny-ing ponies; at meals they sat on either side of her and held her hands tightly while they ate.

My parents' daily ritual was still the same as at Corral de Quati. They came to breakfast, my mother dressed in English riding clothes, and my father in a T-shirt and jeans of some sort—usually very light tan, though he wore frontier pants a lot in the early stages. He always had a bandanna handkerchief in his rear pocket, sticking out.

After breakfast Fuzzy did his exercises out by the pool in this little loincloth he wore. It wasn't a real jockstrap, but a neat little thing which looked more like a cotton bikini. He also did his writing there,

Sunday lunch, Francis Sedgwick with a guest

sitting in the sun in this cotton bikini with a great big sombrero on his head. He was always nearly naked. He had this belief that the human body revealed the discipline and the performance of the person inside. With his enormous thorax and the muscles of his arms and chest and abdomen, and his priapic, almost strutting bearing, the main effect was one of fantastic vitality.

After lunch my parents would always rest until three o'clock and then we would meet at the barn to go riding. At dinner my mother would wear a Chinese mandarin coat, exquisitely embroidered, and satin pajamas. My father usually wore a gabardine suit and a bow tie. He always had the same haircut, a long crew cut, sort of stuck up: a brush cut, I believe it's called. My mother cut it for him. He was very vain about his hair, very pleased that he was not balding . . . everything to do with veer-il-i-ty! Well, he *was* something. When he came to the Katharine Branson School to see me, the girls stood at the windows and stared at him. He was so beautiful. "Swoon! swoon! faint! faint!"

Laguna was also different from Corral de Quati because life was as jolly as it had been at Goleta. It was raffish and violent, but it was very jolly. How funny my father was! He was hilarious. And he had enormous charm. He was a real Don Giovanni.

My father had the feeling that, if he survived, it was by an act of will. He had Don Giovanni's defiant attitude toward fate and consequences. In that sense he was heroic. He had the physical beauty of Don Giovanni, the seductiveness, the taunting quality of Don Giovanni, the *disprezzo* of Don Giovanni. Life was a feast for him and he really was going to drink its cup to the dregs. He bore himself as if all eyes were upon him and he was center stage all the time . . . which he was. He moved in the world and you felt him.

RICHARD PARKER   Duke Sedgwick's sculpture was like him—it had a kind of courage. Great huge statues of horses and generals and God knows what. Very conventional, very academic. But you felt he had no inhibitions, no lack of self-confidence about what he was doing. I don't know why he became a sculptor. It seemed a strange profession for him to indulge in, but he liked studios, I guess.

JONATHAN SEDGWICK   He looked tall, though he wasn't very tall at all. He was only five-eleven. It's your bearing. If you have your energy together, you can be gigantic. He always rode up above everyone else along the side of a hill. But even if he happened to be riding below the others, he still looked bigger. The energy was heavy. My father was a great blaster of energy.

RICHARD RAND   Every year the Sedgwicks had a round-up. Marvelous occasion. Hundreds of people would come, and many of the men would go out with Duke Sedgwick to round up the cattle and bring them in. Real Western scene, right? Lots of children and a great deal of activity. Every person you knew would sit along the fence and watch them rope the calves and tie them down and brand them and all the rest.

After the round-up you had an enormous outside picnic, with picnic tables, and animals turning on spits—something out of an old painting. Everybody got cozy and sat at the tables with the working people. Duke went around with a quart of whiskey, which he would hold up to each of the men there, who would ceremoniously—a sort of nice Faulknerian touch—take a swig and pass it on.

The new gentry out there were from New York and Boston. They came to Santa Barbara for various reasons, usually because they had become discontented with life in the East and its pressures. But in a sense it was a very Eastern scene—a certain cultural snobbishness, the feeling that if you came from the East you were more civilized than the yokels who grew up there. We wore Brooks Brothers clothing rather than sports shirts. We socialized with each other.

So the social stratifying was fierce. If you came from the Middle West, you had damn better come from a meat-packing fortune, or forget it. If you didn't, you had all the bad vibes and no redeeming features. The social lines were very tight. Of course, it was also promiscuous. You were allowed to sleep with just about anyone.

SAUCIE SEDGWICK   At one of my parents' parties I saw my father disappear into the bushes, right in front of my mother, with his arm around a woman—just traipsed off into the bushes in front of fifty people. I was horrified, but my mother never turned a hair. Our French cook, who adored my mother, once surprised my father kissing another woman just as my mother came in. My mother said to her in French, "That's nothing, Monsieur is just teasing, that's nothing."

JONATHAN SEDGWICK   She didn't take her frustration and anger at my father's affairs out on the children. She'd get allergies and needed special diets. She'd stay in bed a lot with what were said to be "low-grade fevers," and she began going to the hospital. Then my father would get scared because he'd think he was going to lose the one who really loved him. My mother finally got to the point where she wouldn't go anywhere. They'd be invited to a dinner party and at the last minute she'd pretend to be sick, or have some other great excuse at the last minute for why she couldn't go.

SAUCIE SEDGWICK   My mother was the shyest person. She liked to hide unless she was in control. She was terrified to walk in alone anywhere. The only place she'd feel comfortable away from home was in a club. She wouldn't dance at a party; she felt that over the age of twenty-five it was not dignified to dance. My father agreed with her that it was not dignified for her to dance.

My mother didn't have the glamor and lightheartedness that Fuzzy saw in other women, but she was a real lady, and she knew that she had what he needed—namely, utter steadfastness. And money. He couldn't have done without either. He would tell me how bad I was and then he would *always* say: "Now your mother, she's a good person." Yet in some way she wasn't enough for him any more. So she became a kind of Mediterranean mother who maintained the family and the hearth. He went out and had flings, but he always came back.

SUKY SEDGWICK   Maybe Mummy had all of those children because Fuzzy wanted to have a little tribe to show everybody. We were paraded around a bit, just to show the guests the children, that's what it was. I didn't know why I hated it so much. I had to play the piano for them. I was Miss Mozart. Edie was Miss Rembrandt. Minty was Mr. Leonardo. Christ, we were all supposed to be God knows what—geniuses to add to Fuzzy's pyramid.

SUSAN WILKINS   My God, the father was something! A cross between Mr. America and General Patton. We were all whinnying little girls in the Fifties, we didn't know anything. After all, we were privileged Wasps who had come out of the mold of private schools. We all had the same basic attitude toward life: we all wanted to be popular with nice college boys, marry a handsome man from Harvard, Yale, or Princeton, have a few babies, wear cashmere sweaters and tweed skirts in the autumn, play a good game of tennis, join the country club, and never be a force for anything.

I spent a week at Rancho Laguna in August, 1954—one of the most extraordinary and shocking times I have ever spent. I went there to be a bridesmaid for Pamela Sedgwick's wedding to Jerry Dwight. Pamela was a tense person who bit her fingernails, a rather shy, slightly horsy-faced girl with brown hair and a rather angular face, which her brother Bobby also had.

We arrived and were immediately ushered into the presence of this "man," this father with his exaggerated views about human beauty. Nobody who wasn't beautiful was allowed around. He began by making comments about each of the bridesmaids, the length of our legs, the size of our bosoms. There were two of us he took a particular liking to—Ginny Backus, who was a knockout, and Shelley Dwight, who was Jerry's sister and had that Irish red hair that caught the sun. So while much of that week was spent in tennis and swimming, which should have been fun, all the time you were being made to wonder whether you measured up or not—whether you cut the mustard. It certainly helped if you were beautiful and rich.

There were a lot of tears that week, a lot of us in our rooms crying—bridesmaids, the bride. *Lots* of tension. I remember it as being physically exhausting. We went from dawn to dusk. The tension was phenomenal. *Phenomenal!* There was something almost mythological about what was happening. Duke Sedgwick reminded me of somebody from Mount Olympus. I'm thinking of Titian's *Rape of Europa* in the Isabella Stewart Gardner Museum. *That* was the feeling. It was a stud farm, that house, with this great stallion parading around in as little as he could. We were the mares. But it wasn't sex. It was breeding . . . and there's a difference, of course. The air was filled with an aura of procreation. Not carnal lust, but just breeding in the sense of not only re-creating life but a certain kind of life, a certain elite, a superior race. There was no romance. It was stultifying. I remember Jerry Dwight saying, "I've just got to get Pamela the hell out of here." I never heard Pamela disloyal to her mother or her father, but I think she wanted to escape. Marriage was the way out for her.

The other aura that seemed to permeate everything was the element of brutality. Great violence! Bobby had his accident when I was there—he fell off a bicycle going down a steep hill and broke his neck. He held on to his head when he got up, which was all that kept his spine from severing. The family was in pandemonium because for a while they didn't know whether he'd walk again, or even live. The father was on very bad terms with Bobby, and there was a whole ruckus about whether he would even go to the hospital to see him—a lot of yelling behind closed doors. A lot of crying. The mother was stunned. Everybody was shocked.

SAUCIE SEDGWICK   Traction didn't work, and Bobby's neck had to be fused. It was a very dangerous operation. Bobby had a dream in which he crawled on his knees down the long corridor to my parents' bedroom at Goleta and begged them, "Please give me another chance, *please*," and they told him, "No, you have had your last chance." When he came out of the hospital, he was in a cage, this huge apparatus, with his hands on the bars and his dark eyes staring out.

SUSAN WILKINS   We learned that Bobby would be able to walk again, and so that problem was forgotten. It was back to business. Duke appeared for the dress rehearsal with his shirt open to the navel. Afterwards we went swimming. I remember this great red hot sun sinking over the pool, and while we were standing around—some of us were already in the water—he came strutting out in a little blue bikini like a peacock, showing us with his arms spread out how he could ripple his muscles back and forth.

I can remember Edie at this poolside episode, the father flirting and Edie being angry about it. She stalked off. She was wearing very short shorts, those long legs, and a man's white shirt, a very thin girl with brown cropped hair, and she said something like "Oh, for God's sake, Fuzzy!" How old could she have been? Eleven or twelve. She was young and she was disgusted. She was so live then; she glided—I can see how she moved—so thin, and suddenly she zipped off, just *phftt*, like that.

It certainly didn't deter him. He would invite us to his studio. It was sort of like the emperor selecting a vestal virgin. We all knew we'd better not go. We all thought that this was against the rules . . . an eighteen-year-old and a fifty-year-old . . . no, no, no.

Duke was a presence—a *fauve*, a wild beast. I disliked him thoroughly. He sometimes could impress you as one of those militant boot-wearing fags. Did you know he used to wear shoes a size or a size and a half bigger because he thought his feet were too small? There was something *malsain*, a Marquis de Sade undercurrent that thirty years later I can feel in my flesh right now. The way he *looked* at people. He undressed every woman he saw. His eyes, they just would become cold. The way he dealt with women was a kind of brutalization. He thoroughly brutalized his wife. He was tough—very, very tough.

EMILY FULBRIGHT   The busts in Mr. Sedgwick's studio made it sort of a rogues' gallery in the sense that many of them were of his different mistresses. It looked like a trophy room in a funny kind of way. You had to prove yourself before you were put on a shelf in there. I was still too young.

The first time Mr. Sedgwick came to pick me up at my parents' house, he was driving a little Mercedes sports car. I was terrified because he drove so incredibly fast. Even at that age—I must have been eleven—I realized he was showing off for my sake, because he shot up this little mountain road at about ninety miles per hour. I arrived at the ranch limp.

SAUCIE SEDGWICK   There was a lot of machismo on the ranch, with my father and then Bobby and Jonathan with their guns and their stuff that they shot, and their ropes tied on their saddles, but Minty had pictures by Botticelli up on the walls and little bits of brocade. He was just a gentle person; he loved to ride, he loved girls, he was very masculine, but my father and brothers made him feel that he wasn't.

CHARLES HOLLISTER   Once Minty and I went hunting deer, high in the mountains, and that night at Saunders Knoll we were in two twin beds and we talked all night about sex. He was telling me that he lived in a world of games. He wanted to know how, being two years older than he was, I had so many neat girls. He wanted to learn how to unsnap a brassiere from behind. With just one hand. He wanted to know about pregnancy. Minty was not getting anything from his father . . . warmth, caring. "How can I have a lot of girl friends?" I said to be honest, be friendly, be warm, be human. And don't play games. The point is that Minty didn't realize that you didn't have to be a Duke Sedgwick; you could be a friend of a woman. You didn't have to score everybody you met. It's a sharing. It's not a conquest. I knew from my father about Duke. He used to conquer, penetrate, ejaculate.

DIANA DAVIS   When I met Minty, I was so pleased that he asked me to come to his family's ranch. My parents were divorced or separated, I don't know. It was a confused time. I was about fourteen. My father had a mistress who I felt didn't want the children to stay in that house any more than we wanted to.

Minty picked me up and we drove over the mountains. I can remember the terrific approach to the ranch. We stopped at a knoll and the whole Valley lay out in front of us and off in the distance we could see the formation of this little civilization. Minty stopped the car and said, "There it is!" I went, "Oh, wow!" Then we drove down. Minty said,

"Come on, I want you to meet my father." It was late afternoon. Fuzzy, as everyone called him, was in a white bikini and all glistening with oil. He was on a mat doing his exercises. I remember that green grass and the pool and this fantastic classical music coming out over the loudspeaker. God! He really was one of the most beautiful men I have ever seen; at fourteen for that to be someone's father seemed so extraordinary. Then out of the woodwork came Minty's older brother, Bobby. You know how beautiful *he* was. And here was Minty, who didn't have that same kind of beauty, but he was very pretty, pretty more than handsome, and then the youngest brother, Jonathan. There was this whole additional group of kids; everybody seemed to have a friend.

Fuzzy liked me, or felt sorry for me. I went to him saying, "Oh, please don't send me back to Santa Barbara." He interceded for me. They seemed to like me. I wasn't causing any trouble. I wasn't sexy, so I didn't make them nervous on that account. I was really a little string bean of a girl who was hardly aware of what was going on in other girls of my age.

While I was back home, a close friend of Mr. and Mrs. Sedgwick came to stay at the ranch with her daughter, and Minty took up with her. He telephoned me and said, "I don't think you should come any more because this girl is here and I like her." I was in anguish. It wasn't so much that I needed Minty as I needed that place to go to. Fuzzy found out that Minty had done this, and the next thing I knew he was on the phone saying, "It's ridiculous, Minty has made an error of judgment. He can't choose her over you." I kept saying, "It's Minty, Fuzzy, not *you* who's making the choice." Suddenly Minty was on the phone saying, "I've made a mistake, it's really you I want here."

Well, I went back to the ranch. I didn't have any pride. I thought Minty was wonderful, my first crush. I was like a little child looking up at him. I can still remember the first pang of having another woman involved in my life. She was sexy. She was blonde; there were breasts and hips and things like that. I looked at her and felt sort of sick and wondered why I was there.

NITA COLGATE   I was staying at the ranch that summer and I remember Minty kept saying that his father was a poor wretched devil, but his mother was the one he hated.

Sometimes the children fought back, but it was sort of pathetic. For breaking a date with a girl named Diana Davis, Minty got punished for what his parents thought was grossly antisocial behavior. The decree was that he had to go to bed every night at ten o'clock.

This one night we were all listening to Fuzzy reading, and at five minutes to ten Minty got up ostentatiously, clicked his heels, and then went over and bowed good evening elegantly to a friend of Mrs. Sedgwick's, shook hands with his mother, and stalked out while Fuzzy, in this steely, rather acid voice, kept on reading.

Finally I wanted to get out of there. I left a week early. I never held it against Fuzzy at the time, but later, when I looked back on what was going on, I realized I had not been in any sort of paradise at all.

DR. JOHN MILLET   Francis and Alice seemed so involved in their family life. They always sent me Christmas cards and photographs and so forth from the ranch, and I'd see these marvelous-looking creatures getting bigger and bigger, all riding horses, looking like gods and goddesses. Wonderful-looking crowd. I thought everything was going hunky-dory now. Then these things began to happen.

10

SAUCIE SEDGWICK   One by one, we started to have trouble. It wasn't easy to rebel, because the parental grip was tight. I was the only one who rejected my parents completely, and I think it really threw them for a loop. I remember saying to my father in my grandmother's car, a huge blue Cadillac like an airport limousine, that I had to live my own life and be responsible for my own actions until I knew who I was and where I was, and that I couldn't stand any more disruption. I was really crawling along on the bottom rung—my father had tried to get me thrown out of Radcliffe for my personal life and I finally had to withdraw from the school. He went to the Dean and told her I had cheated because I was sick in the infirmary during exams, and that I was promiscuous. I guess he thought I was having an affair, which I wasn't.

The real trouble went back a couple of years earlier, when I was engaged briefly to someone my father considered "unsuitable." Ironically, *I* was the one who was unsuitable. I was a mess and my fiancé was a mature veteran who had been something of a hero in World War II; he had lost a leg. He was studying labor law at Harvard Law School. I didn't know that I was rebelling, but I have to laugh at myself, looking back: I was working in a laundry and going around with a Jewish Marxist. My parents behaved pretty respectfully at the time, but it changed their attitude toward me so that they tried to take control of me.

9 3

My father and I had a big argument in the car. He said that if I insisted on having my own way it could mean the death of my mother —she was in the hospital at the time with one of her low-grade fevers. He said, "You'll have it on your conscience all your life that you caused your mother's death." I remember my grandmother pushed the button that closed the glass window between us and the chauffeur.

What made it possible for me to stand up to my father was that a few days earlier he had made a sort of pass at me. We were staying at my grandmother's on Long Island, and we were in evening clothes— he had taken me to dinner at the house of some friends of his, and he had shouted at me all the way there and back in the car, saying he wanted me to go into the WACS. I had been speechless at the party and in tears most of the evening. Afterwards he came into my room and began talking kindly to me. Then he came over—I was sitting on my open bed—and he put his arms around me and his head on my neck and he said, "Don't you think I understand how all these men feel about you? After all, I'm a man, too." I don't know if he even realized that he was making a pass at me. Still, I thought, "Well, you filthy old creep. So *that's* what the trouble is." I never felt anything for him again.

That made it easier for me to escape than the others. But it wasn't easy for any of us in the outside world. When we came off the ranch we used to laugh that we were unable to care for ourselves: it terrified us to take a subway or a bus, we didn't know how. All the apparatus of life was a big mystery; every decision was a bolt from the blue, often disastrous.

HELEN BURROUGHS STERN   I remember thinking it was so awful when Bobby and Minty were sent East to Groton, where they didn't know anyone. Once Minty hid in the Los Angeles airport until the airplane had gone, and he had to be sent along later. Minty was just like his name, he was just "Minty"—little bone structure, pale, white face, and little, watering, frightened eyes that were so grateful. Very ethereal and very pinched; he looked like Oliver Twist. I liked him, the way you just like some people. I said, "You'll be all right. These people are nice, and you'll like it. You'll be able to get cake for dessert, and pies."

HARRY SEDGWICK   Bobby graduated from Groton in '51 and Minty in '56. I didn't see much of them while they were at school, but everybody was taken by them. I remember Minty as being just adorable. There was a great vulnerability and "please love me" look about him. He was such a lovely specimen, just a lovely kid. Girls would flip over him! And Bobby was unbelievably good-looking. He was sort of a composite of all the best-looking parts of his father and my father and our grandfather. I heard that neither of them was particularly distinguished academically, nor were they involved in sports at Groton.

MINTURN SEDGWICK   Francis was terribly ambitious for his sons, particularly when they were growing up at Groton, and they weren't good athletes. One spring Minty turned eighteen and he did not want to go home for vacation. I went out from Boston to see him. He was terrified at first because he thought I was going to try to ship him back to California. Then he opened up and told me why he didn't want to go. Francis had given Minty a special football outfit. Minty said he wouldn't be using it, because he didn't like football. Francis said, "I'm ashamed to have you bear my name." He had not been a great athlete himself, but he pushed his children. It was ill-advised. Minty wasn't built for football.

Francis was very upset. He became quite illogical about Minty's not wanting to come home. He wrote and telegraphed people, including Babbo, with whom he had rarely communicated since his marriage to Gabriella. Francis told everyone that if Minty asked to stay with them in the East, they were not to put him up. When I heard this, I wrote Francis at once that, like any relation of mine, Minty was more than welcome at my house at any time. He was a terribly attractive young man. The poor boy just didn't want to play football.

So Alice came on East. It was the only time I ever saw her aware that she had a strange husband. She was always absolutely loyal. For once, she realized that Francis was wrong about Minty and the rest of them. That was the only time . . . the only time.

JAMES WATSON   Minty's masters at Groton were well aware of the strain he was under. It showed up in his work. When boys with fine minds have academic difficulties, it is customary at Groton, and other preparatory schools at which I have taught, to send them to be tested by an educational psychologist. The boys are given Rorschach tests all day long, and the psychologist then sends a report to the school and to the boy's parents. Very often the learning problem turns out to be something caused by the boy's relationship to his parents . . . and that

Hundred House, Groton School, Massachusetts

Groton graduation photographs of
Bobby (1951), Minty (1956), and Jonathan (1958)

was certainly true with Minty. As is so frequently the case with the parents of these boys, Mr. Sedgwick had plenty of warning, but he didn't take heed.

MINTURN SEDGWICK Francis and Alice almost never visited Groton while Minty was there, but Francis wrote a series of letters critical of Groton. The trouble was, of course, that Minty was under tremendous psychological pressure from his father. There was nothing wrong with the academic standing of the school.

Groton never paid the slightest attention to Francis' letters. No answers of any sort ever. That was the policy and I think they were wise. But Francis was always very, very loyal to Groton until the episode of the blacks came along . . .

You don't know about that? All hell broke loose. The Secretary of the Federation of Protestant Churches wrote to all the prep schools asking them what their policy was on admissions so far as race and religion were concerned. John Crocker, the headmaster, is a Christian from way back and has a wife who is not only a Christian but a very strong anti-segregationist. He wrote back saying that we pay no attention to race at all, despite the fact that we are nearly all Wasps, as they say . . . but we do have Roman Catholics.

Having set the policy, Groton went to look for a black. It was important that particularly the first one be just right. Now, they wanted an outstanding boy, but not *too* outstanding. They didn't want him to be the star of the football team or the best scholar in the class. Howard University selected six black students. Groton got a boy, and he was just right. Of course, the first day everybody was frightfully nervous about the whole thing except this boy, who was completely relaxed. Well, Francis took off about this. He was furious that he hadn't been consulted, so he wrote a letter, unsigned, which appeared on Groton School stationery to the alumni:

GROTON LETTER DATED FEBRUARY 12, 1957

. . . In consistence with Christian doctrine and the teachings of the Bible and in consistence with the human beliefs of two of Groton's most eminent graduates, the New York Governor Averell Harriman and the late President Franklin Delano Roosevelt, Groton announces its irrevocable intention to increase the number of Negroes from a few students to not less than one fourth and not more than one third of its total enrollment.

To this just and proper end Groton boys, parents, friends, and the

National Association for the Advancement of Colored People are invited to help qualified Negro boys to apply. Inability to pay is no obstacle. A Christian character and ability to meet Groton intellectual standards are the sole requirements. Groton pledges, if necessary, the full use of its entire endowment fund towards scholarships for this purpose.

SAUCIE SEDGWICK   My father's view of blacks was "The Negro is first cousin to the monkey, and that is a *fact*." But I don't think it was rage at the headmaster, John Crocker, or at Groton for taking blacks, so much as it was his rage at all institutions or people that wouldn't remain static and conform to his image of them. Look how he behaved when Babbo married Gabriella! Everything had to stay the same or he would go berserk.

MINTURN SEDGWICK   When Francis' letter was sent, the administration and many of the alumni were furious. Of course, there was the big question of who had sent it. There's nothing illegal about sending unsigned letters through the mail, but the Post Office doesn't like it and asked if the school would be interested in finding out who wrote this thing. Naturally, the school allowed that it would be.

Within two weeks the Post Office told the school that their handwriting expert, who had never been faulted, was prepared to swear that the man who addressed those letters also signed himself Francis M. Sedgwick. Well, what to do? Naturally, the few people in the know informed me right off. I just couldn't believe Francis had done such a stupid thing. I heard people say that if they could find out who the hoaxer was they'd ride him out of every club—that sort of thing. The attitude of the school was not to publicize the fact that this reasonably eminent alumnus was the author of the letter. So Francis was clear in that regard. I was advised to try to get Francis to seek psychiatric help.

I faked some business out on the West Coast and went to see him. He met me at the airport, which is about thirty miles from Rancho Laguna. We had not driven more than five or ten miles when he asked, "Have they any idea who wrote that letter?"

I said, "Yes, they know. It's you."

That stopped Francis in his tracks.

Well, he didn't attempt to deny it. He told me that the reason he had written the letter was to draw attention to the problem and that he was following it up with a long letter detailing his objection to blacks at Groton. When I got back to the East, this second letter had already been mailed to all the alumni. The gist of his argument was that, while he highly approved of educating blacks and was delighted they were in Harvard, Groton was sort of a family and you didn't take blacks into your family.

It was a shame. Francis had become very active in Harvard affairs. It was in him to become the president of the Associated Harvard Clubs. He might have gone on to become an Overseer. This killed the whole thing.

Francis was a terribly competitive fellow. He was very ambitious physically, as I was, and he just didn't have the physique; but he worked on himself so that he became awfully strong, stronger than me. I've seen him take a Manhattan telephone book and tear it in two. This is partly a trick, but it requires tremendous strength. First he wanted to be a tycoon. Then he told me once that he must build a statue, paint a picture, and write a play or a book. Three things that would really last.

Uncle Ellery once asked Babbo if he wasn't scared of his son—that colossal, hungry ambition of his—which Uncle Ellery found unnatural and terrifying. Babbo just shrugged it off. Babbo died less than a month before the "hoax" letter. Francis had only seen Babbo once after he married Gabriella. Francis turned up in Stockbridge to have lunch with Mrs. Austen Riggs and Gabriella fled the Old House. She was frightened of a confrontation. I was there when my brother arrived. The conversation was polite, but there was a lot of emotion. Babbo had always wanted to heal the breach, but Francis wouldn't allow it. His letters had been so ferocious: "You can come home again if you divorce that woman." How Francis could shift his moods! I heard from Mrs. Riggs that just after leaving Babbo in the Old House, he kept her luncheon party in gales of laughter.

JONATHAN SEDGWICK   I came back to the ranch from Groton and I didn't know that Babbo had died. My father came out to meet me. He was walking with a cane. He said it was high blood pressure, but it was sadness! He was not letting his feelings out, but there were tears in his eyes. He loved that man. He really loved that man. It was so sad he couldn't tell him. Babbo wanted to hear it. They hurt each other so much.

My father was most threatened by the loving people in his family . . . by the men. He was trying to be masculine all the time. He was very sensual and effeminate actually, but he didn't understand that effeminacy is part of manhood. He felt small. My father told me that he himself had been a weakling—a little pigeon-chested, sickly boy who had been bullied—and now *he* was a man. He talked about the feeling of the pigeon-chested, these feelings of people pushing him around. Well, *he* wasn't going to be pushed around, so he had made his body and his ego strong. He wanted his sons to do the same. Minty always threatened his sense of what manhood was just by being Minty. Minty was sensitive and loving and it was just awful.

Once my father knocked Minty to the floor in my grandmother's apartment in New York City and banged his head against the floor: "Get up and fight me." Minty just cried. It was over Minty not being a man.

DR. JOHN MILLET Apparently Minty began drinking and demanded that his father pay for his psychiatric treatment. Francis told me, "I jumped him and put him down." He told me about this in New York in 1960 when he came to see me about Minty, who was going to be twenty-two in a couple of days. He told me how much he and Alice loved Minty, whom he described as innately timid—getting off a horse at sixteen and asking his mother to ride it home for him. He described Minty as quite artistic, very good-looking, with a nice sense of humor, though verging on the effeminate. Minty had begun to cause them anxiety when he refused to play football at Groton and then when he was turned down by Harvard because he had indicated that facing challenges was a problem for him. At that point Minty went out and enrolled at the University of California at Berkeley, and at the end of two months he had upset his father considerably by spending his entire yearly allowance of twenty-five hundred dollars. He would sleep until one-fifteen in the afternoon, just too late to get to his last class. He left college almost at once and had a very interesting experience in the Army, where he served for three years. After two months of basic training, despite his fear of firearms, he came out with the sharpshooter's medal and best-soldier rating. Then he was assigned to learn Chinese, and though he was four years younger than anyone else and a private, he graduated as one of four people out of a class of forty—with men ranked up to colonel—who had an all "A" rating. Francis got the nicest letter from his commanding officer, who was a Chinese Mandarin. Minty wanted to go to Korea, but was sent to Fort Meade, where he did secret decoding work until his discharge.

He finally entered Harvard in the fall of 1959, and stopped writing to his family a month later. Francis said that in the beginning of January Minty called him from New York City from his maternal grandmother's apartment, saying that he was on medical leave from Harvard with the consent of the University; the school would accept him back after a year's work. He told Francis that he had been advised to go to New York City to live on his own, and he had enough money from a trust his grandmother had set up for each of the children to pay for his upkeep and his therapy.

Francis told me that he made no move to interfere, but he soon became concerned about Minty. He had heard that Minty was giving tremendous dinners at the Stork Club and that his doctor in New York was giving him pills so strong that his driving license was inoperative, so he hired Cadillacs with chauffeurs. So Francis finally called his mother-in-law to tell her that Minty must get out of her apartment. In return, Minty had telephoned Francis two or three times, telling his father to butt out of his affairs—calling him stupid, and being abusive when he was drunk. Minty was particularly aggressive at Francis' suggestion that he come see me.

One of Francis' weapons was refusing to pay for Minty's psychiatric treatment unless he was under my care. I was asked to keep a check on his progress. Shortly after, Minty called and asked for an appointment with me. I wrote Francis: "Well, I finally saw your Minty. He is indeed a most attractive youth, as you described him to be, and I suspect in other ways also the spitting image of his male progenitor, which I suspect is the reason for most of the troubles that you've experienced in your mutual relationship. I believe the boy has great promise, but is of unstable temperament and is not the kind of mule that you can get into action by whacking his behind." I urged Francis to continue to help. "You are pained that he begs for financial help. However, this, at the moment, symbolizes *for him* asking for love. You're indulging him for what is apparently a serious purpose, and for that purpose only, namely, the continuation of therapy at the hands of his own doctor might serve to break the logjam of feelings and substitute this *ex fronti* from *visa tergo*"—direct power from the front rather than by kicking a person in the rear.

SAUCIE SEDGWICK Minty stayed at my grandmother's briefly. Then Roland Redmond, the lawyer in charge of my grandmother's affairs, got him out of there on my father's orders and he spent some time apartment-sitting for Mrs. Albert Spaulding. Gabriella, Babbo's widow, arranged it. Mrs. Spaulding was a very respectable lady with a ravishing apartment in which Minty roared around, very disturbed. I saw him getting crazier and crazier. One day I came in at nine in the morning and found him conducting the stereo with a baton, blood on his pajamas, and I got scared to death. I took him to Payne Whitney, the psychiatric division of New York Hospital, and got him to commit himself voluntarily. That was the first of a number of hospitalizations—Silver Hill, in Connecticut, finally . . . you remember, that's the hospital Dr. Millet founded.

NITA COLGATE   After Minty came out of Silver Hill that first time, he would have supper with us and afterwards he would go to the AA meetings next door at the Brick Church. I had the feeling—having been definitely branded with family problems myself—that we'd gone through the same wars, even though I hadn't had to live through them the way he had. He wrote me letters later on when I was in Bloomingdale Hospital. They were strange, with drawings of sexy naked women . . . three- or four-page letters on small notepaper . . . pen-and-ink sketches like the illustrations you see on the cover of a detective-story magazine. Lurid. I remember them as having the deliberate sexiness of a prostitute—a stripped prostitute. That's the image that comes to mind.

DIANA DAVIS   When Minty got out of Silver Hill, he wanted to see me. I was shocked when I saw him because he was so blown up— alcohol or drugs, I guess. Somehow he wanted to tell me that everything was fine, and to find out about me. He kept saying, "I'm much, much better." We went to his grandmother's apartment for dinner. A number of the family were there. I don't know whether I was there because Minty liked me or because they'd all decided for him, "Oh, she's a nice girl." I couldn't judge our friendship any more. He saw me to the elevator. I remember saying, "I'm glad you're better." I kept thinking it was like when people ask you, "How are you?" and you say, "Oh, I'm fabulous," and inside you're just a total mess.

LUCY SILVAY   He seemed disturbed and would talk about his family incessantly. He told me that he had tried to commit suicide twice: once by taking pills and another time he nearly jumped out a window. We would stay up all night talking—we even discussed getting married, but he never made a pass at me. I was surprised by that because I'd had affairs before.

I only knew him as "Francis." He told me he hated that other name . . . "Minty" . . . the name his family called him.

JONATHAN SEDGWICK I'm sad I didn't help Minty, because he came to me and said, "Help me." I was too cold. I had come out of the Army in 1962, when I was twenty-two, and went back to Harvard. He came begging for help. His thing was that he never was sure people loved him. He couldn't understand people's love. He was a sensitive, musical person who could pick up the wings of a bird and play them on a flute. Girls loved him, they really did, but he couldn't *feel* they loved him. When Minty was younger and would bring a girl friend to the ranch, my father would turn on his sexual side and just usurp all the energy that my brother was putting out on that level and blow him out.

Minty thought too much about loving. I just gave up on loving people, they were too weird. Letting them into me was just ugh . . . they were nuts. So I always stayed open to animals. I could talk to them. They do what I ask. They come to me in the wild. A little fawn came right up to me, man. Blew me out. I wasn't ready for it.

Minty and I went to dinner one night in a tiny little restaurant off Brattle Street in Cambridge. We talked until four in the morning. He asked me how I satisfied girls. My way was just simply I loved girls, I didn't care whether they loved me. I loved it when they did love me, but that wasn't what I was after. Minty was sure they never loved him . . . never, never, never, never.

11

SUKY SEDGWICK   The year Babbo died, Edie was thirteen. She had just started boarding school at the Katharine Branson School near San Francisco. Pamela's husband saw her on a summer vacation and said he just couldn't imagine a more pure vision of absolute beauty possible than Edie walking across a tennis court. She was totally innocent. A young, budding woman with a very childlike consciousness to go with it, which is extremely tantalizing for older men. And I suppose that was difficult for me, too, because she was the apple of everyone's eye when I was coming of age and trying to get some eye on me.

Being away from the ranch turned out to be a terrible wrench for Edie. When she went to the Katharine Branson School, she told me she had nightmares about Mummy. Crying. Just crying about Mummy a lot, I don't know why. I think she hated school desperately. Maybe she felt she was being punished by being sent away. I don't know.

SAUCIE SEDGWICK   Suddenly Edie was taken out of school. I heard all sorts of rumors when she was brought home—that she had mononucleosis, even that my mother thought she was getting leukemia. That would have been absurd, because my mother must have known what the real trouble was. Edie had anorexia.

In our family there were two styles of eating. One was to eat special foods, which my mother did because of all her allergies. Edie ate special foods at all hours of the day and night; even her white rat, named Hunca Munca, had to have special food. The rat's diet nearly caused William and Nancy, the couple who had been with us since Long Island, to leave. The other style was to eat enormously—which my father did. In a way, my father was a model for Edie because he would eat such quantities; then he would burn it off with his exercises and swimming and riding. But Edie vomited it up. She would sit down to a very special meal which she herself would carefully choose and eat helping after helping of, course after course, excusing herself during the meal to go and be sick, to throw up what she had eaten so she could eat more. But nothing reached her stomach, or very little did.

SUKY SEDGWICK   I used to assist on those feasts. She used to call it "pigging." "I've got to go pig now." Eating and stuffing and stuffing and eating and then throwing up.

GILLIAN WALKER   Edie told me what it was like on the ranch alone with her parents, because by then all the children, even Suky, were off at school. She spoke of lying in her room alone with the shades drawn. She loved telling me how her father would come after her and lock her up and force her to stay in bed—a helpless, isolated prisoner, a drugged princess. She dramatized these incidents in a way that made me think she'd been reading nineteenth-century Gothic novels. But since she rarely read, I think these things were really going on.

JONATHAN SEDGWICK   Edie found my father making love with some lady in the blue room . . . just humping away, and it blew her mind. He jumped up and swore at her. She went running to her room. He came charging in and slapped her a few times. He was irrational because he'd been caught in his act. "You don't know anything. You're insane," he told her. Then he made the doctor come right over and give her a lot of tranquilizers. Nobody'd believe Edie because "Edie is sick." Mummy wouldn't believe her—she just had a blockage against things like that. Nobody'd believe her, so she was really a prisoner. Edie wanted to tell people what was happening, but she couldn't do anything. She was too fucked up in her head to be able to do anything. She lost all her feelings because everything around her was an act now. She knew what had really happened, and my father just denied the whole thing. And that *really* hurt her.

When I came back—I guess I was a senior at Groton—Edie was really strange. She was like a little baby, saying, "Look at the neat horse

I'm drawing. See, Jonathan? Isn't it neat?" Her life had gone, except for the horses. So my father shipped her off to another school.

LAINE DICKERMAN   Edie came to St. Timothy's in 1958. As you know, St. Tim's, as everyone calls it, is a small, exclusive school of about 125 girls on a totally secluded Maryland estate surrounded by woods and hills. It's always been proud of its tradition of turning out well-balanced "Christian gentlewomen." At the end of each year the school gives out two prizes, one for "the best scholar," the other for "the best person."

When Edie first came, she seemed like a real leader type. She was the only one of our class to make the Brownie basketball team. She practically lived in the team uniform—a brown tunic with a red Brownie shaped like a plump troll on it. She was *so* high on making the team. The night before the big game at Thanksgiving there is a secret candlelight ceremony in which the newest Brownie, Edie, walked around within the circle of Brownies all chanting:

> *I thought I heard my Grandmother say*
> *St. Timothy's School is coming this way*
> *With a Vivo and a Vivo*
> *And a ribtail, ribtail*
> *Hanging on a cat tail*
> *Vum, vum, vum.*

Edie must have been incredibly pleased with herself; it lasted her most of the fall, her happiest time. The rest of the class admired her. She was our first class president. She dazzled us with her charm, and we all wanted to be her best friend. That Thanksgiving was the peak of her desirability.

But then it became apparent that Edie's friendships were full of courtships and rivalries and jealousies. She would choose only one best friend at a time, do everything with her, and make the rest of us jealous. Then she'd suddenly be attracted to someone else, drop the old friend, and hurt her with scorn and indifference. She had crushes on seniors in high positions and was quite bold about approaching them, flirting with them and trying to impress them. She was so bold that I often felt embarrassed for her. But she got the seniors' attention; they noticed her and treated her like a cute mascot. One of them gave her a ring at exam time for good luck.

Then Edie began to get in trouble. She'd wear the blue skirt when she was supposed to wear the gray one, or sneakers instead of saddle

The Brownie basketball team, St. Timothy's, 1958.
Edie is in the front row, left.

shoes, and then she would refuse to change. She'd explode at people in crazy arguments. I remember her yelling, her face dark, and flinging herself around on the bed. Once I saw her hit a girl who had criticized her. Her temper provoked teachers. She became by turns sloppy and lazy and disobedient, or brilliant and enthusiastic, depending on her moods. The sick times of winter affected her, so that she seemed bitter, not dazzling any more; Thanksgiving was long gone. All the people who'd thought she was so cute and bright were really sick of her. Housemothers who had once been charmed now gave her "tidy crosses"—which were demerits. She seemed to hate herself. Suddenly her eyes would look wild and scary, and she'd cry out, "I can't do it— I've failed."

Sometimes she could be magical. I remember one time toward the end of the winter term Edie and I stayed up late into the night. We sat on the floor in the hall outside our rooms with the moonlight coming through the French doors onto the Oriental carpet. We talked about the seniors, our families, ourselves . . . private, secret feelings in the moonlight. I felt very close and easy with her, without any of the currents of rivalry and jealousy and wild emotion that had made me afraid to be intimate with her. She had on a white slip that night as a nightgown, a strap sliding off one of her shoulders. She seemed fragile, vulnerable, and serious. She invited me to come to the ranch that summer. She made it sound like the perfect life and her family like gods. I imagined all those dark, handsome Sedgwicks. It sounded wild and romantic, not like boring East Coast tennis parties. We imagined adventures we'd have riding all day in the mountains getting sunburned, and then at night we'd wear long white dresses and bare feet and sit at the long family dinner table in candlelight with all those handsome brothers. She made me fall in love with it. I never went . . . I don't remember why . . . the plan just didn't materialize.

That spring at St. Timothy's was so green and rich . . . the dogwoods and magnolias . . . lying in the grass on Sunday afternoons, walking to study hall after supper in the pale light. But Edie seemed subdued. Perhaps her sicknesses in the winter had affected her. People didn't care any more whether she liked them or not . . . her power was gone. In a way, that might have been the time when she was most real, when she was just like the rest of us. I thought of her still as my friend, but not as the prize possession she had been in the fall. Somewhere underneath there was an incredible dark fear, a strangeness that made her bite her nails, pick her face, blow up at her friends, and hate herself. Her feelings were too exposed. I never knew what made her so miserable, but I felt uncomfortable with her. I couldn't absorb it. It was her problem, not mine.

I was both sorry and surprised when Edie didn't come back to St. Tim's the following fall because I thought she'd like being an old girl. But then when I thought about it, I wasn't at all surprised.

SAUCIE SEDGWICK   I saw Edie on the ranch the summer of 1960, the year after she left St. Timothy's. She was seventeen years old and had a kind of Shirley Temple look; she wore doll-like clothes and had a breathless, childish voice. She used the word "cunning" a lot. Or "sweet." Edie had a little baby way when she was with my mother . . . a special baby talk, "Mum-mum." I noticed that she had established her authority on the ranch. She got rid of the furniture in her room and designed a whole suite and had it put in—heart-shaped bedsteads, hideous beyond description—and this was one of the first indications of her relationship with my parents because the rest of us were never allowed to have anything. I was scandalized to find out what Edie was getting away with. She did exactly as she damn pleased. It was always considered absolutely out of the question to sleep late, or walk around the house in nightclothes, but Edie flouted all these things. She had brought my parents to their knees.

I remember that summer I had a poisonous conversation with Edie. We were sitting in the living room at the ranch. She asked me if I didn't think she was the most beautiful one in the family. I was an outsider—you have to remember that this was a family in which I was a monster—and Edie was asking for fealty, for tribute. I said, "No!" I didn't say that just out of meanness. Actually, I thought Pamela was very handsome, with the most beautiful legs, the most talented, and the most special. I said so. That was the only time I remember talking to Edie; I disliked her heartily.

SARA THOMAS   Duke Sedgwick adored Edie. He just couldn't take his eyes off her. He said she was so delicious. She was the only one of the Sedgwicks I ever saw who fixed herself up. She came into the living room before supper with just a small amount of make-up on and she was absolutely devastating. Duke referred to her as "my little chorine," which I thought charming since the word is so antique.

SUKY SEDGWICK   Edie was allowed to use Fuzzy's car, which nobody else was. Fancy that. Mercedes 190-SL. Pretty glamorous. Edie liked to be glamorous, she did! She always did, but it was a dress-up time being glamorous, and "Let's have a giggle. Turn on the radio and pass everybody on 101." That's what we did. With our sunglasses on, feeling like two movie stars. Shit, it was just fun for us. And then we'd get the giggles over some twerp who'd follow us. All it was was just pure fun and letting off steam. Sizzling along the highway with the music blaring and with our fancy scarves over our hair and our big sunglasses on our faces. Oh, shit, we had fun!! It was just fun, it was dress-up time in the car with the music, but there was the fine line, a razor line, too, between our fun and hysterics. Because, coming back from Anderson's Pea Soup diner, I think we screamed all the way home. That's a little exaggerated for just having fun. Somewhere along the line—somewhere, somehow—I seem to remember that the scream-ing turned into tears. It wasn't quite as much fun as it was supposed to be.

Edie had a streak of *Wuthering Heights* in her. She loved violent weather. We went through a thunderstorm on horseback up in the high mountains—I mean, as high up as you can get on the ranch. A whop-ping thunderstorm. I was so goddamn scared, I didn't want to go home alone. I ran my horse all the way home. Jesus, I galloped all the way from the top of the ranch down to the barns. Edie wanted me to leave her alone up there.

When it was a beautiful night, we'd disappear into the hills and sing "Dream, Dream, Dream." We used to sing our heads off when we went riding. It was an absolute escape from the world we were living in. In the evening we'd ride into that sunset! We'd ride along the top-most hills of the ranch and *stare* at the sunset. I mean, we just never took our eyes off that sunset changing. Then it got to be dark, and we were both scared of the dark.

Oncoming night was accompanied always by coyote calls, yowls. Have you ever heard a coyote? Yowls into darkness. That was savagery.

JONATHAN SEDGWICK   I always thought Edie wanted to escape on her horse, but she couldn't get off the ranch. She was penned in. Usually it started with a battle with my father. She always felt that he would come and get her. So she could only run away on the ranch. She would just disappear into the mountains with her horse, Chub, and you never knew where she was. Then she'd come back mellowed out.

SAUCIE SEDGWICK   My parents didn't know what to do with Edie. They were not going to send her back to St. Timothy's, so they decided to take her to Austria. If things didn't go right, Europe always was the solution. The idea was to send her to stay with a noble family in Vienna.

But when they arrived, there was a terrible blow-up in the hotel room. My father became convinced that Edie was really sick. My mother had tried to conceal her eating habits from him until then. He realized that Edie wasn't able to function; she couldn't even cross the street by herself. My father must have gotten one good look at what the hell was going on and said, "No, this is crazy." He became frightened and even threatened to pull the whole family down around my mother's ears if she didn't send Edie to a mental hospital. Imagine the ambivalence of my father—such a destructive, negative force—trying to get Edie helped. Actually, he was doing the right thing for the wrong reason. He was trying to get rid of Edie, pull her away from my mother, who was obsessed with her.

So my mother and Edie came right back from Austria. I think they were only there for about forty-eight hours. I saw them at my grandmother's apartment on Park Avenue. It was a strange meeting. My grandmother was lying senile in her bedroom. Edie seemed superficially sane. Rather than anxious or disturbed, she seemed angry and resigned.

But then at lunch I saw her *heap* her plate and eat in that bizarre way that anorectics do, picking and wolfing . . . and then she would get up and disappear.

When I heard what the choices were—that unless Edie went to the mental hospital at Silver Hill where Minty had been, my father would leave the family. I said to my mother, "You're in a situation where you have to choose between your husband and your children."

She said, "Oh, no, there's no question of leaving my husband. I couldn't."

JONATHAN SEDGWICK   Of course, Mummy knew that Edie wasn't the problem—it was Fuzzy who should have been in an institution. He was just about at the edge of a breakdown: shaky, nervous, running around like a guy with his balls cut off. I'd come from the Army in Germany to see him in London. He was in an absolute panic that Mummy had left him. She had stood up to him. She'd said, "Goodbye, I'm leaving. I'm taking this child with me." He stayed in London for a week and a half, praying that she'd heed his instructions to put Edie in an institution. That's when Mummy gave in; she could sense he was folding. She had an intuition that covered everybody.

SAUCIE SEDGWICK When Edie was sent away, it affected my mother profoundly. She cried. The only times I had ever heard her cry before was when she fired governesses. I heard her crying behind the sliding doors of the library at my grandmother's apartment. They were never closed, but my mother pulled them together, and I heard her in there. I said to her through the doors, "You shouldn't shut yourself off when you're suffering." She replied that she always liked to be in control of her emotions.

My mother put Edie in Silver Hill the fall of 1962 as my father had demanded. I would go to visit her. She worked in the shop at the hospital a little bit, but it seemed absolutely pathetic. She had an awful beehive hairdo. She looked like a drugstore attendant.

Silver Hill was quite lax. Edie made good use of the facilities, particularly the OT, occupational therapy. She made lots of objects—a cheeseboard over there on the table. The design's faded, but there were five mice on it, very deftly drawn. Edie did pretty much what she wanted at Silver Hill and she could leave whenever she wished. Phyllis La Farge's mother's house was nearby—Edie's godmother, I believe—and Edie probably went there. Mrs. La Farge was a solitary woman who fed her big Labrador dogs from her plate with her own fork or spoon. She said that their mouths were cleaner than ours.

JOHN ANTHONY WALKER Edie said that she was the only person at Silver Hill they could never figure out what was wrong with. She was very pleased with that. She felt she could outthink them. She wanted to get away, of course.

PRISCILLA EVANS Most of the people at Silver Hill were middle-aged, there to dry out or get over divorces. There was this old Dr. Terhune who was the head of the place and gave these dumb lectures; he'd written this book of essays and he'd read them to us once a week. About the only other contact Edie had besides myself was with a girl named Virginia who stayed there almost as long as Edie did. They had sort of a rivalry as to who had been there the longest and who was the sickest.

VIRGINIA DAVIS Silver Hill was very swish in my time. Some rich lady kept donating her Hitchcock furniture . . . originals. Every year she would redo her house and Silver Hill would get all this fine furniture. Edie was in the main house. Everyone had private rooms; I think it was something like a thousand dollars a month to stay there, not including psychiatric care. In those days they had no maximum-security facilities and they claimed not to take anyone who was seriously disturbed—no psychotics or schizophrenics or alcoholics. Of course, half the younger crowd there—the people in their forties—were alcoholics, and they could wander down to the Silvermine Tavern any time they wanted and get crocked. I mean, who was to stop them?

Silver Hill was like a country club when Edie and I were there. We were served at dinner, all very proper, from the left, and dinner attire was required. We goofed off and had a grand time. After lunch Edie and I would go into town and she would spend thousands of dollars charging stuff. I mean, thousands! Maybe not at one shot, but a few hundred one day and then a few hundred the next. If you stayed at Silver Hill, the New Canaan merchants would extend you unlimited credit. Edie would buy shoes and clothes and art books, the expensive ones, like the Leonardo da Vinci book for fifty bucks. But she never felt constrained. She acted as if it didn't matter in the slightest.

She had a peaches-and-white complexion, those dark eyes, and dark hair. She used this very pale make-up to accentuate this contrast. I felt all thumbs by comparison with her. She was a very dominant personality. We used to have conversations . . . philosophical discussions, and on this one occasion we decided we were so alike in our heart of hearts that we shared the same soul! There was nothing sexual or anything like that involved, just crazy girls the same age who were together in this messy scene. Edie had the notion that she wanted control over the soul we shared, so one afternoon in my room she took it. For some reason her nurse wasn't around. I can remember going that evening, about four or five, terribly upset, to see our doctor. Both Edie and I had him. I was crying because Edie had taken my soul and I was totally under her control, which put me in limbo all by myself . . . soulless. I'd let Edie have it because she deserved it, being better or prettier or something, and Edie apparently agreed with me.

My doctor was at high tea . . . well, not really high, but his family always had cookies and real cream for tea. He told me it was all a lot of nonsense. He said, "Poppycock. You're being silly. You've got your own soul and she's got her own, and they're distinct."

Edie used to say that she wasn't ill, she was only there because her father wanted to get rid of her. She complained a lot about her family. Of course, I did, too. That was the big thing, hate your family, it was

Edie at Silver Hill, 1962

Drawings by Edie

all their fault. To hear Edie talk, her family was all wild and woolly out there in California. She never spoke much about her mother. I remember being so surprised to hear a friend of mine describe Edie's mother as being this reasonable and sedate lady.

But Edie was mostly interested in herself. She was enormously into taking care of her skin and body; she had Germaine Monteil creams all over the place. The rest of us didn't much care, but she was always very fastidious about her appearance. We wore sweaters and shirt-waist dresses. She wore tights, always. Dark tights.

What was crazy about someone so fastidious was that Edie used to vomit after every meal. Edie would gobble up enormous amounts of food and then vanish up the stairs. She would never admit this; she would run off and do it privately. She knew it was destroying her body, but she told me that was something she wanted to do. Her body was threatening to her. After meals we would go out for walks together. She walked so fast it was hard to keep up with her. I was fat for a teenager—a hundred thirty, forty.

Edie was successful with anything she undertook at Silver Hill . . . externally, that is. We learned any number of different kinds of billiards. But in other ways the place was of no use to her. Her weight kept dropping until she was only ninety pounds, in spite of a nurse kept around to keep her from vanishing. She went on from there to Bloomingdale, the Westchester Division of New York Hospital.

SAUCIE SEDGWICK   They finally had to send Edie to a "closed" hospital, where she couldn't pull any tricks or manipulate the situation as she had at Silver Hill. Her doctor felt that if she went on that way, irreversible changes might take place.

At Bloomingdale her doctor was Jane O'Neil. You couldn't get in to see Edie without meeting with her first. Bloomingdale was a definite place with definite rules, and they meant business. They meant to cure. Edie's diet and activities were monitored very carefully. There was no gentility about it. She began to graduate from one ward to another. Edie blossomed in there. It was the only time in her life that I saw her look the way she should have: natural, beautiful . . . I mean, just breathtaking. I used to come away from there sobbing so that I couldn't see to negotiate that long driveway . . . it was so heartbreaking to see that child in that place. I visited her at least once a week unless my mother was there or somebody else was going. I felt I couldn't abandon her. She would beg me to get her out of there. Beg and beg and beg. Very painful. I would transmit all this to Jane O'Neil.

Jane O'Neil was a big, masculine woman like Edie's first baby nurse, with gray hair and glasses. Vigorous, very vigorous . . . knew what she was doing. She was not going to be moved by desperate cries for help. She wouldn't play Edie's game. Edie couldn't seduce her. As for Edie, she was only interested in getting out. She regarded Dr. O'Neil as an authority figure whom she respected, but she hated being bossed around. She behaved like a normal, unruly girl stuck in a boarding school.

One afternoon Edie took me on a walk around the grounds, which are beautiful, like a great English park. There were no obvious fences or boundaries. Edie was very gay. It was one of the first times she had been allowed to walk around outside the hospital. But after we got back into the building she said that she'd taken me into an off-limits area, laughing because she had broken the rules and involved me in it at the same time.

NITA COLGATE The system at Bloomingdale was hierarchical. The patients were assigned to floors depending upon the severity of their particular case. The most difficult cases were assigned to the lowest floor. It was the only floor with a name—Nichols. When they got down there, people would really give out with their emotions because they couldn't sink any lower. But the people who were on the next floor up always kept themselves under control because they didn't want to fall back into Nichols. You actually graduated from one floor up to the next. The fifth floor was where you were getting ready for the outside. Then you could actually leave for two hours with your husband when he came, rather than have to stay on the grounds. But there was always this fear that you would be demoted to Nichols. After that there was no place worse they could send you, except to the state hospital. When you got to Nichols, all responsibility was taken away from you. You didn't even decide when to wash your hair. That was done on Friday night: you stood in a line and it was washed for you by a student nurse. And your arms and legs were shaved. People were coming to see you on Saturday.

The place was drenched with student nurses. I was on what they call "constant observation"—CO—which meant that no one was going to let me out of their sight even when I went to the bathroom. The lack of privacy was devastating. And yet there were locks everywhere. Oh, yes, locks and locks and locks.

One was so anxious to move up. I went into shock treatments smiling, ever so cooperative. They wrap you in a wet sheet the first time, but I was told by my friends that if you didn't give them any fight they wouldn't wrap you in a sheet after that. It was really like helping with your own execution . . . you'd be sweet and nice because they were doing something for your benefit that was going to leave you with a splitting headache and no memory and a few other side-effects, too, but it was "all for your good, my dear."

Actually, the place was quite ritzy. We sat down to dinner at little round tables with white tablecloths and were served our food. There was occupational therapy in the mornings. There were degrees of responsibility and privilege. The staff there really were behaviorists. Perhaps they didn't view it that way, but when you moved from one floor to the next, you found yourself more on your own. You could choose when to wash your hair. One of the benefits of this sort of tit-for-tat arrangement was that I certainly never want to go back to that hospital. Lots of people go back to other hospitals but not to Bloomingdale. It cured me. It made me feel if I was ever to commit suicide again, it had to be done. No more attempts. No more games.

SAUCIE SEDGWICK   Edie got pregnant near the end of her stay at Bloomingdale and she had an abortion. Kate told me about it. She was very bitter because Edie made my mother go through everything that she disapproved of. My mother was so old-fashioned. We older sisters couldn't have gone to her for anything like that . . . an abortion. If any of us was having an affair, my mother would have turned us out forever.

EDIE SEDGWICK   (From tapes for the film *Ciao! Manhattan*)   *This tape is supposed to be about love, and I guess the distortions of love. The Love Tape. Do you have any questions you want to ask me?*

MAN: *Tell me about the boy you loved first.*

EDIE: *Oh, my God. Bloomingdale. Well, that includes . . . I don't really . . . I held out pretty long before I really had an affair, but I had lots of attention from my father physically. He was always trying to sleep with me . . . from the age of about seven on. Only I resisted that. And one of my brothers who claimed that sisters were there for the purpose of teaching . . . a sister and brother should teach each other the rules and the game of making love; and I wouldn't fall for that either. I just felt . . . I had no reason to feel . . . Nobody told me that incest was a bad thing or anything, but I just didn't feel turned on by them.*

I'd been two years locked up in hospitals. I was twenty when I got out from Bloomingdale and I met a young man from Harvard who was very attractive in a sort of Ivy League way. And we made love in my grandmother's apartment and it was terrific, it was just fabulous. That was the first time I ever made love, and I had no inhibitions or anything. It was just beautiful. I didn't get my period and so I had to tell my doctor. The hospital pass was given to see if you could handle yourself outside. I was terrified to tell him that I thought I was pregnant, but I finally did. I was pregnant. I could get an abortion without any hassle at all, just on the grounds of a psychiatric case. So that wasn't too good a first experience with lovemaking. I mean, it kind of screwed up my head, for one thing. This fellow found out. I was upset . . . and he asked me, and I said, "I'm pregnant. I'm not going to ask you for anything, so don't get uptight, but it's just kind of making me uncomfortable. I don't know exactly what I'm going to do about it." He split, and I didn't see him again until the summer had passed and I went to Cambridge for my first free year.

12

SHARON PREMOLI   Edie swept into Cambridge in the fall of 1963. She decided to study art with her cousin Lily Saarinen. Edie was very elegant. She'd get into her great gray Mercedes and she looked just like an ad. She was sculpting then. The first time I met her she was coming out of Adams House at Harvard wearing a rubber apron covered with clay.

One thing that I thought was amazing about her was that although she was incredibly beautiful, her *hands* didn't seem to belong to her body. She chain-smoked, her fingers had nicotine all over them; she had clay and stuff under her fingernails. Those hands didn't belong to this incredibly beautiful girl.

LILY SAARINEN   She was the most talented young person I've taught art to. She'd come in late and very tired. Sometimes she'd stay an hour; sometimes she'd stay five. She'd have her friends come in, and pretty soon more came. I had the feeling that she needed an audience. She was very insecure about men, though all the men loved her. She was always chic and adorable. Pretty soon my life was Edie because I couldn't do anything else. She worked *frantically*. She wanted to do a horse. She said she'd ridden them all her life and knew every inch of them. Young girls do love horses. It's wonderful to have a great, powerful creature that you can control . . . perhaps the way she would like to have controlled her father. So she worked on this one horse. It looked like a T'ang horse. It took her all winter; it had the most beautiful buttocks. Though that was a world she knew a great deal about—the life of the great ranch—she never seemed particularly interested in doing cowboys.

Edie was about the only one I was teaching that winter. I had to fit my day to hers. She was completely erratic. She'd say she was going to come and she wouldn't. Or she'd come when she wasn't supposed to come. She was a will-o'-the-wisp. Very energetic. High-strung. She never came out with much about herself. But she had so much to give and be creative about. She was full of beans. I think she should have ridden horses in Cambridge. She didn't have any exercise there except to go tearing from one high spot to another, and that's not exercise, is it?

ED HENNESSY   I saw that horse a hundred million billion times! It seemed to me that it never changed form. It was always just perfect. Edie'd say, "Look! Look what I've done to the leg!"

"Oh, yes, Edie, yes. Oh, much better!"

But I could never see what she'd done. That horse went through the whole year. It just wouldn't end, that horse. I wonder if that crazy father of hers ever saw it.

PATRICIA SULLIVAN   The first thing you ever knew about Edie was that she came from this truly remarkable and totally insane family in California. Somebody would say: "Oh. See over there, that's one of the Sedgwicks; they come from California and they're all crazy." Of course, growing up around Boston, everybody's slightly mad. Old families have strange people in the attic. Staying with one family, you're told never to speak to Uncle James. One day a friend of mine looked out and saw a naked man under his car looking at the mechanism of the undercarriage. It was Uncle James.

BARTLE BULL   I first met Edie one evening that fall. I was bemoaning that I had been stood up for a picnic lunch the noon before. I still had the gear for the picnic lunch in the trunk of my car, so when I ran into Edie, I asked her for the next day, and we went to the Mount Auburn Cemetery and had a super time. Oh, yes, Mount Auburn was my regular picnic spot. It's a charming place because the grass is as smooth as a pool-table top, and it's full of flowers and old shrubs. No one is around. Mary Baker Eddy, the Christian Scientist, is buried there. She has, or had, a telephone in her crypt. For years the church paid the telephone bills on the off-chance she'd call up from the beyond, but the light never blinked on the switchboard.

So we sat on that smooth grass, opened up the picnic basket, and we had daiquiris, white wine, pâté, caviar, cheese, chicken—the whole thing—out of two big paper bags. Edie was charmed by it all. We saw each other more or less steadily for the next year or so.

She had recently come out of a psychiatric institution, obviously pleased to be loose, but she wasn't running around wild, either; she seemed quite balanced at the time . . . spending her time sculpting or with her shrink in Cambridge, or fencing with her family members as they came in and out of town. She was going to the shrink at least three times a week, perhaps five, but she was uneven about seeing him. She had a fatalistic sense about her family being doomed.

MINTURN SEDGWICK   Edie came to visit us—the sort of duty visits one pays one's uncle—every once in a while when she was beginning her art studies in Cambridge. The telephone started ringing about three days before. It never stopped while she was there, and it went on for a while after. It was really an eye-opener how many young men were calling. There was one particularly odd young man. I finally said to him, "As an old hand, I think you will make more ground if you pay less attention to her."

BARTLE BULL   She could be quite a different person from hour to hour. What sort of creature am I today? Am I like this? Am I like that? Very mercurial: she could be immensely difficult or very sweet; she could be creative and sculpt and have an organized week; or she could retreat and be chaotic and not do anything. That was part of her charm—that she was so unpredictable.

Sex was a nervous, uneven thing for her. If she talked about it, it was only very lightly: offhand, frivolous. She'd say something like, "I'd better not let So-and-so sleep with me because then he'll love me for the rest of his life" . . . just kidding around.

She was a fantastic dancer. We danced in New York in Shepheard's, and I remember Huntington Hartford coming out of the shadows and trying to pick her up with some of that "Baby, I can put you in lights" treatment. To my annoyance, she found that quite interesting.

Edie at her twenty-first birthday party with Ed Hennessy, April, 1964

We went to Bermuda together. They'd never seen anything like Edie. Most of my friends there were fairly conventional—Bermuda shorts and suntans. Edie was fantastically pale; she would never go in the sun. She was very exotic for Bermuda.

Have you seen those passport pictures of Edie and me? We were at Logan Airport in Boston. We had some time to kill and we got into one of those booths where your picture is taken four times, about a second apart. You can see her sort of schizy quality in the pictures. She said, "We'll do four completely different pictures," and she did just that, bang, bang, bang, bang.

I knew she was going out with different groups. There were periods when, for a time, I wouldn't see her. She would stumble around in some slightly dim Cambridge world.

SUKY SEDGWICK   Edie didn't want anybody too close to her. As soon as there were men who were interested, she would wriggle away. It was physical protection. In the beginning, both Edie and I went to some coming-out parties, but by the end of the year they were all-night orgy things. She ended up at breakfast in long evening dresses. It became kind of a feat. Hers was a non-stop zoom, zoom, zoom. I do remember moments of desperation, but she was consuming different experiences . . . spinning faster and faster.

JOHN ANTHONY WALKER   The really interesting people weren't going to Harvard, but they were hanging around. Edie had the capacity to create instantly the world around her. You entered Edie's world and nothing tangential made any difference: everything else fell away and there Edie was in the middle of a pirouette. I'll give you a scene of Edie. One day I was in the Widener Library Reading Room at Harvard. It was just essential that I study my notes for an hour exam. Edie was with me. I don't know why. To get out of the rain. She started to draw in my notebook. It was almost as if you'd given a child a crayon and a piece of paper to keep her quiet because she had no one to play with. She did this perspective of the Reading Room which was phenomenal. Absolutely phenomenal. She did the whole length of Widener with its ceilings and vaultings, a special rendering of that sort of cavernous place it is.

It was a particular period in Cambridge when there were a lot of fairly bright and beautiful people—as beautiful as Edie—going down-hill as fast as they could and not stopping because they'd fall down if they stopped; they tried to take as many people with them as they could. So you had people like Cloke Dosset, who sat there already frustrated and failed by Cambridge standards, and somewhat bitter.

Cloke Dosset was from the South—all those cottonfields stretching as far as the eye can see, which he would inherit if he straightened up and married. He came up to Boston dragging the tendrils of the South like Spanish moss, out of a Carson McCullers scene. There he was, a sensitive Southern boy in what would be considered an effeminate world by that red-necked aristocracy.

PATRICIA SULLIVAN   The fabled Cloke Dosset! I think he was already out of Harvard by then. A very brilliant man, very promising scholar who had come to Harvard to do graduate work . . . older, balding, but with a kind of ageless quality . . . and as a graduate student teaching a section. His morality and seduction of beautiful boys had reached the point at which the University could not tolerate it, and he was, I'm told, not allowed to enter Harvard Yard. They had a sort of contract out on him. So he was part of the shadowy world that lived on the fringes of Harvard University.

I remember sitting with him in his little apartment at a very small table for dinner. The first course—I remember them as being so elegant—was half an avocado with the hollow filled with sherry or maybe salad dressing. That may not seem all that dazzling, but I grew up in a good, strict Boston household where the first course was always consommé with a soggy cracker in it. So it somehow seemed so wild, so elegant, so recherché to serve an avocado. His mind and his conversation were very original and, I thought, amusing. Tremendous repartee. Probably now I would think it sounded like a rejected act by Noel Coward.

Cloke picked on young men at a particularly vulnerable stage in life. You can imagine the crop of exquisitely beautiful young men who'd arrive in Cambridge every fall out of those small, coddled schools, suddenly in a class with twelve hundred people. It was not like Groton or St. Paul's. They were not protected. So they'd run into somebody who was everything intellectual superiority was supposed to be like—someone who talked about God and Freud and Shakespeare, with a fair number of literary allusions tucked into every sentence. Cloke Dosset did have a fine mind. He'd draw these men in . . . a whole circle around him.

The walls of his apartment were decorated with something like black satin. Strange cocktail parties consisting largely of men who wouldn't speak to women. Many of them had these wonderful names which Cloke would give them: Columbine Streetwalker, Halloween Pederast, Gardenia Boredom, and Gloriana, which is the name of Spenser's Faerie Queene, and Appassionata von Climax. The girls did not get nicknames.

In the early days of this group there weren't any superstar ladies like Edie; they hadn't yet moved into high gear. A few strange, rather flamboyant women hung around in big hats, but they were more along the lines of a Bette Midler. I remember one who was grossly fat who took off with the Shah's nephew, something Pahlavi, and they had a wild night of passion. "I was Empress for a night!"

Up to that point Cloke had not hit upon the idea of the more effective decoy—the sort of thing that a beautiful woman like Edie would provide: I mean, they were bait in the trap. Other women were certainly much more intellectual than Edie, and had a more substantial seductive quality. But Edie had an ephemeral charm that nonetheless becomes implanted in your memory. It was vulnerability and a way of reaching out to the person with whom she was talking that was utterly charming.

What did Edie find in that scene? Well, adoration certainly, and a great deal of safety, and of course there was the feeling of being totally needed and useful to someone without having to make any commitment. Awful, though, to be used as a fly in a spider's web . . . sort of luring people in. You move aside and they fly on into the arms of Cloke Dosset.

Like any fag community, it was tremendously amusing, intelligent, energetic, interesting, and a refreshing change from Saturday afternoon football games—not really, but at the time it seemed that way.

So it gave one a sense of belonging. And it was heightened by the scene being decadent and probably dangerous . . . it was exciting. This is the big world. This is the wicked world.

RENÉ RICARD   Edie loved the very nitroglycerine queens, the really smart ones who knew everything. She wanted high, very sophisticated, brilliant faggot friends who posed no threat to her body. That was a golden period, that year in Cambridge. All those amazing faggots and Edie. She had them all—the prettiest girl in town and the most degenerate men! Most of them stunning.

Ed Hennessy was an astonishing number. I mean, the *things* he would say! The expressions he would invent. One of them was: "You have a flair for the obvious." *He* certainly didn't. When he was an undergraduate, he would go to parties dressed as Bea Lillie, with the pearls and the cloche. Edie loved all that. In the photographs you can see her just *dying* of laughter . . . you know, that smile with the dimples. That smile melted everyone's heart.

WILLIAM ALFRED   Ed Hennessy was a great character of that time. He'd turn up at class smoking black cigarettes and saying things like, "Let's swear a lot tonight." A kind of deliberately outrageous dandy at a time Harvard was not producing many dandies.

ED HENNESSY   You wonder how the girls fit in? I hardly knew myself. Indeed, at the time I didn't realize what I was up to. Years later I realized that what I was really doing was trying to impress boys into thinking that either I was one of them—"You see, I'm straight: I'm going out with Edie Sedgwick"—or that, much more likely, I was out with a girl in order to meet boys. I can tell you one case in particular. There was a freshman—oh, this is embarrassing—Robert Taft Hollingsworth the Third, who'd been to St. Mark's. I was in the Lamont Library in the reading room pretending to study, and this incredibly attractive boy walked through. I *just* about fell apart. I *try* not to get involved in things like this, or even *think* these things. But this boy was too beautiful! Anyway, I could not find his pictures in the yearbooks. Chuck Wein helped me. He had graduated a year or two before, but he had come back to bum around. We were walking together along Mass Avenue when I saw this incredible boy again. I said, "Chuck, that's the *person*—that's the boy I was talking about . . . Chuck!" Chuck and I did our famous pirouette move there on the street. He had taught it to me: as you're walking along and you see somebody very attractive pass you, you do a complete circle as you continue walking and you take another look. We didn't care how odd it seemed. We *wanted* another look. Chuck said, "Since you've got a thesis to worry about, I'll do some spying for you."

So Chuck did a little spying. He followed him into the Harvard Yard to Grays Hall, one of the freshman dormitories. We looked in the freshman yearbook, which I hadn't thought of doing before. There he was! Robert Taft Hollingsworth the Third. Virginia. St. Mark's. So we knew where we were. We found out that Robert Taft Hollingsworth the Third occasionally went to the Casablanca bar. I can't remember how the introductions were finally arranged, but they were, and very quickly things started flying: invitations to things, cocktail parties. He never knew my feelings. And then I introduced him, my love object, to Edie. He fell in love with her! *Aggghhh!* Started calling her up every five seconds and wanting to go out with her. She was furious! I don't think she really understood what was happening. He would call me up, saying: "I like Edie so much. Do you think you could arrange a date?" He had money and a little Jaguar. So then I'd call up Edie, or if he'd tried to reach her directly, she'd call me to complain, "Oh, God, that little goose is calling me again!" I remember that vividly. Even if you're very fond of the girl who calls him that, when you're infatuated with someone, you don't like them being called "a little goose"!

The irony of this is like an eighteenth-century comedy. Edie couldn't bear him. I was in love with him. She wanted to be with me. I wanted to be with him. He would put up with me just to be near her, and vice versa.

Edie didn't want to be harassed by men. She didn't want to be pawed. She didn't want to "have dates." She'd say, "Eddie, get me out of this. Do something." She knew she was safe with me, because we weren't going to go: "C'mon, honey, take your bra off." None of that. We never spoke about this; it was implicit. That's one of the reasons, perhaps, that we loved her. She understood that we were men but we were not going to play sexual games and bore her or annoy her.

JACK REILLY   Edie was always pleading with me to let her into the Casablanca when I was the bartender. She wanted to be there with her crowd, but she was under twenty-one. "Jack, I don't have to leave, do I? Can't I just stay? I love it here so much!" It was like her home away from home. "It's only two more months before I'm twenty-one." She pleaded as if it was everything in life to her. It was very disturbing that anybody would put that much importance on a bar.

ED HENNESSY   At the Casablanca they wouldn't even give her a Coca-Cola. They wouldn't let her sit with us. It seemed a vendetta on the Casablanca's part. One afternoon we went to a dumpy clothes store in Cambridge and bought her a housedress with rhinestone buttons, and a dreadful wig. We put wrinkles on her face. We wanted to disguise her and make her look very old. We worked all afternoon on her. But when we walked into the Casablanca, Jack Reilly took one look and said, "Out!"

That's one of the reasons we wanted to make such a production of her twenty-first birthday. It was so important I can remember the date —April 20, 1964. Edie had just come into a trust fund from her grandmother.

The party was at the Harvard Boat House. Edie danced divinely. Oh, God! Everyone wanted to dance with her, but there was no way. She changed dresses three times during the evening. That confused a lot of people—the party girl, the birthday girl would suddenly be in a different dress. "Do you think someone spilled a drink on her?" Then she'd be in *another* dress. "Oh, my goodness, she must have some very drunk friends. How resourceful to have extra dresses on hand if one gets spilled on!" Oh, she was something. She was something different in Cambridge!

JOHN ANTHONY WALKER   The great time was when Edie was able to drink in the Casablanca legally. The Casa B was an atmospheric place, and the sentimental music, the haze from the daiquiris, the darkness of the place all helped the milieu. You couldn't see who was coming down the corridor. It was like being in the theater: someone would make an entrance. The door was plywood. You came down the stairs from the Brattle movie theater, along the corridor, opened the door, and there was the Casa B. It was Edie's Casa B; there was really no one else in there. Everybody knew her; she knew everybody. When one came through the plywood door, it was into her total world, and what heightened the experience was that one often had come down from the Brattle—that factory of illusions.

When the Casa B closed, you came up the stairs to the back door and you'd be out on the street and you'd go a few blocks to Cloke's apartment, laughing and giggling up to the second floor, turn left, open the door, and there was Cloke, who'd got there from the Casa B before you, and where, like a Southern gentleman, he would give you a gin-and-tonic.

PATRICIA SULLIVAN   I can imagine how an evening at Cloke Dosset's would have deteriorated, but the stories never floated back. Those were the days when everyone was much less candid about their private lives. The worst thing that could be said about you at Radcliffe was that she goes down. That was a blow from which your reputation could never recover.

ED HENNESSY   Edie's brother Jonathan was frightened by Cloke Dosset. That wasn't surprising. Cloke exuded a kind of dangerous vibration. At my parties Porcellian Club clubbies would come up and say: "Who is that?" They didn't know what it was all about. I remem-

Edie and Ed Hennessy

Ed Hennessy as Bea Lillie

Edie and Bartle Bull

ber a sophomore, a very nice Porcellian boy—they seem to be the *most* fragile—whom Cloke saw across the room at the Casablanca and apparently liked. He got his attention just by focusing on him, and then he walked across the room very slowly, snapping his fingers, click, click, click, and finally he got right up to him, and the boy fainted! He was on the crew and a big jock.

Edie and I shared many things. One, that we never read the newspapers, ever. I still don't; I never read a newspaper unless I'm told my name's in it, or my mother's name. Edie and I were so ignorant of current events, it was unbelievable. So witness us—Edie and me—walking on Mass. Avenue just in front of the Unrest Restaurant . . . well, it's called the University Restaurant. Neither of us was feeling too hot. I think we'd been up all night. I'm sure I'd been working on a term paper and she'd been working very heavily on her horse. No. Frankly, we'd just been partying it up.

Edie was carrying her book. She always carried around a copy of *A Tale of Two Cities*. It wasn't a pose. All the girls and boys at Harvard were always carrying around bookbags and opening up books and notebooks. So Edie finally got a book! She decided on *A Tale of Two Cities*. She read: "It was the best of times. It was the worst of times." I think that's as far as she got. But once it was lost . . . "Where's my book?" It was a monomaniacal thing. "My book! My book! What did you do with my book!" I don't know why it was Dickens. It was a nicely bound book. It may have come from her grandmother's at 720 Park.

Anyway, we were walking down Mass. Avenue, Edie with her Dickens, and out of nowhere—and this was the first experience that I can remember of Edie being on camera—came a TV camera, a microphone, and a man with a dreadful question.

First the man asked for our names. "Edmund Hennessy, class of '64 at Harvard." "Edith Sedgwick, I'm studying sculpture." Then came the question: "What do you think of the expression 'Better Red Than Dead'?"

Well, Edie and I looked at each other. We'd *never* heard it before. We had no idea what he was talking about. But we'd given our names and our occupations and we had to do something. So I said into the television camera: "I think in these troubled times that our government has a debt to its people to promulgate certain information. If the populace is not able to assimilate this promulgated information . . . well, it would be just *frightful*," and then I lost myself and faded away.

So then the interviewer, looking somewhat startled, turned to Edie and asked what *she* thought of the expression "Better Red Than Dead."

Edie said, "Well, I think that what Eddie has said just about hits the nail on the head. But I do think," she added, "that the whole concept"—after all, she was carrying her book, *A Tale of Two Cities*—"is entirely ludicrous!"

The interviewer was absolutely shocked . . . but we thought we had pulled it off extremely well. We went to lunch at Lowell House at Harvard, and it was there that we discovered that it was R-E-D, not R-E-A-D. We had thought: "Better Read," and there I'd been talking about illiteracy rates being too high.

About two months later, after Edie's acceptance into the Casablanca, we ran into Tony Hiss and someone who looked like his father. Ed Hood, one of the more worldly people in our group, said, "That must be Alger Hiss." Now, Ed Hood knew who Alger Hiss was. Edie and I knew he was famous, but we didn't know why. Perfect example of two young people—from Santa Barbara, I might add—who have no touch with the real world.

Anyway, we all went back to Cloke Dosset's apartment. Cloke was fluttering about—"Oh, Alger Hiss, oh, Alger . . ." Edie and I were in the kitchen. Chuck Wein was with us and he asked Edie, totally facetiously, "Why don't you go out and tell Alger Hiss that *funny* 'Better Read Than Dead' story?"

So Edie walked out and announced to Alger: "Would you like to hear a story about Eddie and me and 'Better Red Than Dead'?"

My God, everyone froze with fear! I suddenly remembered who he was—an accused Communist, a convicted perjurer, something awful like that. At first Hiss was listening like a cat because he didn't know what Edie would come up with as a punch line. She went blithely on and when she came to the punch line—that we thought it was R-E-A-D, reading books and things—Alger Hiss laughed and laughed like he thought it was the funniest thing in the world. So that was the irony—that the first time around we didn't know what "Better Red Than Dead" meant, and the second time we didn't know who Alger Hiss was.

You've heard about the great lunch at the Ritz? God knows how it got started. Edie *claimed* that her father, Duke, had a charge account there. So she wanted to have this big lunch and charge it to him. We took over the huge round table in the front of the dining room. Everything was shaped round in Cambridge and Boston, wasn't it? We rather doubted Edie could charge it to her father, and we all brought money to make sure the bill could be paid. Because why would Duke Sedgwick, living in California, have a charge account at the Ritz in Boston? Anyway, some phone calls were made and we had quite a crowd. We got extremely drunk—I, particularly. Champagne, prosciutto ham. I don't recall if Edie had her favorite food—which was roast beef with *lots* of Russian dressing. At the time it was her middle name: Edie "Lots of Russian Dressing" Sedgwick.

Anyway, at the Ritz we started inviting people over from other tables. We got a *senator* over. He was with his son; Bob Smith knew the son through the Fly Club. So he came over, this old divine man, who was just in his element, being with young Harvard undergraduates and lovely girls. He may have bought a round of champagne; he was just a marvelous old man.

Then the bill came, and we all held our breaths. "Oh, dear, let's see if Edie can cope." She did a little fiddling . . . and signed her name. The waiters standing around looked down and, oh, their faces just filled with surprise. We said to ourselves, "Uh-oh, she's signing either Charlie Chaplin or Donald Duck. Oh, God, we've got to come out with the cash." The manager was called over. We truly thought we were in trouble. But no! She had written down a hundred percent tip. It was perhaps a two-hundred-fifty-dollar lunch. She'd written a two-hundred-fifty-dollar tip! That makes five hundred dollars. Signed it. So that's why the manager was called over—"racy people at this table." But Edie told him, "No, no, I mean it. I insist."

The next day I realized that Edie didn't really know what a tip should be. Probably had never come up in her life before. She thought one hundred percent was about right. I chatted with her about it the next day. "Edie, did you really mean to leave all that? I mean, did you like them so much you wanted sort of to go *overboard?*" She said she didn't. I don't think she knew. She did have an innocent way. How many times had she gone to a big place and bought or charged a meal?

Well, when the bill was paid, the Ritz party really began. There was much singing—like the Friendship Chains in the Casa B—swaying back and forth. Have you been to the Ritz? I mean, you just don't do things like that. Then Edie stood on the table and sang her favorite song, Richard Rodgers' "Loads of Love," just bellowing out that line "I just want money, and then some money, and loads of lovely love." We stood up on our chairs and began doing the twist. There were some Iowans or something who left in the middle of their meal because they were so scandalized at what we were doing. Undoubtedly Edie had on her picture hat and was standing on the top of the table by then. What's the opposite of *sotto voce?* Well, that's the way she sang to that whole room, stentorian: "I want some money, and then some money, and loads of lovely love." I have the record at home and I cry every time I put it on. She gave it to me. She had it memorized; she used to dwell on that song. The lyrics are very good and quite pertinent: "I never have been handed much / I never have demanded much / I never have expected much / I never have rejected much / I want my dinner, my conversation, and loads of lovely love."

She sang it in the Ritz not to shock anyone. It was just that she felt like singing it. The headwaiter said, "Come back, but not soon again."

We finally left. We went leapfrogging down the stairs and through the lobby. I learned that at some coming-out party. You play leapfrog as you go down the stairs and you show your ass to the hosts. So we did those fabulous leapfrogs down to the *rez-de-chaussée*, and then, just as we were on the way out, Bob Smith, right in front of some Ritz official, reached into Edie's enormous basket purse and pulled out piece after piece of table silverware, saying: "Edie, *now* I see why you can leave hundred percent tips. You steal silverware!"

Edie just turned *blue!* Bob Smith kept pulling it out, one after the other . . . "Look, Edie, all this silverware from the Ritz-Carlton." Then he started giggling.

The Ritz man got angry. Bob Smith had to admit to the officials at the manager's desk that he had done it all as a joke—sliding the silverware in one piece at a time during lunch. Oh, it really shocked the Ritz man standing at the whirlaround door.

JOHN ANTHONY WALKER   When I first saw her in Cambridge, she looked like a Tamil child growing up in South India—huge-eyed, those children are, with faces just like Edie's. I don't care what she did or how wrong she was. She was a catalyst, what is known as a *shakti* in the trade. The female energy which dynamizes: by being in contact with her, the edges were sharper. An evening with Edie would only end when Edie had got to the point of exhaustion, which would be at the end of two or three days. There's that old Yogi axiom: the higher you go, the further you fall. We all know that. She liked walking very close to extinction, always.

Edie had a very hard time handling the world . . . as would be the case with an Olympian god who had taken the wrong exit off Olympus and come down here into this mortal coil. She saw herself as somebody who, if touched, could be annihilated. You have to be very careful. Edie felt this, psychologically—that she must never be touched by the "brute, irredeemable facts of life"—that's a quote of Henry James in Alfred North Whitehead.

I could never have held her. My father was never frightened by any of the ladies I hung around with. Except by Edie. He was perceptive enough to see that I could quite readily spend the rest of my life, and what money he would give me, trying to keep Edie happy and together.

SUKY SEDGWICK   I didn't see much of her even though I lived in Cambridge that year. But I saw her whenever she was in trouble, and that became a pattern. Whenever she was upset, she'd come to me or I'd go to her. She had flocks and flocks of people around her, telephone going all the time, and appointments to be made right and left, people looking for Edie. And Edie was just Edie . . . being Edie, she didn't want to be possessed by anybody, in any shape or form. Just like a fish, zoom, zoom, zoom, escaping in a lot of ways. And amusing herself in the limelight.

Suddenly her glamorous world would evaporate, would shatter. Then Edie would become that hundred percent butterfly creature that she was underneath. The absolute purity and defenselessness that belonged to all the stories she told, and absolute tenderness. There would be openings in the clouds and she would throw her arms around me and cry.

13

HARRY SEDGWICK   Minty was picked up in Central Park in October, 1963, standing up on one of the statues, apparently making a speech to nobody. He had just fallen to pieces. He had a Bible with our family name in it, so they looked in the telephone book and called up my wife, Patsy, who called me. I called Minty's mother out in California and I said, "Alice, Minty's in Bellevue!" I asked, "Do you want me to make a reservation for you for tomorrow night?" expecting her to rush East. She said, "Well, I've got to do this and that, and I've got to be in Boston to settle Suky into the New England Conservatory of Music." I said, "Alice! Minty's in Bellevue. Bellevue's an unhappy place." She said, "Well, I'll call his doctor. Other than that, are *you* going to take care of it?" I was being asked to be the surrogate. Boy, that really shook me.

Minty was just a name on a roster at Bellevue. Nobody cared. He screamed and screamed and nobody heard. He yelled out for help and everybody who counted asked, "Did you hear a noise?" Evidently he'd lie on the ward floor and try to crouch into the corner. He'd crawl to interviews on his knees. He was hallucinating—one thing he kept saying was "Helicopters in the sunlight. The morning sun." He told them he was an addict and an alcoholic and had homosexual impulses. At one point he said, "I'm not sure whether I'm Francis Junior or Francis Senior."

Minty went from Bellevue to Manhattan State. I saw him there, too. He seemed like a tiny little boy in a terribly rough world. He just didn't have the protective skin for that sort of place. It's awful. There's nothing more dramatic than the stark, barred windows and the pajama-clad emptiness of that place. He was sweeping floors. And, of course, the comrades were mostly in pretty rough shape. Minty looked scared . . . furtive. He kept saying, "I don't want to go back to Silver Hill." I spent some time with the doctor at Manhattan State. He was a fairly young guy, but he really spoke with enthusiasm about his patients. They weren't just numbers like No. L 462. He said that in his judgment Minty was certainly not responsive to his doctor at Silver Hill, although doctors aren't supposed to say that sort of stuff. He felt that it wasn't a good idea to continue with that doctor. But when Alice finally came East, she still believed in Silver Hill, so Minty ended up back there.

SAUCIE SEDGWICK   The psychiatrist at Silver Hill was just the kind my parents would go for. He made my mother feel comfortable. Very neutral sort of man, large and calm . . . an insulating presence, as if he were covered in layers of cotton wool. He had also been Edie's doctor two years earlier. Minty would call up and say, "I'm taking medicine, but I'm all out of whack. My doctor says I'm not trying to get well." Minty was so noble; he never asked for help. Never. He was polite to the last instant! He was dignified in a way that would just break your heart.

FROM THE MEDICAL EXAMINER'S REPORT TO THE CORONER, MARCH 4, 1964

. . . at about 7:20 p.m. Ann Ridge, a maid, was asked to check his room to see why he was not at dinner. She found the room in darkness and on investigating saw Sedgwick hanging against the bathroom door—he had fastened the tie around his neck and passed the remainder over the top of the door and attached the knotted end to a metal clothes hanger. . . .

I am satisfied that the said death was not caused by the criminal act, omission, or carelessness of any other person or persons, and that an inquest is unnecessary. In accordance with the statute I have delivered the body of said deceased to Hoyt Funeral Home, New Canaan—awaiting instructions from family for burial.

Silver Hill, New Canaan, Connecticut

Minty, fall, 1962

SAUCIE SEDGWICK   Minty killed himself the day before his twenty-sixth birthday. The telephone rang in the middle of the night. I was asleep. I picked up the receiver and it was my father: "Hullo, Sauce . . . Minty hanged himself this afternoon." He didn't even say "Sit down," or "How are you feeling?" or "I have some bad news." He seemed to be handing it to me in a way that was as shocking and cruel as possible. If I had to give his voice a color, I would say it was black.

He asked me very coldly to tell my sister Kate and nobody else. He and my mother were coming East the next day, and they didn't want anybody to know until they could tell Edie themselves, in person.

ED HENNESSY   Edie was terribly upset. She was *furious* at her father. To the point where she'd go out and kill him. She told me about Minty and his sexual problems, and that he had ended up at Silver Hill because he had fallen in love with another boy. According to Edie, he had finally come clean with Duke, who was harassing him all the time: "What's wrong with you? What's the matter? Stop being crazy, I can't stand it. Stop being depressed. You're a Sedgwick. You've got to stop doing this!" Finally Minty just broke down in tears and told him what the problem was. Instead of sympathizing and saying, "These things happen, let's talk about it," his father got furious and said: "I'll never speak to you again, you're no son of mine!" Within a matter of days Minty killed himself. Edie was just beside herself. She cried. Oh, yes. It was the first time I'd ever seen a lady with black stuff running down her cheeks.

JONATHAN SEDGWICK   We met somewhere in Cambridge. Edie started beating me, hammering me with her fists in the chest, saying, "Come on, cry. God damn you!" She was just pouring tears. She loved Minty.

SUKY SEDGWICK   Edie consoled me. I thought I was going to go berserk when I heard about Minty . . . I really did. I screamed. I just got hysterical. I was in shock—physical, total, mental shock. Edie put her arms around me in the back of the car.

Mummy and Fuzzy were in the front seat. They had picked us up in Cambridge, and were taking us to the Somerset Club, which is on Beacon Hill. It's a very sophisticated, quiet, very Mummy-type place:

very old-fashioned and incredibly porcelain. Think of porcelain dolls and porcelain everything. And somewhat awful when you had just the four of us sitting in that room with that kind of news.

Oh, Edie sure as hell was crying, too. Oh, shit, man, who wouldn't. Minty being . . . Minty was somebody to *us!* We knew who Minty was!

JOHN ANTHONY WALKER   Edie told me Minty had called her just before he died at Silver Hill. He told her that she was the only Sedgwick he could ever hope for. He sort of listed them all. We can infer from this that he was consciously committing suicide; he knew he was going to do it. He called up Edie because she was the last one he could talk with. Nobody wants to die without leaving a message. She was very wrought up.

It was a rainy night, when she came to see me, not long after, and she came to me as a friend, very strung up. She didn't cry. Just an odd sense of anguish. She felt that space was closing in on her. Her family was going to get her, or the universe was going to get her, or with any luck she'd get herself first.

Well, that rainy night I decided the best thing I could do to get Edie out of her depressed head was to take her to a light and frolicsome movie. The Brattle was playing *The Blue Angel.* For some reason I had it in my head that *The Blue Angel* was a Second World War farcical movie that included Luftwaffe planes. So I thought, "Wow, we'll take Edie to a little bit of light German burlesque." Somehow I was crazy enough to think Marlene Dietrich was a comedienne. And then, of course, the name itself—Edie is an angel out of the vast blue. So it was appropriate.

We walked in. It starts out as an extremely funny movie. But then it becomes the most vicious movie. It spares you nothing. It was a trap that we walked into. You remember—the rigid, authoritarian Herr Professor in the college town who goes to the burlesque house to speak to the burlesque queen who's been tempting his students . . . and he falls in love with her, marries her, and joins the circus. For a time you're jollied into this feeling of empathy and camaraderie with Herr Professor and his new world of burlesque, with all these people who are like caricatures. But then it begins to go awry. They are *not* caricatures, and you watch the Professor slowly get enmeshed and crushed beneath the pressure of a totally unsympathetic society that totally exploits him.

At a certain point I looked over at Edie, realizing that this was all going wrong. I didn't have the courage and it didn't occur to me, but I should have said: "Hey, Edie, let's split. Edie, you don't need to take this." She was totally in the movie, she was like drawn up inside herself. She was right up there on the screen. Her eyes, big as they were, were bigger. Her hands were clutched around her knees. She was rigid.

Finally there's that closing scene when the Professor returns to the college town, a total failure: he's lost everything—his academic standing, his integrity, his money, and Dietrich is having an affair with this circus strongman, so he has *this* humiliation also laid on top of him. He comes out on the stage as the magician's apprentice and he begins to flub his lines. He can no longer hold it all together. He's supposed to call out "cock-a-doodle-do"; and the magician produces an egg from his ear. The camera doesn't turn away: you see this sort of mottled, apoplectic face. Finally the magician, to get a laugh, breaks some eggs over his bald head so the yolk runs down his face. That snaps him completely and he starts to cry out "cock-a-doodle-do, cock-a-doodle-do," and they come for him with the straitjacket and put him in his old schoolroom where he had once taught the boys. That's how it ends.

Well, you can imagine what this did to Edie that night. The man carrying the straitjacket! It was a brutal movie; it is almost unforgivable to use a camera like that. When the Professor broke, it was so relentless the way the camera held on him. Next to me Edie said: "Please, God, end this scene," but the camera just stayed there and hung on this man: insane, broken completely, sprung out of his head, crowing at the top of his voice while they threw bottles and things from the audience.

I didn't dare look at Edie. There was nothing I could do. Maybe I should have held her hand and said: "It's only a movie." It was a heavy night for her.

14

SAUCIE SEDGWICK Bobby was in the hospital in Hartford, Connecticut, when Minty died. I don't know how he found out about it, but when he called me—he must have been sedated—he just said, "Poor Minty . . . poor guy."

GEORGE PLIMPTON Of all the family, Bobby was the only one who wasn't at all consistent. He took on guises—like a chameleon. Minty was predictable. Bobby wasn't. I remember Bobby when he got to Harvard from Groton twelve years earlier, in 1951. He was an astonishingly handsome kid then—I mean handsome in the sense that everybody, male or female, stared at him without really meaning to . . . not lasciviously, but because he *was* extraordinary to look at. He couldn't get over it himself. He's the only person I ever met who suffered a true narcissist complex: at that time he carried a small pocket mirror which he would take out and admire himself in without any self-consciousness, the way a beautiful woman will preen herself in a fashionable restaurant. Bobby carried the mirror to the beach at Hendaye down on the Basque coast, for God's sake, and he would slip it out of his bathing suit and look at himself. I don't remember that anyone kidded him about it, or even made slurring remarks behind his back—he was so guileless about it. Everything had to be in order. Every hair in place. A fashion plate. He was a terrific success with the girls that summer, but it seems to me his whole attitude about them was quite perfunctory. I mean, *they* were the ones who appeared to do all the work.

He wore this curious grin. I used to think it was the grin of the cat who swallowed the canary. He seemed blessed with the best life can offer to someone who was just, what? twenty years old: extraordinary looks, a prestigious name, a wonderful and vibrant father (at least that's what I thought), a mother my parents thought was the salt of the earth (with which I would have agreed), a huge number of healthy brothers and sisters, a great education (Groton and Harvard), fine if somewhat exuberant friends, a grace and charm that endeared him to older people, social acceptance (the Porcellian Club), and really with all this he had *everything* to look forward to. But then I realized that the grin was too fixed and strange to have any connection with stability. It was so vacuous. It was tacked on. I thought at the time that he was simply a bit victimized by his liberal education and patrician background—not quite knowing what to do with either . . . which was certainly a common enough phenomenon. Certainly I thought if there were any problems he could straighten them out.

SYDNEY J. FREEDBERG   In Bobby's undergraduate days at Harvard I had an office off the library in the Fogg Museum, where I was a professor in the Fine Arts Department. It was immediately accessible to anyone who wanted to walk in the door. Bobby did so frequently. He would sit himself down and open up a subject of discussion which might or might not be relevant, and then he would very rapidly wander off into philosophical generalizations of perfectly extraordinary breadth and confusion. It was almost impossible to get him to think in a consecutive and disciplined way. But he would insist on bringing up the heavy artillery, involving himself with first principles at the philosophical level. He really was terribly intelligent. One felt that his intellectual derailments were the consequence of psychological motives, not of any defect of mind. Sometimes he would say things that had the most extraordinary acuity, really great intellectual penetration, but he himself was never accessible to his own critical faculties.

Often he brought up his father, characterizing him in a way which I can only describe as pathologically hostile—a relationship dominated by buckets of incompatibility. Duke couldn't see at all what Bobby was about; terribly impatient with him. And Bobby, on his side, was absolutely hostile to his father's insistence upon stringent fiats and all the virtues that Bobby thought were Boy Scoutish.

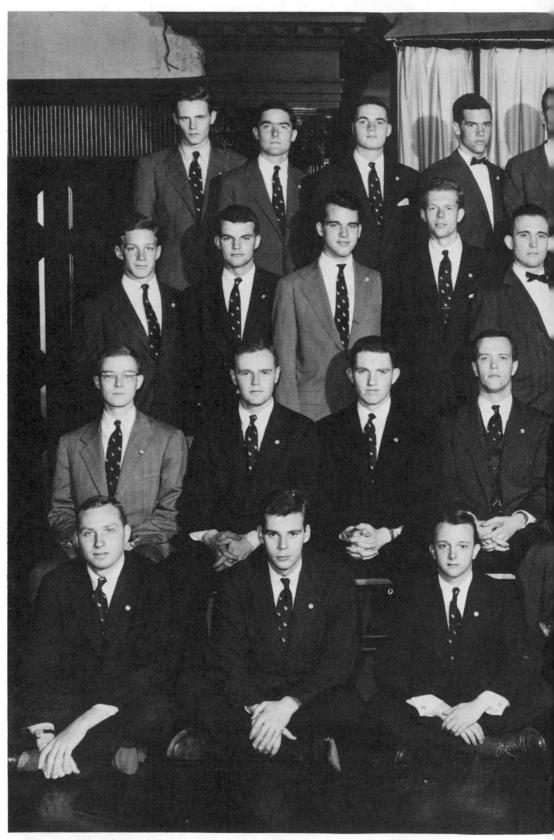

The Porcellian Club, Harvard, 1953. Bobby is in the back row, fourth from left.

WILLIAM ALFRED   The odd thing was that, despite Bobby's obvious difficulties with his father, he carried his father's nickname, Duke, through college. He was a very strange young man. He had these fits of irascibility and actual weirdness. His freshman advisor gave him to me and said, "See if you can't get this guy through his sophomore year." He was taking Fine Arts at the time, and I offered to tutor him. Just before Christmas, 1952, he handed in a paper which didn't make any sense to me. I said, "Read it to me sentence by sentence and then tell me what they mean." We talked it over; it was like giving dictation. After a while he began to get the hang of it. He could write by himself then. But after Christmas vacation at home he just gave up. I was told that his father said things like "You're sort of stupid. You're just a good-looking Airedale. I don't think you can use your brains. Your only hope in life is to marry some rich girl."

"I can't do any more work," Bobby told me. "I've got these terrible pains in my knees." He had taken up so much of my time that my first reaction was to take a book and hit him on the top of the head, he made me so damned mad. He told me, "Every time I go home I get the stuffing kicked out of me, and I just don't see what's the use. I'm going to let everything slide. I just don't care whether I pass or not." I'd never seen anybody collapse that fast. Whatever happened out there must have been awful.

THOMAS J. MCGREEVY   Part of what probably finally set Bobby off was the end of his romance with Randy Redfield. The Redfields were part of the aristocracy of Harbor Beach, Michigan, if you can imagine such a thing. Bobby met her when she was at Radcliffe. They went together for two or three years. She was an All-American sort of beauty —dark-haired, dark-eyed, big-boned, with a very expressive face. She's now the Countess of Toulouse-Lautrec and lives in Versailles and she is very involved with horses. I think the break-up with her had a considerable effect on Bobby.

RANDY REDFIELD   He was having terrible emotional problems. His nickname, Duke, seemed such a totally inappropriate nickname for somebody who was so lost and confused . . . pitiful. He would talk long and hard about the most trivial, mundane things—not quite how-to-get-up-in-the-morning, but almost. He would burst into tears on my shoulder. I think he loved being with me because I listened to him. I like underdogs; I felt very concerned for him. You can't really close a door on someone like that. He was preoccupied with the idea of destroying himself: "It's not worth it. I can't hack it. I would be better off dead. We would all be better off. Serve Father right!"

He was obviously very frightened of his father, and impressed by him at the same time. His father had been commissioned to make an equestrian statue, his first commission in years . . . oh, just a glorious thing, but very frightening for Bobby, because it somehow confirmed a facet of his father's strength.

Mr. Sedgwick disapproved of me. I represented a magnet. He did not tolerate any kind of magnetic field other than his own. And besides he considered the Sedgwicks socially superior to my family . . . socially and culturally . . . because we were from Harbor Beach, Michigan. He laid down the law that Bobby was not to be in touch with me. We'd have these clandestine telephone calls. Bobby would say: "I'm hidden in a phone booth. I love you." We'd arrange to meet. He'd talk endlessly . . . endlessly. The domineering father would come through, of course. I have absolutely not a single recollection of Bobby talking about his mother. Not one! Nor what he did as a child . . . the nursery rhymes, the songs he learned—none of that came through. It was very much a house draped in black.

ALEXANDER SEDGWICK   Bobby and I both lived in Eliot House his sophomore year at Harvard. That spring he had a breakdown. I was in my room and suddenly I heard a ruckus in the hall. Someone was screaming. I came out to see what was going on, and there was Bobby being taken away in a straitjacket to the hospital.

JUDITH WATKINS   When Bobby came back to Harvard in the fall of 1953 after that breakdown, he saw a lot of me. There were a lot of people at war inside Bobby. Fascinating, beautiful, spoiled, lost, and self-destructive. He was a searching person who turned to Far Eastern philosophy. He was thinking of doing what Jay Rockefeller had done: go to Japan and live, go deeply into Zen. He got a kind of tranquility from studying Chinese; it seemed to relax him a lot. But then he would slip out and drive all night to New York and go to the Copacabana.

PETER SOURIAN   He was seeing a psychiatrist in Boston, who kept sending him little notes on slips of paper: "Bob, you are doing better, just hang in there." They were like little cheerleader notes.

Into this situation—I was sharing a suite at Eliot House with Bob

—came Gregory Corso, the poet. He was also in mental pain. Bob was around being depressed and lumbering. He sometimes got rather heavy, an athletic sort of heavy rather than fat, so that when he and Gregory went out for walks, it was like watching a big whale and a pilot fish. It brought out the best in Gregory—which was his gentle side. Bob once said to me, "You know, he soothes me."

Corso had come up from Greenwich Village. He stayed with us there in our suite, which was not generally done. I had two foam-rubber mattresses and dyed sheets and metal poles, out of which I made a kind of elaborate Arab-like tent. That's where Gregory ended up sleeping—in a sort of house within a house. He would write in there during the day.

Sometimes we brought him into the dining room of Eliot House, but usually we smuggled his food back to the room in bowls. He was, well . . . a bit *difficult* in the dining room. He would attack people— I don't mean physically, of course—for being idiots. He had a confrontation with Archibald MacLeish, who was the Master of Eliot House that year. "You're not a poet," Corso growled. MacLeish rather graciously put up with all this.

Then that relationship with Bob began. There was some sort of affinity, the poet with the madman. I hate to say madman because I don't mean that. I mean, after all, poets are healers of a kind. There's sort of a psychic nerve they're touching.

GREGORY CORSO   I loved Bobby . . . not homosexually, but friendship. Nothing else, no. He was a very moody person. Very moody. And stuck on Zen Buddhism, which was the thing that helped cool him. He was the first person I ever saw get into Zen . . . outside of Jack Kerouac and Gary Snyder doing that number out in San Francisco.

I had come out of prison. Out of Dannemora. For what? For nothing. A simple robbery. I was there for three years. Good God, those prison years were the *best.* If I'd gone to high school, I'd've been in there with kids; I wouldn't've learned a thing. But in prison I got an education from the old men on Death Row. Spoke to those people! Man, they knew the books. Stendhal's *The Red and the Black,* Kierkegaard, Hegel. Ate up books like mad. That was the best!

When I went to Harvard, I suddenly learned that rich kids do not have it better than others. They're still locked into something. I was coming from the cold of prison and these people were coming from the warmth of a six-thousand-acre ranch, but, good God, they still can't get out!

Bobby with his friends Gregory Corso (*left*) and Christopher Amanda (*right*)

SAUCIE SEDGWICK   My mother's big concern about Bobby was that his hair was too long, and she wrote him a letter saying that if he went around Harvard like that, people would think he was a homosexual.

LETTER FROM FRANCIS SEDGWICK TO NITA COLGATE, MARCH 9, 1957

. . . Bobby continues to be a fearful and increasing problem. I discovered that in the last 2 years he has spent all his slender capital (about $25,000—wait till he tries to earn that amount!) and he fell into a passion with me over the telephone for not handing him out $3000 instantly "for psychoanalysis" at the same time he was trying to dig $10,000 from Mrs. de Forest for the same purpose (she telephoned us in desperation) and swore he never wanted to see either parent again ever—"they" were the cause of all his troubles. Well!

ALEXANDER SEDGWICK   Around this time you never knew what sort of person you were going to meet when you saw Bobby. One day Bobby would be High Porcellian and the next day a Marxist . . . talking about organizing the workers. He could be open and charming one day, and the next day turn off, withdraw, or be incredibly rude. After he graduated in 1956, he did some graduate work in Oriental art at the Yenching Institute at Harvard. But at the same time he got involved at the Massachusetts Institute of Mental Health, where in helping the underprivileged he began to get interested in radical politics.

JOHN P. MARQUAND, JR.   He got slowly further and further to the left. I remember he came around one night—Barbara and Jason Epstein were there—and he was on an intense Maoist kick. It would be hard to be more intense than Bobby was. That evening he began talking about the incursions of the aggressive Tibetan neo-fascists against the People's Republic of China. I remember Jason saying, "Don't you think that's a little far afield?"

LETTER FROM FRANCIS SEDGWICK TO NITA COLGATE, JUNE 4, 1960

. . . Bobby is reported to have a scholarship from the Ladies Garment Workers Union to study Marxian economics at N.Y.U. next winter. I never expected to be tied to David Dubinsky—a man everyone thinks highly of, but different.
Life wiggles slowly on. . . .

KENNETH JAY LANE   Bobby was an old little boy. In his labor days he wore a sort of thrift-shop zoot suit. Pale gray. We met Saucie at

Parke-Bernet for lunch and she said, "Oh, you're wearing your anti-Christ costume today." He had on a black shirt, a 1940s tie, and his hair was slicked back, very shiny, cheap black shoes, and one tooth out. He talked "dem" and "doses." Terribly funny. He was all profile. His face was so thin that when you looked at him from the front it was like looking at a cardboard cut-out.

THOMAS J. MCGREEVY I didn't see him after college until one night in Kansas City in 1961. I'd gone down with my wife to a black bar, a wonderful place called the Mardi Gras, Eighteenth and Vine. Ella Fitzgerald would come into town to sing at the Music Hall, and then she'd come over to the Mardi Gras and improvise. Everybody'd shout: "The Queen is here . . . here's Ella!" Great place!

Anyway, we were sitting in there. I think it was a night Dizzy Gillespie was in town. Out of the smoke and haze came this gaunt figure and he said, "Hey, Tom, man, how you doing?"

I looked around and it was Bob. He looked like Charlton Heston, only very emaciated, as if someone had *sat* on Charlton Heston.

I said, "My God, Bob, how are you? What are you up to?"

He said, "I'm organizing for the ILGWU. I'm engaged to this black chick and I'm, like, really swinging with it, man—and, like, what do *you* do?"

I told him, "Well, let's see. I'm married to this young lady, Molly. I have two children and I work for my father as a stockbroker."

This didn't seem to bother him at all—this conservative slant to my life. He seemed genuinely pleased to see me. "Oh, Tom," he said, "we're going to see lots of each other. Let's play some tennis."

So Bob and I got out to the tennis courts at the Kansas City Country Club, which is very, very conservative! Sedgwick's tennis outfit consisted of a tight T-shirt and very short white shorts. He came out onto the court smoking a cigarette. He was coughing all the time, and spitting up because of all the smoke and booze in his system. He made so much noise that from the next courts these people playing polite, crisp tennis looked over to see who was playing with this guy breathing green fumes! After about fifteen minutes Bob said, "Hey, Tom, excuse me for a minute," and he went over to the corner and *urinated* against the fence.

Oh, God, we saw a lot of him. I met his black fiancée a couple of times. Finally he wanted to leave her, but he had backed himself into a corner. He'd say, "Listen, chick, I want out; I don't like you any more," and she would turn on him and say, "You're doing that because you're a prejudiced son-of-a-bitch, you honkie." So he stayed around to prove that he wasn't. After he split up with her, he got involved with a beautiful blonde Jewish girl who was married to an older husband and had four children. He used to come over and tell us what a problem it was for him: "This girl loves me, but she doesn't want to leave her children." That's one of the reasons he left Kansas City. Just before he went, he came up to me and said, "Tom, I'm in terrible financial shape; I've got to leave Kansas City so I can get out of this married lady's clutches. Will you lend me two hundred dollars?"

So I did. I didn't know that he'd asked the same of my wife. He also borrowed two hundred dollars from *her* just before he left.

MOLLY MCGREEVY   I saw Bobby after he moved back to New York. His apartment was like poverty-city. It was railroad-car style and there was a hole in the floor about the size of a tennis ball through which you could see the apartment below. Bobby was very depressed. He seemed aimless, no work, quite broke. He had a catatonic tone in his voice. In Kansas City he'd play it cool like an intellectual, but he got excited if you argued with him over some point. But in New York he had only just a fleck of emotion. That was the last I saw of him.

SAUCIE SEDGWICK   I had to put Bobby in Bellevue on August 20, 1963, a few months before Minty was admitted. He called me from a booth in the street and I could tell from his speech that he was in great trouble. He ran out in the middle of admission procedures and began trotting up the sidewalk. That beautiful boy, in his loose gray hospital pajamas. Two guards went and got him.

I called my mother and begged her to help because I just didn't have the means. My husband was earning maybe ten thousand dollars a year at that point, and I was five months pregnant. "If you could see him, I know you would help." I was crying and begging, "Please come."

My father got on the phone. "Stop it. You're upsetting your mother," and he hung up on me.

I was distraught. I called Edie's former doctor, Jane O'Neil at Bloomingdale, to get her to intercede with my parents and she told me very firmly to get hold of myself, that Bellevue was as good a place as any in an emergency and that my parents had a lot to bear. She said my brother could spend the night there and be tested and then be moved to a private hospital after diagnosis. Bobby stayed in Bellevue for ten days, and then he was committed to Manhattan State Hospital, that ghastly institution on Ward's Island underneath the Triborough Bridge.

As far as I know my father never came, but eventually they did pay for him to go to the Institute for Living in Hartford. I only went up there once to see him because I was nursing my son. As I was leaving I told Bobby that I loved him and he cried. He was fat! That beautiful boy was fat from the drugs. He walked like a fat man. His hair was turning gray. He had lost that marvelous physical beauty he had when he was younger, and the feeling of power. And there was something almost . . . it's strong to say . . . eunuchlike about him . . . something soft and unmanly. They had him at work there making those appalling, clumsy ashtrays.

SYDNEY J. FREEDBERG   While Bobby was at the Institute for Living, he wrote me a long letter asking for my help in getting him accepted at the Harvard Graduate School as a Special Student in Fine Arts in the fall of 1964. I had the feeling that if we could attach him to a serious, at least paraprofessional interest, I could give Bobby the feeling that he was committed to something; it might serve not only as a concrete training but also as a very significant kind of psychological support for him. He needed a platform, an anchor. I felt so strongly about his quality as a person and an intelligence that I thought he deserved my taking the responsibility for his coming back, and I succeeded.

MARIANA WINKLE   Just before Bobby returned to Harvard for his graduate work, he went out to his younger brother Jonathan's wedding in Santa Barbara. I had known both Bobby and Jonathan in Cambridge, and the wedding was my first visit to the ranch. Jonathan was going to marry Louise Veblen, who was the daughter of the editor of the Santa Barbara newspaper. Her family lived at the far end of the Valley and were close friends of the Sedgwicks. This was the first time Bobby had been home for years.

One evening after dinner there was almost a physical confrontation between Bobby and his father over me. It started out as verbal play, but after a while I felt like a hunk of meat between two dogs. My approval was not asked for, but that was not what was important. It was father and son hitting heads. I had been talking to Mr. Sedgwick after dinner in front of the fireplace. It was a warm night, but the fire was lit. It had been a kind of engagement dinner, quite a big thing, and everyone had been drinking. It was quite dressy. In those days everyone wore short evening dresses. Mr. Sedgwick and I were having a general conversation about God knows what, but when Bobby entered the room it became very personal . . . about how desirable I was, and to whom I belonged. Mr. Sedgwick said something like, "I got here first. She's mine." Then Bobby called his father an old lecher. Mr. Sedgwick said Bobby always arrived late on the scene and caused trouble. In the middle of this it came out that Bobby had come out to try to make Jonathan's fiancée, and if he couldn't, he would settle for me.

The whole thing started out being sort of friendly. Then it got serious, with the two of them pushing at each other's shoulders. At that point, I got really uncomfortable and I said, "Quit it, this isn't funny any more." When I got up, it broke the tension and that was the end of it. But Bobby stormed out.

I remember Jonathan's fiancée felt uncomfortable with Mr. Sedgwick's attention. She was a very voluptuous sort of girl, who sometimes didn't wear a bra, which in those days was unusual. She said to me, "God, he hugs me awfully hard when I don't wear a bra."

SYDNEY J. FREEDBERG When Bobby returned to Harvard that fall, he was not the graceful person he used to be. He was conspicuously heavier. The whole person had become roughened. That deliberate roughness he'd acquired had stuck. You had the feeling that he hadn't shaved that morning, or that the clothes seemed not so much casual as shapeless. Deliberately he had exorcised a measure of his native grace and cultured background, the quality of that background. It wasn't gone, but he had tried to put it away.

He had invented a way of speech to disguise his background. It was the damnedest noise. It sounded so absolutely unright coming out of Bobby. But then after a while all this play-acting began to pall. I think he felt it was for him a kind of hollowness.

He didn't come and see me as much that year. He was not as dependent. He had matured significantly and didn't need someone to talk to, talk at, be sympathetic with. Despite his appearance, he seemed so much more self-reliant.

WILLIAM ALFRED Bobby had a lovely Mexican girl with him at Harvard—gentle, beautiful, funny. They would come over to my house for a drink two or three times a week, this very beautiful girl riding pillion on the back of his motorcycle. He was an entirely changed person, except that he did have that reckless streak. He rather fancied himself—as all people do who ride motorcycles—in a somewhat vain way. He saw himself with his hair blowing in the wind—that sort of thing. He didn't wear a helmet, though I kept nagging him about it. I'd lost two students because they didn't wear their helmets.

Bobby and the girl had a kind of closeness. The language of looks. Somebody would say something preposterous, and you could see there was a great deal of intimacy between them. She had a faint Mexican accent. She hardly ever spoke . . . a kind of silent Dolores del Rio type. She was working as a secretary, but she had that kind of poise that South American women have when they come from good families. She had long black hair—very full and beautiful—and enormous brown eyes; a quizzical smile. She was kind of madonnalike, but she could be very funny. With her it seemed that his life had opened up. But there was stuff that worried me. He had been doing some strong-arm stuff in a labor organization and told me when he returned that nobody was going to push him around. I remember one night a kid came into my house and made a bit of a pest of himself. Something snapped inside Bobby's head and he took the kid and threw him down my front stoop. He just put him up over his head and threw him down. The kid was a little snotty, but you don't throw kids down the stairs.

JOHN ANTHONY WALKER When Edie used to visit Cambridge, she'd bring Bobby to the Casablanca bar. "Meet my brother." She really loved him. I remember this huge motorcycle jacket on him . . . the size of him . . . the big boots . . . the initial impression visually at a distance was of a Hell's Angel coming through the door. Of course, Bobby wasn't that at all. He would sit in the Casa B with this sweet, gentle smile that you'd only find really on an imbecile, except he wasn't an imbecile. There was something just incredibly sweet, childishly sweet about him, like Prince Myshkin in *The Idiot*. He was a Santa Claus from the skies wearing a motorcycle jacket. A sense of warmth and love and protection. Edie was a little girl looking up at him.

15

SUKY SEDGWICK Cambridge was too suffocating for Edie. She had some opportunities in New York—that's the way I understood it. Bright lights! Hit the big town there and kick up your heels and have fun! She wanted to kick out and do some things. She wanted to be in a bigger space, and New York offered a bigger space for her. Everybody knew Edie. That was even mortifying for me. "You're Edie's sister? You're *Edie's* sister?" Edie's sister . . . Edie this, Edie that, Edie everywhere. She was famous. Cambridge was too small for her.

GORDON BALDWIN Edie was not *that* involved in her horse sculpture; she kept covering it with damp towels and there was a question of whether or not it would dry out irreparably. She felt that the Casa B and Cambridge were "not enough." New York had a real night life. It was a natural migration.

I helped her pack and drove her to New York in her Mercedes-Benz. The car was completely filled with mismatched luggage, boxes, parcels, and such miscellaneous objects as stuffed animals, straw baskets, and a large collection of unpacked hats. On one of the turnpikes Edie pulled into a Howard Johnson's under the impression that it was a long row of phone booths. Her visibility may have been bad with all that luggage, but that was typical of Edie's kind of vagueness.

I think her idea was to model in New York. Much of that summer of 1964 she went to a salon where they literally pounded her legs into shape. Her legs were not good in those days—piano legs—but by the time the course was over she ended up with those legs that were so famously beautiful.

SAUCIE SEDGWICK   Edie was living at our grandmother's apartment at Seventy-first and Park. She saw uptown people. But she felt awkward being at our grandmother's and her bizarre habits were a great strain on the household—the servants were going bananas. Edie would take off on these enormous spending sprees: her closets and drawers were crammed full. I've never seen so many clothes in my life! Never! Never! Just incredible. Edie used the place rather the way we all did . . . staying there the way you stay at a club . . . but it got out of hand.

The apartment was well decorated but not especially pleasant. It was horribly dark because our grandmother refused to live any higher in an apartment building than she could walk down. She had a fear of elevators. She wanted to be within walking distance of an Episcopalian church. So the apartment was on the fourth floor, and the electric lights had to be on twenty-four hours a day. Heavily curtained. The furniture was English and very elegant. Naval battle scenes on the dining-room walls. Pale English vistas. Our grandmother lived at the end of a long corridor. People seldom went to see her after she became senile.

SHARON PREMOLI   She kept to her bed most of the time. Edie told me she read the newspapers upside down. She asked me once what she should give her grandmother for her birthday. I suggested candy, or perhaps she could take her to the movies. A few days later I asked Edie what she had done about the birthday. She said, "I found the most wonderful thing for her. I went into Bendel's and found this beautiful gold evening purse."

I burst out laughing and asked if her grandmother had known what it was. Edie said, "She loved it!"

SAUCIE SEDGWICK   Edie had always dressed to conform to my mother's taste—little Peck and Peck costumes with navy blue sweaters—but in New York one day I suddenly saw her in this little red fox fur waistcoat with a matching hat and huge peacock-feather earrings,

Edie and her limousine

some kind of outlandish bag, black stockings, and high-heeled boots, none of which was in fashion then at all. I was very shocked. I said to her, "Is that the way you want to go around?" She said, "I think it's fun."

JOHN ANTHONY WALKER   Because she had this whole thing about modeling, she tried out for Miss Teenager in one of those teenage magazines. They accepted her with great happiness. Then they found out she was no longer a teenager. It was typical of the helter-skelter life she was leading when she first came to New York that summer.

I remember asking her up for the weekend to Fishers Island. What happened was typical, too. First she telephoned from New London to say that she'd missed the ferry boat to the island. New London's a strange town to be caught in if you've missed the ferry. A railroad town; a harbor stop. In the old days what I would have done was spend the night at the Mohican Hotel and catch the ferry the next day. The Mohican was big and old and very nice, but it was not the sort of hotel Edie would be caught spending a night in. So I told her, "Rest easy. Go to the airport at Groton and they'll fly you across. We'll pick you up; it's a ten-minute flight."

So I went down to the little Fishers Island airstrip to meet her. It had been sort of a drizzling day and the fog began to roll in. The fog-horn you hear on Fishers Island is the same one that Eugene O'Neill heard when he was writing *Long Day's Journey into Night* in New London. O'Neill's foghorn was blowing wildly; you couldn't see the lighthouse. The man in the airstrip office said, "They'll never take off from New London." We were totally shrouded. Just as he said that, there was this purr of the motor up in the air. So the guy said, "Well, he'll never land; he'll never find us." But suddenly we heard the sound of the airplane coming in to land, the increasing roar as it came down closer. Then the yellow undercarriage appeared out of the fog, not more than five or ten feet above the runway. We all went, "Wow!" I could have run out and caught the *wheels* as they went by. Then the undercarriage disappeared up into the fogbank and the sound of the airplane disappeared. I could sense Edie trying to get down at all costs until the pilot told her, "Lady, I don't care who you are, I'm *not* going to land here!"

I went back to the house and wondered what to do. How was I to find Edie in New London? How could I get through to her? All this turmoil . . . with Edie I always felt a considerable responsibility. I think I even tried to call the local lobsterman to see if he could go over to the mainland and pick her up. In the middle of all this there was a phone call—a ship-to-shore relay. It occurred to me that my only contact with Edie that whole day had been sound: the purr of the airplane, and now this disembodied voice from the high seas. Edie said, "The captain says in another half hour we'll be getting in." I could hear the clink of glasses in the background and somebody saying, "West Harbor, West Harbor."

So we went down to the West Harbor dock and in she came, sailing happily out of the fog, on Jock Whitney's yacht. Edie had arranged it somehow. It was a fine entrance. She was totally the center of attraction. I remember exactly how the yacht arrived out of the fog—first of all the bow and all these men in white running up and down with ropes, and then the bridge with the captain, the radar going dot, dot, dot, dot, and the lighted portholes, and then the brass, polished teak, highly formal living room pulled in with Edie in the middle of it surrounded by people in director's chairs.

So we got her on the island. That night we went to the Buckner coming-out party. Mrs. Buckner is the daughter of Thomas Watson, the founder of IBM, the man who said, THINK. I had grown up with the sons, Walker and Thomas. The young children of these families, the scions, raced in these little boats about eight, ten feet long. It was good high-key times. But the fathers on the docks took it very seriously. It *was* IBM versus the National Gallery, or whatever. The nannies came down to watch the races. It really was important to these people watching us in our first competitive acts, and it was always strange coming in from these wet, flappy races, which were rather fun, into this tension. For instance, Walker Buckner once lost a race because he hadn't bailed out his boat. He was made to walk around their place carrying two metal galvanized buckets filled with water so he'd become more aware of how heavy water was—quite a heavy trip to lay on a little kid! After a few years of bailing out the boat, he said, "Fuck it all," and went off to play jazz in California.

Well, that night the Buckners had a dance for their two daughters at Barley Field Cove—Mary Gentry and Elizabeth. It was informally understood that we could go. It wasn't something I had intended to do, but Edie loved parties. She *adored* parties.

I remember they had trucked in a lighted fountain. Perhaps it came from Hammacher Schlemmer. They must have brought it over on the ferry. There was a huge tent, but it was fancier really . . . perhaps a pavilion. You could see out of it to the lawn which rolled down to the water. It was an impeccable lawn. A lot of my life has been involved with the lawns of Fishers Island. This one was a turf lawn, truckloads and truckloads of sod brought over from New London and put down from the house to the ocean. It was very well kept up. It rolled down to the ocean, there was a bit of hard scrabble, then a drop and the beach below it. It was a very comfortable party. Many of the young had been flown in—the graduating class of Groton or whatever. There was a band. Lester Lanin. People dancing. A young man on Fishers Island then wore a white jacket, a ruffly-tuffly shirt, and a somber black tie. Possibly, if you were making a statement of fashion, you might wear plaid trousers neatly pressed.

I believe Edie was wearing leotards; whatever, it must have been a little exotic, because I remember being rather proud to be sitting at that table with her under the marquee; she had become the focus of a certain amount of attention.

The moon rose out of the ocean, spiraling up in the dark. It was the final touch—a nice moon rippling the ocean and turning everything silver. The combination of all this—champagne, the music, an idyllic setting with the ocean below—enchanted the party. Edie was very sensitive to enchantments. Also she was exuberant that weekend; she had so much energy and things were going well. She had been dancing inside earlier that evening, getting more and more extravagant, especially in the foxtrot, and now, outside the marquee on that moonlit lawn, she broke away from the form completely and was doing these totally free dance movements. We looked out from under the marquee and there she was on this deserted lawn—a brilliant green during the day and which had taken on its own tonalities of color under the moon —and she was cartwheeling across it . . . *cartwheeling.* She was an exquisite dancer and dancing purely for herself, a part of the tenuous enchantment of the evening. I remember the music dying down as the focus of attention shifted to her out there, and I suppose that since she couldn't see into the light, she was totally unaware of us.

The next day we were having a Fishers Island picnic at Isabella Beach—one of those picnics where the consommé and vodka come in thermoses and you toast the idyllic summer days with plastic cups. Edie had disappeared. It was a bit spooky. Somebody said, "We saw her go swimming." But she was nowhere in sight on this beach. Then somebody else said, "Is that her? Way, way out?"

Fishers Island people are marginal swimmers, staying between the break of the surf and the paddling of the small children. Once in a while somebody will briskly swim ten strokes out and ten strokes in. But Edie was way out . . . a little dark head . . . such a distance that she was beyond where I could swim if she were in trouble. Was she in trouble? She seemed to be going under and then sur- facing again. I could see the shine of her legs as she dove. It was like her dancing the night before. She was playing . . . totally natural and involved in the element of water; she was like a porpoise. First there was fear for Edie: "She's in trouble." Then it was: "Why, she's playing! Edie's having fun." She seemed only to exist freely in at- mospheres that were removed or enchanted . . . in a particular space that she liked. Most people are happy swimming by the shore; she was happy out there.

JOEL SCHUMACHER   The first time I ever saw her was at a New York party. She was with about six boys and she was in the middle of the floor dancing. The boys were a little Oscar Wilde bunch with big, floppy neckties and their handkerchiefs always flipped out a lot . . . a fey group of guys who were trying to get into society and were riding along with her because she was the new girl in town, and that was very evident. That was the time of new girls in town in New York; every once in a while somebody would arrive and make quite a stir. Edie was certainly one of them, but she went a different way than anyone else ever had. Other girls went through the usual bunch of guys at the club and would maybe marry one of them, or go out and marry somebody else. But Edie went through that immediately. She was in strange places faster than anybody else.

Up until the early Sixties social life in New York was extremely predictable. There was a form to the whole thing: if someone had a black tie dinner, everyone there was in black tie. If people were invited to a brunch they were attired in a certain way. Everyone held on to the values of the Fifties, those standards that had been created by life in and around El Morocco, the Stork Club, by polo players and debutantes —patterns that were followed by the *nouveaux riches*, the Jews, or whatever. No one told the truth. People lied. Society was a group of liars. People pretended that they weren't unfaithful. They pretended that they weren't homosexual. They pretended that they weren't horrible. If you wanted to social climb or socialize in New York City, you had to follow these rules.

Edie came in at the destruction of all those rules. The Robert Sculls were just about to move out of their suburban life in Great Neck and buy the kind of apartment and things to put in it that people from Great Neck had never thought of before. Showing up late to someone's dinner, or never showing up at all, became a way of life. People were going to start shooting up in the bathroom. Freaks were going to become sought after. Overnight you could become famous for having big hair or short skirts or a neon bra. There was such a desperate hunger. Suddenly all these women in little black dresses and men in pinstripe suits from Meledandri and Sills and Saville Row would be rushing down to Trude Heller's on the corner of Ninth Street and Sixth right across from the Women's House of Detention. There they would see Monte Rock. Or they would rush down to the Dom in St. Mark's Place where only the black people used to dance.

The wild stuff began coming out of the woodwork. People showing off. "Look at me! I've got something to say! I am something!" And the more freakish you could be about it, so much the better. Look at Edie. Or Tiger Morse, who was a society girl from a good family wearing very straight clothes, and all of a sudden the next day she was a speed freak with her hair wired, wearing electric dresses and green glasses. And then dead. These insane people wallowed in self-destruction . . . almost as if they were trying to punish their parents and the world of rigid systems that had been so painful to them in their formative years. Edie came into the world of people getting ready to come out and make that kind of statement.

DANNY FIELDS Edie moved from her grandmother's late that fall of 1964 to an apartment in the East Sixties between Fifth and Madison. Her mother came to town and took Edie shopping to furnish the apartment. Suddenly this empty room was full of the sort of ornaments prosperous people have who've been living in the same place for years and years . . . solid crystal paperweights, great fur scatter rugs, fabulous embroidered pillows, one of those enormous leather rhinoceros from where? . . . Abercrombie and Fitch, wasn't it? Elaborate cigarette lighters, really heavy and solid. Most of them never worked; Edie never bothered to fill them. She didn't have affection for any of these things: a lot of them she didn't even understand. None of this was collected with any love or preference, but just provided with a snap of the fingers. She was always sending to Reuben's restaurant . . . blinis and caviar, always caviar. It was almost a game . . . everything had to be the ultimate. I guess she was extremely spoiled, because she was given whatever she wanted . . . a leopard-skin coat that must have come from her parents unless it was from an unknown admirer. A real leopard-skin coat! About the only thing that was her own was a huge horse above her bed that she'd drawn on the wall with pencil.

It was a tiny apartment. Sometimes the garbage was pretty messy in the kitchenette. She would let it go pretty far before she took emergency measures . . . someone would volunteer to reach into the sink and unclog it.

There was a lot of acid around then . . . LSD . . . the first days of it, and most of those people down from Cambridge knew Timothy Leary and Richard Alpert. In the refrigerator they used to keep little brown vials of liquid to drop on a sugar cube. Edie would drive her Mercedes on acid! I thought that was the most daredevil thing she'd ever been into . . . I mean, she'd go up on curbs sometimes, and she'd never pay much attention to traffic lights. It was like everything else: her own rules applied.

CHUCK WEIN   We liked bizarre people because we didn't really take ourselves that seriously, and we were amused about how seriously everybody else seemed to take themselves. That was our approach at that point.

We rode around in that gray Mercedes, staying up all night after the discotheques closed at four. Sometimes I'd drive, but Edie loved to drive herself . . . it was like riding a horse. She told me all about her family. She seemed to love her mother . . . it was almost "the poor dear . . . the poor thing is going to be so worried."

TOM GOODWIN   Edie got into spending her inheritance. It was a time when the first discotheques were opening—like Ondine—and people were beginning to live it up in places like that. We often went stoned drunk to a place called L'Avventura to have these gigantic dinners. Edie loved salmon. And extra lemons for her Bloody Marys. All that extra this and that. She ate vast quantities of shrimp. Shrimp and salad, stuff you would think was healthy. But she had four of whatever it was.

I quit my job at the Right Bank restaurant to be her chauffeur. She paid me one hundred dollars a week. We had first met in Cambridge when she was studying sculpture and had gotten to be friends in a curious non-lover way. It was a bit of a strange arrangement to be her chauffeur, but it seemed okay to me. Then I went *pow* into a taxi in front of the Seagram building and cracked up her Mercedes. I felt so bad, because she loved that car. But it didn't faze her in the least. She didn't get angry. We began traveling in limousines.

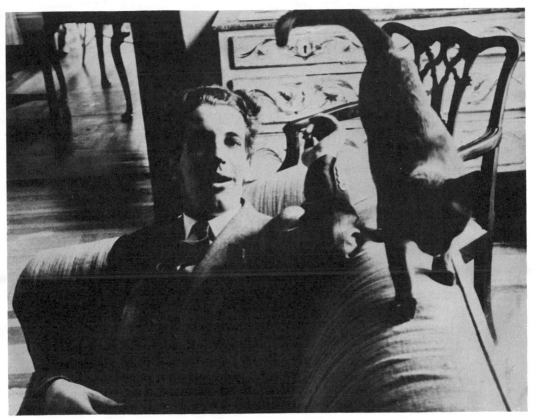

John Anthony Walker

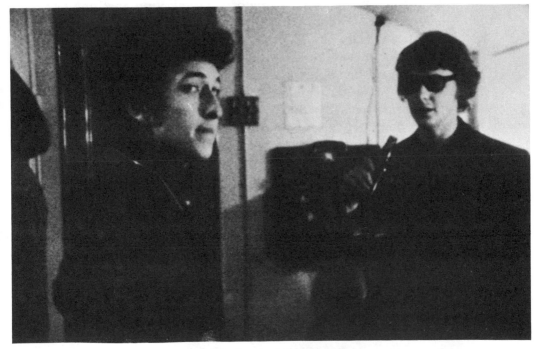

Bob Dylan and Bob Neuwirth

BOB NEUWIRTH   Bob Dylan and I occasionally ventured out into the poppy nightlife world. I think somebody who had met Edie said, "You have to meet this terrific girl." Dylan called her, and she chartered a limousine and came to see us. We spent an hour or two, all laughing and giggling, having a terrific time. I think we met in the bar upstairs at the Kettle of Fish on MacDougal Street, which was one of the great places of the Sixties. It was just before the Christmas holidays; it was snowing, and I remember we went to look at the display on Houston Street in front of the Catholic church. I don't remember how the evening ended. I'm sure it ended logically, or maybe it didn't. Who knows? Edie was fantastic. She was always fantastic. She believed that to sit around was to rot, an extension of the Sixties pop culture from a Bob Dylan song "He not busy being born is busy dying."

Edie went through limousine companies the way people go through cigarettes. She never paid her bills, so the limousine people would shut off her credit, and she'd shift to another company. The drivers loved her madly, because she'd dole out these twenty-five- and thirty-five-dollar tips. This one shiny black Cadillac limousine with a terrified driver would wait maybe three or four hours for Edie to come out of some sleazy artist's loft on the Bowery down beneath a bridge by the Fulton Fish Market with nothing around but trucks and derelict cars.

She had the ability to relate on all levels . . . with chauffeurs or ranch hands . . . understanding the human condition, yet at the same time because of that upbringing of hers, rejecting anything less than *numero uno*. She would order fish and invariably ask the waiter, "Is this fish fresh?" Of course, in New York there's hardly any fresh fish, but whether it was a sleazy little restaurant downtown or Le Pavillon, she would invariably ask that question, "Is this fish fresh?" And invariably the waiter would say, "Of course it is, Mademoiselle." When the fish arrived from the kitchen, Edie would test it with her fork and say, "I'm sorry, this fish is not fresh. Please take it back." But it was so crazy because she'd do this in these pop places where the junior-grade discotheque society went to eat . . . where the fish was obviously fish cakes. She would still send them back. She could do this sort of thing without really pushing it. It's something you learn very early to be able to get away with—a real patrician royalty trip. She could do it without offending. People would knock themselves out to do what she'd asked. Being really ungracious, but she could be graceful about it. Waiters would see to it about the fish. Chauffeurs would stay up with her all night rather than taking shifts.

And yet she was very adept at appearing absolutely helpless, unable to fasten bracelets, earrings; unable to zip skirts, get boots off, whatever. But it turned out she was an exceptional swimmer . . . terrific athlete, you know, for a girl of such a slight build. Totally strong. If there was anybody around with a bottle of pickles or raspberry jam to be opened, she could do it. But she could certainly be helpless, too.

DANNY FIELDS   When the bills would mount up, she'd stuff them all in a big envelope and she'd take a dozen people to the Ginger Man for drinks. The bills would get spread out—the Acme bills in one pile, the Weinbaum's bills here. Thousands of dollars' worth of cosmetics! A lot of giggling: "Oh, dear, how did that happen? I don't remember that drugstore. Oh, let me see, that's the nice Mister So-and-so. He'll let me come back. Oh, I *had* to have all the new colors of the Rubinstein line." By the time the dessert came, the bills were all in disarray and she'd shove them back into her black bag.

It was the gravy train. She didn't know half the people she took to those dinners of hers. Fifteen to twenty people. Friends. Friends of friends. Edie would sit closest to the ones she wished to consult or console, giggle or get drunk with that night. I felt we were taking advantage of her. But people would say, "Don't worry. You don't know how rich she is. Her grandfather built a railroad."

I'd say, "But even if they're rich, don't her parents get hysterical?"

"Oh, her parents are so nutty," they'd say, "they won't even notice. They'll just pay and pay."

So after a while I figured, "Why not?" I didn't feel guilty or as if I was sponging. I felt like we were just redistributing the wealth.

TOM GOODWIN   All the time the money was flowing out. Edie went through eighty thousand dollars in six months—the delicatessen, L'Avventura, the Bermuda Limousine Service. There were various mysterious men who handled her money. I remember going downtown with her one day in the limousine. She was told she didn't have any more money. She refused to let that be a possibility. Her mother and father had all this money, and she should have it, too. She came out angry, indignant.

She would take her friends to her grandmother's apartment. Amazing place. Her grandmother was a vegetable. Edie would make fun of it all and serve us drinks. Edie aced: the young princess needs her food and drinks. And yet at the same time she had a tremendous compassion for crazy people; she talked about them, those "who had seen the big sadness." I remember a long conversation we had about the big sadness . . . the whole thing, you see, which she really saw larger than her own doom. It wasn't feeling sorry for herself, this big sadness, but for suffering outside of herself. And yet she was amoral, a facile liar. She would steal, rob, rip off; she would get herself in awkward situations and lay something on somebody. She could push everybody to the farthest extent of indulgence. Methodically. She could bitch and moan and be prissy and infantile, demanding this and that . . . extra lemons! I remember squeezing endless lemons. She was scared to go to sleep. It was very hard for her to. I saw her desperate and unhappy like a caged animal. Yet she always had such energy . . . I mean, she'd run people ragged. "Let's go. Let's get into the limo!" She never wanted to cool out. She was always, like, pushing everything to the limit.

16

SAUCIE SEDGWICK My father heard about all those shenanigans. He insisted that Edie come out to California for that Christmas of 1964 with the family. But Bobby, who was doing graduate work at Harvard, was not allowed to come home. What Bobby wanted was to be with Edie. He wanted to come down from Cambridge on his big motorcycle and they'd spend Christmas together, just the two of them, and she would show him New York. Edie and Bobby were very much alike. He kept speaking to me about having fallen in love with her. I think Bobby recognized himself in Edie, as if she were living out something for him. Bobby identified with her because she was young and beautiful, succeeding at that time against all odds, and he admired her, too, because she'd apparently found the weapon which absolutely neutralized the magic or power of our parents. What he especially loved about Edie was her outlandishness and her absolute abandon. He respected her for the mobility that she had socially. I don't mean socially, capital S, or *Social Register*. I mean literally that she could move anywhere . . . like a creature moving in and out of those funny-shaped stones in a goldfish bowl.

Bobby told me the reason my parents gave for not wanting him to come home [for Christmas] was that he upset Jonathan. The message was: "Don't disturb the other children. You're a bad influence." Edie had to go. So they all deserted Bobby. He must have felt that. He had

Bobby, July, 1964

really stacked it against himself: he had spent all his money and put himself in every way in an untenable position.

SYDNEY J. FREEDBERG The problem was that he was still self-destructive. There was an element of the suicidal in the way he used vehicles. He had smashed up his sports car earlier. I saw his motor-cycle, like a Harley-Davidson monster, one of the big ones. I encoun-tered him as I was going out the gates onto Massachusetts Avenue opposite the Porcellian Club. There was Bobby and this iron horse. He showed it to me with enormous pride; I expressed my displeasure and concern. I told him it was going to kill him. He shrugged it off. I told him I thought it was extremely dangerous and not the right thing for him to have in his hands.

PETER SOURIAN I was just going out in New York to a New Year's Eve party. It was about seven-thirty. The doorbell rang and Bob came upstairs. He said, "Hi, how about a drink?" I said, "I'm going out." I didn't realize he was in difficulty. He seemed very breezy and relaxed. I didn't pick it up—the cue. I mean, on New Year's Eve when you appear like that . . . I mean, you ought to be able to translate. I wish he had screamed, "Goddammit, what are you going to a party for? You sit here with me." But he didn't. He wasn't the type of guy who was going to tell you. We went down the street together and that's the last time I saw him. It was that night, New Year's Eve, that he crashed.

JONATHAN SEDGWICK Put-your-head-in-the-mouth-of-the-lion trip —he would try it. One of those times the mouth is going to close, and that's what happened. He was riding the lights up Eighth Avenue, just catching them as they turned, and he went into the side of a bus with-out his helmet.

SUKY SEDGWICK What an imp Bobby was. He had been riding his stupid motorcycle. I told him to be careful because I knew Bobby was a violent little character, always thrashing around. He said, "I've got too many mothers."

I prayed he'd die if he couldn't recover completely from that acci-dent. Because I knew Bobby could not be a vegetable. He was in-capable of that, and that would have taken away his Bobbyness. And that couldn't be. So I prayed both ways. That's a pretty awful prayer.

SAUCIE SEDGWICK   Bobby never regained consciousness. My sister Kate went every day to the hospital. I went once, but I couldn't bear it—his head was covered in bandages to the bridge of his nose, and he was hooked up to all kinds of machines. He had one big bare arm out of the covers, and when I took his hand, a stream of tears ran down from under the bandages. The doctor told Kate it was just that his nose was irritated by the tubes.

He died on January 12, 1965—he was thirty-one years old. I heard that the obituary in the *Santa Barbara News-Press* reported that my father said there would be a service for Bobby in the East, but there was no funeral. My parents never came East. My husband and I collected Bobby's things from the hospital—his sheepskin coat, all torn and bloody—and we went with the funeral director to the city morgue to identify him. We stood in a side room looking at a dark wall. Suddenly a light flashed on—just for a second—and there was Bobby lying on this shelf behind a window, like a gisant—a tomb figure—so very long and perfect. I remember his color seemed extraordinarily vivid. I gasped, and the light went off.

Then he was cremated and my father asked me to have Bobby's ashes sent to him, care of General Delivery, Santa Barbara, so that the local postmaster in the Valley wouldn't have to handle them. I don't know where my brothers are really buried. I don't think they're buried anywhere.

JONATHAN SEDGWICK   My father told me he took Bobby's and Minty's ashes up to what's called Center Ridge, which is a high-peaked ridge that goes through the center of Rancho Laguna. He rode up there alone with a little square box. He scattered the ashes on both sides of the ridge . . . I'm sure the wind took them in all directions. It was the backbone of the ranch, that ridge, incredibly steep in places, and we used to gallop the horses down the trails and up the other side. My father must have remembered how much fun we all had on that roller-coaster ridge. He went up there on a tall, regal horse named Tiger. He would have been wearing the old classic Spanish regalia—the visalia saddle, the Tapaderos stirrups, and the fancy bridle with the decorative tassels hanging down. He must have been a formidable sight. Leather leggings. His wide bucking belt. A straw-textured Stetson that he always kept centered very carefully on his head, without the slightest tilt: he always had to be centered.

One day, not long before my father died, we were coming back along that same ridge and that's when he told me what he had done.

17

G. J. BARKER-BENFIELD   Almost at precisely the same time Bobby ran into the bus on New Year's Eve, Edie was in a bad accident out in California. Edie was driving. There was a flashing red light and she didn't stop. A big saloon car drove right into us. The car went into a lamp stand on the next street. My head went through the windshield. The car was totaled. They had it on TV—"How did two people step out of this car alive?" I was cut around the right eye and had to have twenty-two stitches. Edie, it turned out, had broken a knee. But she got out and began removing several hundred dollars' worth of stuff from the trunk of that car which she had bought that afternoon in Santa Barbara, throwing it out on the sidewalk just in case the car blew up.

Edie was very scared that her father was going to use this accident as an excuse to put her back in the loony bin. We talked things over in the hospital room. She decided that we'd leave undetected. Her mother was in cahoots with her. She came and picked us up in a station wagon. Edie's leg was in plaster. Mrs. Sedgwick drove us to the ranch, and then we took our stuff and I drove Edie directly to the Los Angeles airport, where we had a drink, and then she boarded the next plane for New York. I never saw her again.

GILLIAN WALKER   After Bobby died, Edie told me, "I knew he was going to die . . . he killed himself." It was like a part of her, she told me, was standing by and watching the curse play itself out in the family. Her response to it was to suppress the whole matter by going back to the frantic way of life she was beginning to find for herself in New York.

GEOFFREY GATES   Early in January there was a party at Ondine— a twist party—and through the morass of people I saw this rather pretty girl doing the most violent, deliberate kind of twist wearing a hip cast from toe to the hip. I recognized Edie. We lived in the same townhouse on Sixty-third Street. I couldn't believe it. I went over to her table and asked, "What happened? Are you okay?" She said she'd crushed her knee in a car accident.

The smile was wild . . . manic. She kept getting up and dancing, one leg sheer white with only a couple of signatures on it just rooted to one spot on the floor, and the rest of her body spinning around the cast as if she were an acrobat.

She still had a girl's finishing-school appearance, but her face and actions showed that something else was coming up very fast.

BOB NEUWIRTH   The doctors said she'd probably walk again, but with a limp. The fact that she had on a cast didn't stop her. I remember her at Harlow's, an uptown discotheque where the Young Rascals were playing in their Little Lord Fauntleroy suits. She had a sculptor come over and chisel off the cast. Then she sent a few of her escorts to the cloakroom for some coat hangers and tied them to her leg with neckties to make herself a splint. She proceeded to dance for the rest of the night. Her doctor was suggesting she'd be a permanent cripple and she was having none of it.

SANDY KIRKLAND   Edie was very frail and vulnerable. She was just psychologically scattered: she never finished a sentence, she never looked you in the face, she was never there. She wasn't yet getting a lot of attention, so she was just kind of floating around. Very distracted. The only things she talked about were her father and her family and the Santa Barbara scene that she had just left. She had a deep worship of her father, and yet at the same time hating and resenting him because he had . . . well, she felt that he had fucked her around. I don't know whether that was literal or not. If she got drunk, she would talk about him in a very physical way. Perhaps she felt violated by him because she worshiped him so much . . . almost a metaphor for something he was doing to her psychologically.

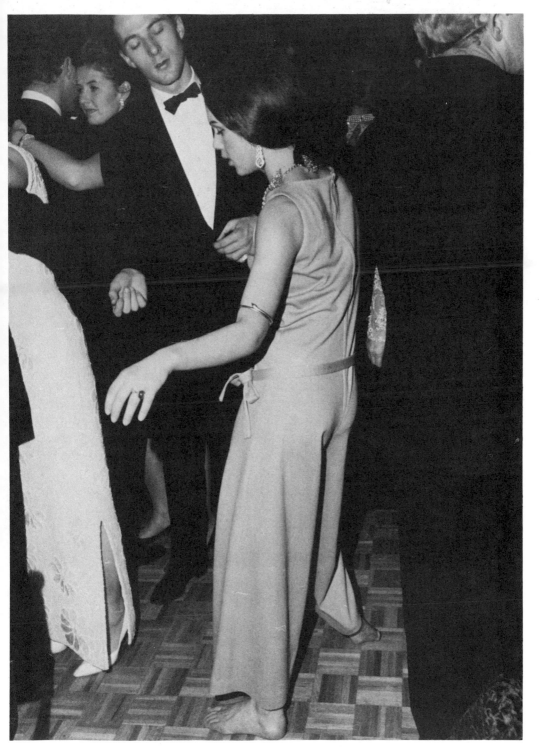

Edie at a society dance, 1964

I used to hang around her apartment with her. Agonizing . . .
even to me then. Chaos! Piles of clothes on every piece of furniture.
Easels. Canvases—she was painting at the time. There was a portfolio of very small, scrunched-up rodent drawings with funny little
monster men. A top hat on one of them. Bleak little pictures. Art was
her ostensible thing, her reason for being in New York, according to
what she had told her parents.

Sometimes I went over there with Chuck Wein, her Cambridge
friend. He would be plotting out the next move of their great strategy—
whom he was going to introduce to Edie that night, what they could
do for her. She would try on twenty-five different outfits, but every
gesture was very slow. Do you remember how she moved? Like a
Japanese Noh dancer—very dreamlike and slow. Lighting twenty
cigarettes and putting them down.

Chuck had a real promoter's vision about her, and she'd act kind of
coy about it. He knew that she had this quality, but that she was totally
disorganized and wouldn't be able to pull it off by herself . . . so he
took over her life.

CHUCK WEIN   She couldn't really cope with the day-to-day reality,
and she always needed to have friends who understood that. Edie provided the glamour, you see, and the glitter . . . when she walked into
some place, the whole room turned. And if they didn't, she'd do something in the next twenty seconds that would make them. She'd giggle,
or she'd dance and spin around.

She was voracious for people. Edie was one of the great devourers
of all time. But her method of devouring was to entice. If you had a
room full of twenty people and Edie came in, there was an energy
uplift. It got everybody off their boring number. Here was this glamorous freak. People were willing to let Edie be the star. They just wanted
to be around her because the glamour was there and it was like a
beautiful-child vibration. If Fuzzy was going to play the game of
"Ranch King," she could play the game of "The King's Daughter." She
played princess everywhere she went.

There was one guy who was madly in love with Edie. Son of the
chairman of the board of some major corporation. One night he was
supposed to be coming to pick her up at the Sixty-third Street apartment. She and I got into this long rap, and he arrived at the door
before I could get out. Edie said, "Oh, he's so jealous and upset. He's
got this whole fantasy about wanting to marry me" . . . he'd taken
her out twice. So I hid under the bed the whole time he was there,

lying under this brass bed with half of Edie's wardrobe and all those boxes from Bendel's. He went through this whole tear-jerking declaration of love . . . high comedy! He was sitting on her big leather rhinoceros; she was on the bed. Poor man! He poured out his entire existence onto her. She knew that he was reaching out and that he was as desperate as she was. He finally left. I came out from under the bed. Edie laughed; she loved it.

KEVIN McCARTHY   She was always going out and glittering in the night somewhere, but the fact that you couldn't rely on her drove you nuts. If she said she was going to see you, she might or might not be there. You weren't equals. If you were a prosaic person, you'd take her to dinner, go to the theater, read poetry aloud together, or even roll around and wrestle a little together, but at the same time there was this feeling that she was from another world. It was intense and sweet and troubled. Maybe she was from the underworld. She reminded me of Montgomery Clift. He once said to me: "I would like to go down into the depths of the underworld, the depths of darkest experience, and come back and tell about it."

CHUCK WEIN   Edie could keep everybody busy getting her things . . . eight guys calling her up from eight different social strata. She'd be off to a jet-set party here and an underground party there, and also rapping to the guy from the deli. And everybody on each level believed that her life on that level was her real trip. She kept everybody going!

Edie meets Andy Warhol

18

CHUCK WEIN It was at Lester Persky's place that Edie met Andy Warhol. It was early 1965. She was doing her dance there—a sort of balletlike rock 'n' roll. We'd had an idea of opening up an underwater discotheque where Edie'd dance her ballet to Bach played at rock 'n' roll tempo. So Andy invited us down to the Factory the next day and he said, "Why don't we do some things together?" Andy spotted her energy. Everybody else was tired and going through the trip.

GORE VIDAL Lester Persky was sometimes known as the Wax Queen. Among his advertising accounts in the Fifties was Six Months Floor Wax. He had a penthouse on East Fifty-ninth Street, and a good income, and a collection of famous writers, like Tennessee Williams and Bill Inge and me, and who else? Jack Knowles later, Capote later. Lester would have parties in his penthouse, to which were invited attractive ephebes . . . everybody looked like John Travolta in *Grease* —but then this was the Fifties. These evenings were true symposiums, in Plato's sense. Lester was, essentially, an educator. "What? You've *never* heard of Tennessee Williams? He's the most famous writer in America." I have many vivid memories of those waxy evenings.

LESTER PERSKY Andy and I became good friends in the early Sixties. He was interested in what I was doing . . . being very successful with these hard-sell TV commercials—Roto-Broil and Glamorene and Charles Antell. Andy once made a film which he called *Lester Persky: A Soap Opera* because he'd been infatuated with my hard-sell commercials. I was sort of an idol, I guess. I was the secret custodian of that period . . . the catalyst.

I'm a big party-giver. In those days I would invite six, and Andy would account for twenty uninvited. We always had candlelight. I never had *any* electricity in the dining room. We ate what Saga, my Japanese houseman who's now dead, would prepare—very rarely Japanese dishes, which weren't fashionable then. He usually did kosher food, which I detest.

Andy would arrive with his crowd. He was busy having superstars, of course. He had Baby Jane Holzer, but she was sort of running out of speed. I told him: "You've got to have a new superstar. You've got to meet this girl Edie Sedgwick. She will be your new superstar."

I arranged to have Edie at the party. She had a friend in tow, Chuck Wein, and they wanted to be involved in film and in theater. She had a certain quiet dignity and a beauty that was quite extraordinary. Although she was always surrounded by these somewhat *manqué* people, she herself always had a fantastic poise. And it was at my house, at this marble table, that I brought the two—Andy and Edie— together. Andy, as I recall, sucked in his breath and did the usual popeye thing and said, "Oh, she's so bee-you-ti-ful," making every single letter sound like a whole syllable, as he does. He was *very* impressed.

RONALD TAVEL   You went up in that tiny elevator about which there were so many stories because people who hated each other would get stuck in it for hours. Once I was in there with Tennessee Williams. I sat down and spoke to him, and he didn't understand a word I said. He kept looking at me and saying, "Yes," which is what he always says to me: "Yes, yes, yes." It's an automatic response.

At that party I conducted myself in a semi-facetious way, which is what I always do, especially with a few drinks. I'd say, "We're here on business. I'm scouting for stars. You interested? I'll write the script. We'll call you up and make a movie." I said that all the time to people. I said that to Montgomery Clift when I met him: "I've been watching your work since 1947, and I think you're ready to make a film with us." He said, "Thank you."

I did the same with Edie. I told her she was Nioka the Jungle Girl, and I pictured her in that kind of setting. She had a beehive hairdo,

Andy at the Factory. Photograph of Tennessee Williams and Lester Persky in background

dark hair, and a leopard suit. She probably wondered what I was talking about. I was very surprised when I saw her show up a few weeks later at the Factory to look for Andy Warhol. I think she was slumming when she first came in—just checking out the scene with a small entourage, to see what was going on.

SANDY KIRKLAND When Edie met Warhol, it was this immediate thing. They were going to make movies. Andy started escorting her, and drew her into the fold really fast. She became this extraordinary camera object, which was incredible for me to see because I had known her only as this waif. She suddenly became a person who went to the Factory, and any time the camera was turned on, she would gravitate toward it like Gloria Swanson at the end of *Sunset Boulevard*. She had this real romance with it. She could be a totally bedraggled, wiped-out wreck, and then the camera would go on and she would just be this magical star. It was crazy, but it was very powerful.

RENÉ RICARD So Edie became the Factory's superstar. Edie and Andy! You should have seen them. But you *did* see them! Both wearing the same sort of thing—boat-neck, striped T-shirts. Andy wore black corduroy jeans, banana-shaped high-heeled boots—terrible boots. I hated them. He never could stand up in them. He never had a good wig in those days, the poor thing. Edie was pasted up to look just like him—but looking so good! The T-shirt. The black stockings. Long earrings. Just the most devastating, ravishing beauty.

Edie brought Andy out. She turned him on to the real world. He'd been in the demi-monde. He was an *arriviste*. And Edie legitimized him, didn't she? He never went to those parties before she took him. He'd be the first to admit it.

ISABEL EBERSTADT He was madly flattered. Although his words communicated so little, one could tell how excited he was. There was this rich, beautiful girl, who seemed to be dressing and looking just like him, and he didn't know what to make of it: what did it all mean? Edie and her entourage seemed to be taking him everywhere in a car. Should he do it? He had a very dependent way of approaching one and saying, "Oh, you won't stop calling? You won't stop coming around, will you?" That was very characteristic of Andy at that time of his life: asking you for advice about where he should go and whom he should see. I think he always knew what he wanted to do. He just wanted to put it in your mouth.

Andy is a terrific snob. He was a fashion creature and he absorbed a lot of the snobbish values of the fashion world. They were still part of him when he met Edie. Some of Edie's glamour to him was certainly enhanced by the fact that she came from a marvelous family. That was amazingly important to him.

TRUMAN CAPOTE   I think Edie was something Andy would like to have been; he was transposing himself into her *à la* Pygmalion. Have you ever noticed a certain type of man who always wants to go along with his wife to pick out her clothes? I've always thought that's because he wants to wear them himself. Andy Warhol would like to have been Edie Sedgwick. He would like to have been a charming, well-born debutante from Boston. He would like to have been anybody except Andy Warhol.

19

DUANE MICHALS   I was brought up in McKeesport, Pennsylvania, where Andy says he comes from, a steel town at the confluence of the Monongahela and the Youghiogheny. Because our rivers were orange I thought all rivers were orange. At night the steelmills lit up the sky; it was always this incredible kind of inferno. The mills made a lot of noise; you could hear the cranes dropping enormous things and booming all the time. There was a certain drama about it, kind of scary, too. When I was a kid, I thought it was terrific . . . just the best place to live. Of course, my family lived in a community that was completely homogenized—Germans across the street, Poles up the block, and somebody we knew lived next to an Italian family, and somebody else next to the Hungarians. It was a wonderful mix—in no sense a ghetto. Down where the rivers meet, there was a section which was really much more of a ghetto. I have read that Andy's family lived down there.

GERARD MALANGA   Andy would always lie to people in his interviews. He'd always say he was out of McKeesport or Pittsburgh. It was never the same place in different interviews. He'd also lie about his age. This outraged me actually, because I was a fiend for accuracy. Then I realized it can be a very Duchamp type of situation, to create a myth for oneself, an identity.

ISABEL EBERSTADT   Andy told me that he was sick a lot as a child, that he had three nervous breakdowns before he was eleven. "Always in the summer, I don't know why," he said to me. He couldn't remember much about his early schooling. His mother was protective and wouldn't let him go out much so he used to lie in bed and play with dolls and dream about having a glass of fresh orange juice in the morning and a bathroom of his own. He started drawing, copying the Maybelline ads of Hedy Lamarr.

CHUCK WEIN   He said he had St. Vitus dance as a child and he lost his hair and couldn't hold his hand steady; he couldn't write on the blackboard. The other kids would beat him up, which made him terrified of socializing. He retreated into movie magazines—the glossy photos and images rather than the printed word.

PHILIP PEARLSTEIN   When I first met Andy at Carnegie Tech in 1945 he was naive and unworldly like any kid in Pittsburgh would be. I had gone to college there before I went into the Army, and then came back for the three years. We were both sophomores. He was younger than the ordinary sophomore because his mother had registered him in grammar school early. And then most of the people in the class were veterans, so we were all older than Andy and the girls.

He was very quiet. He was doing these eccentric drawings that the faculty didn't like—Aubrey Beardsley–type things . . . only wavy lines. It wasn't that he refused to conform; like any young kid, he was just doing what he did naturally. The faculty, I gather, had wanted to throw him out of school at the end of his freshman year. I think he had trouble with his academic courses. It was mostly a communication problem; he didn't quite understand what they were saying.

We were in a class together—it was kind of a therapy course where you'd talk about how an artist finds images that will be meaningful in terms of his life, and how to project them. That's when all of us really began drawing a lot, particularly Andy. His style began developing— a kind of unique style in response to these problems. In our senior year, Andy and I collaborated on a children's book project. I wrote the story —it was going to be called "Leroy"—about the worm inside a Mexican jumping bean. Andy made the illustrations, but in the finished artwork he misspelled it and it came out "Leory," which was much nicer.

I got to know Andy pretty well. He would come over to my house to work because he didn't have room at home. There were some nieces

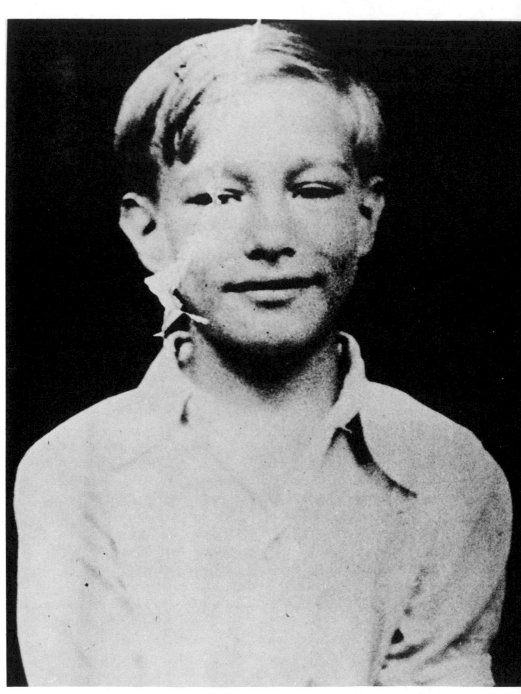
Andy Warhol, age twelve

and nephews who wouldn't let him work in peace, and they'd destroy his work. His brothers made fun of him—they thought he was strange because he was doing art.

When we finished school Andy's first idea was to be an art teacher in the public school system. Then he got a job doing displays at Joseph Horne Department Stores and he began studying fashion magazines in depth—they gave him a sense of style and other career possibilities. So I talked him into going to New York that summer of 1949. He said he wouldn't go unless I went, he just didn't feel secure enough. We each had a couple of hundred dollars.

One of our teachers at Carnegie Tech was Balcomb Greene, a big-name artist from New York. He lined up an apartment for us on St. Mark's Place—right off Avenue A. It was terribly hot. A six-floor walkup. Two or three rooms. Cold water. Bathtub in the kitchen. Andy had a terrific portfolio of drawings he had assembled, and by the end of the first week he had an assignment from *Charm* magazine for a full-page drawing of shoes. He got these jobs constantly.

All the time I lived with Andy, he was very quiet and went to church a couple of mornings a week. Occasionally, we went out to the movies, and those were the only times we'd have aesthetic discussions, if you could call them that. I remember Andy saying once that a movie we'd seen on Forty-second Street was terrible. I said that I didn't think it was possible for any movie to be uninteresting, no matter how dumb; there was always something going on that was interesting. He didn't answer, but perhaps that made an impression.

ANDREAS BROWN   Andy was very naive, very innocent, but very determined. He was extremely ingenious about ingratiating himself. He would go to the advertising agencies with a little bouquet and he would give each receptionist or secretary just a single flower in that wonderful mute way. Everybody else dressed in Brooks Brothers suits and carried beautiful leather portfolios, but Andy always came in ragged clothes, and he often carried his work in a brown paper bag. Everybody felt sorry for him.

GEORGE KLAUBER   I used to think of Andy as a hanger-on. There were times when he had nothing to do, and I used to take him places on weekends. He should never go to the beach because he had a skin problem. He would get burned fiercely. One of the comic images I have of Andy is remembering him in a white shirt, no tie, chino trousers, and sitting on the beach with a black umbrella over his head. That was East Hampton. We used to stay in a rooming house on the other side of the tracks.

HENRY GELDZAHLER   One of the strange commissions Andy had during the Fifties was doing the weather on television—his hand on the screen drawing clouds, or the sun, or sparrows in the rain. I always thought that one of the reasons Andy was so pale was because he had to get up so early, at five o'clock in the morning, to be at the TV station to get make-up put on his hand.

PATRICK O'HIGGINS   During his shoe period Andy's new apartment in the Thirties and Lexington was one floor up. Two rooms. Very simple indeed. No furniture. Like a room out of the set of *On the Waterfront*. In the kitchen I think there was a picture of Christ pointing to his Sacred Heart, and that's about all. Piles of magazines. Movie magazines. I remember thinking, "How strange, why would he keep such things?"

As soon as he made a few dollars, he brought his mother to New York. She was a Czech lady, spoke English brokenly, so she spoke Czech to Andy, who answered in English. She looked a little like a Buddha, a solid, square figure of a woman with her hair pulled back in a gray, almost white bun. She looked like Madame Helena Rubinstein without all the trappings.

There was only one bedroom. I know for a fact that Andy shared it with his mother. He told me so.

PHILIP PEARLSTEIN   Andy wanted to have a show at the Tanager Cooperative Gallery on Tenth Street—at the height of its glory then. I was a member. He submitted a group of boys kissing boys which the other members of the Gallery hated and refused to show. He felt hurt and he didn't understand. I told him I thought the subject matter was treated too . . . too aggressively, too importantly, that it should be sort of matter-of-fact and self-explanatory. That was probably the last time we were in touch. The next thing I knew came the Campbell's Soup can. Andy and I just lost contact altogether.

EMILE DE ANTONIO   Andy was doing very well. He started to collect things. He moved out of his apartment and bought this decent-sized townhouse on Lexington and Eighty-ninth Street, next to the National Fertility Institute. He installed his mother. Her presence wasn't real; it was ectoplasmic. When she did float through, Andy would sort of guide her away. Andy told me that she cleaned the house compulsively: got up at five o'clock in the morning and cleaned everything and then started drinking. She went to bed very early.

On empty nights I'd walk up Park Avenue and over to Andy's. He poured Scotch whiskey, but he never drank it. He looked like a super-intelligent white rabbit. Paintings appeared. *Dick Tracy. Before and After.* One night two paintings were put up, one against the other. One was a Coke bottle, nothing else; the other was limned with the brushy strokes of an East Tenth Street failure, second-generation Abstract Expressionism.

ROBERT RAUSCHENBERG   I first met Andy, very shyly, on some-body's back porch in mid-Manhattan with D—Emile de Antonio. D Antonio had already been instrumental to Andy in a number of ways: he convinced him that he had the courage and the talent to give up his commercial-art success. Andy had a kind of facility which I think drove him to develop and even invent ways to make his art so as not to be cursed by that talented hand. His works are like monuments to his trying to free himself of his talent. Even his choice of subject matter is to get away from anything easy. Whether it's a chic decision or a disturbing decision about which objects he picks, it's not an aesthetic choice. And there's strength in that.

D was also there to console Andy in the beginning, because it's a big change to move from being a top illustrator into "I don't know if this is art or not." D stuck by him and exposed his work for the first time to people who were seriously involved in art—gallery owners and a few museum people—and Andy became a phenomenon.

GEORGE SEGAL   The first time I saw Andy's paintings—strange comic-strip paintings—Lichtenstein had just had his showing at Leo Castelli's gallery. We said, "What the heck is this? *Two* guys involved with comic strips." Then the next paintings I saw were Andy's repeti-tions of dollar bills. We were amused by that because this Japanese girl Yayoi Kusama was already at the Green Gallery with her repeti-tions of penises. So such ideas were in the air: the notion of repetition, of serial. Fine. When the dust finally settled, the one who said it best would be the one with the most conviction to deal with the idea.

This is the document the State of Pennsylvania provided when asked
for the birth certificate of Andrew Warhola, born in 1930.

Mrs. Julia Warhola
with two of her sons

Andy Warhol,
high school portrait

Andy and his mother in his apartment on Lexington Avenue

Andy's gift to Truman Capote, 1954

WALTER HOPPS. In early 1961 Irving Blum and I were staying in New York with David Herbert—we were all art dealers, but David was one of the more pioneering of us and had his ear to the ground as to what was really going on. He was mobile, let's say, in the uptown New York gay world, as well as observant and mobile in the serious world of painting. Two different worlds. Sometimes the same. In the course of going about our business, looking into Jasper Johns and Bob Rauschenberg and rounding up some other stuff, David Herbert kept telling us, "Look, there's someone you should see. His name is Andy Warhol." It seemed like a funny name to me. He kept insisting that we should both go and visit this . . . this person.

Well, at the door was a peculiar, fey, strange-looking person. I sighed, thinking we were in for a cute time of it, and my reaction was reinforced as we went down hallways and I saw peculiar stashes of a kind of chi-chi gay taste . . . crannies full of gumball machines and merry-go-round horses and barber poles. I said, to myself, "Good Lord, this guy is a cute, rather effete decorator," which was not especially novel since public taste was already on the edge of Tiffany glass. Everywhere in this townhouse, variations on this kind of taste were collected. We went into a foyer and looked down the hall at a great collection of material that seemed to reflect this . . . a stash of Forties wedgie shoes, which seemed kind of kinky. The townhouse, gloomy and large, was peculiarly unfurnished. It was more of a collecting depot, a warehouse of things. I said, "Gee, it looks like you collect a lot of gumball machines here." He was some strange, isolated figure in his laboratory of taste experiments.

I started to look at some of the material. I was being a little nosy. Irving Blum was rolling his eyeballs at the ceiling, like, "Oh, my God, I didn't want to lead you into *this;* this is not your cup of tea." Actually I was fascinated.

Then Warhol led us into what seemed to be virtually a windowless room. It was a paneled library, but the bookshelves were empty . . . no pictures on the wall, nothing. Like it was being moved into or moved out of. What really made an impression was that the floor—I may exaggerate a little—was not a foot deep, but certainly covered wall to wall with every sort of pulp movie magazine, fan magazine, and trade sheet, having to do with popular stars from the movies or rock 'n' roll. Warhol wallowed in it. Pulp just littering the place edge to edge. As we walked in, the popular music of the time was blaring from a cheap hi-fi set-up; there was a mess of cushions, blankets, and maybe a little mattress. I don't remember that there were any chairs.

I think we squatted, or maybe there was a little chair for one of us. But the extraordinary sight was all this pulp pop-star literature, and the thought of Warhol wallowing in it.

We didn't know what to talk about. Neither Blum nor I knew who this person was or where to go with him. No art encountered us.

And we felt uncomfortable.

Warhol started to interview us! He wanted to know what we were doing in New York. "Well, we're looking at paintings." "Oh, what paintings?" Then it got to a particular focus. He asked, "Oh, what do you think of Jasper Johns?" I answered, "I think he's a very serious man indeed." Every remark I made was challenged: "Oh, you really think so? Why is that?" There was a kind of funny, bitchy edge to what he was asking. It was as though we had to pass a number of tests so that he could feel free to show us something.

Finally, one of us said, "Well now, do you have anything to show us at all?"

Up to that point Andy had been pushy and questioning . . . quite forward and talkative to a degree I have never heard since. "Well . . . uh!!! Yes," he said, after a bit more dissembling.

He got up and walked over to the corner where there was a kind of closet door, and he literally had to get down and scrape away the magazines. He got the door open and came out first with a couple of smaller paintings. They were surprising enough. One was a stretched canvas or a piece of white linen, with a lot of bare space, which gave an unfinished effect—not the look of a Rauschenberg, but that's what popped to mind. It was a Royal typewriter! Very carefully rendered, so that though there was some scumbling and other stuff around the edges, it looked just like an advertising illustration of an old-fashioned Royal typewriter. We looked at it in surprise. "Hmmm, that's interesting," we said, and the other things one says. But we *were* interested.

The second painting he brought out was a slightly different approach to paint application. Dick Tracy and his sidekick, Sam Ketchem, done in a sort of smeary, painterly way . . . a blow-up of these cartoon figures partly painted out but with loose paint on it.

All right! Finally he brought out the third thing, which looked like it was perhaps eight or ten feet tall, a rolled piece of linen . . . fine linen. He unrolled this thing out on the floor, over all that fan magazine junk. It was astounding! It was a larger-than-life-sized image of Superman flying, carrying Lois Lane, a blow-up painting in full color of a comic-book image. Flat, smooth application of the color. It didn't look anything like a painting. It wasn't composed. It was just a big-sized scale of a comic-strip box! Well, that was already strange. We'd never seen anything like that at all. And there was something about the Superman image that did vary from the comic strip. In the strip, Superman himself and the characters are all kept in the same scale; he's not larger-than-life. In this painting of Warhol's, as I recall it, Superman is much bigger in scale than the Lois Lane he's carrying in his arms: she's not doll-sized, but miniaturized. We were just astounded. We looked at it a while, but even before we'd finished looking, Warhol rolled it up and put it away. That was that. We'd had a peek at the material, and now he'd cut the evening off. Odd. We'd arrived ready to get out of there as soon as we could, figuring this was going to be a bust-out, but now that we were intrigued, Warhol was concluding things. To get us out of that room he suggested that he had an interesting little book we might enjoy, that his mother—up to this time we'd never heard of Andy Warhol's mother—had done. We were taken to another room, downstairs, I think. Like a creepy scene out of *Psycho*. Andy went off into some shadowy corridor, talking off there . . . I've often wondered if as in *Psycho* there really *was* a mother . . . and he finally came back with this strange, campy little privately printed book called *Holy Cats* done in this curious kind of gay illustrator's technique . . . quite unlike the stuff we'd seen upstairs. By now we were totally confused. What did this have to do with anything? He gave us each a copy and then he said, "Oh, I must have my mother sign them for you!" He took them back and disappeared into another room again and got them signed. There was some fumbling around, a delay. To this day I don't know whether his mother signed, or if he just went in there, fumbled around, and signed it himself. It was signed, "Andy Warhol's Mother."

I have never seen that Superman/Lois Lane painting since. He put things of that kind away. He had many more tricks up his sleeve. He didn't need to compete with Lichtenstein. If someone else was doing such things—fine, let them do it.

IVAN KARP   One day in 1961 two or three young people came into Leo Castelli's gallery, where I was working, looking for a drawing by Jasper Johns. One of them was this curious character with a shock of gray hair and a very bad complexion, who purchased after negotiations a drawing of a light bulb by Jasper Johns for the price, I believe, of three hundred fifty dollars. His name was Andy Warhol. He was very reticent and shy: he seemed extremely perceptive about what was going on in the art world. He asked me if there was anything else of unusual interest in the gallery. I took out a painting by Roy Lichtenstein to show him. It was a painting of a girl with a beach ball held over her head. This curious little pictorial ad still appears in *The New York Times* every Sunday as an advertisement for a hotel in the Poconos.

Andy, looking at it, said in shock, "Ohhh, I'm doing work just like that myself." Wouldn't I come to his studio and take a look at these curious things so related to Lichtenstein's work? Very shortly thereafter I went to this townhouse, where he had about thirty or forty paintings of various cartoon subjects, some done in the Abstract Expressionist style and some very plain and numb. He asked me for my reaction. I told him that I preferred the works without the splashes and splatterings, that if one were to work in a cartoon style like this curious character Lichtenstein, one might as well go all the way. He said he felt the same way, but that he was paying homage to the Abstract Expressionist movement with these paintings; he would prefer to reject them if he felt an audience could be responsive to work as cold and brutal as simple cartoony subjects.

Andy's studio was a rather scrumptiously bizarre Victorian setting. The lighting was subdued, the windows all covered, and he himself sort of hovered in the shadow. He played the same piece of rock 'n' roll music at an incredible pitch the entire time I was there. It was a song called "I Saw Linda Yesterday." Andy told me he was playing it until he could understand it, which meant that eight hours a day he played that song at full volume.

I was fascinated by his curious and elusive presence. He was very shy about showing himself. During my subsequent visits to his house he offered me a choice of elaborately festooned masks to wear while visiting him. They covered his eyes and nose like at the *bal masqué* of the eighteenth century. I am not one to put on a mask. I don't know what the purpose was, but in Andy's case I think possibly to shield his face. He never had what you would call a seemly complexion, though part of his attractiveness was the roughshod character of his face in juxtaposition to his complex sensibility. It made him almost saintly looking.

ANDREAS BROWN He had sort of a W. C. Fields rather bulbous nose, so he had himself a nose job. A friend of mine saw him in the hospital with his face all bandaged up. Andy was embarrassed and quite angry that this guy, who had heard he was sick and wanted to surprise him with some candy and flowers, had tracked him down at the hospital, because he was trying to do it all secretly.

EMILE DE ANTONIO   One of the driving forces behind Andy was his infatuation with celebrity. He was always writing fan letters and mash notes to people like Tab Hunter. One day he came to me and asked, "Don't you think it would be wonderful if I had an underwear store?"

I asked, "What do you mean, an underwear store?"

"Well, we'll sell famous people's underwear," he said. "Cary Grant's, Tab Hunter's . . ." Andy said the underwear would cost ten dollars if it were washed and twenty-five if it weren't.

TRUMAN CAPOTE   It had to be in the late Forties, or perhaps 1950, but certainly it was when my mother was still alive. Anyway, I started getting these letters from somebody who called himself Andy Warhol. They were, you know, fan letters. I never answer fan letters. If you do, you find yourself in a correspondence you don't want to have; or, secondly, you find these strangers turning up on your doorstep; or, thirdly, if you don't keep up with your letters to them after the first, they write hurt, vindictive letters wondering why you've stopped. But not answering these Warhol letters didn't seem to faze him at all. I became Andy's Shirley Temple. After a while I began getting letters from him every day! Until I became terrifically conscious of this person. Also he began sending along these drawings. They certainly weren't like his later things. They were rather literal illustrations from stories of mine . . . at least, that's what they were *supposed* to be. Not only that, but apparently Andy Warhol used to stand outside the building where I lived and hang around waiting to see me come in or go out of the building.

One day my mother was visiting from Connecticut. She was sort of an alcoholic. Somehow or other my mother spoke to him out there on the street and she invited him upstairs to the apartment. I walked in later, and he was sitting there. He looked then exactly the way he looks now. He hasn't changed an iota! He had been having this conversation with my mother, who was a bit looped. So I sat down and talked to him. He told me all about himself and how he lived someplace with his mother and twenty-five cats. He seemed one of those hopeless people that you just know *nothing's* ever going to happen to.

Just a hopeless, born loser. Anyway, it was friendly and pleasant, and then he left.

He started calling me every day after that. He'd tell me what was happening to him, and his troubles, and about his mother and all those cats, and what he was doing. I didn't want to be un-nice or anything, so I sort of put up with it. Then one day when he called up my mother, she told him not to call any more. She was drunk at the time. Like all alcoholics, she had Jekyll-and-Hyde qualities, and although she was a basically sympathetic person and thought he was very sweet, she lit into him. So suddenly he stopped writing or calling me.

I didn't hear from him or about him until suddenly one day D. D. Ryan bought a gold shoe Andy had dedicated to me in a show and sent it to me as a Christmas present. She told me, "Oh, he's becoming very well known, very on-coming." Even then I never had the idea he wanted to be a painter or an artist. I thought he was one of those people who are "interested in the arts." As far as I knew, he was a window decorator . . . let's say, a window-decorator type.

Then I ran into him on the street. When I had known him in his previous incarnation, he seemed to me the loneliest, most friendless person I'd ever seen in my life. He was surrounded by seven or eight people, a real little entourage around this person I had really thought quite pitiable.

Then he started sending me pictures again, including a portrait of me that if you look at you can tell I didn't sit for him.

I think, looking back, that at a very early age he had decided what it was he wanted: fame—that is, to be a famous person. His drive was simply that: fame was the name of the game . . . not really talent. Not art. Whereas with me I think it was the other way around: an intense preoccupation with an art form, which in turn led to fame. Mind you, I'm not saying that Andy Warhol doesn't have any talent, because obviously he has *some*; he has to. But I can't put my finger on exactly *what* it is that he's talented at, except that he's a genius as a self-publicist.

DAVID BOURDON Despite his growing success Andy was intimidated by the art-world people, especially the Abstract Expressionist group that hung out in the Cedar Bar. That generation of artists had struggled for so long for the little amount of recognition they got, only to be eclipsed by Pop Art, that they had this tremendous amount of animosity, especially toward Andy. That a shoe illustrator should be given a show at the Stable Gallery rubbed a lot of artists the wrong way. Andy was very wary of those people.

WALTER HOPPS   The Abstract Expressionists took the stance of workingmen—Franz Kline packing a lunchpail and marching to the other end of his studio. This sort of blue-collar approach was carried on from Bill de Kooning to Larry Rivers and Mike Goldberg. That's what the Cedar Bar in the Village was all about . . . no chic, no chi-chi, no frills, no nothin'! It was bright with a kind of yellowish light, dirty, and it was for serious drinking, talking, and arguing.

By the end of 1962 Pop Art was exploding in the American consciousness. The movement happened overnight, and Andy was very much included. That spring *Time* magazine took the lid off of it for the mass media with an article called "The Slice-of-Cake School," generally decrying and instantly making controversial this new manifestation. Andy had his first show of the Campbell Soup cans out in the Ferus Gallery in Los Angeles.

I remember how really insane the opening was at the Sidney Janis Gallery in New York in November, 1962, for a show called "The New Realists" that combined all these *new* American Pop people—Warhol, Rosenquist, Segal, Lichtenstein, Tom Wesselman, and others, along with European supposedly Pop people, the first time they had all been seen together in New York. Jean Tinguely's work—you know, the artist from France who makes the mad machines—sort of set the tone of hysteria. He had an icebox that had been stolen from an alley outside Marcel Duchamp's secret studio, and when you opened it, a very noisy siren went off and red lights flashed. This icebox really had nothing to do with Pop Art, but it set the noise and tone that was to continue all the way through the Sixties.

GEORGE SEGAL   Sometime in 1963, for some peculiar reason I could never understand, Salvador Dali and I were both invited to a mid-morning housewives' TV program to discuss Pop Art. Everyone in the magazines thought it was fun-and-games—a mockery and celebration of American vulgarity. I didn't think so, and Dali, to my amazement, came out with this long gobbledygook that Pop Art was really an obsession with death and nihilism. I found myself absolutely agreeing with him. Jasper Johns had just done *Tennyson* and *No*—paintings that were dull, dense negations, pulling shades down. *No,* you can't see me; *no,* you said no to me; *no,* I don't want to get old; *no,* I don't want to die. This is what his paintings were saying to me—nothing to do with entertainment, fun-and-games, or the celebration of vulgarity. Warhol's early images of Jackie Kennedy, Elvis Presley, electric chairs, those car crashes—everything was done in pastel colors, thin, bright, scintillating, but since they were about the most dense, horrifying feelings, they made a shatteringly effective statement. And Marilyn Monroe—a double obsession with style, beauty on the same extraordinary level to be admired with death and negation. A shocking juxtaposition, and I think effective.

JASPER JOHNS   I liked Andy's Brillo boxes—the dumbness of the relationship of the thought to technology—to have someone make those dumb plywood boxes and then paint them. I mean, artists have had other people make things for them, but nothing quite so simpleminded. Yet those boxes must have involved a lot of thought and decisions on his part—how they were going to be made, and certainly the colors. I have one of the first ones, which is a different color than the ones he finally came up with. He came to see me once in the early Sixties when I lived on Riverside Drive and brought me a present. It was a sculpture of a Heinz Tomato Ketchup carton. Then a while later he said that the one he'd given me wasn't right; he would like it back so he could give me one that *was* right. I didn't return it.

LEO CASTELLI   Jasper made a tremendous impression on Andy. He really understood how good Jasper's drawings were and, even more important, the impact that Jasper's *mind* had on him—the use of the flag, the numbers . . . one of the great basic events at the end of the Fifties that influenced everybody.

JASPER JOHNS   When I was growing up, I knew I wanted to be an artist. It meant being an interesting person who was doing interesting things to which people paid attention, and not being who I was at that time—someone living in a little town in South Carolina. I knew that you didn't do it there. I was anxious to get to New York, and I came on the Silver Meteor, the fastest train going. But I did not leave and forget where I had been. I never did anything terribly dramatic; I didn't run away; I didn't dismiss the past. Is it important for an artist always to keep a connection? I think so.

You asked me if we need more than one Warhol in this century. Well, I guess if we need them, we will make them. Haven't got much time left, though, in this century—just about enough to make a young one.

20

DANNY FIELDS   By the end of 1963, Andy moved into a loft on a floor of a factory building on East Forty-seventh Street—I think they made hats there. He didn't dub the studio "The Factory," like a christening; it was just what people started calling it. What I most remember about the Factory itself is the aluminum foil that covered the walls, and the stuffed couch. Stone floors, a lot of paintings, a lot of standing around, a movie projector and cans of film. Some Salvation Army furniture to sit on. When the Velvet Underground was there, they had rock-band amplifiers, drums, and stuff. A coin wall telephone by the door; it was extremely important: there'd always be a line of desperate people, calling in or out. The Factory was totally open; anybody could walk in. At one point they put up a sign, DO NOT ENTER UNLESS YOU ARE EXPECTED, which everyone ignored. There was always an ebb and flow of people . . . like a crowd on a street corner or Sheridan Square.

WALTER HOPPS   There was always a shortage of places to sit. There was that decadent overstuffed sofa on which a lot of the sex play of the movies was shot, but that quickly filled up: people lying on it, lounging, and so forth. I think there were a couple of director's chairs, maybe more. Andy never sat down. One always had the sense of him standing, or pacing around slowly. This was Andy the sleepwalker in the mid-Sixties, on his feet all the time.

Everyone around him was ravaged on drugs, though I never saw Andy smoke a joint. One night I was at the Factory at a screening of some of Andy's films. Cecil Beaton was there with his friends, filling up whatever comfortable places there were to sit, apart from that damn couch. The floor was filthy in that place, and the movie was pretty long and boring. In the gloom I saw what looked like a rolled-up carpet and I went over and sat down on it. I sat there for a while until Andy came slowly over and said, "Uh, uh, I guess he's so out of it, it doesn't matter, but that's . . ." and he mentioned a name. I was sitting on some guy who was lying on the floor as straight and symmetrical as a rolled-up rug—his jacket so tucked up about him that I had mistaken him for a carpet! I mean, this guy was really wiped out.

HENRY GELDZAHLER   A clubhouse. It became a sort of glamorous clubhouse with everyone trying to attract Andy's attention. Andy's very royal. It was like Louis XV getting up in the morning. The big question was whom Andy would notice. There are artistic personalities who need enormous amounts of people around them where they're working —Hockney, Rauschenberg, Warhol—I imagine like Peter Paul Rubens, who always had bunches of people around. Andy can't be alone.

I first met Andy when he came to the Metropolitan Museum, where I was a curator, and in the next six years we saw each other just about every day. It was magic: we knew that we were on the same wavelength. He immediately knew that I knew things that he could use . . . "smart stuff," he called it. He used to say, "Oh, you know so much. Teach me a fact every day and then I'll be as smart as you are." So I said, "Cairo is the capital of Egypt." He said, "Cairo is the capital of Egypt."

My favorite was a telephone call at one-thirty in the morning. "Henry, I have to talk to you." I said, "Andy, it's one-thirty in the morning." "We have to talk," he said. "Meet me at the Brasserie." I asked, "Is it really important?" He said, "Yes, it's really important." So I said okay; I got dressed, took a taxi, and met him at the Brasserie. We sat down at a table. "What is it?" I asked. "I have to talk to you. I have to talk to you." "Yes? Yes?" "Well," Andy finally said, "say something." That was it—a cry for help of some kind. Sometimes he would say that he was scared of dying if he went to sleep. So he'd lie in bed and listen to his heart beat. And finally he'd call me. But it was amusing, too, in its mad way. He did like to hear me talk. Sometime that year he was asked to do a radio interview at WBAI and he asked, "Can I bring a friend along?" So I joined him at the microphone. They would

Edie dancing at the Factory with Donald Lyons

ask a question and he wouldn't say anything. So I'd lean forward and say, "What Andy means is . . ." and I'd answer it. Once in a while he'd say yes when the answer was no. Then I'd say, "When Andy says no he means yes," and then explain. At the end, the interviewer said, "I'd like to thank Mr. Geldzahler from the Metropolitan Museum for being with us today, and Mr. Andy Warhol." Andy grabbed the microphone. It was the first time he spoke in the whole interview. He said: "Miss Andy Warhol."

Andy can't be alone. That's what the Factory was really about . . . providing a baffle of friends.

DANNY FIELDS   There was always a pecking order: who in those caravans of cars went in the car with Andy. There was always the immediate circle—the prime ministers. In Edie's time it was Chuck Wein. Whatever boy Andy was in love with, whatever superstar women were most in the limelight. Perhaps one new beauty being looked over, someone very young and innocent. No blacks, they weren't hip enough. A group of boys from the Cuban aristocracy—a bunch of them were discovered in Central Park. It was certainly Action Central. Whoever was supposed to be hot shit could come in. The Duchess of Rothschild would come trotting through with all these fabulous people, the rich, the beautiful, the foreign stars, reporters.

The major figures were all vying for Andy's affection: who was going to be the beloved object. There was always trouble between the competitors. Andy loved this stuff. It was like a gladiatorial contest. He'd just lick his chops and sit back and watch these people have at each other and pretend he didn't know anything about it. He would let them crawl all over each other's egos and bodies and reputations to get closer to him. Quite a collection.

BILLY NAME   People would ask me what my name was and semifacetiously I would say my name is Name. I thought it was cute and I'd never seen anyone use the name Name for a name. I used to think like that; I would have these spontaneous original ideas.

I was working as a lighting designer off-Broadway and I had an apartment on East Seventh Street. I used to cut all my friends' hair. These hair-cutting sessions turned into hair-cutting parties. Everybody would crowd in and have a great time. I had covered the entire apartment with silver foil; I had some spotlights up. It just looked very cool to me. Andy came once and he asked if I would do the decor for his new studio, the Factory, just the way I had done my apartment.

It took me so long to do the Factory that I just stayed there. I converted one of the two toilets into a darkroom. I slept on the floor. We had sofas and furniture at the Factory, but I was a very erratic person, not terribly conventional. I wasn't used to sleeping in bed.

PAUL MORRISSEY   Billy Name. Such a curious person. He lived in a toilet for four years, a black-painted toilet with no real light inside. He sat in there reading mystical texts and the cabala, things like that. He almost became a leper—totally caked with sorés because of a lack of light and vitamins. He was a good photographer because he had a kind of great sensibility. He'd been in the toilet for so long! He'd only come out very late at night so nobody would see him. Every now and then people would get a peek at him. Somebody would say, "I saw Billy Name. He was coming out of the toilet!" I would complain, "Andy, he's going to die in there, and the papers are going to say: ANDY WARHOL LOCKS MAN IN TOILET FIVE YEARS." Poor Andy sort of inherited him.

ONDINE   When Billy left the Factory, his mother put him into a retreat, Graymore or someplace like that, for about a week. He was working out there when they asked him to paint a fence. He stopped in the middle of it, because he didn't know whether the fence wanted to be painted or not. So he couldn't do it. There are certain *issues* for him. He was possessed by lesser spirits, spirits of the earth. You could hear them, you could hear them raging through his body. His eyes turned yellow; his hair was growing in concentric circles; he was getting scabs on his face; his fingernails grew. There was some kind of fire going on in Billy's brain. Even his involvement with the Factory finally ended. A note turned up in the back room: "I am fine. Goodbye."

DANNY FIELDS   Then there was Gerard Malanga with his bullwhip. Whenever we went to a poetry reading, there would be Gerard with his bullwhip wrapped around his arm. People only knew of Gerard as Andy's assistant. He was a poor Italian boy from the Bronx who grew up with his own fantasies of possessing the social life and beautiful girls and rich women who were socially above him. Finally, he had access to them.

Andy was very hung up on Gerard and dependent on him. He was certainly the Prime Minister for a long time. Gerard was it, and he was very jealous of anybody who came around.

ISABEL EBERSTADT   Gerard Malanga hung on by his fingernails. He was a very tenacious character for many years. He really served Andy very well. He was more usable in the end than almost anyone. He had inestimable virtues as a pornographic star, being constantly ready for action of any sort. He had a certain style and taste, he wasn't a bad writer, so he was a perfect lieutenant. It was just that Andy couldn't bear having anyone around too long.

ONDINE   Andy and Gerard would have their fights because Gerard hadn't painted the silk screen or because he was being lazy. Andy'd say: "Gerard! I'm sick of you laying in bed. I'm not paying you a dollar and twenty cents an hour for nothing!"

GERARD MALANGA   Andy and I worked on a lot of major artworks together, major in the sense of size because it took more than one person to work on a huge canvas to make a silk screen. I gave Andy some ideas for certain canvases and regarding the processing. On the Elvis Presley silk screens the image appears slightly imposed over itself, maybe three or four times. That was an idea I picked up from a photographic process and introduced to Andy. I gave it a sort of psychedelic strobe effect by shifting the silk screen over just a little bit and screening again so that the second time it would be superimposed over the first, and then doing that again for a third and maybe a fourth time. Cecil Beaton had done something like that in one of his early photograph books—a kind of trick stop-motion effect.

Andy got his subjects from all over. He had a friend who worked for a girlie magazine that had gone out of business. He gave Andy his complete file of what were actually UPI photographs—eight-by-ten glossies. A lot of Andy's work came out of that file—the Marilyn Monroe portrait, the disaster series, the electric chair. I found his cow on the corner of Seventh and Twenty-third Street in a bookstore which burned down some time back. It was in one of those trade books for farmers with pictures of agricultural equipment and new ways of milking cows. I figured Andy wanted a sweet-looking cow, and I found one in there.

He found his famous flowers in a botanical catalogue. He said, "Here, get this made into a silk screen." A woman recognized her photograph of the poppies and felt she deserved something from him. I could understand her feelings about the matter. It was years before the whole thing was settled out of court.

Andy on the Factory couch

Billy Name cutting Edie's hair on the Factory fire escape, with Ondine tape-recording

ISABEL EBERSTADT   When I first knew Andy they were working on the Marilyn Monroes. Malanga and Billy Name did most of the work. Cutting things. Placing the screens. Andy would walk along the rows and ask, "What color do you think would be nice?"

ONDINE   How he made those paintings was so helter-skelter. Do you remember Harriet Teacher? She was one of the queens of the avant-garde. Very weird girl. Very small. Intense. Controlled. She always had a dog with her—a huge dog named Carmen Miranda. One day she came up to the Factory with Carmen Miranda and asked Andy if he would mind if she shot his Marilyn Monroe paintings. He said no, it was okay.

There were about seven Monroe canvases stacked one against the other on the floor. Harriet put on a pair of white gloves, took a pistol out of her motorcycle jacket, aimed it at the middle of Marilyn Monroe's forehead—standing about fifty feet away—and shot a hole through all those canvases. Right in the middle of the temple. Perfectly on target. Lots of people were watching . . . Billy Name, Morrissey, Warhol . . . no one could believe it. It was a small, beautiful German pistol; it was just lovely. After she'd fired it, she said, "Thank you," and sat down. Warhol came over to Name and me and he said, "I didn't think she'd do it. My God!" After a while Harriet left with Carmen Miranda. She put the white gloves in the pockets of her motorcycle jacket. She was very neat about the whole thing.

Marilyn Monroe looked marvelous after she'd been shot. Just beautiful. The holes in all the heads were clean. Real clean. Andy sold them, of course. There's nothing he doesn't sell.

DANNY FIELDS   Ondine was around a lot at this period, always ready for some Factory party with the cowboy hat and the vinyl boots. Ondine? A brilliant actor-comedian. Very brilliant. From Queens or Brooklyn; he's from an Italian family, a doting mother. He was one of the first great Mole People—those who moved through a transitional stage from beatnik into a more stylized and campy version. We called them Mole People because they only seemed to come out at night; they all wore black—black turtlenecks, pants. Some leather. Their skins were light, and they were very intense. A lot of them were into dance. A sort of severe kind of New York nighttime creative craziness. Ondine came out of that.

It was the violent speed era, and people could fly off the handle at anything. They were into intense paranoia and could easily strike. Violent people. A lot of them died young: they jumped off roofs, or slit their throats; cracked up cars and motorcycles.

Andy used Ondine as the Pope in *Chelsea Girls*. I gave him his name—Pope—because to me he was very regal, always in command, a very high authority. He had his ups and downs. Later on, Andy helped him get this job at Carnegie Tech. He's very together now. He's mellowed out. Drinks a little bit, but no more speed.

ONDINE   I'm called Ondine after the character in the Giraudoux play. I came out of the water one day at Riis Park with seashells on, and they called me Ondine.

The first time I met Warhol I had him thrown out of an apartment. I said, "I do not want this voyeur in here." He looked like a gray specter. I didn't give a good goddam who he was. There were the beginnings of an orgy and he was staring. What does Warhol stare at? He stares at the world. But that night he was staring at what was starting and I just thought that was unfair: there was a certain look in his eye; it wasn't wonder, or wanting to get involved, or not being able to be involved . . . he was just *watching* with this watching eye, and I said, "Get him out of here, man. I don't want to see him! He's putting a damper on the whole party." They got rid of him. That made him love me in a strange way. I had put my foot down.

I was the Pope in *Chelsea Girls* when Andy had reached his golden throne, when he had absolutely a halo. People recognized me from the film. They'd walk up to me on the street and say, "Hiya, Pope!" Just anybody. I mean, four Negroes in the subway. "Hiya, Pope!"

DANNY FIELDS   The other noted figure at the Factory from Harvard was Chuck Wein. He represented Edie's past and present somewhat the way Andy represented her future. They both resented that they weren't more of the other. Andy wanted to be in her immediate past, her rich, powerful, Waspy past, and Chuck wanted to be a part of her future. They fought for her soul and her loyalty and her attention. She turned more and more to Andy because he moved in the New York circle, and away from Chuck, who represented Cambridge and that crowd. But Chuck, though transitional, was not to be overlooked. He was very powerful within the structure of the Factory itself—the prime minister. He had walked around the world to see the bottom of volcanoes; he was mystical and talked about extraterrestrial beings

Paul America

Chuck Wein, Andy, and Edie

Brigid Berlin and Viva

Danny Williams

Henry Geldzahler

Andy and Gerard Malanga

Richie Berlin

Billy Name

Lou Reed

Paul Morrissey

Walter Hopps

Andy and Rod La Rod

and astral parapsychology and synchronicity and vortexes. A snow job! But he was really good at it—smart, magnetic, and very sexy. He thought of Edie as a Trilby kind of creation; he was going to be her von Sternberg. But I'm sure he was in love with her. He needed her as much as she needed him.

TOM GOODWIN   One of the things that Chuck was terrific at was getting Edie to do things on film. He understood that Edie was best at just being Edie. She was totally involved with her self-image . . . or her vision of her self-image. It was like that awful voyeuristic thing of the one-way mirror. But what was beautiful was the way she did it. Chuck had a real sense of timing with Edie. All the stuff in Andy's films of Edie being Edie is Chuck. That's not Andy. Andy was kind of fascinated with the whole thing, but it was really Chuck's saying, "This is good, run it." Was he using her for his own advancement? I don't know, that's always the director-actress problem.

GERARD MALANGA   Chuck Wein brought in Danny Williams with his kind of genteel Harvard schoolboy look, brown hair. It sort of happened that Danny was responsible for the wiring at the Factory. He had this desk and it was like walking into an electrician's hardware store, boxes labeled with plugs and wires and screws and nuts and tools . . . very Kafkaesque. This Harvard graduate putting plugs into sockets. He was always sweating, his T-shirt dirty, and his hair was stringy. Part of Danny's seediness was that to take a shower you had to run to the YMCA across the street. If you didn't, you just started collecting dust.

   He finally went off and killed himself. He parked his car by a cliff on Cape Cod. His clothes were there, which leads me to believe that he took them off, dove into the water, and swam off to drown. I remember one detail about his death: his parents sent Andy these two brass doorknobs. Somehow they knew that Danny wanted Andy to have those doorknobs.

ONDINE   Paul America was another *strange* cup of tea. He was everybody's lover . . . he was marvelously satisfying to everyone. Imagine having that type of curse. People would go to sleep in his arms . . . Richie Berlin, me, just everyone! He was the personification of total sexual satisfaction. Without a brain in his head. Just beautifully vapid. He was a wonderful creature. Anybody who wanted anything from Paul could get it. He was there to satisfy. And he did.

PAUL AMERICA   I met Edie Sedgwick at a discotheque called Ondine. It was my first night in New York, actually. A friend of mine had
told me to meet him there. I only had two dollars, and the drinks cost
two something. So I was waiting at the bar for my friend, realizing my
time was short. He turned up and asked me to sit with everybody in
the back—Chuck Wein and Andy and Edie; they were having a dinner
party because Edie had been on the Johnny Carson show that night.
When they went back to the Factory, I went with them, and I stayed
for three years. Most people didn't know I lived there, because I was
taking speed—I figured if I took speed, I wouldn't be paranoid—and
I only slept about twice or three times a year. If I felt I needed rest,
I'd take a bus somewhere. I would sit down for a few hours. That was
enough rest. I'd go up to the Cloisters or down to the Staten Island
ferry. Sitting up was more comfortable than lying down. So I'd just sit.
It was restful to be in one position knowing I wouldn't have to move
right away.

I put together a motorcycle for Andy. He gave me that name, Paul
America. When he gave me the name, I figured it was all right. Except
I went through a period of paranoia about it. I mean, every time I saw
that word—and it's everywhere—I related it to *myself*. The country's
problems were *my* problems. I think that if I weren't called Paul
America it would have been easier for me to register in hotels. Most of
the time the desk clerks said, "Okay, Mr. America."

Andy was very secluded. He would come into the Factory and stand
off by himself. Sometimes I would go up to him and suggest something
that we could do, and he would listen very nicely and ask Gerard to
give me his reply. It was pretty strange. He wouldn't talk with me
directly. He looked down on me, I guess. Took me for a fool, which I
guess is what a lot of people do. Andy didn't dig me at the time. Like,
every time I opened my mouth he made me feel paranoid. So I laid
back. I said, "Go on, you fool," and I would just sit and watch when I
could have helped him a good deal.

HENRY GELDZAHLER   Paul America was a wasted creature after
they had finished with him. They finally washed their hands of him
and let him float away. He's a poor burned-out thing living in a commune in Indiana and trying to pull himself together. Not long ago I
sent him a check for two hundred dollars and I got back a big package
which looked like a small coffin, about four feet by two feet by two
feet. When I opened it, I discovered the cast off his leg. He'd broken it
falling out of a tree, or sliding in the snow. It was sort of off-white

and covered with writing which I didn't read. I opened and closed it and it's in the back there. I don't think I'll ever open it again. I don't know exactly how to throw it away. It looks like part of somebody, and I'm afraid if I throw it away I'll be arrested. It's like the Australian joke about a boomerang: how do you throw it away?

DANNY FIELDS   No one ever wasted Paul Morrissey! Incredible eye and sense of satire. When he starts carrying on, everything in sight gets knocked down. He is an excellent filmmaker.

VIVA   Everyone at the Factory was constantly speculating on Paul Morrissey's sex life. He played the male role of the Virgin Mary in the theological hierarchy, with Andy going as God the Father, and Billy Name as God the Holy Ghost; I never decided who played God the Son.

ONDINE   Paul Morrissey was the first person to say *outright* to Warhol: "I am your disciple." Nobody else involved with Warhol would think of saying it that way because Andy was the *queen* of passivity . . . the absolute son of non-existence. He was just divinely not there.
   Morrissey sold him a bill of goods . . . this commercial shit.

VIVA   Paul was a real nine-to-fiver—the only one. He wanted to make money, be commercial. He dealt with the press. Paul could deal with everybody. He was quick . . . very quick. That was it. There was nobody else. So he got rid of anyone who was unfashionable or uncommercial. Gerard discovered him, but he says now, "I brought that viper in."

GERARD MALANGA   Originally we thought Paul Morrissey could be kind of useful to Andy on a technical level, but he rose very quickly. He became a sort of hatchet man . . . great charm and quite humorous, but from the beginning I think he was maneuvering to get Chuck Wein out of the way. I know one thing that Paul hated was when Chuck put LSD in all the omelets and scrambled eggs after we'd shot *My Hustler*. It was Paul's first film. Chuck didn't tell anyone until after we ate the eggs. We were out there on location on Fire Island. A huge vat of scrambled eggs. Paul to this day will deny getting high on LSD. But he was found under the boardwalk curled up in a fetal position. Andy would also probably deny being high on LSD, yet I found him at six in the morning rummaging through the garbage cans. I asked, "What are you doing?" He said, "I'm looking for something."

Ondine and Andy

Graffiti in the Factory bathroom

DANNY FIELDS Brigid Berlin was another extraordinary part of what was happening in New York in the early Sixties. I hope she gets recognized for the great artist she is. She and her sister, Richie, are the daughters of the Richard Berlins, he was the head of the Hearst Publication empire. Brigid was into all sorts of things—she was into trip books.

Trip books were a big thing. You worked on them when you were on amphetamines. You'd fill in the blank pages. Sometimes you'd get a friend to do a page, or you'd fiddle around—little poems, decorations. Each page was a trip. Beautiful drawings. A collage of photographs from the *National Geographic*. A piece of cotton pasted in. Somebody's pubic hair. Toothpicks. Spangles. Blotches of color. The books got so fat they wouldn't close.

MARIO AMAYA Andy himself was keeping a record book back in the late Fifties. They were drawings of cocks. He did a foot book, too. In '68 or '69 he was doing Polaroid shots of all his friends' penises. He asked me if I would expose myself and he did a Polaroid shot.

KENNETH JAY LANE He did both my cock and my feet. One day after work he came over for tea. He told me, "Oh, I saw Diana Vreeland today. I went up to her on the street and said, 'Mrs. Vreeland, can I draw your feet?' She said, 'Oh, Andy, how are you?' I said, 'Can I draw your feet, Mrs. Vreeland?' She said, 'Oh, Andy, you don't want to draw my feet. They're too small!' "

ANDREAS BROWN One night I went out for dinner with a girl friend of mine to a restaurant in the Village. Andy came in with an entourage of ten or twelve people for dinner, Brigid Berlin among them. They sent over a bottle of wine and we sent back a thank-you note. Brigid came over to the table and asked us to autograph one of her famous trip books, her scar book . . . that is to say she wanted to make an impression of any scars my girl and I might have with an ink pad and then transfer them to her book, where we'd sign our names and explain how we got the scars. Communication between the two tables was established. Andy suggested that maybe we'd like to come to a little party they were all going to for drinks. We went along. A television set was turned on in the living room. Drinks were served. Then people slowly began to disappear into the back room. Andy got his Polaroid out and began taking pictures of people carrying on sexually back there. It started off with people running around in the nude, but eventually it began to progress. We were encouraged either to participate or just come on in and observe. Andy was in no way participating or showing any enthusiasm; it was almost as if he were bored. He was taking photographs and sort of nodding . . . encouraging the thing to go on, and all the time observing the degree of participation and interest of all those around. Andy was being a cool, detached, aloof observer. But at the same time, he was the ultimate instigator, the person who really held the party together. Without Andy you wouldn't have had the floating crap game moving from the Factory to the restaurant to the apartment and to the back bedroom. So he was the Big Director in the Sky in one sense: moving everyone around on the set.

TRUMAN CAPOTE Actually, if I had to make a really good guess, I'd say that his thing is being a voyeur. He's very interested in pornography. I know he has a big collection because he trades—like kids who trade bubble gum cards—with someone I know who has a truly great collection which I've seen part of: it would take a month and a half to see it all. I know one of the things the two collect are photographs of famous people in the nude, which isn't exactly pornography, but they do a lot of trading in that. I've seen one collection of these—an album of famous people—and it's rather amusing because they're mostly taken of people who didn't know they were being photographed . . . like in locker rooms.

DANNY FIELDS Brigid Berlin was into a whole series of themes with her trip books—her cock books, which had impressions of outlines of people's cocks on the page, her belly-button books, her scar books. Really incredible! Many people contributed because she asked *everyone*, even her parents' friends, so that in her trip book she had contributions from J. Edgar Hoover and the Duke of Windsor—not the imprints of their cocks, for God's sake, but J. Edgar Hoover's Christmas card, for example, and a note from the Duchess of Windsor to Brigid's mother.

Brigid was also into tapes—taping orgies and taping herself fucking and other people fucking and stuff like that. Very big on that. I've heard them all. Whenever I called her up, I had to listen to those things on the phone—what people said to each other. The most outrageous tapes. Everything is filed and catalogued. It could go into a museum the way it is; they wouldn't have to hire someone to sort it out.

BOBBY ANDERSEN   In the Factory they all had a special language. Brigid and her sister, Richie, initiated a lot of that lingo. They called it "taking a poke," an expression made up by Brigid when they took a shot—what the street people called "getting it off." If you were being bad, you were on a "ravage." Not able to "fold one's napkin" was a metaphor for not being able to cope. When anyone went too far, the famous line was "The rant runneth over." Brigid would say: "Take a poke, my dear. It's divine." I think that's why everyone called her Polk—it came from "poke."

It was sort of a children's game—like little kids playing and showing their behinds. Richie's ass was famous because no one could get a needle through it.

RICHIE BERLIN   My sister, Brigid, gave herself a poke in front of everyone in *Chelsea Girls*. If Brigid could be one person in the world, she'd be Andy Warhol or Mrs. Andy Warhol. So she gave herself a poke, and my mother was off on a lah-de-dah about her firstborn playing a "lesbian-pillpopper-Molly-junkie-gopher" and it was, "Really, it was just mortifying!" My mother went to see *Chelsea Girls* in a Carey limousine, unidentified as a person, and said, "Disgraceful."

DANNY FIELDS   I loved Richie. Smart and great. She was short and boyish. She wore a mohair kneesock and tied it around her neck in a double Windsor knot in a color coordinated with whatever little outfit she was wearing. Very short hair. No make-up. She was like a wire. I got a kick out of seeing her because she was always into something intense to talk about.

RICHIE BERLIN   I rarely hold opinions more than a few hours. Finishing leaves me with a despair. But I also make wild, rather intriguing collages that fascinate me by their separateness. Don't remind me that I turned out wrong because I had a nanny who washed my wee-wee out with Q-tips and I wore hats and coats to match . . . I feel best when alone with pocket money, quite thin, agile, and slightly vicious . . . I've always believed in live high, die, and have a wonderful corpse.

In one of my sister's tapes she claimed she's talking to Henry Kissinger and he was coming on to her, trying to make a date. My sister Polaroided Tiger Morse's funeral at Frank E. Campbell's funeral home. I think that's a bit much.

Chuck Wein and Andy

John Palmer, Carol James, Gerard Malanga, Marisa Berenson, and Edie

We never had separate identities, I was always Brigid Polk's sister. But I gave Brigid her first poke. . . . I have a dog, though. *He* is separate . . . Toto . . . a Yorkshire Terrier who has been with me for eight years and wears eyeglasses. I dress him up. He makes you want to call me Dorothy. He has a tape recorder in his shoe and Mark Cross loafers. He wears coats and hats.

DANNY FIELDS   The Factory mascot was a little boy whose mother was Nico, a singer with the Velvet Underground, and whose father was the French film star Alain Delon. There weren't many children around. Nico took him everywhere. He was an unhappy kid. Very angry. He was only four or five then; I'm sure he's changed.

Also in the Velvet Underground was Lou Reed—a little devil, a great talent. Everyone was certainly in love with him—me, Edie, Andy, everyone. He was so sexy. Everyone just had this raging crush . . . he was the sexiest thing going. He was a major sex object of everybody in New York in his years with the Velvet Underground.

NICO   Lou Reed was very soft and lovely. Not aggressive at all. You could just cuddle him like a sweet person when I first met him, and he always stayed that way. I used to make pancakes for him. I had subletted a place on Jane Street when he came to stay with me. That's when we first did the Electric Circus on St. Mark's Place; at the time it was called the Balloon Farm.

Lou was absolutely magnificent, but he made me very sad then. . . . He wouldn't let me sing some of his songs because we'd split. He tried to make it up to me later with that Berlin album . . . I'm from Berlin originally and he wrote me letters saying that Berlin was me.

DANNY FIELDS   After Nico came Viva—very special, very smart, very crazy, and a good mother.

VIVA   Andy was at this party. I screwed up my courage and asked him if I could make a movie. I thought I'd make a few Warhol movies and become a big Hollywood star—starting at the bottom, with Andy my first step toward my ultimate, incredible glory and fame and riches and stardom. Andy said, "If you want to take off your blouse, you can make a movie tomorrow. If you don't want to take it off, you can make another one."

I was afraid if I didn't take off my blouse that very next day he would forget me completely. So I put these round Band-Aids on my nipples and took off my blouse. They loved me; they all thought it was an incredible *acting* technique they were seeing.

DANNY FIELDS   Then there was Alan Midgette, the one who impersonated Andy . . . very charming with a movie star's kind of glamour. He looks part Indian, which accounts for his striking looks. You wouldn't think *he* could get away with impersonating Andy on the lecture circuit.

ALAN MIDGETTE   It happened very spontaneously—walking into Max's Kansas City at about two-thirty in the morning. Paul Morrissey asked me, "Do you want to go to Rochester tomorrow and impersonate Andy at a lecture he's supposed to give there?"

I said, "No." I was so used to the idea of not receiving anything for whatever I did at the Factory that the idea of doing a lecture in place of Andy was not interesting at all until Paul said, "You would get six hundred dollars. We'd give you half of the lecture fee. We'll go on a tour of colleges." "Well," I thought, "six hundred dollars for one day's work is not bad, and I'm always up for fun like that."

The next day Paul asked how we could make it work. I said, "We'll spray my hair silver and put some talcum powder on top of that. Then we'll get some Erase, the lightest color they have. I'll put it all over my face, eyebrows, lips, up my nose, in my ears, and over my hands and arms. Then I'll put on Andy's black leather jacket"—he'd handed it to me in Max's Kansas City the night before—"put the collar up, put on the dark glasses, and that's it."

So it worked. Paul sometimes called me Andy by mistake. He couldn't tell the difference at times. He came along with the film which was the main part of the Warhol presentation. The idea was to show it to students on this tour of colleges and they would ask me questions.

It was easy to impersonate Andy because to the questions I'd always say "Yes" or "No" or "Maybe," "I don't know," "Okay," "You know, I don't think about it," which is the way Andy would have answered the questions anyway.

So I passed. I passed at one o'clock in the afternoon on a clear, sunny day in a gymnasium in Rochester. They had a packed audience.

Paul projected the film. I sat in a corner with my back to the audience. I decided that was the easiest thing to do. I chewed gum a lot, because Andy did. It gets your face moving quite a bit, so the audience couldn't tell very much about it when I had to turn around to answer questions after the film was over. The first one was: "Why do you wear so much make-up?" I said, "You know, I don't think about it." They let it go.

I think perhaps the thing began to blow up in Salt Lake City when "Andy" was supposed to talk to three thousand students. As we landed, we heard over the loudspeaker, "Please be careful getting off the plane. Watch out for your hats because it's really windy today."

Sure enough, when I got off the plane, the wind blew off all the talcum powder I'd put in my hair, just blew it right out like a puff of smoke. All these people were standing there waiting for us. I got into a car and this guy started taping me. He was very shy. Finally he said, "What is that stuff on your face?"

I said, "I have a skin condition."

He got very embarrassed, and said, "Oh, I'm sorry."

At one of the universities the students wanted to do an interview with Andy for their television studio. I was trying to get my face in a position where the viewer really couldn't see the form of it. As I stared at the monitor, I suddenly realized I looked exactly like Marcello Mastroianni.

The thing finally broke when I was in Mexico. The next thing I knew, the story was in *Time* and *Newsweek*. It was all over the place. I haven't seen much of Andy since then. It's not the kind of thing we ever sat around and laughed about.

ONDINE Andy loved this guy called Rod La Rod. Isn't that perfect? Every time Andy appeared with his camera, Rod La Rod would throw it down and beat up Andy, and they'd have this fistfight right on the set. They'd smash each other to ribbons. Then they'd make up. It was just wonderful. They'd found each other. They were divine. We kept telling Andy: "Oh, God, he's awful for you."

Andy'd say, "I know. I know." It was so amusing.

Do you remember when Lester Persky gave a party in the Factory for the fifty most beautiful people? People came like Montgomery Clift . . . just thousands of people there . . . the really great stars. I'll never forget the door of the freight elevator opening up with Lester Persky and Tennessee Williams standing there with their arms interlocked carrying Judy Garland. Everybody refused to recognize her. Simply refused. The only people that were paid any attention to were Edie, myself . . . people in the Warhol contingent. Nureyev, at one point, asked Judy Garland to twist. They got up. Everybody turned away. Just totally. The whole party was involved with drugs and the new kind of celebrity. Even Nureyev was considered very old hat.

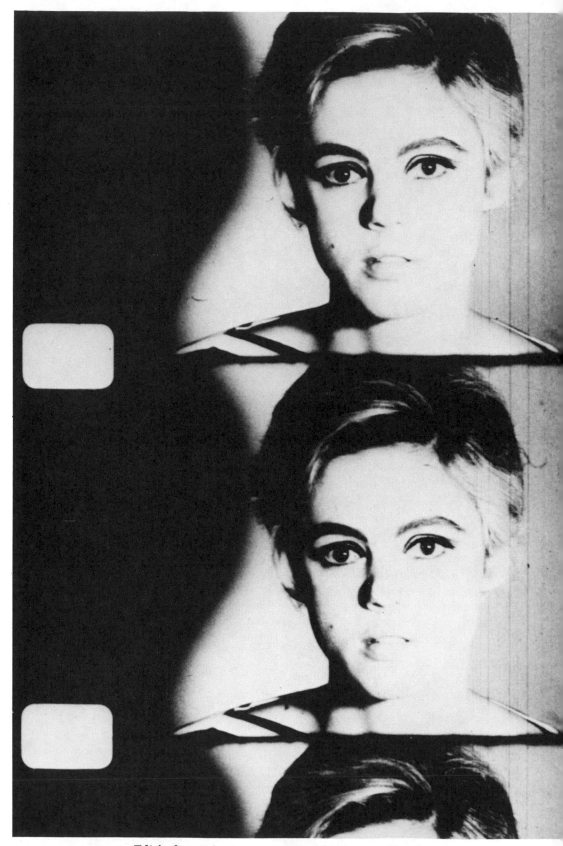

Edie's three-minute screen test at the Factory, March, 1965

21

DANNY FIELDS   When Edie entered the Factory scene, I thought it was nice that the Cambridge boys had imported their own private princess. It seemed a nice transfer of domain because, before that, she'd just been a Cambridge legend. She was rich, glamorous, beautiful, and she was instantly adored.

Edie was the First Lady and Andy's prime companion, so there was an on-going struggle for her favor and attention . . . a rivalry for her affection. She was the greatest of the superstars.

RENÉ RICARD   The term "superstar" was coined and invented by Chuck Wein. The big words then were "super" and "fantastic." Jane Holzer may have started "super." Certainly that was her big word. It was the first time the words "super" and "star" were coupled together. I've found it only once before—in an obscure fan magazine from the Thirties.

DANNY FIELDS   The superstar was a kind of early form of women's liberation. They were so smart, beautiful, aristocratic, and independent. Edie, Nico, Viva, and the others. They were like Garbo and Bette Davis in that system of the Thirties. They were indulged by everybody. They were as smart as any of the men around. Everybody, from little boys to old faggots, fell in love with them . . . just as those stars of the Thirties inspired their leading men, the directors, the producers to fall in love. They were definitely superior beings and very involved. They're the women we all want to worship. I mean, Virgin Marys. At the same time they were very destructive people—self-destructive and other-people-destructive. They were riding the whirlwind.

VIVA   None of the superstars really had a role in the Factory. Edie, I figured out, who was non-Catholic, was never actually a part of the *true* family. And, being a woman, she played an inferior role. In the Catholic Church women are supposed to play a big role—I mean, we have the whole nunnery and so on—but women have *no* voice in the running of the Church. They can never be priests. Their dirty menstrual bodies cannot possibly touch the sacred host.

The popular view of Andy is as a Father Confessor, but I don't go along with that. He was more like an attention-giver. If you had a father who read the paper at the dinner table and you had to go up and turn his chin to even get him to look at you, then you had Andy, who would press the "on" button of the Sony the minute you opened your mouth. And we were encouraged to perform. The Factory was a way for a group of Catholics to purge themselves of Catholic repression . . . and Catholic repression in the Fifties was so extreme that the only way to liberate oneself from it was to react in the completely opposite direction, and then hopefully level off after that.

Andy Warhol would try to pick out men for me. He'd say, "Now go with this one, go with that one." All these men in whom I had no interest whatsoever. He was always coming up with these guys I think he was interested in. He would try to get *me* to go off with them. He'd say, "Big cock, big dick. He's got a big cock, go with him." And yet if you so much as tried to touch Andy, he would actually shrink away. Shrink. I mean shrink backwards and whine. Many times I used to make a grab at Andy, kiddingly, or touch him, and he would cringe. Whine, "Aw, Viva, awww." We were all always touching Andy just to watch him turn red and shrink. Like the proverbial shrinking violet.

I tried to grab his cock, I mean through his pants, of course, just to watch it shrink. Or touch him on the shoulder. Anything. Any touch was like a burning poker. It just got to be a joke. You could even reach your hand out and pull it back the way you would from a hot iron, and not even touch him, and he'd shrink. That was the conditioned reflex.

Baby Jane Holzer in *13 Most Beautiful Women*, 1964

Viva

ISABEL EBERSTADT   I had the impression that Andy's relationships were not overtly physical. He always said that he "couldn't bear to be crunched again." He'd had some unhappy relationship in his younger days and had decided to withdraw himself emotionally as much as possible. So he worked out this curious formula where he lived as a voyeur.

I was moving out when Edie was moving in. Andy was as taken with her as I think it was possible for him to be with a woman. Edie spoke to me a little about the world she'd left in order to be with Andy: she claimed her father had forced her and her sister to sit in a sphinxlike position with bared breasts on the top of columns flanking the entrance to the driveway when guests came to their place in California. Edie's story was that her father would beat them brutally if they moved. A lot of what she used to tell me turned out to be true. I really became confused about how much was true and how much was fantasy.

JANE HOLZER   It was getting very scary at the Factory. There were too many crazy people around who were stoned and using too many drugs. They had some laughing gas that everybody was sniffing. The whole thing freaked me out, and I figured it was becoming too faggy and sick and druggy. I couldn't take it. Edie had arrived, but she was very happy to put up with that sort of ambience.

DANNY FIELDS   Edie fit wonderfully into all this. What was great about her was that she was attracted to the most brilliant and crazy people—Ondine, Chuck, and Andy. She was really a poet's lady. Most of these people were probably gay, but they were seriously in love with her. She was very beautiful, which anyone can respond to. And she made them feel like men. She would come on helpless, which brought out their strengths.

ONDINE   One night after we had just made a film Edie and I walked into the film co-op on Forty-fifth Street—the Mekas thing. Jonas Mekas, the underground filmmaker, was sitting at a table, and he *fell* off the seat when he saw us and scalded himself with hot coffee. He couldn't take the idea that this whole stardom thing—Edie, this poor little rich girl, and I, this vicious street thing—were actually happening in *his* world, *his* realm. It must have been a very glamorous moment because we both looked so beautiful, and he just was knocked off his seat.

HENRY GELDZAHLER Andy always picks people because they have an amazing sort of essential flame, and he brings it out for the purposes of his films. He never takes anybody who has nothing and makes them into something. What he did was recognize that Edie was this amazing creature, and he was able to make her more Edie so that when he got it on camera it would be made available to everybody.

22

GERARD MALANGA   Andy never actually directed a film. He was a sort of a catalyst genius who would get people to do things for him in front of the camera. But he never went for anything like rehearsals. All he did was turn on the camera button and turn it off. Andy had it in his head that it was like magic. He wanted everything to be Easyville. He thought of himself as Walt Disney, you know: just put your name on something and it will turn into gold . . . some kind of alchemy.

RONALD TAVEL   *Vinyl* was Edie's first Warhol film. She arrived at the Factory just as Gerard Malanga was doing his little torture job in *Vinyl* on Ramsey Hellmann, this runaway kid from Canada. They'd brought in some real sado-masochists to do the number right, with razor blades and candles. They were very serious, with their leather and all that. Edie had come in at the last moment—no rehearsals, nothing. I thought she was going to demolish all the work I had done. Andy propped her up on a huge trunk, smoking a cigarette, and occasionally she flicked her ashes on this boy who was being tortured. She sat there, sort of stretched out, and the camera just went berserk looking at those eyes. The outfit she wore was certainly calculated . . . she had no breasts, but she had legs that didn't quit, so why not show everybody the legs all the time? What do you do with legs like that in the middle of winter, I don't know . . . freeze to death?

Andy filming

The film became like one of those vehicles for a famous star, but it's somebody *else* who gets discovered . . . like Monroe in *Asphalt Jungle*. She had a five-minute role and everyone came running: "Who's the blonde?"

GERARD MALANGA   In *Vinyl* I was giving my long juvenile-delinquent's soliloquy when Andy threw Edie into the film at the last minute. I was a bit peeved at the idea because it was an all-male cast. Andy said, "It's okay. She looks like a boy." And it worked out fine. She had covered her automobile-crash scar with a decoration like a tear drop. She said something you could barely hear on the sound track, otherwise she didn't say anything. She didn't get in my hair.

ONDINE   The whole last scene was filmed with people on poppers —amyl nitrates—*Boom!* It seemed like the entire room was stoned. I mean *just out of it*. When the film was over, we went off in the hallways and up on the roof. I was in the hallway with Pierre's lover, who was really beautiful. Pierre was up on the roof with somebody else. Somebody was in the bathroom with somebody. People did things on the couch.

In the middle of all that, Edie was staring, just staring. She couldn't believe it. She was talking to Warhol, who was eating his hamburger, there was no way she wasn't aware of it.

Well, after we saw a few reruns of *Vinyl*, some of us got an inkling of what was going on there with her in the Factory . . . a power that we hadn't even suspected.

RONALD TAVEL   I wrote a great number of the Warhol films. Warhol and I were very uncomfortable together. I never knew what to say to him, and he never knew what to say to me. In fact, we almost never said anything. The only time we really worked together, co-directing for about a week, was with *Kitchen*. Andy really liked it; he said it was the best script that I had done, and he liked it as a vehicle for Edie Sedgwick.

As best as I can articulate about the average Warhol film, the way to work was to work for no meaning. Which is pretty calculated in itself: you work at something so that it means nothing. I did have one precedent—Gertrude Stein. In much of her work she tried to rob the words of meaning. So my problem as the scriptwriter was to make the scripts so they meant nothing, no matter how they were approached.

Edie and Gerard Malanga in the torture sequence, *Vinyl*, March, 1965

I worked on getting rid of characters. Andy had said, "Get rid of plot." Of course, Samuel Beckett had done that in the Fifties, but he had retained his characters. So I thought what I could introduce was to get rid of character. That's why the characters' names in *Kitchen* are interchangeable. Everyone has the same name, so nobody knows who anyone is.

Andy and I would sit side by side like two Hollywood directors and tell the actors what to do, and sometimes Andy'd turn to me and say —especially when Roger Trudeau would hug Edie—"It looks just like a Hollywood movie." That would bother him. He went for that sloppy, offhand, garbagy look. Edie forgot her lines a lot. If she didn't know a line, she was to sneeze. That was the signal, so that someone behind the refrigerator could whisper it to her. There were other techniques—pages of script hidden among the junk on the kitchen table, or in the cabinets, so if the actors forgot their lines, they could go and pretend they were looking for a cup or a glass.

NORMAN MAILER   I think Warhol's films are historical documents. One hundred years from now they will look at *Kitchen* and see that incredibly cramped little set, which was indeed a kitchen; maybe it was eight feet wide, maybe it was six feet wide. It was photographed from a middle distance in a long, low medium shot, so it looked even narrower than that. You can see nothing but the kitchen table, the refrigerator, the stove, and the actors. The refrigerator hummed and droned on the sound track. Edie had the sniffles. She had a dreadful cold. She had one of those colds you get spending the long winter in a cold-water flat. The dialogue was dull and bounced off the enamel and plastic surfaces. It was a horror to watch. It captured the essence of every boring, dead day one's ever had in a city, a time when everything is imbued with the odor of damp washcloths and old drains. I suspect that a hundred years from now people will look at *Kitchen* and say, "Yes, that is the way it was in the late Fifties, early Sixties in America. That's why they had the war in Vietnam. That's why the rivers were getting polluted. That's why there was typological glut. That's why the horror came down. That's why the plague was on its way." *Kitchen* shows that better than any other work of that time.

GEORGE PLIMPTON   Any number of influences must have been involved with Andy's filmmaking. I remember riding in a large freight elevator with Andy in the early Sixties—it may have been the one that rose slowly to the Factory—and mentioning in passing that I had been reading an account in *The New Yorker* of an Erik Satie musical composition being played over and over for eighteen hours by relays of pianists in a recital room in Carnegie Hall. Apparently the composer had specified that this was how he wanted the piece— which was only a minute and a half long—performed. I mentioned it to Andy only because I thought he might be vaguely interested— after all, he was doing these eight-hour films of people sleeping. It never occurred to me that he knew of this concert, or of Satie, since it wouldn't have surprised me a bit if he'd never *heard* of Satie. His reaction startled me. He said, "Ohhh, ohhh, ohhh!" I'd never seen his face so animated. It made a distinct impression. Between ohhh's he told me that he'd actually *gone* to the concert and sat through the whole thing. He couldn't have been more delighted to be telling me about it.

JOHN CAGE In September, 1963, we had ten pianists to play one of Satie's "Vexations" in relays, including me and one music critic who thought he could play the piece and wanted to get in the act. I forget his name. He was very friendly, but he made more mistakes than the others. Viola Farber, the dancer, played the first twenty minutes. While she played, someone on her left was sitting on the bench ready to slide over and pick up the piece so there wouldn't be a hitch in it.

The effect of this going on and on was quite extraordinary. Ordinarily, one would assume there was no need to have such an experience, since if you hear something said ten times, why should you hear it any more? But the funny thing was that it was never the same twice. The musicians were always slightly different with their versions—their strengths fluctuated. I was surprised that something was put into motion that changed me. I wasn't the same after that performance as I was before. The world seemed to have changed. I don't know quite how to say it. A moment of enlightenment came for each one of us, and at different times. People would say, "Oh!" as it would suddenly dawn on them what was happening. The audience varied. It started with four or five and ended with seventy-five. I stayed there for all eighteen hours and forty minutes. I may have gone down to Chinatown to get something to eat. There was one person who stayed the whole time except when he went to the men's room. He had brought his food and his shaving equipment. After it was over, I drove back to the country and I slept for a long time, something like twelve hours. When I got up, the world looked new, absolutely new.

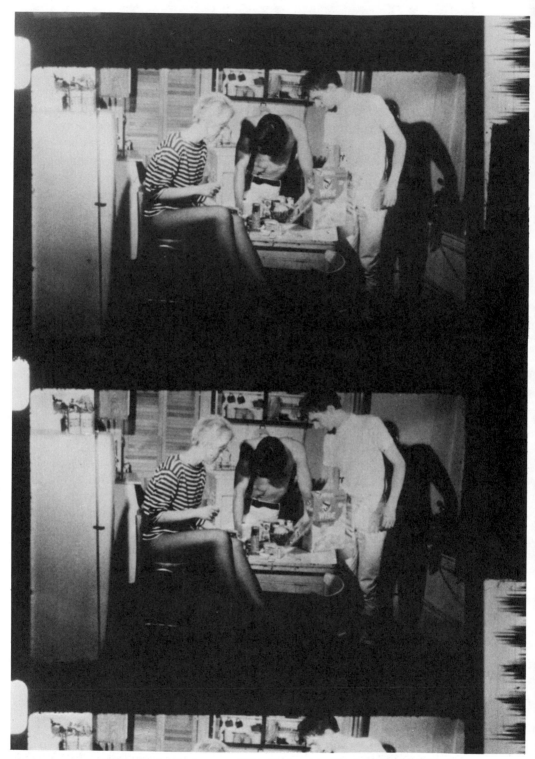

Edie, Roger Trudeau, and René Ricard in *Kitchen*, May, 1965

I hadn't realized Andy was there. But even if he wasn't, it doesn't surprise me that his work followed the same lines. Of course, artists are encouraged by other things that happen, but mostly by what is either in the air or already inside them. Andy has fought by repetition to show us that there is no repetition really, that everything we look at is worthy of our attention. That's been the major direction for the twentieth century, it seems to me.

RONALD TAVEL　Warhol used to say, when he was interviewed, "We make a film a week," but it's not true. I kept a calendar and it shows that we made a film every *two* weeks . . . which is a big difference. Sometimes Warhol wanted me to move quickly from script to script, and I'd say, "But I have to see the film we've just made!" Obviously, I had to learn from what I'd just done before I could move on to the next project. So as soon as I saw the completed film, he would tell me what he wanted next, just the subject: "I want something on Juanita Castro," "I want something happening in a kitchen," "I want a screen test," and so forth.

One of the things Warhol was always talking about, and I was, too, was what you can do that hasn't been done before. Unexploited territory. Sado-masochism, transvestites—such things came in not only because they were novel but also theatrical . . . all image and display. For example, Anthony was a genuine sadist. Incredibly exotic-looking and devastatingly beautiful. Women just couldn't control themselves. "My God, you're good-looking." He was into things that are hard to take seriously. Into wheelchairs. Into all this therapeutic material . . . crutches, carts . . . and he'd stand on the street and look at this stuff through the display window of the hospital-supply stores and he'd be ecstatic!

His apartment was on the Upper East Side. It was very small, two rooms, and just candle-lit. The walls were painted like a Rousseau jungle—the entire thing, ceiling, walls—so that you were in a lush Rousseau jungle right down to the little tigers staring at you. A candle swung on a chain, suspended, and as it swung, it illuminated a portrait of St. Barbara, the black saint, with her slashes. I asked, "What's she doing there?"

He said, "Well, look at all the slashings. Read up on her."

He had torture racks in there. A filmmaker friend and I were there one day to do research and Anthony wanted to put us on the racks. It was quite something. He talked a great deal to us. Sado-masochists are very gentle. They always want you to try things out because they feel that most people, even if they have such inclinations, are so repressed that they can't even experiment. After all, no one's going to come out and say, "Here's what I'd like to do," if they haven't done it before. So he had to guide us. He did things like put us on the racks, stripped, and then he'd throw wood alcohol on our genitals, which is quite something to go through. It came as a total surprise. He said, "It's good. You'll feel good. It's wonderful." And then suddenly SPLASH. But it was not good. It was not funny. You go tearing out of the place.

Out of this research came *Horse*. The film was made around Tosh Carillo and Gregory Battcock and one or two other people. Dan Cassidy, the poet, and Larry Latreille. With Tosh Carillo I thought I had discovered a new Turhan Bey. But it turned out that the horse was probably the star of *Horse*. Andy had called some agency and asked for a pony. In came this enormous stallion, very nervous because, though they are trained, bringing a horse up to the Factory in a freight elevator and making him stand still for hours, with a camera and people milling around, can make a horse very nervous indeed. This horse was there with his trainer, who kept feeding him whatever they give them—tranquilizers, I guess. The horse stood in front of a painted Western setting that looked terribly real. That bothered Andy because he kept saying, as he looked through the camera: "I'm telling you, it looks exactly like a Hollywood Western," and he didn't like that. He kept telling me to lower the mike and the boom so we'd have that showing in the picture frame. The actors were under great tension because of that huge stallion. They had no idea what was happening. All they were told was to dress vaguely Western; just *suggest* being a cowboy. So they came in, of course, dressed to the hilt like cowboys, and we had to take off a lot of their paraphernalia. We wrote their lines out for them on these big idiot cards. They had wanted to see the script, but we didn't want that. They were under great stress because they were sitting there practically *under* that horse and they had no idea what they were supposed to do or say until they saw what was written on the idiot cards.

All of a sudden I put up this direction which was: APPROACH THE HORSE SEXUALLY EVERYBODY. So everybody stood up, *en masse*, and *assaulted* the horse . . . probably quite tentatively and gently, but not to the horse, which struck out and kicked Tosh right in the head. Under normal circumstances he probably would have fainted. But he kept right on assaulting that horse.

What I was doing with this idea was working on a whole theme about cowboy homosexuality and masturbation and asexuality implicit in the Old West with no women about, and with their love for horses and everything. But I also wanted to make a point about racial prejudice. So the next stage direction I put up on the idiot card was YOU NOW ATTACK TOSH. He could be taken for a Mexican-American, you see, although he's Hawaiian. When the actors saw that sign, they left the horse and they nearly killed Tosh on that concrete floor. They released all the tension and fear they'd had under the horse, and they used Tosh as an outlet for it. Oh, they just beat him up! First Gerard and I put up a sign: STOP. ENOUGH, which nobody saw, of course, and then we had to run onto the set and break it up, screaming: "Stop! Break this up! What are you doing?"

EMILE DE ANTONIO   Andy's like the Marquis de Sade in the sense that his very presence was a releasing agent which released people so they could live out their fantasies and get undressed, or, in some cases, do very violent things to get Andy to watch them. In one of Andy's films somebody was blowing a black guy and being buggered by another guy at the same time. It may be what she had always wanted to do, but I doubt she wanted to do it on the couch at Andy's studio with a camera on hand.

He was able to bring that out in a lot of people—people doing weird things in those early films who wouldn't have done what they were doing for money or D. W. Griffith or anybody else.

TRUMAN CAPOTE   I'll give you an interesting analogy here. Have you ever read Carson McCullers' *The Heart Is a Lonely Hunter*? All right. Now, in that book you'll remember that this deaf mute, Mr. Singer, this person who doesn't communicate at all, is finally revealed in a subtle way to be a completely empty, heartless person. And yet because he's a deaf mute, he symbolizes things to desperate people. They come to him and tell him all their troubles. They cling to him as a source of strength, as a kind of semi-religious figure in their lives. Andy is kind of like Mr. Singer. Desperate, lost people find their way to him, looking for some sort of salvation, and Andy sort of sits back like a deaf mute with very little to offer.

GEORGE PLIMPTON   I got involved—somewhat against my better judgment—in trying to put together a retrospective of Andy Warhol films. My co-producer was Peter Ardery, just out of Harvard, who was the managing editor of the *Paris Review*. He was a film buff, and absolutely fascinated by what Warhol was doing during that period. He was certainly the instigating force of the two of us, and it was through his efforts and prodding that for five hundred dollars we purchased the rights to everything that Warhol had done in film up to that time. It was a low period in Warhol's career. Five hundred dollars apparently meant a lot.

The films arrived at my apartment in two large cardboard cartons. Most of them were hundred-foot reels which lasted for three minutes on the sixteen-millimeter projector which we set up in the living room. The projector worked overtime. We spent hours looking at what we had. I was discouraged. I thought it was really all very bad —just what one might expect of someone, however clever, who's picked up a movie camera for the first time and has started to learn how to use it. There were the usual standard home-movie shots of people mugging for the camera, little half-done scenes with the principals suddenly breaking down and giggling with embarrassment, and most of it out of focus, of course.

Then one day we put a film on the projector titled *Beauty Part II.* It came on one of the larger reels and lasted sixty minutes or so. It had a sound track. It was electrifyingly different . . . I suspect it was one of the first attempts in the Factory to do something more than simply point the camera and hope for the best.

In the film the camera was focused on a bed throughout. There were no cutaways or different camera angles or anything sophisticated like that: the camera was trained on the bed like an artillery piece. I seem to remember the bed as being of the hospital variety, with a white sheet on it, upon which lay Edie Sedgwick and a character from Warhol's Factory named Gino Piserchio. He looked like the Spanish bullfighter Cordobés—a dark, small, but muscular figure wearing a pair of Jockey shorts, as I recall; Edie was almost naked as well—wearing a bra and panties, both of black lace. She looked absolutely ravishing—that pale, long-limbed girl on the bed, with her great, dark eyes, and I remember the contrast . . . almost a study of contrast . . . with the white of the bed sheets, and the girl on them—really quite an elegant, almost aloof beauty she had—contrasted with the general tawdriness of the scene and the dark goatherd-type guy next to her. I don't recall that he ever said very much. His function in the film was to paw at her from time to time, not violently but rather sleepily, as if he had started awake from a half-dream and thought it might be nice to indulge in some leisurely lovemaking before slipping back to sleep. One had the feeling the two of them had been on the bed for a very long time.

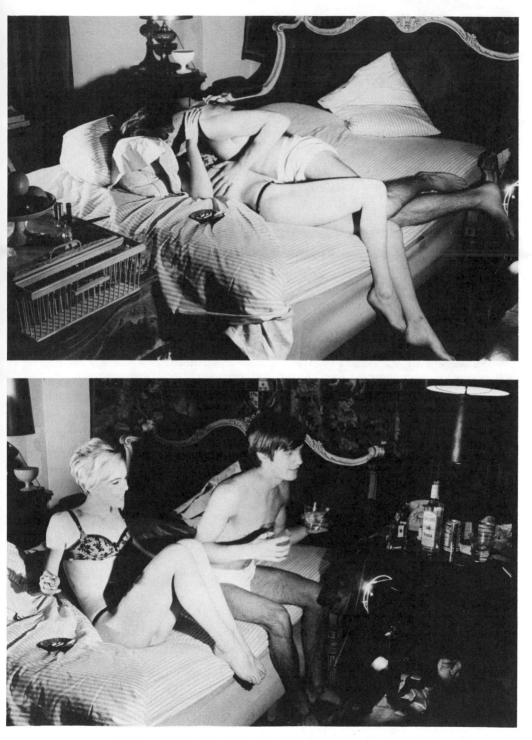

Edie and Gino Piserchio, *Beauty Part II*, July, 1965

There was a third character in the film—he was an older man from the Warhol entourage, Chuck Wein, who was sort of Edie's guru at that point—and the concept here, I thought, was the genius of the whole project. He was to be seen in the foreground of the film, just a shoulder showing in a lower corner of the frame, or the side of his head—the form of a man sitting on a chair in the shadows and watching the bed in front of him, very much the set-up of an *exhibición* in some cheap Havana hotel in the pre-Castro days.

But he wasn't really so much a voyeur as a sort of inquisitor. I remember his voice—nagging and supercilious and quite grating, which may have been the fault of the sound track, too. A lot of the questions, rather searching and personal, were about her family and her father. On the bed Edie was torn between reacting to the advances of the boy next to her and wanting to respond to these questions and comments put to her by the man in the shadows. Sometimes her head would bend and she would nuzzle the boy or taste him in a sort of distracted way. I remember one of the man's commands to her was to taste "the brown sweat," but then her head would come up, like an animal suddenly alert at the edge of a waterhole, and she'd stare across the bed at her inquisitor in the shadows. I remember it as being very dramatic—at least, compared to the other stuff we had seen—and all the more so because it seemed so real, an actual slice of life, which of course it *was*.

I couldn't get the film out of my mind. I had known Edie during that period. I went to Sunday lunch once to her grandmother de Forest's. Edie had on a lipstick color that was silvery and moist and I thought it made her look wan and ill. We always had an easy and civilized time, though. But I remember that evening when Peter and I watched the film for the first time—that when it finished, the end of the film flapping as it turned on the take-up reel, I turned to Peter and I said incredulously, "I don't know that girl. I don't know anything about her at all."

23

RENÉ RICARD   It was the high point in Edie's career. She was the girl on fire with the silver hair close to her head, the eyes, the Viceroy in her fingers, the sleeves rolled up, those legs, yoicks! . . . all you saw was her!

PATTI SMITH   The first time I saw Edie was in *Vogue* magazine in 1965. I was seventeen or eighteen then. You have to understand where I came from. Living in south Jersey, you get connected with the pulse beat of what's going on through what you read in magazines. Not even through records. *Vogue* magazine was my whole consciousness. I never saw people. I never went to a concert. It was all image. In one issue of *Vogue* it was Youthquaker people they were talking about. It had a picture of Edie on a bed in a ballet pose. She was like a thin man in black leotards and a sort of boat-necked sweater, white hair, and behind her a little white horse drawn on the wall. She was such a strong image that I thought, "That's it." It represented everything to me . . . radiating intelligence, speed, being connected with the moment.

Edie as a "Youthquaker," *Vogue*, August, 1965

Vogue, August 1965

People Are Talking About . . . YOUTHQUAKERS

. . . Edith Sedgwick, twenty-two, white-haired with anthracite-black eyes and legs to swoon over, who stars in Andy Warhol's underground movies. "It's like watching a Henry Moore sculpture out of focus," said Edith Sedgwick, who toyed with the movie name Mazda Isphahan for *Poor Little Rich Girl.* With Pop artist Andy Warhol on camera, undergrounds roll out like crepes: *Vinyl* is in the can; *Vacuum* about to turn "when we find a pure white kitchen." *Rich Girl* was made in Miss Sedgwick's apartment, where she is shown here arabesquing on her leather rhino to a record of The Kinks. . . . In Paris Warhol's gang startled the dancers at Chez Castel by appearing with fifteen rabbits and Edie Sedgwick in a black leotard and a white mink coat. In her deep, campy voice, strained through smoke and Boston, she said: "It's all I have to wear."

PATTI SMITH I would read about these discotheques. I would come all the way up to New York to loiter in front of a discotheque, watch people go into Arthur's or Steve Paul's The Scene. For me it was like seeing Hollywood. I saw Edie dance once. It was the big moment of my life. I think I said I had to use the bathroom, and some weak guy at the discotheque door let me through. I remember I had on a green wool mini-skirt. For New Jersey I looked pretty hot, but I didn't look so hot there. What I remember most of all were their earrings. I thought they were really neat dancers but unusual. We didn't dance like that in New Jersey. I was brought up in a really black area and we were really great dancers. I thought they danced like weird chickens. They just didn't have that fluid nigger grace that my friends and I possessed. Everything was angles. Everybody was skinny, and it was elbows and angles and knees and earrings. It wasn't a question of my wanting to be them. I just liked that they existed so I could look at them.

ROY LICHTENSTEIN My wife, Dorothy, and I went to a Halloween costume party given by the painter Adele Weber, dressed as Andy Warhol and Edie. Andy looked somewhat different then—leather jacket, blue jeans, funny sunglasses, and funny shoes that were all broken up . . . silver paint on them. Easy to imitate. I sprayed my hair with silver paint and I powdered my face to look very pale. When people said anything to me at the party, I said, "Oh, wow!" or "How glamorous!" Even though Andy can be unusually articulate, I reduced his repertoire to those two expressions. Dorothy wore hot pants and very high heels and put on a lot of silver glitter. She had short hair like Edie's. Andy does exactly what I don't do. *He* was his art. His studio was his art. Edie was part of his art, and a lot of other people. I was an old-fashioned artist compared with him. When I looked at Andy, I looked at him as a tourist would, I guess . . . with wonderment. How glamorous. How strange.

VICTOR NAVASKY   I was on a David Susskind panel on his television show. "Who's In and Who's Out" was the topic for the night, and Edie as Girl of the Year was on it, along with Gloria Steinem, Russell Baker, and I forget who else. Susskind began the show by making fun of Edie. "Why do you dress like that? Why do you . . . ?" And she was answering half defensively and half in a Warhol way. Her whole life was a media event.

New York *World-Telegram*, August 18, 1965
Gotham-Go-Round, Joseph X. Dever, Society Editor

EDIE SEDGWICK AND ANDY WARHOL,
ROYAL MEMBERS OF UNDERGROUND MOVIES

Chez Catharsis: At a low decibel point amid the deafening sound of the Executives trio last night at the Scene, we shouted into the ear of Edie Sedgwick, silver-topped queen of the underground movies: "Where is the *real* Edie Sedgwick—home with a book?" The bob-haired, 20-year-old heiress from California looked to see if we were serious, then shouted back: "The real Edie is where the action is. Fast cars, fast horses, and people doing things!" With that, she watusied away, her trademark leotards lost in a swirl of hip-huggers, tight blue jeans, Pucci slacks, and little-girl mod dresses. That swinging catacomb on W. 46th St., the Scene definitely was where the action was last night. . . .

ANDY WARHOL   She was always making fun of the kind of clothes she wore—saying that not wearing underwear, and things like that, was her way of showing that her family didn't give her any money. Actually, she invented all those new clothes and stuff. She always looked so good. Edie was a beauty, gee!

WENDY VANDEN HEUVEL   She came to a party at my mother's. The maid said, "Can I take your coat?" She said, "No, I don't think so. I'm a little cold." Later Edie told me the real reason she didn't want to take her coat off was that she wasn't wearing any clothes under it.

I was about five years old at the time. I thought it was funny that she would come to a party with no clothes on, just a coat. We had funny conversations. I would say "Hi," and she would say "Hi," and then I would say "Hi," and we'd just keep on saying "Hi," "Hi," "Hi," to each other. It seemed like she had so many friends, but when you really looked at her face, it was like she never had *any* friends.

ANDY WARHOL   She always wanted to leave. Even if a party was good, she wanted to leave. It's the way they work now in St. Moritz: I mean, people who spend fortunes to have parties can't wait until they're over so they can go somewhere else. I don't understand that. Can't wait to go . . . and there's no place to go. These people in big, expensive cars can't wait to get to the next party . . . and there's no next party. They just get up and leave. It's really funny. But Edie was like that. She just couldn't wait to get to the next place.

One night, when the parties were over, I guess she didn't want to sleep with somebody, so she asked me to share a room with her. She always had to have her glass of hot milk and a cigarette in one hand. In her sleep her hands kept crawling; they couldn't sleep. I couldn't keep my eyes off them. She kept scratching with them. Perhaps she just had bad dreams. . . . I don't know, it was really sad.

New York *World-Telegram*
September 14, 1965

Gotham-Go-Round, Joseph X. Dever

. . . Clip-coiffed Edie Sedgwick upstaged *The Vampires* on screen at the Lincoln Center film festival last night as she swept in on the arm of pop artist Andy Warhol. Edie's outfit included her usual black leotard plus a trailing black ostrich-plumed cape like a camp version of Mme. Dracula. . . .

Life, November 26, 1965

FASHION:
The Girl with the Black Tights

This cropped-mop girl with the eloquent legs is doing more for black tights than anybody since Hamlet.

The Girl with the Black Tights

This cropped-mop girl with the eloquent legs is doing more for black tights than anybody since Hamlet. She is Edie Sedgwick, a 22-year-old New York socialite, great-granddaughter of the founder of Groton and currently the "superstar" of Andy Warhol's underground movies. She used to wear her tights with only a T-shirt for a top but lately has taken to wearing them with mid-thigh-length dresses—"the simplest, stretchiest ones I can find." Her style may not be for everybody, but its spirited wackiness is just right for lively girls with legs like Edie's.

A favorite outfit of Edie's last summer combined her black tights with a white-banded T-shirt and floppy hat.

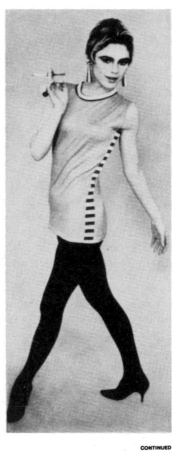

Though she still goes for an occasional T-shirt like the one at center by Cole ($4), Edie is now on a dress kick. The pale dress above, with halter neckline, is made of wool knit by Rudi Gernreich ($35). The checked silk print at far right, also by Gernreich, has a turtleneck that ties over the head ($155).

CONTINUED

Life fashion layout, November, 1965

RENÉ RICARD   I was one of Edie's escorts the night the limousines pulled up to The Scene, where she met Mick Jagger. I was there, and you don't know how I felt, seventeen years old. It was an extraordinary moment! Edie Sedgwick, the most famous girl in New York, and Mick Jagger, the most famous singer and the one everybody wanted to fuck! And there he was.

We were at least two hours late at The Scene. Edie was always brilliantly late; Andy would wait for her; he'd never say a word. He trusted her aristocratic instincts. He always said, "She knows what she's doing." When she'd arrive, it would always be when the tension was at its greatest. Everyone at The Scene was saying, "Edie's going to meet Mick. It's Mick and Edie . . . New York's big girl and England's big boy, and they're going to be together."

Edie was wearing the Gernreich dress she had modeled somewhere —breathtaking and in such great style—made of a cinnamon-colored, satiny football jersey. Her sleeves were pushed up and she wore a million bangle bracelets and very high, high heels. Earrings. We went down the stairs. Edie never, never carried anything when she went out on these evenings; I don't even remember a coat.

It was in front of the coat-check place that it happened. Mick Jagger was there and Edie was there, facing each other. She said, "How do you do? I just love your records." Well, what *do* you say? And he said, "Oh, thank you." Then, all of a sudden, there was an explosion of people and every corner of The Scene emptied into the tiny vestibule where we were standing. People were pushing and banging up against each other. The flashbulbs were blinding. Edie was able to get to the ladies' room. The poor thing! She was appalled by the crush. I don't remember what happened the rest of the night. All I know is that the picture of the two of them standing together in The Scene, the dingiest and most disgusting place in the world, is imprinted on my retina because it was so glamorous!

JOHN ANTHONY WALKER   I saw very little of Edie when she was in New York. I remember the irritation of once trying to phone her when she was at the top of the crest and being answered by a social secretary. Crazy, hard, tough chickie, I guess, in an iron-gray suit. I don't know what she had on, obviously, being at the other end of the line, but that was my speculation. I was angry because she kept saying, "Miss Sedgwick." Edie was not Miss Sedgwick . . . ever! I didn't want to make an appointment with a Miss Sedgwick, so I didn't.

ETHEL SCULL   Edie and Andy were at an opening at Lincoln Center with the cameramen as hysterical as if Mrs. Kennedy was making an entrance, lunging at the pair of them. Edie just preened . . . absolutely enjoying every minute of it. So did Andy, who sat humbly with his head down, wearing his leather jacket, and whispering to Edie what to do. Directing her. I could hear him say: "Stand up. Move around. Pose for them." He knew just the right moment for her to say, "We must go in. We must leave." Edie loved it. I once asked her, "How does it feel to be a superstar?" and she said, "It's frightening and glamorous and exciting at the same time. I wouldn't change it for anything! After the bad and sad times in my life, it's something I want to do." At intermission that night she stepped out into the aisle of the State Theatre in her black leotards, doing her kind of free-form dancing . . . no music . . . with the whole audience watching.

ROBERT RAUSCHENBERG   I met Edie at an opening. In any situation her physicality was so refreshing that she exposed all the dishonesty in the room. I was always intimidated and self-conscious when I talked to her or was in her presence because she was like art. I mean, she was an object that had been very strongly, effectively created.

SAM GREEN   Perhaps the greatest triumph of that year for both Edie and Andy was the Warhol Philadelphia exhibition. We stayed at Henry McIlhenny's house on Rittenhouse Square—Edie and Jane Holzer, Andy, Kenny Lane, Isabel Eberstadt, Taylor Mead, Gerard Malanga. A more bizarre group you couldn't have found in Philadelphia. On Sunday afternoon we all appeared at his house. We overlapped with the ladies' tea for the Philadelphia Ballet. We all sat as far away from the other group as we could in a huge sitting room filled with Charles X furniture and great French Impressionist paintings on the walls—both groups just horrified that the other was there.

The butler came over to our group. He was very tall and proper, very stuffy, and about seventy-five years old. He had this great book out. Very grandly he asked what we were going to have for breakfast the next morning. Gerard had never been asked that question before, so he didn't know what to reply; I wouldn't have, except I'd stayed there before; Edie knew what was going on, but I don't think Andy did. Of course, Taylor Mead began rolling his eyes and carrying on. Nobody answered the butler, and he finally had to insist. Staring at Taylor

Long earrings are fast coming back into fashion, a fact that delights Edie because she has been wearing them all along. This set by K.J.L. ($40) is seven inches long. "I swish them the way other girls swish their hair," says Edie. Her huge rings are also from K.J.L. Edie's evening dress of matte jersey resembles a stretched-out T-shirt (Rudi Gernreich, $110). Sleeves push into folds at wrists.

Life fashion photograph, November, 1965

Mead, he said, "Sir, may I have your order for breakfast in the morning?" Taylor looked him up and down—the forty ladies on the other side of the room sitting under Toulouse-Lautrec's Moulin Rouge painting were all waiting for his reply—and he said, "You." The butler, without a pause, said, "Yes, sir, and will there be anything else?" Taylor said, "Well, maybe I'd like some caviar and a quiche Lorraine." Andy wanted ice cream, and some flowers for his bathwater. Gerard wanted whatever Andy had.

WALTER HOPPS   That Philadelphia exhibition of Andy's was one of the most bizarre mob scenes I've ever witnessed. In New York, even with the avant-garde, the shows were relatively sedate . . . a kind of inured if not blasé quality about the presentation that kept them from being at all scandalous. But this out-of-town show of Warhol's! Quite astonishing! It was the first survey of all his work—held in the reasonably sedate setting of the little Institute of Contemporary Art there at the University of Pennsylvania. It was crazy. It was the first time I saw a young avant-garde artist have a show mobbed as if it were a movie premiere . . . all kinds of people clamoring to get at Andy as if he were a star. The kind of adulation, curiously, that would be associated with a Salvador Dali daydream. Dali would have loved to have pulled off such a thing and, as far as I know, never quite has.

SAM GREEN   For the preview the press came with their television cameras. It was the biggest thing that happened in Philadelphia *ever* . . . terribly sensational, with lots of cameras and people. The television lights in the crush began to fall into the paintings and tear them; people were crushed up against them.

So I realized that the public opening the next night was going to be even *more* frantic. At the last minute I decided the only thing to do was take down all the pictures so the paintings wouldn't be ruined. So the grand opening was in fact just people! Andy was mobbed. We were pretty scared because we arrived late from drinks and thousands were jammed into the museum. It was a mob scene and they were all out for blood. Somehow, once inside, we managed to get to an old iron staircase that led up to the ceiling—it hadn't been used for years and was sealed off at the top by the ceiling itself—and there we were, stuck up above the heads of this unruly crowd pushing and shoving and swarming and carrying on like the mob scene in *The Day of the Locust*. The police were keeping the crowds off the stairs with their sticks. Edie was wearing a Rudi Gernreich dress, a long thing like a

Edie meets Mick Jagger at the Scene

Edie at the Warhol exhibition, Philadelphia, 1965

T-shirt with sleeves that must have been twenty feet long, rolled up and bunched at the wrist. Then, in this incredible performance, she began baiting the audience: she began to let her sleeves down over the crowd like an elephant's trunk and then to draw them up again . . . teasing the crowd and working them up. And dancing and talking into the microphone, giving interviews.

While this was going on, an architectural graduate was trying to break through the fake ceiling above us so we could get out through the library private stacks, over the roof, and down the fire escape and out where the police could protect us. He was up there on the floor above with crowbars, ripping up the floor. That's how we escaped.

Edie was astonishing. She was really in show business, giving all those people something to look at . . . and it was crucial because they had been getting more and more unruly for hours, angry, first of all, because there were no pictures on the wall. So she, in fact, became the exhibition. Andy was just terrified, white with fear. Edie was scared to death but she was adoring every minute. She was in her element. She carried on this sort of forty-minute soliloquy into the microphone. She called out to them, "Oh, I'm so glad you all came tonight, and aren't we all having a wonderful time? And isn't Andy Warhol the most wonderful artist!"

PATTI SMITH   I went to Philadelphia to Warhol's opening at the museum. I came in from south Jersey on a train and I guess we took the bus. To me it was like slitting open the belly of a discotheque and walking in. Edie was coming down this long staircase. I think she had ermine wrapped around her; her hair was white, and her eyebrows black. She had on this real little dress. I think she had these two . . . unless I dreamed it . . . big white afghan hounds on black leashes with diamond collars, but that could be fantasy. It was all like being shot up. She seemed so connected. That's why I thought she was great. She had so much life in her. Her movement was fluid, and she was like little queenie.

People think it's all superficial, but I thought and still do that my consciousness about it was great. I always thought that the world of the upper class was really fantastic. I was from a working-class family with no affiliation ever with the middle class. So I really didn't resent the upper class. I thought they were great, their style, and the way they moved . . . and Bergdorf's. I thought Edie was great. I even had a crush. I wasn't into girls or anything, but I had a real crush on her.

ONDINE   There's no way people can stand outside a museum and chant "Edie and Andy." But they *were* out there, chanting and screaming. They were *that* relevant.

Edie told me afterwards: "Ondine, I cannot believe that they were out there chanting 'Edie and Andy! Edie and Andy!' " She said it was like an insane response from a whole culture. I said, "Well, that's what it is. These people are relating to you for a very good reason." If you're going to be that kind of culture hero, my *God!* Assume the mantle. Wear it! Be the culture hero. Edie was, literally, the queen of the whole scene. Totally the best of them all.

24

SAUCIE SEDGWICK   At first our father adored Edie's publicity. I've seen a letter in which Fuzzy refers to her as a Youthquaker—a phrase out of *Vogue*: "Edie is 22, going whither, God knows, but at a great rate!" But still, he lapped it up. He hoped she really would become an important actress.

Did you know Fuzzy actually met Andy Warhol at the River Club in Manhattan? Edie arranged it. Ernest Kolowrat would remember what happened. He was a kind of literary witness to the Sedgwicks . . . an audience. Ernie adored Fuzzy. He once said he'd love to marry Edie so he could live happily ever after and see Fuzzy.

ERNEST KOLOWRAT   At the River Club that evening Edie kept getting up from the table throughout dinner to telephone. Finally I asked, "What the hell's going on?" Fuzzy said, "Oh, she's trying to get Mr. Warhol to join us." It was a sudden brainstorm of Edie's that Fuzzy should meet Andy. It was the night of the Floyd Patterson–Cassius Clay fight in Las Vegas when Clay really taunted Patterson and made him suffer. Fuzzy was standing by the bar downstairs off the dining room watching the fight on television and flinching with every punch.

I remember two remarks Fuzzy made about Andy Warhol while we were all waiting. At about ten-thirty in the evening, when he still hadn't shown up, Fuzzy asked, "Do you suppose Mr. Warhol has had his breakfast yet?" Another one was: "Do you suppose the doorman should be told about him so he'll be let in?" Fuzzy wasn't specifically teasing Edie. I think it was sort of like whistling in the dark because he was nervous. Andy represented a threat and challenge at the same time. Fuzzy was a conservative, and the idea that perhaps Andy was sleeping with his daughter was very disturbing to him.

Fuzzy and I discussed the injustice of somebody like Warhol hitting it just at the right time with a good gimmick while Fuzzy was out on the ranch painting and sculpting wonderful stuff in a classical manner and not getting the recognition he should have. I think Fuzzy understood it, and outwardly he was never bitter. When he talked about it, he always smiled. But I knew that, inside, it was biting at him. I always thought the tragedy of his life was that he should have been the President of the United States, and when he settled on the more specific goals of painting, writing, and sculpture, he had a much more specific disappointment in not being adequately recognized in those fields. He was an immensely sensitive man who was being torn apart by what was happening. So you can imagine what an effect Andy Warhol's arrival must have had on him—when the gray eminence finally arrived.

Edie brought him in and introduced them. Andy shook hands very limply, very weakly. Fuzzy was very generous, awfully nice. Tried to get him drinks . . . Andy this and Andy that. Andy didn't say anything. He whispered a few things to Edie. The River Club, with that wonderful view of the East River, was very much Fuzzy's turf, and that made Andy very uncomfortable. I don't know whether he shakes all the time. Does he? Well, he was very nervous. Quivering. After the first five minutes Fuzzy didn't say much to Andy, he kind of gave up. We sat around chatting for about twenty minutes. Then Edie spirited Andy out of there—she said it was too much for him. Afterwards Fuzzy and I were standing at the bar and he said to me with a great sense of relief: "Why, the guy's a screaming fag. . . ."

Edie was very nervous that night. It was a tremendous event in her life, and I suspect in Andy's it was . . . almost devastating, meeting Fuzzy on his home ground. For anyone as internalized as Andy, someone as externalized as Fuzzy must have been very threatening.

ANDY WARHOL   The father was so handsome. He was telling us about these sculptures that he was doing—a big horse or something like that. Edie was happy to see him. It wasn't really anything that dif-

Francis Sedgwick with his cowboy statue

Andy Warhol in his studio

ferent. It was really nice. She was always saying funny things about him, but he seemed really great. He was, I guess, the most handsome older man I've ever seen. She might have said he was sick with some- thing . . . I couldn't believe her. People always say things and you don't know if they're true or not.

SAUCIE SEDGWICK   Edie was looking for an alternative. Andy War- hol was a kind of alternative convention. She said once that she didn't understand why our parents felt so threatened: she wasn't doing any- thing against them, she just wanted to find a new way of life, not *their* way of life.

But her "new life" became, in a bizarre way, a reflection of many of the features of her life with my mother and father. It revolved around a dangerous, powerful man who was in control of everything in sight and who dictated the style: We do this, we don't go to that; we go to these places, we don't go to those places; this is where we are secure and those people out there don't exist. Even the inversion of the sexual theme was there. Edie felt a strong sexual relationship to our father. But it was impossible. The same thing was true with War- hol. It was impossible. He was androgynous, as Edie herself was. A kind of perverse Peter Pan.

I don't know if Edie really understood that Andy and his ilk were going to inherit the earth. But intuitively, she must have felt that it was possible. My father's world still had tremendous power because of convention and tradition and so forth, although his art had been out since Daniel Chester French. But once you said: "Well, that's not the way it is, and that's not the game, and those are not the rules— after all, we're all just people," that must have been a hydrogen bomb to my father! That rejection of rhetoric, that deadly banality made Andy a final weapon against my father. There was no way my father could get to Andy Warhol.

JOEL SCHUMACHER   There were other father figures in New York at that time—the acid doctors. A friend of mine—well, an ex-friend of mine—told me about this terrific doctor where you'd get these vitamin shots—Dr. Charles Roberts. I used to run into Edie there. I went one night, got this shot, and it was the most wonderful shot in the world. I had the answer: I mean, it gives you that rush. There were vitamins in it, and a very strong lacing of methedrine. I'd never heard of methedrine or speed. They never told you what was in the shot anyway. It was a slow evolution. I went there first and got a shot. I went a week later and got another one. And maybe one week later I was feeling kind of down, and I went twice a week. Eventually I was going there every day, and then I was going two or three times a day. Then I went four times a day. Then I started shooting up myself.

Dr. Roberts was the perfect father image. His office, down on Forty-eighth Street on the East Side, was very reputable-looking, with attractive nurses, and he himself looked like a doctor in a movie. He was always telling me of his wonderful experiments with LSD, delivering babies, curing alcoholics . . . and he was going to open a health farm and spa where all this was going to go on . . . and naturally he was stoned all the time, too. He wasn't a viper. I just think he was so crazy, he truly thought he was going to help the world. He wasn't out to kill anyone. *We* were the ones going in and getting the shots. I

mean, anyone can set up a booth on the side of the road reading: I'M
GIVING ARSENIC SHOTS HERE, but *you* have to stop and take them.

Over the years that he was riding high, tons of people went to see
Dr. Roberts. But there was a little crowd of favorites. When you were
a favorite, it meant that you were allowed special privileges. Even if
the waiting room was filled with twenty people, you got right in. When
you were addicted, being able to get right in was very important. You
got bigger shots; you got shot up more than anybody else, and
you became more of an addict. It was wonderful to be part of this
special group. Edie fit right in. The minute she hit there, she became
a special Dr. Roberts person.

I'll give you a description of what it was like to go to Dr. Roberts.
The time is two-thirty in the afternoon. I'm going back for my second
shot of the day. I open the door. There are twenty-five people in the
waiting room: businessmen, beautiful teenagers on the floor with long
hair playing guitars, pregnant women with babies in their arms, de-
signers, actors, models, record people, freaks, non-freaks . . . waiting. Everyone is waiting for a shot, so the tension in the office is beyond
belief.

Lucky you, being a special Dr. Roberts person who can whip right
in without waiting. Naturally, there's a terribly resentful, tense moment as you rush by because you're going to get your shot.

You attack one of the nurses. By that I mean you grab her and say,
"Listen, Susan! Give me a shot!" You're in the corridor with your pants
half off, ready to get the shot in your rear. Meanwhile Dr. Roberts
comes floating by. Dr. Roberts has had a few shots already, right? So
in the middle of this corridor he decides to tell you his complete plan
to rejuvenate the entire earth. It's a thirteen-part plan, but he has lots
of time to tell it to you, and as the shot starts to work—Susan having
given it to you—you have a lot of time to listen.

In Dr. Roberts' room would be Edie . . . so thin that she cannot be
given her shot standing up; she has to lie down on her stomach. It was
a big shot—all those vitamins, niacin, methedrine, God knows what
else—for a little girl, so she had to take it lying down.

Meanwhile everyone who's back in the corridor for the second or
third time that day complains that the shots they received that morning haven't worked. Out in the waiting room you can hear the people
complaining that they haven't even received their first shot yet.

And Dr. Roberts is still going on. In the middle of his thirteen-part
plan he decides to tell you about a movie he saw on television . . . in
detail. You, however, are telling him your ideas for whatever *you're*

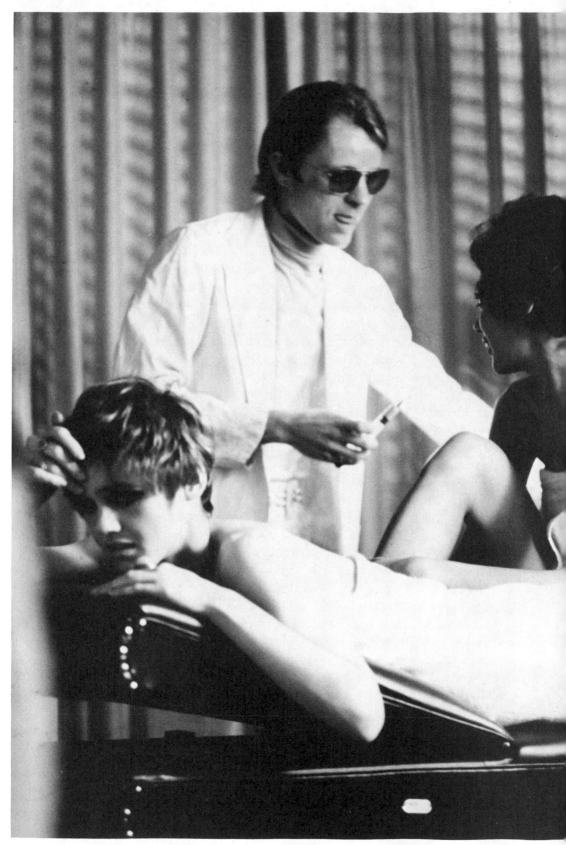

Edie at Dr. Roberts' from *Ciao! Manhattan*

going to do. But then Dr. Roberts begins to describe his idea for a plastic Kabuki house. Someone else is showing his sketches for redesigning the Boeing 707 with a psychedelic interior. Big doings at Dr. Roberts' all the time.

Now you decide to go back out through the waiting room, right? Now you have all the time in the world. Life is a breeze. You've used the sun lamp. I mean, you were in a great rush when you came in; now, finally, you decide you'll leave.

But there in the room are all these people who are *not* Dr. Roberts' special people and who still haven't been serviced. They're there to spend as much money as you have, but they're not part of the "in" crowd. So they're drifting off into craziness because they haven't gotten their shots. A couple of people are wandering around . . . their poor systems are so riddled with the methedrine they got half an hour ago they feel is not working that they've come back for what Dr. Roberts calls "the booster." The basic Dr. Roberts shot goes from ten dollars to fifteen dollars. As your resistance to the drug gets to the point of diminishing returns, you move on up. There is a big shot for twenty-five dollars, and if it doesn't work, you go right back and get "the booster" for five dollars. That's what some of these poor people are doing—standing out there waiting for the booster. But *you* . . . you are flying high, having just had your twenty-five-dollar special, and you walk out into the outer office and say: "Hi. Oh, *hi!* What a beautiful sweater! Gee, you look wonderful! How *are* you? Oh, hi! Isn't it *wonderful* to see you! What's happening?"

Before leaving, I'd often go and find Edie in Dr. Roberts' sauna. If we'd been up all night on drugs, the sauna and steam bath were wonderful things. We'd go out and walk for blocks and blocks . . . just be together, because we didn't know what we were saying half the time.

The speed thing was so wonderful because everyone was walking around scared to death . . . scared because they couldn't sustain that pace. And so these shots from Dr. Roberts and all those other speed doctors gave you a false sense of being together. You could face everybody when you went out at night. You could dance all night. It was like "the answer." Nobody knew much about speed in those days.

Once Edie's mother came to Dr. Roberts'. I remember she was on crutches. She looked like Betty Crocker—gray hair with a little hairnet, a blue print dress, and little glasses. She looked like a librarian from the Midwest standing next to Edie with her cut-off blond hair with the dark roots, thigh-high boots, a mini-skirt, and a kind of chubby fur jacket that looked like it was made out of old cocker spaniels. There they were—the two of them. Mrs. Sedgwick had come to see if Dr. Roberts was taking good care of her little girl . . . and I guess he must have conned her, because Edie kept going there. I guess the parents paid for her treatment: it cost a lot for those shots.

EMILE DE ANTONIO   Her mother didn't seem to know anything about Edie's life—except that it was no good. One day in the Factory, Edie said, "I've got to go and see my mother or else she's coming here. She wants to put me away!" I said, "Is there anything I can do to help?" She said, "Come with me." So we drove to her grandmother's on Park Avenue. Edie was afraid to go up to the apartment. So her mother came down. We all stood in the lobby. Her mother had this stick . . . a cane. She seemed unnecessarily harsh to me—I mean, in the way she was speaking to Edie. The discussion was about Edie's rights; there was talk about hospitals. What I really remember is Edie's mother hitting the floor with the cane with vehemence.

Edie seemed moderately rational; she talked very nicely. You had to know she wasn't, but at the same time she was just as rational as the rest of those people seemed to be.

RICHIE BERLIN   Edie took this rush of vitamins . . . so many vitamins that she smelled of them. It was during that whole era, darling, of "Where shall we go before we go to the Hippopotamus and before we go to Le Club?" I mean, everybody in the eyelash set went to Dr. Roberts to get their hearts started! To keep thin and keep it going. I kept saying, "I will *not* have a shot. I will not . . . that's all there is to it." Well, after my first one I walked all the way to the Village. I flew around the house. I cleaned. I charged in stores. I didn't even know I was in Bloomingdale's; I just had to acquire more and more things. I wrote notes. I wrote a sixty-five-page letter telling somebody I wanted him. I knew exactly where my head was going the whole time. If anyone had asked, "What do you mean, Richie? What do you mean? Get to the point," I would have said, "I have to write you a note." If they had said, "My God, you know, you are a very close friend of mine. I am not at my age, at thirty-nine, going into the bathroom to sit on the john and wait for a *note!*" I would have said, "Well, you just have to. That's all!"

CHERRY VANILLA   Often people got introduced to Dr. Roberts as a present. Going to him was the great gift of the time. If you really loved someone, you took him to Dr. Roberts as a gift and let him feel the feeling. Or if you were trying to make somebody, you'd go around to Dr. Roberts, and after the shots you'd get very oversexed and you'd fuck. People used him in that way. His office was a social focal point.

I've forgotten who took me there first. Someone said, "Hey, Cherry Vanilla, let's go over to Dr. Roberts'." Cherry Vanilla is a name I thought up when somebody asked what I'd call myself if I wrote a column for a rock magazine, and I said, "Cherry Vanilla . . . scoops for you!" Everybody loved it. Anyway, someone said, "Come on, Cherry Vanilla," and we went over to Dr. Roberts'. I was fascinated. All these freaky people were sitting around, rapping their brains out in the office, in the middle of the day.

Then Dr. Roberts moved his office. He had a sauna and a big mirrored room with a dance floor and a barre. Four floors. Never completed. You'd get your shot in the hallway, sometimes from the nurse. You and your friend could go in together and both get them at once, and even give each other shots. It was all big fun-and-games.

I became like an acid queen. I loved it. My looks got crazier and crazier. I started getting into things like pink wigs, teasing them up to make them real big and like bubbles. I'd wear goggle glasses and real crazy make-up: spidery lashes and white lips, and micro-minis. I saw a micro-mini on Edie and immediately started cutting everything off. Kenneth Jay Lane earrings. Big Robert Indiana LOVE earrings . . . giant love paintings on my ears. Little bikini undies, a band around the top; and we made these silver dresses that were just silver strings hanging on us. I was surrounded by a lot of gay boys in designing and decorating who would always give me a hand in pulling some look together. I would go out half naked with see-through things. You took a scarf and wrapped it around you and thought you were dressed.

I gave Dr. Roberts a shot once. In the ass, in his office about five o'clock in the morning. I had been playing records at Aux Puces—I was the disc jockey there—and he had come around to visit and said, "If you come back to my office with me, I'll give you a shot." It was a freebie, which was nice because those shots were not cheap.

I really got into having a needle in the ass. Just the feeling of it. I got into the pain of it. You got the shot, then this taste in your mouth, and you got a rush and you knew you were getting high. It was all very sexual in a way, and very "in" and social and stylish to do it. So I went back to his office with him and I gave him one and he gave me one.

I don't know what he shot me up with, but it was something I had certainly never had before. I was really very numbed. Maybe it was cocaine. Sometimes he would shoot you with LSD. You never knew what he was going to shoot you with. He'd throw a little surprise in every once in a while. So we got involved in a rather heavy sex encounter.

All of a sudden there was blood everywhere. I was bleeding like crazy. He laughed and said, "Oh, I think you should go and see a doctor." Very bizarre. I started freaking out. I thought, "Oh, my God, this man has done something to me. He's killed me. I'm going to die here in his office, all shot up with drugs, and it's going to be a disgrace and terrible." I told him I had to get out. He said, "No, no, you can't leave. I'll fix you. I'll give you a shot." I said, "No, no, no more shots!" I got dressed. I never thought he was going to let me out. Perhaps he was scared I would go to the police.

When I did get out, I ran around the corner to Aux Puces. Some of the staff used to hang out there very late at night taking LSD. Sure enough, they were there. We called doctors. We couldn't get anybody. Then the bleeding began to subside suddenly—about seven in the morning. I never actually knew what happened. I had been cut inside —scratched with something, fingernails or jewelry . . . probably by accident. I think we both just got carried away.

Of course, I never frequented Dr. Roberts' any more. That really kind of brought me to. I think that's the last time I ever had speed in my life, or whatever it was Dr. Roberts gave me. I never touched a diet pill or anything like that ever again.

Until then, it had been like living on the edge of life. It promised a good life without any tomorrow. You really believed that you were going to travel in this bubble right out to the end of the stratosphere. You weren't going to have to cope with the normal structures of life and getting older and making a living. Life was supposed to be completely different.

EDIE SEDGWICK (from tapes for the movie *Ciao! Manhattan*) *Dr. Roberts says, "Hello, girls . . . how are we today? Are you all ready? Okay. Hop up. Put all your weight on this leg. Okay? Ready? My god, this rear end looks like a battlefield."*

You want to hear something I wrote about the horror of speed? Well, maybe you don't, but the nearly incommunicable torments of speed, buzzerama, that acrylic high, horrorous, yodeling, repetitious echoes of an infinity so brutally harrowing that words cannot capture the devastation nor the tone of such a vicious nightmare. Yes, I'm even getting paranoid, which is a trip for me. I don't really dig it, but there it is.

It's hard to choose between the climactic ecstasies of speed and cocaine. They're similar. Oh, they are so fabulous. That fantabulous sexual exhilaration. Which is better, coke or speed? It's hard to choose. The purest speed, the purest coke, and sex is a deadlock.

Speeding and booze. That gets funny. You get chattering at about fifty miles an hour over the downdraft, and booze kind of cools it. It can get very funny. Utterly ridiculous. It's a good combination for a party. Not for an orgy, though.

Speedball! Speed and heroin. That was the first time I had a shot in each arm. Closed my eyes. Opened my arms. Closed my fists, and jab, jab. A shot of cocaine and speed, and a shot of heroin. Stripped off all my clothes, leapt downstairs, and ran out on Park Avenue and two blocks down it before my friends caught me. Naked. Naked as a lima bean. A speedball is from another world. It's a little bit dangerous. Pure coke, pure speed, and pure sex. Wow! The ultimate in climax. Once I went over to Dr. Roberts for a shot of cocaine. It was very strange because he wouldn't tell me what it was and I was playing it cool. It was my first intravenous shot, and I said, "Well, I don't feel it." And so he gave me another one, and all of a sudden I went blind. Just flipped out of my skull! I ended up wildly balling him. And flipping him out of his skull. He was probably shot up . . . he was always shooting up around the corner anyway.

SUSAN WRIGHT BURDEN   We were invited up to Hyannis Port to a Kennedy party and we all went over to Dr. Roberts' to have shots to get up for the trip. Bob Neuwirth, Edie, and me . . . can't remember who else went. That summer Dr. Roberts had an office on Long Island. He was always very into getting people up for what they were going to do. Whenever one of his patients was going to appear on TV, they'd spend the day at his office and do the sauna to get prepared for the event. The doctor was in on the trip to Hyannis Port and he planned the super-shot for everybody.

Somebody had sent a plane down for us. We were all terribly late. We didn't have our wardrobes quite together. The plane waited at the airport for a couple of hours until we turned up.

BOB NEUWIRTH   It was Joan Kennedy's birthday party in Hyannis Port. They wanted us because of the ladies—Susan Burden, Edie. Big Kennedy-compound birthday party. Tents set up in the back yard, local inept rock group of sixteen-year-old kids, smashing guest list.

I can remember Lillian Hellman smoking cigarette after cigarette. Jackie. Sam Spiegel, the producer. But it wasn't Hollywoodish. It was an East Coast kind of party. It was a foggy night, right? I was the only one who wasn't dressed properly. I had on summer clothes—a light turtleneck. The only other person there who wasn't dressed was this guy in a black Japanese bathrobe who turned out to be Sargent Shriver. I spent most of the evening in front of the fireplace at Teddy Kennedy's drinking and discussing this great plan I had for giving free eight-millimeter cameras to the ghetto in order to get a good inside view. I was very hot on people making their own movies.

Edie was a smash. She had absolutely no respect for anyone; she had herself a great time. She was a scamp, but totally social—one of the few people in contact with all the elements of the party.

26

ONDINE   One day in the Factory I said, "This is ridiculous, but I'm penniless. I'll do anything." Edie said, "Oh, I need a maid." Andy said, "Oh, do you think you need a maid?" Edie said, "I do." So I became her French maid. My salary was something like thirty dollars a week, which was enough, I guess, for a male maid. I needed just enough money to buy amphetamine and I was fine. You see, the dealers used to come to the Factory. They were nice—not street dealers. Very elegant. Rotten Rita would appear frequently. He looked like an advertising executive who'd gone awry; he'd come out with this big soprano voice. There was one called the Turtle. He only sold drugs to friends—three hundred dollars a pound for amphetamine. Almost always amphetamine, never anything else. He was called the Turtle because he had one bone missing from his back, so his neck did not quite appear above his collar.

Those were the days I lived in Central Park. I'd wake up by the lakes and swim in them. I was really out of it—very far out. Then I'd go to the West Side, where I had a couple of opera friends who did nothing but listen to music and shoot up, and after that to Edie's house on the other side of the Park in the Sixties.

She'd invariably be asleep. I would have to wake her up. That was my main duty as a French maid. She was barbiturated and there was no way she could get up except resentfully. I had this nervous ring on the bell—zzz-zzz-zzz-zzz. She would finally answer it: "That you,

Ondine?" I'd say, "Yeah, it's me." When I got up there, she'd start coming to and ask if I had any amphetamine. I'd give her some and she'd be fine. In her leotards she'd start doing her exercises. Then we'd play opera and stuff. I introduced her to the world of opera. I would always play Callas. I'd make her something to eat. She mostly ate roast-beef sandwiches and potato salad. A couple of mornings I made eggs. She'd sniff the amphetamine or put it in her coffee. That would start her to come alive. She'd begin to talk. She would open the *I Ching*. We threw an *I Ching*, the two of us collectively, and it was called "Pushing Upward, No. 46." It was a difficult one and really very strange. When we played the *I Ching*, I'd put on her earrings. Do you remember her earrings? The most fabulous earrings, and she'd say, "Here, take them." I'd put them on for the *I Ching*. We loved the *I Ching*. It was very serious about rulers, and about being truthful to the Prince. At that point we thought Warhol was the Prince. It's a very strange book.

We sat on her hippopotamus, called Wallow. It was this big leather hippo. He was so divine. Or was it a rhinoceros? I have no idea, but it was one of those things. We'd talk about Wallow. Then she'd go to the Victrola and play Joan Sutherland's *Traviata* and next I'd play Callas' *Traviata* just to see; then we'd play the Beatles. This went on and on and on. And phone calls; every minute there were phone calls. Dates. People. Thousands of people who wanted her to do layouts for this and that.

My duties as a French maid were really just to get her up for all of this, give her a cup of coffee, and then talk to her. Mostly talk to her. Because she *had* a maid. She had a colored woman—I don't remember what her name was. Jane? Once I whispered to Edie, "I'm going to put some amphetamine in her tea." Edie said, "Oh, that would be fabulous!" So we put this drug in her tea, and the woman started vacuuming the house, but she didn't have the vacuum plugged in. The opera was playing so loud she didn't miss that there was no sound from the vacuum cleaner. She went nuts on this one little rug. She vacuumed it for like two hours. She was *so* involved in getting spots off this and that. She polished the faucets in the bathroom. She cleaned out everything in there. We sat there for two hours roaring. After she finished, she said, "Oh, I'm just so exhausted, I really need a beer or something. I don't know why I feel this way. I just want to talk." So we gave her a beer, and we had this marvelous conversation with this just wonderful person . . . talked about her life and husband and all these people. Just on and on.

I was Edie's French maid for about four months. After I stopped,

Victor became her French maid. Edie constantly accused him of steal-ing things . . . which he did or did not do, I have no idea. She could be mean to people. I remember her keeping Victor in the bathroom for about an hour and a half, trying to find a diamond ring that she had misplaced. *She* had misplaced it, but she accused him of stealing it. "It's got to be in the bathroom!" Edie really used him. "Get in that bath-room. Look for that ring!" She was marvelous for him. It was just what he wanted. Everyone did it to him.

You won't find Victor now. Down the hatch. He was a very pretty guy, but he was just out of it. He was just totally crackers. His favorite movie star was Jane Russell, the pin-up star. So *he* liked to be pinned up on walls. He was very famous for that. People would come in, shoot him up, and pin him on a wall . . . like he was the original cruci-fixion.

Then I moved to the Upper East Side into a friend's house who was probably the most original and fabulous prostitute in New York City. Her name was Leah. All I could think about was Leah. Women: Leah! I entered into a love relationship with her. I'd catch her on the side with girls, making it. I found out later that Edie and Leah were very good friends, and I had this feeling that she was making it with Edie and another girl, too. Just that quiet thing where nobody knows about it. Just not spoken about. Women do that so well, but men make a big stink about it. Leah owns a big castle in France now. She's totally insane. Warhol tried to film her once and she smashed every camera he had. "I told you not to come into my bedroom. It's where I work."

There were orgies downstairs in Edie's building. Three females and three men, and the men would all be having sex—the girls sort of watching . . . everyone so drugged and drunk. Edie and I went. Leah telephoned me there one night. She was screaming. I asked, "What's the matter?" She said, "Someone is fucking me in the ass," and she started yelling that peculiar painful yell. I said, "Get over here quickly!" She came and joined in. I'll never forget the look on Edie's face. She was in Wonderland. Just demented. She couldn't believe it . . . just freaked by the scene.

Often Edie and I would talk about how marvelous it was being with Warhol. Things would come up. Other people were telling her that she should concern herself with being a very famous star . . . putting it in her mind that she was the greatest thing since Greta Garbo or Mari-lyn Monroe—she owed it to herself to be that famous. She didn't know what to do. She began to get qualms. She told me I was her guru at one point, and I said, "I refuse the challenge. I'll be nobody's guru, darling.

The back room at Max's Kansas City

I can't even guru myself." She really wanted some guidance very badly; she wanted a spiritual moment. And nobody gave it to her. I just wasn't qualified. I felt the greatest thing I could do for her was to be her friend. Strictly her friend.

RICHIE BERLIN   I used to visit Edie in that apartment. I wondered from the first about her. You know, what's her scene? What is she into? Is she straight? Is she gay? Is she Edie Sedgwick who charges and shops a lot and has fun? Is she Andy Warhol's superstar? I thought that was a putdown, but it really held her up.

I heard her talk and the tone of her voice. Is she well born? Is she a buttonhook child? Somebody once told me that'd be a fine name for a book. *A Buttonhook Child.* That's said of certain children. Right? The smocked dress; the buttonhook to do your shoes. "Isn't she absolutely darling?"

Edie had eyes as big as teacups. She'd bat them twice and immediately you'd say, "Oh, darling, come in," and you'd run her a Vitabath or whatever. She'd call the drugstore downstairs, "Tuna salad heavy on the mayo, hold this, hold that," and then she'd ask, "Can I have a poke, please?" and you'd give her a poke and then she'd ask, "Do you have anything to wear?" She was my size, right? The phone would be ringing, a thousand times, and I would say, "She's ready. She's here." She'd be dressed and looking fantastic in my clothes. When she was poked up and ready to go out, she was La Sedgwick. But I said to myself every time she left, "What a loss. What abuse," as if I were my own mother taking over my head.

What fun she was to be with! All my friends are the most divine mixture of horrors. Darling, you have no idea what it was like, to get up, get into a Donald Brooks dress, put my Zuckerman coat on, get my gold shoulder earrings out, get my Margaret Jerrould pumps on, and go around with Edie to Lord & Taylor's on the ground floor with my paranoia and tell them I'm rich . . . "Mrs. Richard Berlin's daughter. No, don't be silly! I don't carry identification with me. You can call up *all* the stores; they know me instantly. I've *got* to have those things," and those things would start coming down the chute. Edie would go with me on the "trips"—a Hedda Hopper, a shoplifting tour. She'd pop those eyes at them—the storekeepers waiting for the merchandise to be packaged, and I'd always be waiting for that click to come down the tubes telling the manager that we were to freeze at the counter. My picture was on the cash register of the Notions Department of Bloomingdale's.

To go into a store was like Broadway. This was it! You'd go in and you're up for the Academy Awards on the ground floor. It was their number against yours. There was nothing to make you feel marvelous like a quick purchase. Bath products. A little of this, a little of that. Edie didn't care. She'd say, "Listen, we'll go and get these fabulous things. We can trade them for cash for Dr. Roberts."

I used to trade Daddy's old Knight of Malta medals for vials of amphetamine. Eva Braun's barrette she got from Hitler that he'd bought somewhere. Brigid sold Daddy's Calvin Coolidge letters for twenty-five dollars. Anything for a poke or a pill. One day I swallowed the cufflinks from my new Brooks Brothers shirt. Somebody said, "Here," and I took them as if they were Miltowns or something. Had to have a pill. I've got to get my heart started.

EDIE SEDGWICK (from tapes for the movie *Ciao! Manhattan*) *I think drugs are like strawberries. That was something I was very much a part of, but at the same time there's that incredible nightmare paranoia . . . it drives human beings crazy. It frightened me to see it around me . . . I had everything that could be moved stolen by speed freaks. Things began to disappear. The Queen Bee Speedfreaks and Amphetamine Annie had found out where my apartment was. All my jewelry was stolen and all my expensive clothes. Dior, Balenciaga . . . just tons of originals. By the way, have you heard anything about my furs? Everybody's wearing them.*

GENEVIEVE CHARBIN When I lived with Edie, she would give me a pill in the morning to get me up faster so I could start doing things for her, like running to Cambridge Chemists to buy her eighteen cases of make-up or going to the laundry for her. My first image of the day was this little voice saying, "Genevieve, here's your breakfast." I'd look up and see Edie arrive with her hair all upside down, in a dirty negligee, with that funny little bird walk, holding a tray with an impeccable breakfast on it—orange juice, a little napkin, eggs and toast, and a little plate with a pill on it, next to the coffee and the orange juice— the first thing within reach so you'd be sure to get it right away.

Edie was not the kind of person you could leave sitting in the corner of a room reading a book by herself. There was no peace to be had. We'd cackle about the night before. Most of the day was taken up with talking to Andy on the phone, both of us. Andy was a real blabbermouth on the phone. He carried on. He told you every little thing he did from the second he woke up. He would compose exercises with Edie. Andy did one hundred pull-ups a morning—which does not surprise me because he had an incredibly strong back.

Then there were calls; interviews. People were interested at that point. Men from the night before she'd given her name to. She never would go out with anybody but Andy at night. So it was funny listening to her get out of these entanglements. She'd claim to be busy; she'd say she had to go to the Factory and shoot a scene. She kept turning to me: "How do I get out of this?" That was very sweet.

We really did not do much during the day. Edie would spend hours doing her face. She did it very well, because she could go out for twelve hours, leaving in the afternoon and not returning until the next dawn, a hundred parties in between, and her make-up would never budge. Absolutely flawless. I remember waiting two hours for her to get out of the bathroom. I didn't want to disturb the star putting on her face. There were a few unspoken rules, and that was one of them. The last thing that went on was the gold glitter. Gold dust. She loved the way it glittered. She would come in and say, "Let me give you some of this," and she'd put it all over my cheeks. "Isn't it terrific?" In the late afternoon we would leave for the Factory. It was always very busy there. Then we would go to the parties at night.

BOB NEUWIRTH   The great hangout in the city was Max's Kansas City. It was at a strange location—Park Avenue South and Seventeenth Street—for a kind of artists' restaurant. The guy who owned it had been a manager of a steakhouse downtown. He picked the location so you wouldn't get mugged, but he opened it with an eye for a clientele of painters and writers from downtown. During the Pop Sixties it became a famous place to hang out. As soon as it became public knowledge, there was a lot of business. But it was terrific because people in coats and ties would be kept waiting out on the sidewalk while artists and scroungy people were given tables immediately. It was part of the whole appeal of the place. The back room became a base for Andy.

A close friend brought Bobby Kennedy to Max's to meet Edie. Bobby only stayed a few minutes because his bodyguard ordered him out of there. He had smelled something mysterious in the air. Bobby was having a good time. He was ready to boogie. Bill Barry, his bodyguard, suddenly said, "Senator, we must leave." Bobby looked surprised and a little annoyed. "But I've just ordered a drink," he said. Bill Barry's voice hardened and became urgent. "Senator, we must get out of here at once," and he whisked Bobby out of Max's. Apparently he had smelled marijuana. We sat there astonished. It all seemed ridiculous.

HELEN HARRINGTON   You remember the lady who killed herself— Andrea Feldman? Loved to take her blouse off in Max's Kansas City all the time. She took her shirt off so often to show her tits that the people sitting around Max's would say: "Oh, not your tits *again!*" One night Jane Fonda was sitting in the back room and here came Andrea hopping across the tables with her shirt off . . . everyone calling out, "Booooo!" They'd seen them so often. Eric Emerson was always taking his pants down and showing his ass and his cock, with again everyone saying, "Ughh, must we see *that* again?!" I liked Eric. He didn't quite know what to do. He was one of the creatures that made the atmosphere there sort of special. He got more bonkers as the years progressed. You'd see him and he'd be drinking a glass of piss! He finally OD'd.

VIVA   Like many of the people who hung out at Max's, Andrea Feldman had no money and no place to live, even when she had a leading role in a Warhol film. She finally demanded money and said that Andy gave her some cheap bracelets instead . . . when she threw them on the floor, somebody beat her up. Next thing I heard she was in a mental institution. Next thing I knew Andrea had jumped out the fourteenth-floor window of her uncle's apartment, clutching a bible and a crucifix. She left behind a number of suicide notes, several addressed to Andy. The only phrase that escaped censoring was, "Goodbye, I'm going for the Big Time."

PAUL ROTHCHILD   The back room at Max's was pure theater. People dressed for it. Those red fluorescent lights. The first really broad expression of frank homosexuality in New York City I saw there at Max's—embracing, kissing, great jealousies displayed for the world to see. Before, it had been a confused, almost proper, European kind of homosexuality, but with the Warhol wave it became very theatrical, direct, and out front. Then at the tables you saw the seedier side— people shooting up coke, speedballs, the great pill contest: "How many

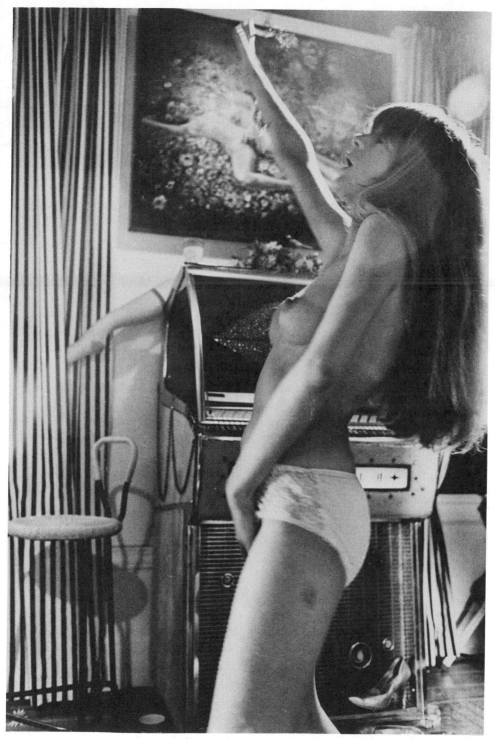

Andrea Feldman

could you drop at Max's and still walk out?" Though I never saw Edie shoot up there, she was one of the queens of Max's. No question about it. She evoked a kind of warmth. Everybody felt very tender toward her . . . protective and cozying her.

TERRY SOUTHERN   If you wanted to describe the back room of Max's in a, God forbid, negative way, you'd use words like "desperation" or "hysteria"—that sort of thing. Going the positive route, of course, you'd talk about "sensitive," "intense," or just plain "hilarious." It was like a carnivorous arena. There was always this buzz along the Rialto: "Andy's coming! Andy's coming!" . . . all on this weird level of "Maybe I'll catch Andy's eye and he'll make this ultimate film or painting of me . . . I'll be the next Edie or the next Baby Jane."

There was a moment, a brief, flaring instant when Edie was like really the tops. She would walk in the back room of Max's Kansas City and everybody would whisper: "Here comes Edie." Fuck fantastic. Much more important in her head than winning some dumb-dumb award like the Oscar.

27

SANDY KIRKLAND   There were problems. The others would turn off Edie and not give her the attention she needed. Part of her understood, but she was still very hurt by it. I can see her in my mind's eye at the back of the Factory, where there was a bathroom, back there alone, abandoned, and she'd be dancing around, spaced out, weird.

HENRY GELDZAHLER   I suppose Edie thought of herself as a caterpillar that had turned into a butterfly. She had thought of herself as just another kid in a big, rather unhappy family, and all of a sudden the spotlights were on her and she was being treated as something very, very special, but inside she felt like a lump of dirt. Then when she was being paid less attention to, she didn't know who she was. That possibility of destruction was built into the weakness of her personality. We have to get used to the reality that we're alone. If you can't get used to it, then you go mad. And she went kind of mad.

I came to her apartment a couple of times, which I thought very grim. It was very dark, and the talk was always about how hungover she was, or how high she was yesterday, or how high she would be tomorrow. She was very nervous, very fragile, very thin, very hysterical. You could hear her screaming even when she wasn't screaming—this sort of supersonic whistling.

GERARD MALANGA   The first hints of the split between Andy and Edie came with the making of the film *My Hustler* in July, 1965. Chuck Wein conceived of this film for Andy. He didn't write anything in it for Edie—not surprising since it was a homosexual film—but he did include a brief sequence with Genevieve Charbin. I don't know what Chuck's motives were, but Edie complained.

DANNY FIELDS   She wanted to move on. She was as great in the little movies made in the Factory as anyone was in a four-million-dollar movie from MGM. So Edie used to wonder: "Should I go to Hollywood? Should I break away from Andy? Should I get a real agent?" People were toying around with her. All sorts of leads. But she'd meet them and come back and say, "Oh, God, they're such assholes! I can't work with them. I have to be with my friends. I want to be with people I love. I could never love those people. They're all stupid. Morons. Forget it."

That's not your most professional of attitudes. I'd say to Edie: "You *have* to do it. If you want to make it in show business, you have to deal with morons. It doesn't matter if they don't like you for exactly the right reasons, or pamper you the right way, or are too stupid to appreciate you for what you really are."

But it was hard to get away from the Andy thing. It was so much fun; it was party time. She felt she couldn't make the transition into the real crap you have to deal with in order to make it.

Once you were in those silver aluminum rooms in the Factory, you were in the world . . . like going through the looking glass in a way . . . a point of contact where everything is happening and one is recognized and creative.

RONALD TAVEL   Edie started to annoy me when she asked what the scripts were about. I'd say to her, "It's not your business. Besides, I have to sit down and think about it myself. I am not altogether sure, and we're working on intuition. If you make me sit down and really think through what I'm doing, you'll spoil the process. It's coming off the top of my head and I'm letting it flow very quickly and I don't want to think about what it means. I hope it means nothing."

She would object right away and say, "I don't know what that means, to say it doesn't mean anything."

I'd ask, "Well, can you conceptualize that we're trying to work on a film that will say nothing? That's the point: to say *nothing*."

Edie performing with the Velvet Underground at Delmonico's, for the New York Society
for Clinical Psychiatry, 1966. Lou Reed, Edie, John Cale, and Gerard Malanga

She'd say, "No, I can't."

Once, when she saw the script of *Shower*—probably the best one-acter I've ever written, in which Edie and Roger Trudeau spend the whole thing in the shower—she started screaming, "I will not be a spokesman for Tavel's perversities!" That was the first time I'd ever heard my work described as perverse. I was to hear it in years to come from some of our best-known critics . . . but that was the first time anyone *cared* enough to say such a thing. "I will not be in it!" Edie cried, and marched out. "I won't do this!"

Actually, I had the feeling that Edie didn't really mind *Shower* as much as she said . . . that she'd been pushed to complain by Chuck Wein, who wanted me out of the Factory to get my job as writer-director of the films.

The end really came when Edie tore up the script of a movie called *Space*, saying she wasn't going to memorize anything. She started to read a few of her lines: "What is all this about? How stupid!" and tore it up, right in front of everybody. That's when I walked out. That may have been the last time I saw her.

RENÉ RICARD   The Warhol people felt Edie was giving them trouble—they were furious with her because she wasn't cooperating. So they went to a Forty-second Street bar and found Ingrid von Schefflin. They had noticed: "Doesn't this girl look like an ugly Edie? Let's really teach Edie a lesson. Let's make a movie with her and tell Edie she's the big new star." They cut her hair like Edie's. They made her up like Edie. Her name became Ingrid Superstar . . . just an invention to make Edie feel horrible.

VIVA   I always used to feel so sorry for Ingrid when she was being groomed to be a superstar because she was afraid she wouldn't succeed and she'd have to go back to New Jersey and work selling refrigerators.

DANNY FIELDS   You had to love Ingrid. She loved her name, Ingrid Superstar. She got it the first day when she walked in, dressed in aqua satin. And you had to feel sorry for her because she didn't really know that they were making fun of her all the time. Then after a while she became so acceptable that they weren't making fun of her; they really started to consider her as a human being and someone they liked.

It was nice. She got carried away with everything. It was wonderful to see it happen. It was like through a child's eyes. "Oh, I made the columns today." To be elevated to any sense of ritziness was just wonderful for her. She was such a good-natured person that it was sort of nice having her around, because all the other girls were social- ites or actresses or something, and she was a natural. But I can't believe that Edie took her seriously or felt threatened by Ingrid Super- star. Edie was on to better things, so she hoped—like the movie she wanted to make with Bob Dylan.

JONATHAN TAPLIN   Dylan liked Edie because she was one of the few people who could stand up against his weird little numbers: she was much stronger than the sycophants who were hanging around him at the time. He was always in an adversary relationship with women. He tested people . . . perhaps to find out about himself. His transi- tion from folk purity to the rock insanity was overwhelming him. He needed to know: who was he? Dylan respected Edie's spirit, and her strength in being able to deal with him, and that she didn't wither. You know that song of his, "Just Like a Woman"? They say he wrote it about Edie.

BOB NEUWIRTH   I know that Bob Dylan expressed an interest in doing a film with Edie—a non-Warholian film. At that time there was a lot of interest in Bob starring in a movie—the great directors were after him. But Dylan has always had a need for the mystique of pri- vacy—the Garbo Trick.

PAUL MORRISSEY   The Dylan relationship came up one night when we saw Edie at the Ginger Man. It was early in 1966. She told us that she didn't want Andy to show any of her films any more. By that time she'd made about eleven films with Andy in only four months. Then things started to go sour, and her last film before *Chelsea Girls* was called *Lupe*, about the actress Lupe Velez, who drowned with her head in a toilet after taking a huge dose of Seconal. Edie had a small role in *Chelsea Girls*, but she came in later to ask us to take out the section of the film she was in. She told us that she had signed a contract with Bob Dylan's manager, Albert Grossman.

It was a very peculiar period. Andy was going through a transi- tion. He was always trying to make more money to support his filmmaking, and he had gotten involved with a new discotheque and was managing a new band, the Velvet Underground. We let them rehearse at the Factory. Suddenly they were taking up more and more time. We started to make little movies with them. They needed a singer, and by accident we ran into this girl named Nico, who had known Dylan in Europe and had been brought over from London by Grossman. He used to come around to the Factory with his assistants, supposedly to listen to Nico practice, but for some reason he had lost interest in her. It was Edie Sedgwick he wanted to put under contract. So he'd ask, "Do you have any of those old movies of Edie Sedgwick we've heard about? We'd love to see them." They wanted to see what she looked like on the screen, but doing it very sneaky and behind our backs. Actually, Edie was all part of it, which we didn't know then. Dylan was calling her up and inviting her out and telling her not to tell Andy or anyone that she was seeing him. He invited her up to Woodstock and he told her that Grossman hoped to put her together with him. She could be his leading lady. So she said to herself, "Ah, this is my break."

She signed with Grossman at Dylan's urging. Apparently Grossman had said that he didn't think she should see Andy so much any more because the publicity that came out of it wasn't good. She said, "They're going to make a film, and I'm supposed to star in it with Bobby." Suddenly it was Bobby this and Bobby that, and we realized that she had a crush on him. We thought he'd been leading her on, because just that day Andy had heard in Sy Litvinoff's office—our lawyer—that Dylan had been secretly married for a few months—he married Sara in November, 1965. Everything was secret in those days for some reason . . . all phony secrecy. So Andy couldn't resist asking, "Did you know, Edie, that Bob Dylan has gotten married?"

She just went pale. "What? I don't believe it! What?" She was trembling. We realized that she really thought of herself as entering a relationship with Dylan . . . that maybe he hadn't been very truthful. Probably none of it was true—Dylan never had any intention of making a movie with Edie, or starring her.

So off she went, and we never really saw very much of her after that. Andy never showed her films any more. He took out her piece of *Chelsea Girls* and we substituted a little thing with Nico with colored lights going across her face—an abstract kind of totally minimal film of Nico looking for a half-hour into the camera. It's got some Velvet Underground music with it. It's the last thing in *Chelsea Girls*, a very beautiful ending.

VIVA   It must have had an effect on Andy—Edie leaving him for Dylan, or whoever. He was probably in love with Edie, with all of us —a sexless kind of love, but he would take up your whole life so that you had no time for any other man. When Edie left with Grossman and Dylan, that was betrayal, and he was furious . . . a lover betrayed by his mistress.

BOB NEUWIRTH   She never made a film with Dylan. After Edie left Warhol, I was actually the first one to make a film with her. We made it on Easter Sunday in Eric Dolphy's old loft near the Fulton Fish Market—a Chaplinesque, satirical movie of Edie making breakfast, and ending up with her wearing a nine-thousand-dollar leopard-skin coat and walking her huge rhinoceros, that big footstool of hers outfitted with four roller skates, up Fifth Avenue in the Easter Parade, pulling the rhino along behind her on a leash. It was very early in the morning. We'd been shooting since daylight. At one point on Park Avenue she tied her rhino to a fire hydrant, and the police, as a joke, gave it a ticket. I have footage of them giving her a ticket for parking her four-wheeled rhino, or actually her *sixteen*-wheeled rhino.

RENÉ RICARD   I made a film with Edie about nine months after she left the Factory. Andy suggested, "Let's do a movie with you as me in it. *The Andy Warhol Story.*" I really hated Andy by then. I realized his was a passive exploitation—that it could be humiliating and horrible. He had been asking me to do this for a long time and I had refused. But one night I took an Obetrol—a very powerful twenty-five-milligram amphetamine pill, the best. They were very hard to get, rare and very good. It's a good high, very gay, very lovely speed. That night we were making this Tiger Morse movie, part of a twenty-four-hour, four-star movie in which I was supposed to be an extra. "Don't do too much talking," I was told. Well, the pill got me hysterical and I was amazingly good at it. Andy fell in love with me for it. Once again he said, "Oh, you're so good tonight; let's do that movie I've wanted you to do."

So I finally said okay. The only reason I agreed to do his film was to get even with him.

I said, "Okay, let's go to my place and do it." I was living in a very beautiful apartment on Fifth Avenue with Avery Dunphy, who was being kept in this luxurious place by a doctor who was mad for prissy Wasps. Mirrored coffee tables, a huge white silk-satin couch. Beautiful, right? What Avery wanted to be was chic—which was all anybody wanted at that time. Having Andy Warhol make a movie in that apartment, even though it wasn't his, was very chic. I called Avery and told him what was happening—that we were on the way. I told him, "I want orchids. I want the place filled with orchids."

He asked, "Well, where am I going to get orchids at this time of night?"

I told him about a place in the East Sixties that's open until midnight. I figured I'd do it right. Right? I didn't have any money, but at least I could have orchids. Besides, I was trying to get even with Andy. So Avery went out and bought the most exquisite orchids you've ever seen. He bought orchids to *die* over. I know the difference between good orchids and vulgar ones, and these were expensive and good—from Hawaii or Vietnam, which is where Paris gets its orchids.

When we all got to the apartment, Andy asked, "Who do you want in the film with you?"

I said, "I only want Edie Sedgwick. Who else is there in your life but Edie Sedgwick?"

Andy said, "I don't know if we can get her."

I said, "I won't do it without her."

I took another pill and I got *wired. Wired!* There's a point when you take speed when you talk a lot, and yet there's also a point where you take too much and you don't talk. That's the point that second pill got me to.

So Andy got Edie on the telephone and offered to pay for her taxi, and about three hours later Edie turned up. I didn't want to make the movie when I saw her. She was wearing a dirty blond fall. She looked like the cheapest piece of filth. Here was my Edie, *my* Edie, and I was making a movie with her—*co-stars!* No longer was I an extra, and she looked like hell! She was wearing a kind of Marimekko-type dress, and mean! She, too, hated Andy at that point: she had been eighty-sixed.

When she was with the fairies, she was on speed and she was Edie, she was "on." When she was with Bobby Neuwirth, who was a hetero, she was on downs, and Edie on downs was not pretty.

Well, when she arrived at the apartment, the cameras started rolling. I had my own personal vendetta against Warhol, and so did she. And I was *playing* Warhol. So I played him the way he behaved to the people under him. She played herself according to how she felt about him then. The things she said to me were horrible. I don't remember them. I don't even remember what *I* said. I was awful. I have nightmares about what I did in that movie . . . saying things about Andy that were true, how he disposed of people. Paul Morrissey, who was behind the camera, was white with rage. I went through the paintings . . . how Andy doesn't actually do the paintings himself. Stupid things like: "Gerard, get me an egg. Do you want to know how I paint my pictures, you people out there?" I'd crack the egg in a glass and then I'd say to Gerard: "Cook it! That's how I paint my pictures."

We did one reel and stopped. Then Andy in his sick, masochistic, dreadful way—after all, here were these two people on camera saying the most ghastly things about him—said, "Let's do another reel." He had been standing holding his fingers in his mouth, which he does when he's anxious, and he was *loving* it . . . getting the truth.

So we did another reel, and in this one it got violent. Edie started it. At some point I gave her some orchids. I said, "You're not dressed up enough for this movie. So do something. Take these flowers."

She took them and crushed them. I got very upset. And I—me, René Ricard, not the Andy Warhol me—was just made demented by that. I love orchids. It was a personal thing from me to her. I said, "You really need to fix yourself up, my dear. Put them on you somewhere."

She cried out, "I hate them! I don't want to be beautiful!" She wrecked the flowers. Edie was hating me. We were both hating each other because of the roles we were playing . . . I loved Edie, but I couldn't *stand* being in the movie with her the way she looked. She was horrible in the movie, and mean. The things *I* was saying were so horrible.

Paul Morrissey suddenly reached out from behind the camera and ripped my clothes off me—a new white silk shirt and new pair of white linen pants. He ripped them. The camera was turning. Paul was out of the frame. I guess he was livid because of the things I was saying about Andy.

So we finished the film—two reels. Edie rushed home. I didn't care about her at that point. My clothes were a ruin. I was a mess. I was wiped out by the pills. Dazed.

You'll never guess what happened then. Andy Warhol at that point was close to a guy called Rod La Rod. He was handling the sound on this film. They asked me to see the rushes in the Factory. I sat there watching it—Paul, Andy, Rod, and a few of the other serfs were there—and I saw what they had done to it. Edie's voice is there, but when I speak, you can't hear it. They were in glee.

28

PAUL MORRISSEY At the Factory we got an eviction notice. The building was going to be torn down. Actually, it was a good thing. The silver spray paint kept crumbling off and deteriorating into silver dust. It got sort of bad to breathe after a bit, and it was hard to clean. I lived downtown on the East Side, and I went shopping around for a loft. I found one which Andy liked at 33 Union Square.

When we moved, the couch was the last thing carried down and put in the truck. It was a famous couch. It appeared in Andy's earliest films. He used it in photographs and paintings. The people who rented the truck were going to move it the next day. During the night the truck was stolen. So the people who stole the truck got it. It was a great couch.

DANNY FIELDS The new Factory was white. It was elegant. It had shiny wooden floors. It had a spectacular view. It was like moving uptown even though it was actually downtown. It was totally unfunky—minimal. It was more of a place to get things done by organization rather than by the spontaneous generation that was so much a part of the old place. There were receptionists. They were trying to keep out the maniacs. It was definitely another era.

FRED HUGHES We tried to keep the new Factory functional. About the only exception was a stuffed Great Dane we found in a junk shop. The junk dealer said it was Cecil B. De Mille's dog. There was a screening room in the back with big, tall doors. I was there when Andy was shot. My first thought was that it was a bomb. I got under this table. We were always frightened because the Communist Party was in the same building and somebody might throw a bomb in the wrong window.

MARIO AMAYA It was a typical scene, people drifting in and out. There wasn't any structure to the afternoon. I was impatient. I'd stayed on another two or three days in New York just to see Andy about the possibility of doing a retrospective abroad, and, as usual, he was very tentative about everything. So I hung around, smoking cigarettes. Several people came in and out; one of them was this woman. Nobody was in there at the time except Fred Hughes and Andy, who was over by the windows. It was a very warm day; the huge windows were all open, and I remember undoing my tie. New York had a lot of snipers at the time—we'd been reading about them in London—so when I heard these shots, I assumed that someone was shooting at us through the windows. I dropped to the ground. I heard Andy shout out: "Oh, no! Oh, no! Valerie, oh, no!" I thought, "Oh, God, that girl he was talking to must have been shot!"

The next thing I remember was looking up from where I'd fallen to the ground to see what was going on, and this woman was standing over me with the gun pointed straight at me. She was wearing trousers, a jacket, and her hair was down. Luckily, she was a bad aim and the bullet grazed my back, going in and out in a very freak way, and by a miracle it missed my spine by a millimeter.

Anyway, I didn't know what had happened. I didn't even know I had been shot. Very odd. I remember thinking, "Oh, isn't that lucky, she's using BB's instead of real bullets." Crazy things go through your head to guard against your own fear or hysteria or whatever's happening in your mind. Actually, the gun looked so little. Like a dinner gun . . . a woman's gun. When those ladies were going to murder their lovers, they'd arrive in a great, long gown and a little evening purse, out of which they'd pull this tiny little gun. I looked around and saw these double doors in the back of the Factory. I said to myself, "If I can get through those doors, I'll be all right." Luckily, they weren't locked.

Paul Morrissey was in the hall. He seemed very spaced out. "What's going on? What's going on?" He was absolutely ashen.

I said, "A crazy woman is shooting."

We looked out through a glass window in the doors and saw the woman pointing the gun at Fred Hughes. It was absolutely terrifying. Afterwards Fred told me that he had said, "Valerie, please don't shoot me. I'm innocent," whatever *that* meant.

Just then the elevator which opened up into the whole space of the Factory appeared, empty—we didn't know why or how, whether by accident or chance, or whether she pushed the button—and she beat a retreat into it.

We came out from the back, and there was Andy lying on the floor laughing. Sometimes when you're hurt badly, you have a reverse reaction . . . an hysterical kind of laugh.

It seemed to take forever for the ambulance to arrive. They didn't have a stretcher. Andy said something very odd: "Don't make me laugh, it hurts too much." No one was making any jokes. God! We finally got him down into the ambulance, and it wasn't until then that I realized I had been shot. Someone said, "My God! Look, your coat's torn!" I took it off, and it was soaked with blood. I thought if I was still standing I must be all right, but anyway I went in the ambulance. By this time, Andy was unconscious. He'd lost an awful lot of blood. The ambulance driver said to me, "If we sound the siren, it'll cost five dollars extra."

I said, "Go ahead and sound it. Leo Castelli will pay."

The girl handed herself in. In Times Square. She claimed Andy had promised her a starring role in his next film. She headed up this thing called SCUM, the Society to Cut Up Men. She had some sort of lawyer who tried to make it a fem-lib case, saying that she had been treated badly by these awful men. Andy and I used to say that we were the first feminist casualties.

ANDY WARHOL   I was always frightened of strange people. I always thought she was strange, but one of the Women's Lib people said she was so talented we thought, "Well, we'll invite her over." I guess it was a mistake, because she was just sort of nuts.

HENRY GELDZAHLER   When Andy was shot, my mother called me in East Hampton and asked, "Have you heard Andy was shot?" I said, "Oh, how awful! Is he all right?" She said, "They said on the radio he was in a hospital. He was shot by a girl named Valerie Solanis. Do you know her?" And I said, "Yes." She said, "I wish you didn't." I said, "It's too late, Ma." Mothers are divine.

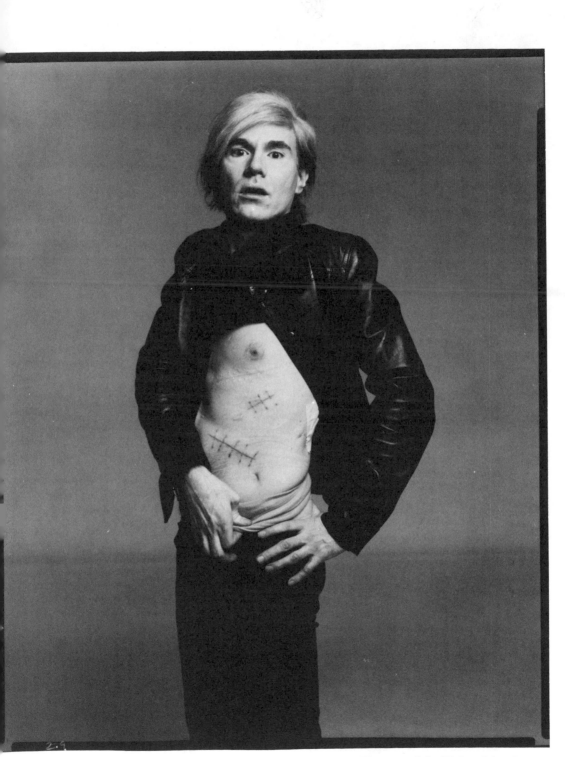

Andy Warhol, artist, New York City, 8/20/69   Photograph by Richard Avedon

Valerie Solanis was an activist early on. She'd written a script for a movie that she thought Andy should produce. When that door was slammed in her face, she just flipped.

BILLY NAME   I was in the darkroom and I heard this big bang. I came out and saw Andy lying on the floor. I was really upset. I hovered over him. I had this protector complex for Andy. I just loved him so much. When he went to the hospital, I used to go and stand outside the hospital window. I just felt like he was my own wizard.

BARBARA ROSE   On June 3, 1968, I was on the phone with Emile de Antonio and he said, "Andy's been shot."
   I said, "Oh, D, cut it out."
   He said, "I swear, Andy's been shot."
   I said he was crazy.
   A couple of days later we were on the phone again.
   I asked, "What is it?"
   He said, "Bobby Kennedy's been shot."
   I said, "That's not possible."
   I was home alone with the baby. I couldn't go out. My husband, Frank Stella, came back from the studio with the papers. Kennedy was critical, Andy was critical. Frank said, "Bobby's going to die and Andy's going to live. That's the way the world is."
   I said, "Oh, Frank, how can you say that?"
   "You'll see," he said. That was his essential intuition: he saw the whole thing as an American parable—a kind of real American story.

DAVID BOURDON   Andy was in the hospital with a fifty-fifty chance of survival. As soon as he was out of intensive care I got a telephone call—Andy calling me from his room. He wanted to talk. He wanted to find out what sort of press coverage he'd been getting. He knew that I was about to do an article on him for *Life* magazine, and he wanted to know how *that* was coming along. Actually, the piece had been finished and it was in the house before Andy was shot. We had all the photographs, the layout, everything. Then Andy was shot. The *Life* editors were ecstatic. It was going to be a lead story—eight or ten pages—a major space in the following issue.
   But then Robert Kennedy got shot. Andy's story was killed, and the cover story came out on the Senator . . . which was the obvious choice. The following week the Andy story was much less exciting to the

Billy Name leaving the Factory

editors, and they said to me, "Well, the only reason to run the story now would be if Andy . . . you know . . . died."

So Andy kept calling me up: "Are they going to run the story *this* week?"

I told him, "Andy, they're very mean. They'll only run the story if you die. I'd much rather have you alive, even if it means that my story doesn't get published."

Andy wouldn't believe me. He kept saying, "Oh-h-h, can't you get it in anyway?" He wanted it both ways.

PATRICK O'HIGGINS I saw the scars on his stomach. Avedon took a picture of them and they show up black on white. But when you actually see them, these ghastly tracks and scars and holes are white on white—white on that pale stomach of his. No red welts. Pale, pale as could be. Not a hair. I think he's an albino.

BARBARA ROSE He became another person after the shooting. He didn't take another risk after that. Up until that time he lived a life of extreme risk. There's no question the shooting was a suicide attempt; he provoked it. He was waiting to be shot. Oh, the whole thing was set up for Andy to be killed. It was part of the kind of closet theater that went on there. It was inevitable, absolutely inevitable.

JEAN STEIN When Henry Geldzahler and I went to visit Andy at the Factory we talked for a while about the Sixties. Andy said, "We saw so much of the Vietnam War because it came up and down Forty-seventh Street. The demonstrations went right past the Factory on the way to the United Nations." I asked him about sin. Andy sat quietly staring at the table: "I don't know what sin is." He paused, then turned to Henry, "What is sin, Henry?"

TAYLOR MEAD Andy died when Valerie Solanis shot him. He's just somebody to have at your dinner table now. Charming, but he's the ghost of a genius. Just a ghost, a walking ghost.

PATTI SMITH They always talk about the end. I guess that's when they pulled the silver down from the wall.

29

JOEL SCHUMACHER   After Edie split with Andy and the Dylan thing collapsed, she desperately wanted to model. She looked so incredible at that period . . . not unlike Twiggy, but much sexier and much more the American girl.

She was the total essence of the fragmentation, the explosion, the uncertainty, the madness that we all lived through in the Sixties. The more outrageous you were, the more of a hero you became. With clothes, it was almost a contest to see who could come out with the most outrageous thing next. "I'm going to make a dress out of neon signs." "Oh, well, I'm going to make one out of tin cans!" "Oh, yeah? You *are*? I'm going to make one out of sponges!" "Oh, yeah? Well, I'm going to make one out of a *toilet*."

And then everyone would fight over who was going to wear these things. I remember we opened a Paraphernalia shop in Cleveland, Ohio, and for the opening fashion show I had done a dress of mirrors. There was another dress with the word LOVE cut out down the front of it. A couple of the girls began fighting over who was going to wear what. Marisa Berenson was very upset she wasn't going to wear the mirror dress.

So you had to show these things off, and not only that, but you had to do it all night. You had to dance . . . and you had to dance fabulously. And everything you read—every paper, magazine—told you how fabulous it was to be young; youth was *it*. And so you had your mother and your grandmother wearing tin-can garbage dresses with red metallic fishnet hose, and they were trying to go out all night and do that sort of thing, too.

RICHIE BERLIN   Diana Dew, the electric-dress designer for Paraphernalia, had those dresses where the tits would light up; or you could flash the crotch and *that* would go off. But they weren't foolproof, and one night two girls went totally off in Max's! I mean, *right* off. They went BOOM! It's true.

BETSEY JOHNSON   All of the clothes at Paraphernalia were experimental. Always changing. It had nothing to do with the customer. It had everything to do with the time, the moment. We were giving the customer something brand new, something that she didn't have a clue she wanted. It was all very spaceship. "What would you wear on the moon?" That was the big question of the Sixties. Everybody felt real future, real positive, real up, optimistic, and the whole Timothy Leary drug trip. Edie and Andy were just the ultimate, you know. Edie and the rock 'n' roll groups were it. The Stones, the Beatles were where you could hear it. John Cale from the Velvet Underground. Paraphernalia was where you could buy it.

Edie was my first fitting model. Very boyish . . . in fact, she was the very beginning of the whole unisex trip. Backless bathing-suit dresses. I remember doing those on Edie. All the silvers, like the silver fish dress. I liked leotardic clothes—body-conscious clothes. The jersey-bodied T-shirty silver second skin. That was Edie. Her body was very important to her. . . . I've got pictures in this album. Here's Edie in the "skeletal"—silver outlining the collar bone, the arm, the pelvis . . . a kind of bone layout. I mean, that's *timeless*. Spacey. Timeless. Here's the "Story of O" dress, you'll remember, with the grommets up the front, the leather "Noise" dress that had all these metal grommets clashing. Here's the body-composition dress. Color compositions based on the body. I have all of these clothes up at home in Connecticut. But they're wrecked. The kids in the family have been wearing them for Halloween.

GLORIA SCHIFF   Somebody told me that Edie was adorable and available to be photographed for *Vogue*. I remembered from either a previous photograph or a previous description that she was an enchanting, beguiling little girl.

Edie modeling a Betsey Johnson design

We did the session out in Brooklyn Heights, where Gianni Penati photographed her. She and I and the hairdresser all had a rendezvous at the *Vogue* offices in the Graybar Building at eleven o'clock, which was a late hour for a sitting, but I thought it would be easier on her because she might be the sort of person if the hour was too early would not show. It's happened before.

She came dressed in a very Bohemian, very unsoigné way—a pair of blue jeans and possibly a pea jacket of some kind. The elevator man would certainly not have turned to look at her. No way! Some of those young girls can turn up in a rather conspicuous way. Twiggy would always appear beautifully turned out, along with her agent; there was always some sort of excitement in the hall when Twiggy or one of those girls would walk in. Professionals come with a bill, and their nails are done, and so is their hair. But not Edie. She came as an innocent. Her childlike hands were so funny, but she had no blemishes or discolorations. Her make-up was terrible—you didn't really want a lot of make-up on that particular kind of face. Some people are very angular and Gothic, with tremendous contours and lids and enormous noses and big mouths, profiles, and they don't smile. Then you want make-up, because you're really painting a canvas that doesn't move. Edie had a face that wasn't a canvas; it was moving all the time. It never stopped.

On the way out to Penati's studio I remember sitting in the car thinking: "My *God*, we've got a child! I mean, she's completely childlike."

Penati creates a very nice atmosphere. He flirts, he's mad, he's fun. He says, "Ahhhh, you're so beautiful! They never told me you were so beautiful!" That kind of thing. He's a mad Italian. "Ahhh, there is the sex image of all time." He's adorable, and he has tremendous sex appeal. Totally charming and very childlike. He would be totally keen about a girl like Edie because she had a nymphet quality which he always adored.

She loosened up and became very with it . . . giggling and laughing, kind of oblivious to the camera, and you realized what wonderful things could happen to her as a model or a star . . . visualizing her dressed in different outfits or in other locations. I thought, "Oh, God, she'd be so much more beautiful in evening clothes." There was a tremendous range in how she looked and the way she projected.

There was also a paradoxical side to her. She contradicted herself all day long. She'd be flirtatious with Gianni, then she'd be a child, clinging to me: she'd be cocky, then shy, then competent. She'd go through a whole range of emotional behavior, which is typical, isn't it, of a lot of stars. I adored her smile and the little fawnlike quality she had. What is amazing is that her face and her looks in these pictures are totally contemporary. They could appear in any fashion magazine tomorrow. They have no date to them. Don't you agree? She was wise with her energy. Surprisingly wise.

We had an idea what we wanted to do with her. I knew we wanted to put black lingerie on her and that she would be terrific; she was so blonde and pale and light. Her hair was a bit of a problem because she hadn't done very much with it. Her hair was not in what is called "first-rate" condition. Fortunately, this charming little hairdresser called Ingrid from Kenneth's brought some hairpieces. Since the photos were black and white, there was no problem matching the hair, and the wilder and the larger the hairpieces Ingrid put on, the smaller and more beautiful Edie's face became—like a little bird's. Her eyes were black, like a snake's. She was just unbelievably appealing and photogenic—especially with Gianni Penati's lighting, which was very lenial—that means the light illuminates half a face, the other diffused. That is very Avedon or Penati, and it's very helpful if your face isn't absolutely perfect in proportion, and is a little Modigliani and off-balance. Any imperfection is somewhat concealed. We put some blush on her and lots of mascara and gloss on the lips to give them some life, and the rest was all her. It was a personality sitting: she was a personality girl. It wasn't as if she were truly a model or a movie star: she was an enchanting, remarkable creature of the moment.

Some of the pictures weren't used in the magazine. There was one in which she was wearing this corsetlike lingerie, a black one with suspenders; a little like that wonderful movie with Marlene Dietrich—what was it called?—*The Blue Angel*. Edie Sedgwick captured that quality in this black lingerie with the white stockings and her white skin. It had a little of Berlin in it; a little bit of something that was strange and not totally American, not totally collegiate or soigné . . . a little messy, a little bit out of control.

She wasn't very strong. You felt that. Oh, dear, this girl . . . she talked about her life and her friends and the way she spent her time. It wasn't sound, obviously, it was going to lead to trouble. She was very mixed up. But I was mad about her.

I remember going with the pictures to Diana Vreeland, who was the editor-in-chief, saying, "We've got a star! There's no doubt about it, she is terrific! A great model! We should do a whole issue on her."

Edie in *Vogue*, March 15, 1966

DIANA VREELAND   She had a little dance step in her walk; she was so happy with the world. She was charming. She suggested springtime and freshness. She was very clean and clear, and her hair was pulled back, almost *Alice in Wonderland*. Freshness and proportion and a sense of the sort of rollick of life, you know, the fun of life. She was a Youthquaker, wasn't she?—one of the true personalities of the Sixties. Only twice in this century has the youth been dominant. The Twenties and the Sixties. Youth came through; the language changed; the music; the humor. The writers and painters produced something totally different from the years before. The two eras have a lot in common. In the Fitzgerald era, Prohibition was on; everybody was as wild as a March hare; everybody had great Stutz Bearcats, and Mercedes—great, enormous cars roaring through the night; youth was wild, rich, extravagant, and marvelous . . . though, unfortunately, it added up to very little . . . I think the Sixties will add up to much more.

I don't call it a violently sex period. You might say, "Well, everybody slept with everybody like kittens." It was just possible. Don't forget, the Pill changed the world. Certainly, though, it was a very intensive moment of the beauty of the body. No question. Every girl thought every other girl was beautiful; every boy thought the other boy was beautiful; every boy thought every girl was beautiful; every girl thought every boy was beautiful.

But if you're an *honest-to-God* model, you go to a gym before you come to work; you have one boyfriend who buys you your dinner. You go to bed good and early. No nonsense. You'd never see one in a nightclub.

That wasn't Edie, though Edie had a wonderful look about her. Lovely skin, but then I've never seen anyone on drugs that didn't have wonderful skin. There must have been some frustration. She was after life, and sometimes life doesn't come fast enough.

GLORIA SCHIFF   There was some sort of problem about continuing with Edie at *Vogue*. Perhaps the magazine's policy became involved. The whole thing kind of collapsed. It was never pursued again. We lost a moment when we could have captured it . . . which was sad. She disappeared from our lives. Edie's timing was a fraction off. She almost did become a part of the family at *Vogue*. If that had happened, she would have had tremendous protection. But she was identified in the gossip columns with the drug scene, and back then there was a certain apprehension about being involved in that scene . . . people were really terrified by it. So unless it involved very important artists or musicians, we played it cool as much as we could—drugs had done so much damage to young, creative, brilliant people that we were just anti that scene as a policy. Not that we weren't sympathetic . . . God!

TRUMAN CAPOTE   Anyone who gets involved with the world of fashion has her own self-destruct built into it. The constant beat, beat, beat, and this girl wandering through it, the total victim, believing it all and destroyed by it through no fault of her own.

EDIE SEDGWICK (from tapes for the movie *Ciao! Manhattan*) *I was Girl of the Year and superstar and all that crap. I'd do things like . . . Everything I did was really underneath, I guess, motivated by psychological disturbances. I'd make a mask out of my face because I didn't realize I was quite beautiful, God blessed me so. I practically destroyed it. I had to wear heavy black eyelashes like bat wings, and dark lines under my eyes, and cut all my hair off, my long, dark hair. Cut it off and strip it silver and blond and all those little maneuvers I did out of things that were happening in my life that upset me. I'd freak out in a very physical way. And it was all taken as a fashion trend.* Vogue *photographed me on top of this enormous leather rhinoceros that I had in my apartment on Sixty-third Street, in leotards and a T-shirt, as a new costume. And then the newspapers took it up because Andy and I ended up appearing in the same places. And I was kind of turned off for the time being, going out with men, because I was very upset that two of my brothers had committed suicide—two that I loved very much. And it kind of screwed up my head, so I just didn't want . . . I just freaked out for a while. . . .*

I'm a little nervous about saying anything about "the Artist" because it kind of sticks him right between the eyes, but he deserves it. Warhol really fucked up a great many people's—young people's—lives. My introduction to heavy drugs came through the Factory. I liked the introduction to drugs I received. I was a good target for the scene; I blossomed into a healthy young drug addict.

30

GERARD MALANGA   This is what I wrote about Edie in my diary on
Monday, October 17, 1966:

> . . . Call Edie . . . Edie invites me over. I've never seen her more
> beautiful. She puts on a pair of red leotards and a red tight cotton top.
> I weed out the seeds and twigs from the pot and fill one-eighth full
> Camel with the Acapulco Gold. We get extremely high. She tells me
> how she wanted to run away from the mad publicity for an entire
> year, how it all frightened her, how transparent it all was, and how
> some of them are so desperate for the faceless publicity—stark raving
> mad seeking acquisition they want so desperately. How sorry Edie
> feels for them. How composed she remains . . . I leave Edie falling
> asleep in her apartment. . . .

And here's what I wrote two days later:

> Got up at eleven, picked up silk screen transparencies and bring
> them up to Andy for inspection, visit Edie in Lenox Hill Hospital who
> two days earlier, having left her falling asleep, her apartment caught
> fire.

GEOFFREY GATES   At about eleven-thirty one night I got a call from
Mary Ann Nordemann, who lived across the street—an old friend of
mine—screaming in my telephone, "Get up, your house is on fire!" I
yelled and jumped out of bed to run for my door. I saw smoke hang-

ing around in my apartment. Just as I reached the door, it disintegrated. Fireman Hennessey, who seemed about eight feet tall, had been knocking on my door and simply decided to come on through, which he did. Just a shower of wood and a huge fireman there.

Apparently Edie had taken an overdose of something, let a cigarette go, and when the fire started, she was lucky enough to make it out of the apartment. It was a very intense fire. I don't know what was burning in there—maybe the rhino. She had been taken off to the hospital. I found a *Social Register* in someone's apartment and tried to reach a Sedgwick somewhere to tell them what had happened. From Santa Barbara I was given a very nervous brush-off by whoever answered the phone. Another Sedgwick in Massachusetts just totally freaked out. He just didn't want to hear about it. "I have no interest whatsoever in this matter." That was one of the nightmare aspects of the whole episode—calling up these known relatives and being told there was no interest whatsoever. Finally I reached her uncle, who happened to be here in New York from Boston. Minturn. He was pretty distressed, and dealt with the situation.

MINTURN SEDGWICK   I was in New York staying with friends and my hostess—a highly intelligent and very nice person—received the phone call; instead of rushing to my room, she took the precaution of calling the Lenox Hill Hospital beforehand to find out how Edie was. She was off the danger list. I went to the hospital the next morning to see her. She looked fine. She was lucky; just a bandage on the inside of her arm.

Edie looked very cute. Perfectly lovely. I asked, "Is there anything I can do for you?" She said, "Bring me my make-up." She gave me a list as long as your arm.

I ordered it from the hospital pharmacy, paid for it, and sent it up. When I came back at five in the afternoon, she'd put it on—dark stuff here and there—and she suddenly looked like a death's head.

JANE FIELD   I asked Mr. Gates, who lived opposite Miss Sedgwick, if I could put her furs and clothes in his apartment. I worked for Mr. Gates, but I'd come in from time to time—a few times a week—to clean up her apartment. Sometimes Miss Sedgwick would tell me her problems. She told me about one man—the man she was in love with. He'd walked into a nightclub with another woman. She had tears in her eyes when she told me about it. All I could do was tell her to pray.

Sometimes she'd have tears in her eyes and then I'd have tears in mine. I always felt helpless because I couldn't help her. She was so generous. She paid me more than it was worth. I'd say, "Oh, you don't have to do that!"

"Oh, take it, Jane." She'd practically force it on me. "You've cleaned up. It was such a mess."

She had gobs and gobs of pills. One day I went in there to do some cleaning. What I saw made me close the door and go away. She was sitting on the floor with all these pills around her like in a half-circle . . . cross-legged in a sea of pills. She was in a dopey mood. I stayed there long enough to see her reaching for one, and I left.

While I was working in her apartment after the fire, these two men came creeping up the stairs and began rummaging through her closets and drawers. They had no underpants on and you could see their heinies through the holes in their blue jeans. They acted like leeches. Maybe they got away with some of her clothes and glass ashtrays.

JUDY FEIFFER   Edie claimed she was lighting candles when the drapes caught on fire. She lit candles every night . . . on the mantel-piece . . . like a child who doesn't want to sleep in the dark.

I went to visit her in Lenox Hill. She was frantic to get out. She responded to that hospital like some mad, frenzied small animal. She was going to call the cops. At all cost, at any cost, whoever was on the board of directors, whatever her contacts were, whoever she knew, she was going to get out of that hospital, and that day. She began a high-pitched campaign and she got out. Twenty-four hours— that was it. She knew the way to get out.

EDIE SEDGWICK   (from *Ondine and Edie*)   *It's a wicked hospital. I got stuck in there with seven women, all Jewish, all old, all screaming: they wanted flowers, cookies; they wanted their children to come and visit. And waking up with someone having an operation right next to me. I couldn't move because I had the tube in my mouth and the tube in my fluid evacuation. They wouldn't give me anything to put me to sleep. You get used to these things. I had to hear them all night. One of them recited . . . it was like a tiger licking.*

JUDY FEIFFER   After she got out of the hospital, she said to me, "I have an accident about every two years, and one day it won't be an accident."

BOB NEUWIRTH   After the fire, Edie moved to the Chelsea Hotel on West Twenty-third. I think she went there because of its sense of tradition and historical impact, and also the artistic milieu. I'm sure her family wanted her to live uptown at the Barbizon Hotel for Women. There were other people in town who wanted her to live at the Sherry Netherland. But the Chelsea gave her a sense of freedom, of artistic license. She knew everybody who lived on her floor, and on all the other floors. She was a star there . . . like Kay Thompson when she lived at the Plaza and wrote *Eloise*. Edie was the genius in residence.

VIRGIL THOMSON   The lobby of the Chelsea used to have very large, exuberant pictures of the Hudson River landscape school. It had perfectly enormous black furniture with leather upholstery. In the middle was a round settee with a pyramid in the center and a palm on the top of it. Of course, now the lobby is falling apart . . . pretty dingy.

Everybody's lived here at one time or another—usually when they were young but not famous. Tennessee Williams, Thomas Wolfe, Dylan Thomas, Arthur Miller, Edgar Lee Masters, who was my next-door neighbor, and Gore Vidal. All were here, most of them unknown, at different times. I met Bob Dylan here once. That's when I discovered, much to my surprise, that though he sounds in recordings like a real lowdown Southern mountaineer, he is a perfectly nice Jewish high-school graduate from Hibbing, Minnesota, who speaks correctly and with manners. His public personality is one purely assumed on his part.

For a long time the traveling rock bands stayed here. You could tell they were rock bands because they wore their concert clothes— purple velvet pants—all day long to get them dirty.

From time to time there do appear the most sensational Negro pimps, very tall, and with high heels, slender, with the most beautiful tailoring, and picture hats, wide picture hats. Every now and then they get put out. If they get themselves into the dope trade, they always get put out.

Of course, one of the happier attributes of the Hotel Chelsea was that it was so inexpensive. The St. Regis was about forty dollars a room in the Sixties. A single room in the Chelsea could be had then for twenty dollars. It would have been a good place for someone with financial problems.

BOB NEUWIRTH   Edie got cut off about the time she started living in the Chelsea—no more allowance—so we got her a professional money manager, Seymour Rosen. He advised her . . . not a young guy, but a middle-aged man who took care of money matters for a lot of show-business people. He got her bills in order; he lined up her creditors and got them not to sue. He tried to get her family to contribute to the easing of the financial situation, but at that point they weren't ready to trust anybody.

So she had no money coming in. The only people she had to turn to were people from her own social circle; some of them were generous and some weren't. To give Edie a check for a thousand dollars was like giving most people ten. Very hard to envy Seymour Rosen his job. He really adored her.

SEYMOUR ROSEN   I visited Edie from time to time, and then she would come by to see me, depending on her needs. Maybe two or three times a week she'd come by to say hello, and to steal fountain pens, just for a lark, apparently: she had a thing about them; she stole all the fountain pens off my desk.

I remember those times when we went down to the Fiduciary Trust. She looked like a twelve-year-old boy. Asexual. We took the wrong elevator at the bank one day and ended up in the record-keeping department. Everybody was working at the accounting machines and calculators. She was dressed in her usual style. We walked through there; everything stopped. She was wearing what came to be called Capri pants. Nobody was wearing them yet. The hip-huggers. Bare midriff. People weren't even wearing them on the beaches. Really stopped traffic at the bank. We met with an officer. We were sitting across from his desk, and he kept staring at *me*. He couldn't look at her, he was so embarrassed. They're a very conservative, straight-line, Wasp organization . . . really old-line.

She couldn't travel on public transportation. Just couldn't handle it. Only by limousine. I took her on a bus one day just to try to get her to learn how to use it. She got off after a few blocks and called for the limo. Not even a cab! Bill's Limo Service. She was clutching me. Very, very uncomfortable and nervous.

So I would take care of Bill's Limo. I tried to keep the creditors in line by doling out as little as I could to keep them happy. Some of them were very nice. Cambridge Chemists. Lovely, lovely people: souls of compassion. Also the place across from Lincoln Center, the Ginger

Man. They, too. She was into them for quite a bit. We worked out a payment. People were nice to her. I think it was those eyes.

Occasionally Edie would throw a fit. She'd call up, screaming hysterically on the phone, to ask for one hundred fifty to two hundred dollars *instantly*. Conceivably, she was fighting with her connection. Once there was a big scene in a hotel lobby—big, messy scene—and I had to send somebody over there with a few hundred dollars to quiet things down.

Her mother was very concerned about Edie's welfare. Once I met with her when she came to see Edie in the Chelsea. The Chelsea's a very depressing place, to begin with. Her mother wanted her out of there. I remember she kept talking about the ranch: why didn't Edie come out? I thought her mother was a hell of a nice lady. She was very solicitous toward Edie, plumping pillows, smoothing her hair, and Edie was reacting the way most daughters do when a mother is solicitous.

31

BOB NEUWIRTH   She'd been in the Chelsea for a few months when she went home to Santa Barbara for the Christmas of 1966—a magical time for all loonies anyway—to visit her parents. It was an unfortunate idea. They had some queer old New England Wasp family idea of, well, it's okay if she spends thirty thousand dollars the first year and forty thousand dollars the second year as long as she gets married the third year and gets herself suitably taken care of for the rest of her life. But when it appeared that she was not going to get herself a nice young polo player, and didn't want to either, it became a question of her parents' not being able to afford to have her independent.

JONATHAN SEDGWICK   She was really weird when she arrived at the ranch. Like a stick, no body at all, and wearing the shortest skirts I've ever seen, super-fake eyelashes hanging so heavy her eyelids drooped.

She was an alien. She'd pick up what you were about to say before you'd say it. It made everybody uncomfortable. She wanted to sing, and so she would sing . . . but it was a drag because it wasn't in tune. A painted doll, wobbly, languishing around on chairs, trying to look like a vamp.

You could see not only the insecurity but the need for love . . . but it was so hard to accept her. She had two selves. I wanted the inner to come out; my father was mad at the outer. Poor Edie, both the inner and the outer, got mad at my father. I wasn't there when they had the fight.

EDIE SEDGWICK (from tapes for the movie *Ciao! Manhattan*) *I went home to California because all my friends were home for Christmas and I didn't want to be by myself in New York. It was a very unpleasant experience. . . . I was on drugs in New York, and out in California I tried to refill a prescription. My mother found out about it and talked to her doctor, who said, "That's very bad." It was Eskatrol, which is a variety of speed. I'd been used to strong shots, and I used a lot of pills to keep from shaking the balance I'd arranged in my system.*

That night my parents woke me up every few hours for maybe five hours and gave me a couple of Nembutal. I had just been out one day and I was determined not to have a fight with my father, and hopefully not with my mother, so I didn't argue about their giving me the pills or anything.

If I disagreed with my parents, I said so. And they couldn't take that. So they figured, "Let's just tone her down and give her some Nembutal." I must have been very stoned when they finally woke me up and said, "You have a temperature of 105." They had put a thermometer in my mouth. I didn't even think *. . . you know, I just believed them. They said an ambulance was coming to take me to Cottage Hospital, which was where I was born in Santa Barbara. I'll go and be treated and whatever, just be cool about everything. Outside, there was a police car! I asked where the ambulance was, and the policeman said, "The ambulance had an accident on its way over the San Marcos Pass. We'll take you to the hospital."*

It was one of those regular police cars with the screen between you and the driver. We started off from the ranch. Then I noticed my father was driving his big 300-D Mercedes behind the police car. It seemed strange. If I'm supposed to be comfortable and I'm sick, I'd be a lot better off in that big car lying on the back seat than in the back of a police car. I didn't understand it. What I didn't know was that my father had given a report to the police that I was homicidal, suicidal, threatening bodily harm to my sister and my mother, and that I ran around screaming naked. Well, the last part of it appealed to me, but I hadn't done any of it. So we went not to Cottage Hospital, where I was born, but to the County Hospital.

Edie's paraphernalia

BOB NEUWIRTH   I tried to reach Edie on the phone in California. I pushed and probed, and after a while it turned out she was sick and couldn't come to the phone; finally I discovered she was in a hospital. "Well, listen, is she in a medical or a psychiatric ward?" It turned out she was in the psychiatric ward. All very confusing. I knew she was not crazy or trying to kill herself.

Edie's father finally came to the telephone. He seemed rather proud when he told me how he had committed her. I guess it was the only way they could think of controlling her . . . hand out the job to a professional. If you can't get your windows clean, hire a window-washer. I told him that I had several lawyers in Los Angeles. If she wasn't at home to answer the phone the next afternoon I was going to get the lawyers, who were poised in Los Angeles to rescue her. He tried to neutralize the situation by saying, "Well, please come out here, and if you can't afford it, I'll send you an airplane ticket." I remember saying that putting her in a psychiatric ward was so out of keeping with the holiday spirit. Something I said worked: they let her come home.

When I finally reached Edie on the phone, she called out to me: "Get me out of here! I'm a prisoner." Shortly afterwards she was on a plane back to New York, where she arrived smiling and completely covering up the discomfort she had experienced at home. She had a certain puritanical way of not letting her blues get in the way of her life-style.

DOMENIQUE BOURGEOIS ROBERTSON   She came back to the Chelsea after her bad experience in California. I was living there with Robbie Robertson of The Band and I interviewed Edie for a French-Canadian newspaper, *Photo-Journal*. Edie sat at the make-up table in the middle of her kingdom, with the most absurd collection of bric-a-brac surrounding her. Lighters. I remember a cigarette lighter shaped like a toy telephone. There was an open closet full of bizarre fur coats with square shoulders, a straw basket full of strange hats, a box of wigs. She unrolled a small Japanese carpet and began her modern-dance exercises. She said it was the only real discipline she imposed on herself. I remember thinking of her as a strange, fragile doll about to break, a kind of tragic clown. She said she'd refused two Hollywood contracts, one of which had her co-starring with Nancy Sinatra and the other with Burt Lancaster. She went on to say she didn't intend to become a monster of publicity, and that she was more interested in her cat, who was called Smoke. He was iron-gray, and Edie said he was wild and fierce like a young lion, or maybe a black leopard—"a symbol," she felt, "of life, presence, and pride."

I left her doing her exercises. I remember the phone ringing and someone reminding her that her limousine had been waiting for over an hour.

NORMAN MAILER Edie tried out for my play, *The Deer Park*, but she wasn't very good. That is to say, she was very good in a sort of tortured and wholly sensitive way—the sensitivity of a movie actress. She gave immense amounts of herself to each phrase, each sentence, each thought, and never did the same thing twice. That she'd had no stage experience was obvious. She used so much of herself with every line that we knew she'd be immolated after three performances. When we turned her down, I must say she didn't seem terribly downcast. I think she had a sense of how impossible it would be.

PATTI SMITH A few months later, Edie and Bobby Neuwirth parted company. I never asked why. Bobby was often in destructive relationships, but not because he was strong or heavy like a Svengali. It's usually very fragile people who bring out the fragility in somebody else, especially in a tough place like New York. It's like being injured. It's rough to be an injured person in the city.

BOB NEUWIRTH Edie was desperate because she felt her edge was going. She didn't want to make any more fatuous films with Andy. But the establishment moguls didn't think she was capable of handling big parts. She was hot at one point and she hadn't capitalized on it.

Anyway, we drifted apart. It started off with her mistreating herself. I couldn't believe that a person of such intelligence would mistreat herself to that extent. But I'm sure, reflecting on it, that it was caused by desperation and a lack of outlet for that incredible energy.

EDIE SEDGWICK (from tapes for the movie *Ciao! Manhattan*) *It was really sad—Bobby's and my affair. The only true, passionate, and lasting love scene, and I practically ended up in the psychopathic ward. I had really learned about sex from him, making love, loving, giving. It just completely blew my mind—it drove me a little insane. I was* like a sex slave to this man. I could make love for forty-eight hours, forty-eight hours, forty-eight hours, without getting tired. But the minute he left me alone, I felt so empty and lost that I would start popping pills. He had more or less quit using drugs . . . When I first knew him, a friend of his used to come up with him to my apartment and they'd do a number in the bathroom. This guy eventually died of a heroin overdose, and Bobby left drugs alone after that. But if I wasn't practically in the act of lovemaking, I would be thinking of how to get hold of drugs. I really loved this man. . . .

What happened was that Bobby said, "Let's go to a party. They're making an underground movie," and he said that I, the Warhol heiress, queen, star, socialite, blah, should be there. Bobby really wanted to go. I had a bad scene with him. I pulled out a knife and I wasn't going to let him out the door until he made love to me. I always get really dreadful. But we finally went. I went through it all. I was furious—this after about two years of our continuing relationship. Finally I said, "Now I'm going to leave this party. I'm fed up." He said that was all right: he'd met all the people he wanted to meet, and he'd watched the film being shot. So we got into my limousine and he said, "Where would you like to eat?" I thought I was going to explode. Where would I like to eat? I screeched at him, "Why the hell can't you make up your own mind where we're going to eat? Why do I have to make all the decisions?" I was just livid, out of hand. I got madder and madder as we drove along, and just as we drove by the Chelsea Hotel I did something. I've never done anything to hurt anyone, and yet I was so furious that I pressed the button and rolled down the window screen—the glass plate between the front and back seats—and I told the chauffeur that the man in the back was molesting me; he was a junkie!

I was so horrified by what I'd said, so flipped out by that, that I jumped out of the car into the path of the oncoming traffic, certain that my head would be crushed. All that happened was that I got bruised, badly bruised, but no broken bones. I mean, I was conscious, not destroyed at all. But I'd done such a terrible thing! I couldn't reconcile that. I had been about to explode. The hotel people came out, and they and Bobby carried me in. I had to pretend I was unconscious because I couldn't comprehend the fact that I had tried to get him busted, to hurt him seriously.

He was the only person I had ever gotten violent about. I take out whatever violence comes into my system much more heavily on myself than on anyone else. But that was a pretty tight squeeze. I really craved making love to him.

BOB NEUWIRTH Man, that was a terrible night. Some little model had called to say she was at the airport and asked where she should go. Edie had taken the message from my answering service and she thought I was not being straight with her. She was in a fury. She burned her cigarette out in my face. It was at some club. I dragged her out into a limousine. She tried to throw herself in front of a truck. It was a horror story in that limo. She was having a fit. When I finally got her to the Chelsea, she began playing the non-violent role, and I dragged her across the street—it was slushy the way New York streets can get—and into the lobby. I handed her over to the bellboy. "Take her up to Room 105."

Frankly, I was sure that as soon as she got upstairs and a hold of herself, she called up one of her limousine services and took off for one of the social scenes that were on that night.

RUTHERFORD JOHNSON Bobby Neuwirth and Edie were at the end of their affair. She was putting him down and he was not showing up very frequently. If you're in an unhappy love affair, dope can come on like magic. Edie was getting hooked. She was at an early, innocent stage—she'd depend on me and this chick who was the connection to turn her on. I'd come from the East Village and knock on Edie's door. I would "hit" her up. She wasn't a real junkie, so she couldn't do it herself. If she'd been a junkie, she'd have been out trying to score.

With Edie, I'd shoot her up, in the ass. It's called "skinning it." It's a very sexy thing, a girl's ass, and though there was no question of taking advantage of her, certainly there were sexual overtones: shooting up is very sexual—you get the flash, like an orgasm.

If you're obsessed with a person and helpless, there is a way out—to fall in love with heroin. The other person can have no control over you. You have a new lover and a new honeymoon. You feel beautiful: it comes on like an illusion, like the few minutes after a terrific balling. The honeymoon can go on for days or weeks.

But then you get hooked and you run around chasing the heroin, and it becomes just what you've escaped, like waiting for your lover to call . . . and then you're in the bad part of the habit, which can go on for years. So it's like a bad love affair—you suffer. You see, it's immaterial if it's heroin or sex. It's very basic: the two are interchangeable.

SUKY SEDGWICK My sisters Kate and Pamela left me alone with Edie at the Chelsea . . . I was supposed to keep her away from her pills. She was having DTs, or whatever the hell they're called. So she put something in her mouth. I tried to fish it out, and she bit the hell out of my finger. It was agony. My sisters had good reason for leaving, but somebody should have been with me. If Edie'd been younger than me, it would've been different. Oh, God! I don't know how long they were gone, but it was no joke. I didn't know what to do. When Kate and Pamela came back, I just hightailed it. I was scared to death.

32

JOHN PALMER   We had no one to play the lead in a film we were planning called *Ciao! Manhattan*. I was talking with Chuck Wein in Bob Margouleff's office—Bob was to be the producer—and Chuck said, "Well, what about Edie?" I said, "Sure, she'd be terrific." He said, "Oh, my God, do you think she could do it? These days she's so spaced and stoned and wiped out." I said, "Yeah, that's true, but we don't have anybody else, so we might as well get her." So we got Edie and, sure enough, she was spaced.

ROBERT MARGOULEFF   I originally wanted to make a little $47,500 movie. I had the money for it. I could have done it without too much of an economic strain. I had run into Chuck Wein one night in this East Village coffee shop and we had sat and rapped. Chuck could really talk a line. He said, "Well, let's make some films together." He told me he had done all this work with Andy. The Factory used to fawn on Chuck: he was their god, their guide to the underworld, the spinner of tales, the manipulator of rhetoric, the grand astrologer, the seer of the white light, and, generally speaking, the leader of one of Andy's competing subcultural groups.

So we decided we were going to make this skin flick called *Ciao! Manhattan*. Chuck was going to write the script, right? It was conceived as a sort of *vérité* underground movie. I knew that everyone came from the underground, but I decided we were going to do a professional job.

DAVID WEISMAN   Edie was living down in the Chelsea then. We all went down there to see her. It was important because we wanted to film her in the Be-In—the big anti-war demonstration—the next day, when there'd be thousands of kids in Central Park. It was a state visit to the Chelsea. That toothless poet, what's his name? Gregory Corso. He was there asserting himself with Edie as the momentary agent-guru, advisor, decision-maker. "Well, now, what do you want Edie to do? What's she supposed to do in this film? What's this film about?"

We were trying to tell her what a great part it was . . . what a great star she was . . . that sort of thing. It was very babyish. I don't think she had read the script. I don't think she *ever* read the script.

So we left some little nymph, some gay kid, up there to make sure Edie got dressed and came to the Park at the right time for the Be-In. The Be-In was in the Sheep Meadow—just jammed. It was April 15, 1967, with the whole hippie thing, just wonderful. Edie was so *wrecked* when she got there. Chuck said to me, "Okay, Dave, your responsibility's going to be to keep your eye on Edie."

I said, "Bullshit. Come on!"

In ten minutes she'd got away from me! Lost her for the whole day. That was my first hint of what it was going to be like trying to deal with Edie and the loonies.

Still, we got the movie under way. I don't believe anyone, at least out of that crowd, ever believed there was going to be a movie until they actually saw the camera. But once we began shooting *Ciao!* and we had a dolly in the Park—everything very professional, a big thirty-five-millimeter camera instead of that silly little camera Andy used to have—it all seemed very official. So we had the movie going and all of a sudden we got pompous. We actually had this contract-signing number in Margouleff's office. Edie came dressed right up to the hilt, a splendid chinchilla fur, just the image of what she thought it was all about: PAHHHHH! Hollywood premiere time, klieg lights, the works. We all lined up, and pictures were taken. It was all part of the indulgence.

ROBERT MARGOULEFF   It started out such a worthwhile project. In a way, the film was a very accurate representation of what the whole period was about: it all comes through—the madness, the alien-

CIAO! MANHATTAN

Speed. Madness. Flying saucers.

ation, the rage, the shock, everything these people were going through. But it got crazier and crazier. Everybody on the set needed a poke, first once a day, then twice. We actually set up a charge account at Dr. Roberts' office.

DAVID WEISMAN Dr. Roberts used to shoot up the entire cast. He was the official astrologer-doctor; he had a horoscope in one hand and a syringe in the other. Probably the biggest day of his career was when he shot up part of the cast for the big orgy scene in the health club.

RICHIE BERLIN The vitamin doctors were the Jesus Christs of the city. I never had so much junk in my life. They wanted somebody to do the sex scene in the movie with this boy.

I had never gone before the cameras. I was very nervous. I had thirty cc.'s of amphetamine through my Lederhosen, and I was perishing with so much rouge. It took me sixteen hours to get out of my room and to the health club. We did the scene in a rubber raft. I was streaming with sweat, and they kept handing me more grass, more hash. I said, "I'm so stoned." I said, "My mother is going to perish." They threw me into this raft.

So they said, "Just carry on and give yourself up to total abandon." I decided I didn't really care, because my reputation was beyond repair and reproach. All I had to lose was twenty-five dollars allowance a week, and I'd already lost that. I didn't figure on running *Harper's Bazaar*, which my father published. So I did it. I can tell you, I'm nearly the *last* person in the world who would ever consider doing a sex scene for a movie in a rubber raft in the middle of an indoor swimming pool at the health club. But that's the way we wound up with it.

I said to Edie, "What do we do in this scene? You're the star, I'm going to follow you." Then Carter Manson gave me a large injection. Edie took more right before she went into the raft . . . pure amphetamine, pure. We were wearing all the chains, all the jewelry. I had on my evening pumps, and when they put us in the raft, it was, you know, "Come on, Richie, make it with Edie." I asked Edie, "Do they want us to sleep together on a raft in Chuck Wein's movie?" She said, "I think so." I said, "Wait a minute. I just so happen to have . . ." and I reached for a Batman capsule on the end of a gold chain with some Seconals or Tuinals in it, and I handed her one, saying, "My dear, *quel* hoot that we should sleep together in Chuck Wein's film."

Then Edie was going to do it with him, the star, in the raft, you see, but instead she dropped off the raft and did the most *fabulous* backstrokes the length of the pool, and then breaststrokes, and I called to her, "My dear, what else do you do?" She wanted out of it. She was like pixie-dust lust. She was doing what she did best—swimming. "Edie, my dear, *quel* hoot!" So I ended up with the boy making love to *me* on the raft. It was all too much. I was dehydrated.

I remember screaming at Genevieve. She called out, "Do you want me to turn the camera off?" and I said, "I couldn't care *less*. I intend to *die* in Chuck Wein's film." I began to sink to the bottom of the pool . . . all those drugs, the sex on the raft, all the gold jewelry that Edie put on me when she went swimming.

MARY BETH HOFFMANN   My sister, Viva, had said to me, "Look, why don't you come to the health center when we're filming this scene in a swimming pool?" So I went along. I didn't get out of there for forty-eight hours. It was like being a prisoner. All during these bizarre goings-on, the father of the producer—Mr. Margouleff, I think his name was—appeared from time to time with these *haute bourgeoisie* plates of hors d'oeuvres—smoked salmon and caviar. Great quantities of them—the sort of hors d'oeuvres that professional caterers supply. He also provided great bowls of fruit punch. So it was like a very formal cocktail party he was putting on. Every time he would come in, someone would call out, "Hush, he's coming. C'mon now, everybody." He'd appear with his wife and a big dog and all this strange, funny food. Everybody'd shape up and carry on like everyone knew exactly what the film was about. The dog was *enormous*. I heard years later that the dog ate up all the takes and that was why the film never materialized.

EDIE SEDGWICK (from tapes for the movie *Ciao! Manhattan*)   *Oh, wow, what a scene that place was—that heavenly drug-down-sexual-perversion-get-their-rocks-off health spa. I was already so bombed I don't know how I got there. I got down to the pool, where all the freaks were. I met Paul America at the pool and I told him we were probably in danger if we stayed, but we were so blasted we forgot what was good for us and what wasn't, and the whole place turned into a giant orgy . . . every kind of sex freak, from homosexuals to nymphomaniacs . . . oh, everybody eating each other on the raft, and drinking, guz-*

zling tequila and vodka and Scotch and bourbon and shooting up every other second . . . losing syringes down the pool drains, the needles of the mainline scene, blocking the water-infiltration system with broken syringes. Oh, it was really some night . . . just going on an incredible sexual tailspin. Gobble, gobble, gobble. Couldn't get enough of it. It was one of the wildest scenes I've ever been in or ever hope to be in. I should be ashamed of myself. I'm not, but I should be.

Sex and speed, wow! Like, oh, God. A twenty-four-hour climax that can go on for days. And there's no way to explain it unless you've been through it; there's no way to tell anyone who hasn't tasted it. I'd like to turn on the whole world for just a moment . . . just for a moment. I'm greedy; I'd like to keep most of it for myself and a few others, a few of my friends . . . to keep that superlative high, just on the cusp of each day . . . so that I'd radiate sunshine.

ROBERT MARGOULEFF Shooting got so unpredictable. There was one scene in which Paul America was supposed to drop off Jane Holzer at the helioport at the Pan Am Building. We filmed him driving up and letting her out and then driving off. He was supposed to drive around the block and be available for more footage to the scene. But he just kept on going. We didn't hear from Paul again for about *eight* months until finally David tracked him down in Allegan, Michigan, where he was in jail. We had to get permission from the Governor to film him in jail and try to integrate that into the footage.

PAUL AMERICA I was high on some weed, I guess. There was a road map in the car. I figured they were taking advantage of me, so I was ready to leave the scene. I drove to my brother's farm in Indiana. I knocked it out in fifteen hours.

EDIE SEDGWICK (from tapes for the movie *Ciao! Manhattan*) *Paul is such a strange, zombielike guru. I hate him, but I have this strange fascination, this kind of love and sexual addiction for him. I remember on the way to the Cloisters . . . poking up speed in the car. I saw him as like some vision of a Martian . . . somebody from outer space. Maybe it was because he took so much acid that he had this strange alienation from the human race. I'm not sure what attracted me to him unless it was a kind of admiration brought about by the drugs which I was so heavily inundated by. But that morning at the Cloisters was truly beautiful. It was great.*

Edie and Viva on a raft during the orgy scene from *Ciao! Manhattan*

GENEVIEVE CHARBIN   Before he went to jail, it was Paul America who took a hand with Edie. Paul had been on heroin, but he had gotten off of it, and, as it turned out, he took up residence with Edie in the Chelsea and he got *her* off it as well. He was very firm with her.

He's a fascinating person. Quite a handful. He was almost too dangerous and mind-blowing to ever let him out of sight for a second. Can't get bored with *him*. His psychic balance is very delicate—like Edie's, but *very* delicate. You could almost say—though he comes from where, God knows, New Jersey?—that he had just landed from another planet. Almost a total telepath, I would say—you cannot tell him a lie. You can't even begin to open your mouth to tell a lie . . . because this look that comes into his eyes is like that of an intelligent child's eyes.

But if he got overdoses from people, he'd go over the brink. He wanted to do violent things or kill because of it. You never knew if the next moment he wasn't going to leap on you and cut your throat. Once he arrived at my door and pulled out a giant plumber's wrench, a really big wrench, from under his raincoat. He held it up raised over my head. But that's as far as he went. He was looking for money. I let him ransack the drawers. He found some checks left over from an old account riffling through them. I said, "What are you going to do with those? They're no good." He said, "Oh, never mind." He huffed out, taking a radio with him.

He would have to leave town when he got violent and end up in some sort of commune. Then he would come back to New York high-spirited and with the strength of a god. Incredible. Then he'd give you more devastating looks than ever. Crazy again. The cycle kept repeating itself.

Edie had her relationship with him when he'd just returned from the country: he was healthy, strong, and gentle. Lovely. He got her off heroin by keeping her busy. Their relationship was really nice for a while. Then it got ticklish because after a month in the city Paul gets to be unbearable, paranoid, insane . . . and so they finally split up. But while it was going, it was terrific. Edie was in seventh heaven with him.

PAUL AMERICA   Sometimes Edie and I had money for speed and sometimes we didn't, so sometimes we would buy it and sometimes we would just take it. Often we went to Brooklyn to pick up the speed at this dude's home we called the Captain. He had a still set up in his apartment to make speed. The batches were different and some of it was probably dangerous to take. So he would have people try it. The kids hung around. We tried most all of them. The Captain dried the stuff over the oven after it had condensed. Most of it came out brown or yellow. The good stuff was normally white. It wasn't no problem because we were already high on some good stuff, and the rest of it would go through us. Edie was into that. Most of the time people who haven't been doing a lot of it will be a little reluctant to take anything. But Edie was right there. She didn't care.

One of Edie's sisters and her husband came one night to the Chelsea and stayed for a little while. We smoked some marijuana and had some drinks. They said, "We don't think you should live here. We want you to come back home." We gave them all the reasons why she should live there. When the dude left, he said, "Take good care of her, man."

We had some good times. We would go to the Park and have a picnic. Or lock the doors to be sure no one was coming into the hotel. But those times never lasted very long. Somebody was always coming over.

I threw a lot of people out who were bothering her . . . who had come to rip her off. I threw them out as soon as they came in. She didn't dig that, because she dug the scene of a lot of people. She called the bellman and tried to have me thrown out. So I left and didn't come back.

DANNY FIELDS   It was a marathon over at her place, just taking a lot of speed and sitting there for a couple of days. Edie was into making little things—stringing beads and pasting things down.

Leonard Cohen, the poet, was living down the hall. I thought it would be nice if he met Edie. He was into incense and candles, and he did a lot of reading which he got from the magic witchcraft place on Twenty-third Street on how candles should be arranged—the whole Buddhist mystical concept. He burned a lot of incense. The Chelsea didn't like it much; they were always trying to throw him out. He used this smoky kind of stuff which floated down to the lobby, and they were always calling the fire engines.

I took him down the hall to meet Edie. Zoë, her friend, had fallen asleep on the floor. The speed had given out and she'd collapsed on this tube of glue, which had sprung open under her, and she'd become glued to Edie's floor. Every time she'd turn over in her sleep, her shirt would stick. Edie was on the phone. She had a cat with her, Bob Dylan's cat's son. Smoke, his name was. So I brought Leonard Cohen into this scene. What was interesting to him was this line-up of candles Edie had on the mantelpiece. He was troubled when he looked at them. He said to me, "I don't know if you should tell her this, or if I should, but those candles are arranged in such a way so they're casting a bad spell. Fire and destruction. She shouldn't fool around with these things, because they're meaningful." It was very complex. It had to be someone who had really been into candle-arranging and voodoo Haitian candle numbers to figure it out. But when Leonard told Edie, she said she didn't want to hear about such things, that was silly, they were just candles. That was ironic, wasn't it? I mean, her life was full of warnings, probably. It was very soon after that the apartment caught fire and the cat was lost.

DAVID WEISMAN   Edie was nude, covered by a blanket, lying on the floor of the lobby. No one would touch her. People running in and out. It was such an insane night. I took her right down to St. Vincent's Hospital, where they wouldn't admit her. They said her burns weren't sufficient. Dr. Roberts was called; he was out in the Hamptons. He came in at seven o'clock in the morning and gave her some first aid and some injections. Her burns weren't as bad as what happened to the Chelsea . . .

BOBBY ANDERSEN   Her description of the fire was terrifying . . . how she'd awakened and the entire room was in full blaze. I believe it because I went to the hotel to rummage through the ashes to see if there was anything salvageable, and there was nothing left. Where the bed had been was a hole where it had burned through to the floor below. She had obviously been asleep in her bed and had set fire either to her bed or the rug and eventually it had all burned right through. She got up and tried to get the lock open, but she gave up and hid in the closet. When the smoke got into the closet, she took another try at it and burned her hands on the knobs, which were white heat, and then she collapsed outside in the hall.

PAUL AMERICA   Edie told me that she was trying to bake a sweet potato and the oven exploded.

GREGORY CORSO   She did not die in the fire. The cat died in it. The cat was named Smoke, and he went up in smoke.

EDIE SEDGWICK   (from *Ondine and Edie*)   *The second fire, they wouldn't come near me. They would not. I went into the lobby at the*

Chelsea. They said, "Wait until the ambulance." They gave me an oxygen tent. I had bruises across the scalp. We started to St. Vincent's, where my brother Bobby died.

ROBERT MARGOULEFF   After she came out of the hospital, she had nowhere to live, right? Her parents had cut her off; the movie had taken every penny I had. I finally put her up in my apartment on East Fifth Street. The place always smelled of Italian cooking from the neighbors downstairs. There was never too much hot water, and always a stream of people. I had to get someone from the East Village community who would take care of her and go on trips with her and be a sort of companion. I couldn't do it myself. I was out all the time trying to keep the *Ciao! Manhattan* zoo parade going. I got somebody by the name of Bobby Andersen.

33

BOBBY ANDERSEN   I met Margouleff just after I got out of the hospital, where I was seriously ill with hepatitis and told every day that I wasn't going to make it and was all prepared to die. I came out all traumatized. Very strange. Margouleff came along. I was so weak already from exhaustion I was ready to fall down in the street. I had lost my apartment and everything in it. He walked up to me and he said, "Hello, you big tomato." I said, "Get the hell out of here. Leave me alone, you creep."

He could see that I was not feeling well and he took me home to his apartment. I never left. I stayed there for three and a half years. When I met Margouleff, he was importing Hercules movies and dubbing them in English at ABC City. When he said that he was going to make an above-ground underground film, we all made a lot of faces and everything. He said someone called Edie Sedgwick was going to star in it. I'd never heard of her. I envisioned this blonde, pigtailed, freckle-faced, homely, wire-rim-glasses type from the name: Edie Sedgwick. It didn't sound very glamorous or pretty.

You should have heard the way Margouleff carried on about her! He hated Edie. He couldn't compete with her. She was so erratic, at least as far as he was concerned. He couldn't understand that anyone could get that high on drugs. . . . he never had even a drink. And here were all these people around him with needles in their asses and every-

Edie after the Chelsea Hotel fire

thing, shooting amphetamine. I don't think he understood all that vibrancy, all that stimulation that the drugs get going in them.

That was how I got involved. Apparently Edie wasn't showing up; they couldn't get her to learn lines, or do this or that. She had been burned in the Chelsea fire, but no one wanted to take care of her. Everyone had refused. So Margouleff asked me if I wanted a job that paid twenty-five dollars a day to make sure that she got up in the morning, had her face washed, and turned up at the studio in proper attire and behaved herself.

I said, "Sure!" I figured I'd be a real male nurse and real nasty.

Margouleff's was a very strange apartment. He owned it and paid the rent. After that it was my apartment. Every room was different: a psychedelic room, a Victorian room, a Georgian room. The kitchen was the best. It had a tin ceiling. The walls were painted as an American flag. I spent a month's work on the refrigerator to make it look like a Coke vending machine.

Margouleff used to tell everybody that I was his houseboy, which I thought was very insulting. I fixed the apartment up; I decorated it; I ran it. It was in the East Village, a fabulous ramshackle six-room railroad flat, and one day I walked in and looked down to the end, where sitting at the harpsichord was this breathtaking blonde that I could see from six rooms away . . . frosted blonde. I walked over. She stood and asked, "Who are you?" I said, "I'm Bobby. I live here. Who are you?" She said, "I'm Edie Sedgwick. Are you my nurse?"

She had these two people with her, one a boy named Anthony Ampule and a friend of his named Donald, who was a professor. On the harpsichord they had this big pile of methedrine, which they were scooping up and mixing into water. Anthony Ampule was called that because he was able to get ampules of liquid amphetamine from his doctor. I don't know what his real name is; even today he's called Anthony Ampule. They were standing there at the harpsichord measuring out their methedrine. I looked at Edie and I said to myself, "Well, how *fabulous!* This fabulous creature!" She was so *electric* . . . just wonderful; I decided about four minutes after I knew her that she was not an Edie, she was an Edith.

She didn't go out that night. She hadn't brought much of anything with her. She had these great big baseball mitts for hands because of the Chelsea fire, all covered with gauze and bandages. I went out to Max's Kansas City and brought back some food for her. Double shrimp cocktail. A chocolate malted, which they made only for her there.

Mickey Ruskin, the owner, would go in the back and melt the ice cream and beat it and make her a chocolate milkshake.

That was how I met her. I was so pleased. I just thought she was wondrous instantly. So I wasn't a hideous male nurse at all. We caught on like wildfire and got along so well it was wonderful. At Max's they used to call me Edie's nurse, but I didn't mind. We'd have drinks there and put it on Margouleff's account. Terrible! Those were the days of signing for everything on anybody's name. Everybody was very rude about it.

She kept telling me that she expected, when the mitts came off, that she would have grotesque, deformed, webbed hands. When Dr. Roberts finally took the mitts off, she was excited and very surprised. Her hands were in perfect shape.

She looked fabulous in everything! At Max's it was as if Queen Elizabeth had arrived. I remember going out with her in the afternoon when she had on what she called her mini evening gown. She'd seen a full-length velvet gown in the window at Bergdorf's trimmed in egret feathers. She went in and bought it, and because the mini skirt was in such vogue then, she had the evening dress cut to mini size and had the feathers put back on. That was her "mini" evening gown. Over that she wore a black ostrich-plume coat, peacock-feather earrings, and black satin gloves up to here with ostrich-plume bows on the top. For broad daylight in the East Village she was incredible! With a huge black straw hat over it.

We went to Coney Island like that. She took her first and only subway ride in New York. The people on the train just loved her. She never sat down the whole way out—the train was so crowded we stood all the way from the East Village to Coney Island. She was in all that mad regalia with a bikini underneath so we could go swimming. The people loved her. She was talking to everyone and getting along. We rode in the first car so she could look out of the window in the front. She was fascinated by the tunnels and the weaving of the train and the clacking. Just fabulous. She'd never experienced anything like it.

We did everything. We had cotton candy; ate hot dogs at Nathan's; we went on the parachute jump, the roller-coaster; we went swimming in the surf and lying in the sun. We collected shells and rocks and brought back two completely chewed corncobs for souvenirs. We did everything. The funhouse. She was just incredulous . . . all wild-eyed and goo-gaa. The distortion mirrors. And the laughing and the laughing.

She screamed all the way up and all the way down the parachute jump, the big peacock-feather earrings standing straight out from her head. We got on the log sluice ride with those big silicone logs, and you came down this big sluice, and water splashed over her feathers and hat and everything, and she just loved every minute of it. I took her on the ride where the man in the gorilla costume chases after your car—one of those spook-house things. She just *loved* him, carrying on with him and asking him into the car with us.

On the carrousel she rode the swan—a double- or triple-seater with the silhouette of a swan on either side. She said, "Birds of a feather ought to stick together."

We went swimming—leaving all this velvet and feathers strewn all over the beach in the midst of these Puerto Rican people and black people and everything. We went way over our heads swimming. Then we came home on the subway with all the rush-hour crowds. The front car both times. Oh, she just loved it! We came home so exhausted.

She was happy at Margouleff's. I never left her for a minute, even when she went to work. We'd go to the banks together. I remember going down to pick up the trust-fund checks and having her pay for the cab with a pearl-and-diamond ring one day. He refused to wait. He took the ring when he read the carat weight inside.

She had on a big star-sapphire ring which she said was worth twenty-five hundred dollars. It fell out of the setting three times to my knowledge, and she kept putting it back in. The fourth time it fell out onto the dance floor; she got annoyed with it and just stomped and pounded it into the dance floor and threw the setting across the room. She left the sapphire embedded in there. Edith wasn't bothered by things like that. She was just fabulous!

We used to share the same bed every night. It wasn't that I had to watch her, we were just that close. In the morning I used to try to feed her omelets and stuff, but she just wouldn't hear about it. She wanted cold shrimp and milkshakes. I'd say, "Edith, please. You're on the Lower East Side, honey. Come down a little."

"I just want what I want . . . what I'm used to."

"Come on, honey," I'd say. "You're making it very difficult for me. I have to make you up, bathe you, I have to do all this crap. I have to have a good time with you, and yet you want me to go out and buy fucking gourmet food at nine in the morning."

In the beginning I had to help her put on her make-up because her hands were these big mitts. I had to put the eyelashes on, and zip her up, and help get her bra on, and this and that. I knew how to do make-up because I had studied it at the Fashion Institute. She'd sit on the stool in the kitchen with five hundred bottles of make-up spread out on the counter. I made her tell me exactly what she wanted. She'd point with her big stumps and say, "Make it darker there," or whatever. She was very big on the black make-up. At the time she still had a few light burns on her face that I covered up with foundation make-up.

I used to have to bathe her. I'd put plastic around the bandages with rubber bands to keep them tight. She'd been there a week and she hadn't taken a bath. She'd say, "Oh, my bandages . . . this, that, I'll get this wet." She went through stages where she was very unclean, though she never smelled. I guess she was just so high on amphetamine it never registered. She always looked immaculate and beautiful.

In the evening we'd help each other get dressed for the parties. I used to really get off making her very fabulous and beautiful. She'd go in my closet and get things to dress me. She'd go in her boxes and crates and dig out all these things. Scarves were very big then. And jewelry. I wore her trousers because we were about the same size in pants. After her hands were healed, she would comb my hair and I used to do her hair. She got me to grow my hair back blond. It was white then, because they had convinced me that I was going to be an underground-movie star. I was very stupid and affected all the time. My hair was snow white, along with my eyebrows, my eyelashes, my sideburns . . . everything was white. People would come up: "Oh, if I only had hair like that . . . I'd give my right arm for it."

I'd say, "Well, it costs seven dollars a week . . . you can have it."

They just didn't believe it wasn't real. No, I didn't have a pierced ear then, but I had a front tooth missing due to drugs and bad diet and poverty. Ruined my whole mouth. These teeth are all artificial.

Sometimes we'd spend two days getting dressed and we'd sail right past the party we were going to. That's a common amphetamine phenomenon. It's not that everything's slowed down. In fact, everything's carried on at a rapid pace; but it's a problem of trying *every* combination, trying on every stitch with everything . . . until finally getting a complete outfit and being all ready to go and suddenly deciding that maybe you'll just change the scarf, and then you do that and realize that something else doesn't go with the scarf, so you change that something else, and you become completely disoriented. You spend all night getting dressed, and by then you completely forget where you're supposed to be going. By the time you're done, you're so exhausted you lay down and go to sleep.

If you stayed up too long on amphetamines, your vision could play tricks on you. Every car you passed with bucket seats had two people sitting in it. Every tree had someone behind it. You'd see people in the windows waving at you. You'd walk down the street and hear people calling your name. "Bobby, Bobby, Bobby," and I'd look all around and there'd be no one there. Then there were also voids. During a conversation you'd realize that you'd just blacked out for a moment—a whole gap in which you hadn't heard anything.

There's no remembrance of what you do under those barbiturate overdoses. You get up, move around, roam, and do things. Once I got up in the middle of the winter with no shoes on, nothing but a pair of slacks and a raccoon coat. And I walked for blocks for a pack of cigarettes, pounding on the front door of shops at five in the morning, insisting that they open up, and flagging a bus down by standing in front of it and making it stop: "Drive me to my street!" I remembered nothing. Tommy Slocum, the Indian boy who lived with us occasionally, followed me to make sure that nothing happened to me, and told me the next day what I'd gone and done; I just didn't believe it.

When Edith first came to live with us, I had never given anybody any kind of needle in my life; I just didn't know anything about it. When Edith said, "My dear, would you give me a poke?" I said, "Sure, tell me what it is."

She took me into the bathroom when she had the needle all ready. I went, "Oh, no, no, no, no. I can't do this." She said, "Sure you can, it's very easy."

We went back and forth for twenty minutes before I was able to stick it in her behind. It was like stabbing somebody, to me. I was *so* frightened. I kept asking, "Does it hurt? Does it hurt?" She kept saying, "No, no, no, no, no." She was holding on to the sink. She was all dressed; she had on navy blue corduroy pants and a Pucci halter top and a matching turban, and of course the pants were down so I could push the needle in her behind. I tried three times. I really almost fainted and fell off the toilet seat. I kept saying, "Don't you want to swallow it or something?"

After a while I could give her an injection any time. In fact, I got pleasure out of giving people needles after a while. It was always made to sound very cute and "toy" to pull your pants down for the shot— "toy" meaning childlike. Very nursery school.

But getting poked really did hurt Edith because she began to develop a lot of scar tissue on her fanny and she had to use big, thick needles to get it in. There's foreign matter with a lot of the street drugs, and it sort of sat in her fat tissue. These are all things I've learned since then.

My dear, beautiful Richie Berlin's behind! They used to call it Rocky Mountain Range and everything. Rhoda Buddha's Rocky Mountains— Rhoda Buddha was Richie's nickname. She could give herself shots. But Edith refused to do it herself. She didn't want to take that step down the hill.

When I first met them all, I wouldn't have them touch me with a needle. I took a couple of pills once in a while; I would get high on those, and it was fabulous. They kept showing me this powder and saying it's the same thing. Finally I let someone give me a poke; it put me in St. Vincent's Hospital. I almost lost my leg. She had used a very long hypodermic, and because I have a very small behind, it went right through the muscle where it belonged. I was almost paralyzed for life. Gangrene and everything. In return for which they called me up at the hospital and told me to eat a lot of fresh fruit! That's how serious it was to all of them . . . all these people working on *Ciao! Manhattan*. They thought it was just hilarious.

Then I got going on it. Getting pokes. I remember going into the Brasserie restaurant and having the little old bathroom attendant do it for me. I was so spaced out I couldn't do it myself. I told him I was a diabetic. He said, "Oh, ah can't do dat. Ah can't do dat." I said, "Look, I'll just hold it here and you walk up behind me and hit it with your hand." I had it in place for him. It was a machine like a small pistol, just the cutest thing. It's like holding a water gun against your behind and squeezing the trigger. So anyway the bathroom attendant closed his eyes, and *pop* he went and hit it.

When Edith lived with me, she had a purse she carried around for the drugs—a picnic basket that was about two feet wide and a foot and a half deep which was filled with hundreds of little zipper bags, plastic bags, plastic boxes, bubblegum bubbles, a lot of it to hold syringes, cotton balls, little vials of alcohol, amphetamines, pills, tranquilizers. Everything was inside of something else. That's an amphetamine dementia. Lots of order. You find something that fits in this box. Then you find something that this box fits in; everything goes inside something else, and it's all very mazy but tight and orderly. It's known as being anal compulsive. It's an amphetamine trait. Most people who take amphetamines are very neat: they'll fluff up a pillow to make it look nice while you're still sitting on it. They empty ashtrays. Edith could spend hours unloading her purse. And then start packing it up again and forget what she was looking for when she started. Incredible! Anywhere. On the sidewalk, on the street, in a restaurant, a bar. Hundreds of things would come out to be unscrewed and looked in and

then screwed back up and replaced. *So* many things. It was like carrying an entire life-style with you . . . like living with a camper van
on your back. Oh, it was definitely an amphetamine thing. They all did
it; they all had tote bags. I had a tote bag. I don't mean to exclude
myself from all of these things I'm talking about, because we were all
the same.

She took the basket with her when we went out. We went out a lot.
One night we went to see Jimi Hendrix give a special performance at
Steve Paul's The Scene. Edith had talked about it for days in advance.
We went in Margouleff's gold Cadillac, which we parked illegally on
Eighth Avenue. We had no reservations, but she did a whole production demanding to see Steve Paul, letting them know just who she was,
and we got a special ringside table in a corner, kind of private but
public so you could be seen at the same time. Edith was very quiet
through the whole thing. She spent most of the performance going
through her wicker basket, opening plastic bubblegum capsules that
she had buttons in, and loose hypodermic needles. While this was going on, Jim Morrison, the rock star, got up on the stage and went
through an adoration number. He took down Hendrix's pants and
went down on him right up there on the stage. At first everyone's
mouths fell open. When it was over, they applauded and screamed.
Edith thought it was absolutely fabulous, but disgusting. Did Hendrix
mind? Oh, no, I guess not! Well, what man *would* mind? Those people
were so very uninhibited anyway, they were all so stoned. I don't think
Hendrix had an orgasm. None of those people were able to reach an
orgasm easily because of the quantity of drugs they were on at all
times.

Edith took so many! Along with her amphetamine usage, she took
barbiturates to go to sleep. That's why she had so many fires—because
she was in such a barbiturate fog that it would cause a roller-coaster
reaction and eventually she would nod off with cigarettes. In the Margouleff apartment alone she went through three mattresses and about
five fires. It was incredible how fast she could set a bed on fire with a
cigarette. The trouble was you'd have to wait for her to pass out to
take the cigarette out of her fingers. She'd get really indignant and
bitchy if you tried while she knew what you were doing.

Yet you'd leave the room, gone just two minutes, and BOOM, the next
thing you knew she'd be asleep and there'd be smoke coming out of the
bed and a hole in the mattress this big. Sometimes she had convulsions
and scared me half to death . . . wicked. She'd say all the things in
her subconscious that had been bothering her . . . that she'd been smil-

ing at people and kissing their asses for nothing. She'd let it all out. She attacked Margouleff viciously; she'd call him a "cheap kike" to his face. She was *wicked!* "You rotten kike, you cheap bastard, Jew mother-fucker, small-time entrepreneur!" Oh, yes, once in a while she'd get a good one in.

Margouleff would say, "Get her to bed. Tie her down if you have to." He seemed very practical about the whole thing. But then all of a sudden, sitting there, he'd begin to shake. He was so upset about that whole experience. Just incredible!

Edith's parents, of course, were terribly concerned and I think very sincere about what was happening to their daughter. There were telephone calls to California. They turned up on the telephone bills . . . Margouleff screaming: "I'm not paying for this! I'm paying her a salary. That's *enough*." Mrs. Sedgwick—I felt like I was talking to my own mother. She wanted me to report to her. "Well, how badly burned is she?"

"Well, it's all right, Mrs. Sedgwick. The doctor is doing a lot and he says there won't be any physical damage . . . maybe a little nerve damage."

Then she'd hem and haw and I knew what was coming next. "Is she on drugs?"

When I'd just met Edith, I'd say, "Well, Mrs. Sedgwick, she's off drugs and she hasn't been on them." That's truly what I thought. All the time Edith in the background would be giving me signals with those big bandaged hands. If I ever got even *near* a topic that was sensitive, there was a lot of waving of those big baseball mitts.

"She's not on heroin, is she?"

I'd say, "Oh, *no*, not on heroin" . . . and Edith would go "Mmmmm," waving her hands in the air.

"Is she drinking? Is she still an alcoholic?"

"Mrs. Sedgwick," I'd say, "I've never seen her pick up a glass with anything but fruit juice and milk in it."

"Oh, thank you," Mrs. Sedgwick would say. "I'm so glad she finally has someone who cares."

I wondered how many times she'd said this to someone on the phone. She must have been through it a hundred times. I could tell she was going through a great deal of grief . . . I mean, she was a real mother, and I felt sorry for her.

Then Edith would get onto the phone and I'd listen in on the extension so Edith and I could talk about it afterwards.

I never met anyone who wanted to go home so much. She used to show me pictures of herself on cruises and in Europe . . . pictures of her on an ocean liner. She must have been at least thirty to forty pounds heavier. I could hardly believe it was the same person. She'd say, "Isn't it incredible?" She looked so much like little Miss Innocence; a healthy All-American girl, and what a lovely debutante. But Edith didn't much like herself like that. She would say, "Aren't I ridiculous? I look like all the rest of them. Don't you think I'm more fabulous now?" Well, I agreed. She *was* more fabulous.

Oh, I was totally awed and impressed to have such a glamorous, exciting woman in my company. I was totally infatuated and madly in love with her. One night—it was the night she had so many drugs she had convulsions and set fire to the bed—we curled up to go to sleep; I put my hand under a T-shirt she was wearing. She responded. But so very gently. Hardly any physical movement at all. It was totally boring and uninteresting—like having sex with a child. She didn't even know how to kiss. She was very fond of kissing around the hairline with little gentle kisses.

When Edith was with someone she really liked and she was on speed and wide awake, she must have been the wildest fuck in town. Amphetamines make you very wild and degenerate about sex, they really do . . . very creative and demented. It's like an eight-hour non-stop stretch of sniffing amyl nitrate. You have no idea. No idea! So wonderful, so inspired, so uninhibited . . . it's one of the truly inspired sex accessories there ever was. You became a sex addict—it's divine. That's the main reason so many of that crowd took it, because that's what they all had in their minds ninety percent of the time: sex. Totally sex-oriented. Amphetamine was only fabulous for that. Everything else that it did for you was boring.

But this night with Edith I was very disappointed. She didn't even remember it, never mentioned it: which was a little heartbreaking. I don't think she really knew how to be in love with anybody . . . not just because of what happened that night. She didn't know how to be *in love*. If you don't love yourself, you can't love anybody else. Sex to her that night was about as useful as when I gave her a bath or combed her hair or helped her across the street; I was like a Boy Scout. But she was very drugged. How much can a dead body enjoy a piece of sex?

It was strange. She thought nothing of exposing her lower sexual area, but she always covered her breasts. Even that night we had sex, she kept the top on and took her pants off. Her breasts were about the size of pears; very small breasts . . . which is very attractive on certain women. Especially for me, because I don't know what to do with very large breasts.

I thought she'd be kind of great. Absolutely great. She was so dynamic on so many levels. Sexually, physically, since she was very lithe, very muscular. And the face. I've always been in love with the face. The face is *everything* to me. I've been to bed with more trolls that had beautiful faces. I even picked up somebody with a beautiful face who turned out to be a deformed dwarf with no arms and one leg—I swear to *God*—a man I met in a bar. I couldn't tell that just about everything on him was artificial. He was just beautiful; he could sing opera like a *professional*, he was so talented. He was quite short. *Very* short. He came back to my apartment, and I thought he was walking funny. I was so dumb. This beautiful, beautiful face! You have no idea what I went through. When we got to my room, he took off his arms and dropped them to the floor. On one side, the left side, he had a whole hand coming out of his shoulder. On the other side he just had this little finger sticking out of his body. I laugh about it now, but . . . oh, my God! Then he unhooked his leg. I was sitting there in total shock. Then he stood on the one leg that was really there, balancing on this little leg, and, shaking as he leaned way forward, these little fingers pushed his underwear down: and I fainted! I absolutely fainted. He had two cocks that grew together and then separated into two heads. I just slid down to the floor. He was saying: "Do you mind if I take a bath?"

I said, "No. Please do. Take a bath."

So he hopped in and filled the tub—God knows how he did it . . . I mean with *what*? One of those little appendages?

I must have waited five hours for him to come out of that bathroom. When he was in there, I never heard a sound. I kept listening; I was waiting for the water to splash, anything. I said, "Oh, my God! This *thing* is dead in my bathroom! It drowned!"

He finally came out and I put him to sleep on the couch. He was getting off on what he was doing, taking everything off and shocking me. The next day I told him, "Please. Listen. If I could *buy* you a contract at the Metropolitan Opera so you could sing, I would. Anything! But you have to leave!"

There was always a stream of people turning up at Margouleff's apartment—maybe not as strange as the opera singer, but just as twisted! Lots of them came to hustle Edith. Mostly under the guise of getting drugs for her. She was always very trusting, and also open to receiving something new to get high on. She'd hand out hundreds of dollars and the people going out to get the drugs just wouldn't bother coming back.

She was really a terribly absurd person . . . people just conning it out of her, or just borrowing it, or stealing it. I remember only once I actually abused her. I took two dollars off her when I was broke. I was never so ashamed of anything in my life. I went to Max's to meet some people. She gave me hell in the morning for it. She said, "I had five dollars when I went to sleep and there's only three left." I said, "Well, I took two dollars out of your pocketbook." I was never so ashamed of anything. What can I say? They were very strange times. I have no idea how long Edith stayed with me. It seemed like a lifetime.

34

HUDDLER BISBY   In 1783 a European shipping tycoon built a stone castle on a cliff on the Jersey side of the Hudson River . . . he was hanged as a spy shortly after the construction was completed. By the neck until dead.

By 1965 all that remained of the castle was the ornate Victorian guest house with its stained-glass windows, elaborate wooden gingerbread trim, a small moat and endless stone walls, extremely well suited for imaginary aerialism in Fort Lee, New Jersey.

The castle was like a psychedelic hotel. Haight-Ashbury East. The long winding driveway almost always featured one sort of Day-Glo bus or another. In the early Sixties it was occupied by two young artists, Tom Daly and Peter Max. They made posters showing what the world looked like through the eyes of a person who lived in a psychedelic hotel on a cliff on the Jersey side of the Hudson River.

The best thing Edie does in *Ciao! Manhattan* is a scene in the very early dawn. She's walking on a brick wall near the Fort Lee castle. An imaginary aerialist, balancing on an imaginary high wire. The way her muscles are moving, fluid at that time, it's very hydraulic, very much in tune with the wind.

Edie's success as a drug geisha was based on her ability to handle high-speed drugs at high speeds . . . at *very* high speeds. Difficult to do. The secret of her charisma was that she was only really beautiful when she was running not just at fifteen miles an hour, or fifty, or eighty-eight, but at fifteen hundred.

With people doing it together, each drug experience is like a group hypnosis, like we tune to each other until we're one radio. But even so, there's got to be at least one professional specialist in the broadcast, an anchor, a source of stability. Edie was one of those people who held you down, kept you from going nuts, because it didn't matter to her that you were going fifteen hundred miles an hour, she was okay at that speed.

ALLEN GINSBERG   The producers had the idea that since the film was about Manhattan, and they'd found a castle that overlooked the city, it would be interesting to do an imaginary sylvan scene, or rustic scene, or barbaric scene, or Fontainebleau scene, with a group of nymphs, satyrs—naked as if savages from another planet, time, century, era, mode of consciousness—looking across the Hudson River at the glittering light of fish-shaped Manhattan. I never got the idea of the whole film. All they wanted me to do was chant mantras across the river to New York. I thought that was harmless—in fact, might even do some good: a contrast combining nakedness with self-confidence, presence, or majesty of some kind that comes from grounding in meditation and mantra—an aspiration toward a spiritual approach including and beyond dope, sex-craze-hysteria.

It was unclear what was being done: some young people wandering through a forest toward a precipice overlooking Manhattan. Was I supposed to be a sort of naked satyr-king leading a band of hippies through the woods to overlook modern civilization? "The Fall of the House of Usher"? The natives peeping through the bushes? *King Kong*? Something like that was going on. Now, what they got on the camera I never saw.

JEAN MARGOULEFF   I was really shocked by some of the things I saw. An example: one fine day on the set they had Allen Ginsberg sitting on a log with all these young people around him while he was doing his karma or his mantra, whatever, with all these young ladies and men around him, and he was in the buff. He was absolutely *naked*. They photographed him that way and I said to my son, Bob, "If you put *that* in the film, please do not put our name on it in any way, shape, or manner, because I just don't want to be associated with that kind of thing. I don't care if his name *is* Allen Ginsberg." It isn't the kind of

Allen Ginsberg, in a scene from *Ciao! Manhattan*, in Fort Lee, New Jersey

thing that was done in my generation, and I don't know how much younger Allen Ginsberg is than I am, but it certainly isn't becoming in *his* generation either. Or any generation.

My son, Bob, had told me that *Ciao! Manhattan* would cost us about fifty thousand dollars. It ended up costing about three hundred fifty thousand dollars. The film began, so I thought, as a day in New York in the life of Edie Sedgwick, and it wound up trying to portray the entire scene of that era—the counterculture, the short-short skirts. The first time I ever met Edie she was wearing the first real silvered hairdo I ever saw, and she wore this abbreviated-abbreviated costume, which indicated to me that she was somewhat uninhibited. Very daring. She would walk around the studio in the buff. We talked quite frequently. For the most part, she was really a little out in left field. She talked about her life—but very sketchily. I don't think she understood what was going on. She thought her father was a very evil man on Monday, and on Tuesday he was sitting there holding God's hand.

Of course, I was so much older than the whole group. I tried on many occasions to straighten things out, but it was very difficult to impose my point of view on a generation I just really didn't understand. To this day I don't understand those so-called groups that were prominent at that time. That was a time of confrontation rather than consultation.

The film had no story line. Nobody really knew what they wanted. Their minds, their attitudes were somehow circular; everything would go around and around and never break out. Chuck Wein, who was the writer, was perhaps a very brilliant man in his field—but I don't know what his field was: I never discovered it.

They borrowed my Cadillac for an hour and it came back six months later—a shambles. They used it until it fell apart. They lugged their mattresses around in it; they filmed from it; they used it all over town. They destroyed that and they destroyed my son's Porsche and a couple of other cars. If your ambitions are to see something successful come of your son's ventures, I guess you become a little supergenerous. I just couldn't control the thing.

BOBBY ANDERSEN   Fort Lee is where Edith reached the point where they all decided they were through with her. It was at the end of the shooting. She was at her most divine, her most fabulous, her most inspired . . . but she was unbearable. They must have shot every scene a hundred times. She just had no concept of what she was doing. She held it up for hours and hours. She had to do her exercises, she had to do this, she had to do that. I just loved every minute, egging her on: "Don't pay any attention to them. You're having a good time, Edith. That's all that matters. It's about time you had a good time"—as if she'd never had one before! We danced most of the day and we disappeared in the castle attics for hours. With a photographer. Taking photographs, and posing, and gossiping. We had so much fun hiding from them in these secret rooms in the fabulous old house.

As for Margouleff's parents, I think they really almost *died* from it! About a week before Fort Lee, I'd been up at their offices where they were extremely hostile to all of us. especially their son Bob. They kept dragging him into little rooms, off to the side, and I kept hearing screeches and shrieks. I mean, to go through so much money and find they'd been spending it on a bunch of drug addicts who sat there cutting the film into tiny one-inch strips showing some pigeons in the air and saying, "How fabulous!" They cut I don't know how many hours and ended up with two squares of celluloid of pigeons that they thought were the *best*. Just sat there on the floor, all wired up.

ROBERT MARGOULEFF   More and more they got into these crazy things. There was this scene which was supposedly on a beach. So they took my studio and filled the entire place with sand. Tons and tons of it. The place was destroyed. I had a really nice office which was absolutely ravaged, right? I was horrified. I was straight: I had short hair, I wore three-piece suits, and my office—the one they dumped all the beach sand into—was full of antique furniture. My partners ran for the hills. I used to run around with a broom, always sweeping up, trying to keep the place in at least some semblance of order.

Finally I sent the whole crew on vacation. I thought, "Well, hell, why not?" and they went to some volcanic island in the Mediterranean for a week while I got the studio cleaned.

That film reduced me to chicken-salad sandwiches, a little one-room office over a bar on Third Avenue, and holes in my shoes. It really changed the course of my life.

BOBBY ANDERSEN   After the film project began to go to pieces, Edith wanted to get back with Andy. She saw him a few times—making up with him—and they did a little film together. The *Ciao!* people got paranoid about it because they heard Andy was going to release it and call it *Ciao! Manhattan*. They were absolutely terrified. A close friend of Andy's had come around and said, "*Dears,* I want you all to know that Andy has already filmed, edited, and published *Ciao! Manhattan*. It is very soon to be released with Edie Sedgwick, and it is the REAL *Ciao! Manhattan*."

ONDINE   We filmed a scene—a small scene—that was later called *Ondine and Edie*. I don't think it will ever be seen; it's in Warhol's closet. I was the one who asked her to do it, because I had the feeling that if Edie was going to make it, she really should make it with Warhol. But I didn't realize there was so much pressure and that so much had gone on between her and Warhol that it was no longer viable. Once Andy makes up his mind against you, you don't return in a Warhol film. But in this case he tried.

Edie had gotten really nervous. It's absolutely the most excruciating piece of footage you'll ever see in your life. It's a whole reel of the total collapse of a person . . . Edie trying to be charming and delightful, smoking cigarette after cigarette, talking to me about things she thinks I'll enjoy, playing actors and actresses weirdly . . . and it just didn't work. It begins to get really painful because she is so obviously coming apart at the seams. Just coming apart! My lover and a couple of other people watched it at the Factory once and they asked Warhol to please take it off. Someone said it was literally the most painful movie he'd ever seen in his life.

GREGORY CORSO   I got on Warhol about Edie. It was at Max's Kansas City. He happened to be sitting alone. I was with Allen Ginsberg. I said to Warhol, "You suck, you know that? You make these chicks into superstars and then you go off into your own thing and you drop them . . . literally, like that. You pick these little birds out and make superstars out of them. And look what happens to Edie!" I really got on his ass. Ginsberg whispered to me, "Gregory, you're laying too much weight on this man. It's really not his fault. Don't you think you should apologize to that man?" I said, "No way."

PAUL MORRISSEY   Sepp Donnhauer, a big rock 'n' roll promoter, was there when we filmed that night, and right afterwards Edie took off with him in a car and drove to California like a hippie beatnik.

35

DANNY FIELDS   The Castle is very high in the Hollywood hills. The land was completely neglected. A swimming pool down the hill was full of algae and moss. It hadn't seen the touch of a gardener in years. Bela Lugosi's house is right across the street, which looks like a Mayan pyramid and was designed by Frank Lloyd Wright. The Castle has a two-story-high living room, a fake-gold-leaf vaulted ceiling, big windows, a grand piano, a spiral staircase, and off it are several weird, irregularly shaped bedrooms. There is a tower room. It all looks like it was made of papier-maché. In the living room you could hear a roll of toilet paper being unrolled up on the third floor. It was a famous haunt for rock 'n' roll people when they first went to Hollywood. They could rent the whole place. The Jefferson Airplane stayed there. So did the Velvet Underground.

We drove up to the Castle. Edie had left Sepp and was going with Dino Valente then—he wrote this one song, "Come on, children, let's all get together, smile on your brother." It became a classic, but it was a one-shotter. Edie was with him up at the Castle. As soon as I got up there, she was after me: "Oh, do you have any downs?" I said, "Nope." "Aw, come on, I just need a Tuinal to get through till tomorrow. I need three Tuinals a day and I've only had two. Last night I took six and they didn't work." In fact, I did have some pills with me, but I wasn't going to let her get near them.

Relationships were built entirely on drugs . . . the only thing going. "Do we have any junk for tonight?" I hid my suitcase under my bed that night. I took the pills out and hid them somewhere in the room. A few hours later, and don't you know, Edie found them? They were all gone. She must have had a nose for them, because she didn't even have to rip the room apart to find them.

MICHAEL POLLARD   When I met Dino with Edie at the Castle, he looked at me and said, "Hey, man, ants, man, ants. Watch out—ants!" He said "ants" like he was drowning in them.

NICO   After Dino, Edie was very much in love with Patrick Tilden. He was Bob Dylan's best friend. Bob had been staying at the Castle before the Velvet Underground moved there. Bob's song "Leopard-Skin Pill-Box Hat" is written about Edie. Everybody thought it was about Edie because she sometimes wore leopard. Dylan's a very sarcastic person . . . It is a very nasty song, whoever the person in it might be.

When Edie and Patrick fell in love, I thought it was a very romantic thing. She lived downstairs in Severn Darden's old room, the spookiest room of all. It was haunted. There was a pentangle in the entrance. I heard the shrieks and funny noises . . . I hear things rather than feel them. Every morning at four, at the same spot, somebody . . . the ghost . . . would make this noise like a broomstick pounding on the floor.

I met Jim Morrison while Edie was staying with me, and he had a fetish for red-haired shanties . . . you know, Irish shanties. I was so much in love with him that I made my hair red after a while. I wanted to please his taste. It was silly, wasn't it? Like a teenager.

PAUL ROTHCHILD   Everything at the Castle was theater. Jim Morrison was another colossal madman pursued by his own demons. He was a tester, too, like Dylan but much more cruel. He took Nico up in a tower, both naked, and Jim, stoned out of his mind, walked along the edge of the parapet. Hundreds of feet down. Here's this rock star at the peak of his career risking his life to prove to this girl that life is nothing. "This is theater. I'm doing this theater for you." He asked Nico to walk the same line and she backed down. Edie would have walked it.

The filming of *Lulu*. *(Above)* Bob Neuwirth putting the finishing touches on Edie. *(Below and opposite)* Edie with Richard Leacock.

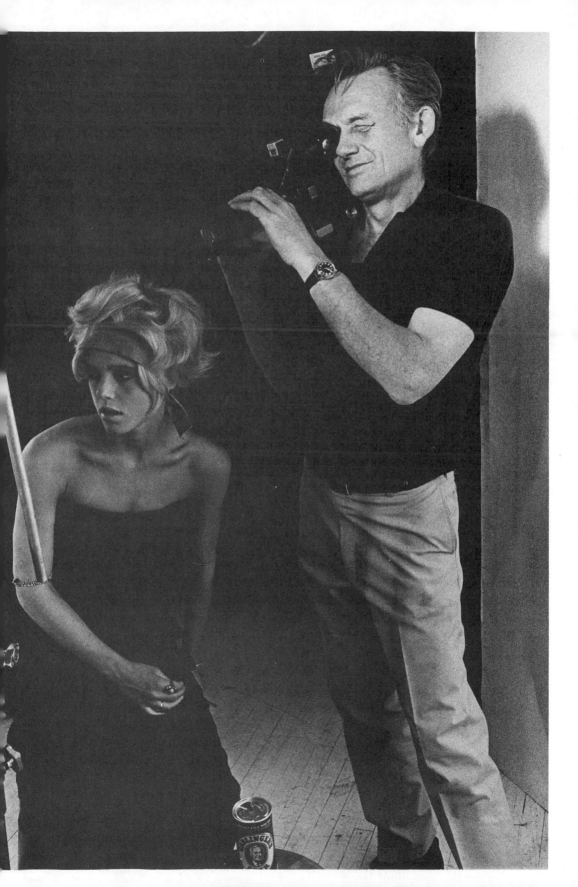

RICHARD LEACOCK   I called Edie in August, 1967, and asked her to play the part of Lulu in the film sequences for Alban Berg's opera, which Sarah Caldwell of the Boston Opera Company had asked me to do. I bought Edie an airplane ticket and she arrived first-class with a bandaged bare foot and what looked like a nightgown on. She was absolutely desperate because she had been on some drug, and if she withdrew from it she would have convulsions. Everybody had to run around like crazy to get what it was she needed. About four in the morning she decided she wanted a chocolate milkshake with two scoops of ice cream and an extra blob of something else. I adored her from afar. For those closer to her it was more complicated. I asked Bobby Neuwirth to come along with us on this filming—in a sense I saw him as a nurse, which was not really fair because it drove him crazy. I remember him saying, "Don't ask me to be a nursemaid. I can't do it. I can't take it."

Edie had never read the script, never heard of *Lulu*, had no idea what it was all about. I was certainly taking advantage of the fact that she was living through this.

SARAH CALDWELL   Ricky Leacock and I wanted to try to use some of the techniques of the Czechoslovakian film and theater—of the actors walking from the stage and onto the screen and off the screen and onto the stage. But mostly we wanted to capture the essence of Lulu in a way that is very difficult to do without the use of closeups. The unreal images of Lulu, the frightening things that one didn't even want to talk about, could be shown more clearly on the film than they could be shown in life.

Ricky went to find Sedgwick and we used five or six film sequences in the opera which he did with her. He started shooting them as very literal film and then he filmed the images reflected on Mylar, which produced a strange image that came and went. So the deeper one got into Lulu, and the stranger her whole relationship to the world became, the further out the film was.

Before the opera, when the public began to come in, the actors turned on some films and sat down to watch. Animalistic films. We had an incredible film of a snake swallowing a rat. There was a scene of a lioness chewing some raw meat which is just one of the most "ugh" kind of things. One member of the animal kingdom feeding on another. And a few nice death scenes. It was brutality.

We were trying to set a mood. The opera starts with a ringmaster in a circus who announces that this is a play about animals. And then

the animals turn into people. Each character has its animal corre-
spondent. They are tigers, bears, monkeys, lizards, and earthworms.
Lulu is a serpent.

Sometimes the audience got very involved and went up on stage
to ask the actors why they were showing the films. They would answer: "Why do you think we're doing it? Would you like to see that
again?" And the actors would turn back and show something particularly horrible. The audience is watching a horrible play unfold. But
enjoying it. Enjoying it as Lulu destroys each one of the men in her
life until finally she is destroyed. But there's no question that in the
audience there's a sense of almost relish as these things happen, which
is another frightening comment on the piece and how it affects people.

Lulu ends up as a prostitute in London, where Schigolch, the old
man who pretends to be her father—he's really the first man in her
life—becomes her pimp. After Lulu solicits Jack the Ripper, a closeup
of his face on the screen reveals that he is Dr. Schön—the man who
earlier in the opera gave Lulu a gun and tried to get her to commit
suicide. . . . She killed him instead. The final scene is very dark, but
I remember vividly his killing her and cutting her into nice little
pieces. On the screen the audience could see the shimmering, distorted
image of Edie's head with a red wig on a greenish-white sheet, and
then slowly a huge pool of blood spreads around her head.

Lulu is finally destroyed. But you can't wipe out the Lulus of the
world. They go on.

BOBBY ANDERSEN   After *Lulu,* Edith returned to New York. I knew she wanted to see her father before he died—all those trumped-up fantasies about going out to California to visit him when she lived with me at Margouleff's. She kept telling me how they had kept him alive for a year on depressants and painkillers and he was withering away with cancer.

Edith would ask her mother if she could talk to her father, but he wouldn't come to the phone. Mrs. Sedgwick would say, "Your father has to do this . . . he has to do that . . . he isn't feeling well. Edith, you don't know what you're doing to your father." All she ever got was "your father, your father, your father." Just hammered up her back.

Edith begged. Cried. Quite a few times. He would *not* speak to her. She had so many mixed, tortured emotions about that man. She loved him, she worshiped him; she hated him.

Her mother would say, "He can't come to the phone. Edith, please, don't put me through this."

Sometimes Edith would wait until she'd hung up and then she'd cry. Sometimes she'd get really furious and outraged and scream about it. She'd turn cold and clinical as she'd describe her childhood and the things they'd done to her.

She told me that her father once tried to punish her by taking her out to the corral, tying her to a post, and whipping her in front of all the servants and the ranch help. She made her father sound like a sadistic Bluebeard, how incredibly unbearable and cruel he was . . . I'm sure she was exaggerating, because people on amphetamine tend to do that a lot. For example, she showed me all these fabulous equestrian sculptures that I now understand her father did and said that *she* had done them . . . pulling out these photographs of enormous sculptures to show me. In those days I just didn't think it was possible for people to sit and fabricate things like that, so I was very impressed and awed. I kept saying: "You really did that? You did that yourself? With your little hands and your little body and your little person?" She kept saying, "Oh, and you should have seen some of the other things I've given away to doctors at the hospitals where I've stayed." Well, that's an amphetamine thing . . . to fib. It could show a desire to duplicate her father in herself, couldn't it?

She had her children's books with her . . . her name inside in scratchy little handwriting. Nursery storybooks . . . most of them English imports from these smart little California bookshops. She cherished them. "This is from this time of my life . . . these are from my childhood when I was a little girl."

She showed me other photographs. "This is my home, this is from my childhood, this is my father's . . . this is my mother's . . ." Home, home, home, home. All I heard about was the name of the ranch: Laguna, Laguna, Laguna. Her horses. How big and wonderful it all was.

JONATHAN SEDGWICK   The ranches always seemed to have one great fat oak tree that was the center of things—the houses sort of curled around them. Incredible trees. We figured they went back to the time of Columbus. At Rancho Laguna, the tree there had wide branches that sheltered Edie's room. It had periwinkle underneath it, very green, which the dogs loved to romp in. It was beautiful. It was like the centerpiece of the family. I know Fuzzy pumped a lot of money into keeping that tree alive. William Kennedy, the butler, told me he spent twenty thousand dollars. One time when I came back from Groton, my father and I were walking by the tree. Just then my father looked up: "You know, when that tree dies, I'll die." That stuck in my mind. I tend to see symbolism in things. When I went back to the old ranch at Corral de Quati, I noticed the tree there had been tremendously pruned—big limbs were missing.

SAUCIE SEDGWICK   My father was rushed to the Cottage Hospital in the middle of the night with what they thought was a kidney stone. They did an operation and found out he had cancer of the pancreas. It's known as "silent cancer" because by the time you have any symptoms it's too late. The cancer had eaten through some tubes that work the kidneys. The following summer he needed another operation.

He did another sculpture: St. Francis receiving the stigmata. Everyone said he was absolutely heroic. Kate told me that he kept trying to do those exercises of his. It must have been like watching an animal whose back is broken. She said it was painful to see because he didn't have the strength to do much except to keep going as best he could.

What stopped him was his sons' deaths. I think he was just eaten alive with guilt. He abused them both terribly, but he must have thought that they would survive and become what he wanted them to be. He had always kept illness at bay, but the moment the real thing—death—got into his family, he died.

HARRY SEDGWICK   Fuzzy suddenly realized he'd destroyed people. He sent out a Christmas card with some Greek saint, or some character in song and story, who apparently had destroyed his children. Killed them all. Alice stopped the mailing but a few did get out. I know there was great talk in the family about it.

MINTURN SEDGWICK   I went to stay with Francis and Alice near the end of Francis' life. I heard him say, "You know, my children all believe that their difficulties stem from me. And I agree. I think they do." I can see him saying it just casually to me—I think there may even have been other people there. He stated it; he felt it; he knew it.

SARA THOMAS   He never sounded afraid or in despair. When Duke talked on the phone, he always sounded like himself. Once in a while when I called him, he'd say, "It's not a good time." But he always had a vaguely jaunty way of talking about things like that, so it didn't embarrass me to talk with him about it. You never got the feeling that he was afraid of dying. Or that he didn't believe he was going to.

But he did worry about his wife. He said, "I don't know what's going to happen when I'm not there to organize the ranch. I hate to leave her. She tells me she won't leave it. I don't want her to stay there with all those memories."

The statue of St. Francis by Francis Sedgwick at Mission Santa Barbara

HELEN BRANSFORD He may have had *some* concern for Mrs. Sedgwick—I mean, obviously he would—but he was the same old Duke to the end. Friends of the Sedgwicks were shocked because he took up with a young married woman, Ann Morrison, from a first-generation Catholic background. Her father is now a successful businessman in Santa Barbara.

HOLLY HAVERHILL Ann Morrison saw a lot of Duke toward the end of his life. She's really smart as a whip. What was involved with Ann and Duke I had no idea. Naturally everyone in a small town like Santa Barbara has a different story. She's extremely attractive. She's always gone directly after what she's wanted. Sexual energy. She's terribly interested in clothes—able to be chic, or easy and casual in blue jeans. They never made any pretense about their interest in each other—Duke and Ann. You'd meet them having lunch together, walking down the street arm in arm. She was obviously a person who made him *feel* better; he had fun talking to her.

JONATHAN SEDGWICK In one year my father aged forty years. Just a shrunken little old man. Absolutely white hair! When I went to the hospital, I had no feeling, man. He wouldn't let me give him love! So what could I do? I wasn't going to sit there and just say, "Well, the weather's fine today." So I said, "Ah, that must be a bummer having nothing inside you but tubes." He went, "Yeah." I wanted to say, "Why the hell are you trying to stay alive?" I could talk to him square-out. No love. Like, when I first knew he had cancer and we were out riding, I said, "Must be really strange to know you're going to die in a couple of months." He said, "Yeah. It's pretty heavy." That's all he said.

In the hospital he wanted Ann. My mother was shut out. The person who cared the most was Ann. She had access to my father at any hour. My sister Pamela tried to keep her out, but couldn't. She went and read to him every day.

ANN MORRISON We read short stories—Balzac, Stendhal. He loved to read. He was always correcting my English. He could tell stories, stories about people he knew all over the world, and he would tell them in a very Harvard-like way, every sentence structured beautifully so it made the listener chuckle and laugh.

JONATHAN SEDGWICK My father's way of letting out his pain was with laughter or by telling people his troubles . . . just blurting them out. It embarrassed and upset my mother, because she didn't like family things to be heard by everybody. He'd tell everybody, with a sort of nervous laugh, that Minty had hung himself and that Bobby had destroyed himself on a motorcycle. Then, just before my father died, he gave this sculpture to the Mission in Santa Barbara. It was of St. Francis receiving the double stigmata. St. Francis was really him. He never liked his name, Francis. So maybe he was purifying it by putting the "Saint" in front of it. He dedicated that statue to the memory of my two brothers. I think it was a way of purging his guilt. Even though you build up a lot of bad karma, you can get rid of it by giving.

ANN MORRISON Toward the end Duke became much more Catholic in feeling. In fact, a Catholic priest, Father Virgil, saw him just before he died and gave him the last rites. There was a big Catholic service in the Santa Barbara Mission.

JANE WYATT Duke died on October 24, 1967. Father Virgil officiated at his funeral service. The Santa Barbara Mission was absolutely jammed to the very last pew. They had a perfectly beautiful service. The priest said wonderful things about Duke—about all the different facets of being a husband, a writer, a financier, a painter, a sculptor, a rancher, and so on. The music came from a man up in the choir loft. They thought of having monks singing from up there, but they had a single man with either a harmonica or a guitar playing cowboy laments—"There's a Long, Long Trail," or "Get Along, Little Dogies." The tears were just rolling down everyone's face.

SUKY SEDGWICK Mummy was absolutely stoical . . . in fact, Mummy is that way. Since that time I've gone back, and she reads Shakespeare and cries, and that just distresses me, because I know if Mummy can cry that means the dam is overflowing. She'll be all right, but she's got so much behind her that . . . that it just topples over the top of that tremendously enormous barrier.

JONATHAN SEDGWICK My father asked me to do three things. One, to take care of my mother; two, to scatter his ashes on the ranch . . . I can't remember what the third was. I got part of it done—

spreading the ashes. I traveled across the mountain with this little box that used to be my father which weighed about fifteen pounds. I had the awareness that he was there with me. I found a place where I could do it, and I threw the ashes into the wind. Into the wind, man, and a lot of it came back into my face, in my mouth, and I was *eating* my father. That was the weirdest trip I've ever been through in my life. I couldn't get it all out! It was like tons of it went in my mouth. It was weird. Of those three things he asked me to do . . . well, I didn't do anything but scatter the ashes. I wish I could remember what that third thing was.

37

RENÉ RICARD   Edie was in Gracie Square Hospital when her father died. Everyone said, "Fuzzy's dead . . . finally. Thank God. Now maybe Edie can breathe." But it didn't have that effect on her. It was a heavier weight. She kept going in and out of hospitals.

One of my theories is that Edie never had to worry about what she was doing or what was going to happen to her because she always knew the bins were there in which to collapse. I never heard her speak badly about the bins, you know. That's the sad thing. She was convinced that they were necessary and helpful.

L. M. KIT CARSON   I had written a film called *August September* about a rock 'n' roll assassination and I wanted Edie to be in it. A lot of good people were involved in the film. Michael Pollard, who had just made *Bonnie and Clyde,* was in the film. He had met Edie in California and he was in love with her, mostly because he knew Edie had been involved with Bobby Dylan. Michael was in a semi-Dylan phase at the time. By the time she was in Gracie Square other people in the film were in love with her—the director, the producer's lawyer—a guy named Bob Levine who is a very straight kind of lawyer. One day he brought her flowers and then stepped out of the room, dashing tears from his eyes because she was so beautiful and there was so much obviously there.

When they let her out, we began living together. One thing I remember . . . well, how she smelled. In sex your body takes on a certain odor. Edie had a particular smell that came out in lovemaking . . . a sweet but somewhat sickly smell, like orchids. I always thought it had something to do with her burns and the chemicals involved in reconstituting her body. To fuck her was like fucking a very strong child, a twelve-year-old girl . . . athletic and coltish.

We finally moved into the Warwick Hotel, registering there as Mr. and Mrs. Carson because she was afraid they wouldn't let her in under her own name. She thought she was on a hotel blacklist for burning her room in the Chelsea. She had kept me up for about a week straight. Then one day in the back of the toilet I found the little plastic top they put on hypodermic needles, and I realized she was on speed. I really got pissed off. I had a kind of messianic Jesus Christ complex . . . getting involved with girls who are victims and trying to save them. So I got the drugs and took them away from her. We stayed there for two more days without her being allowed to shoot up, and I watched her disintegrate. I had to hold her down on the bed; she writhed; she bounced off the walls. She turned from being Edie, this beautiful woman, into a monkey. It got very violent. We were both being violent, threatening to jump out the windows and kill each other. I told her I was going to kill myself if she didn't stop it. I guess I was trying to make myself into the victim that she would have to save, turning into Edie Sedgwick, doing an Edie Sedgwick number. She got insulted because I was threatening her.

Finally I called her doctor and said, "She's driving me crazy." I told him I was losing a lot of weight, and that I was a wreck. I was over the edge. "What can I do?" I told him I couldn't take care of her and she wouldn't voluntarily commit herself anyplace any more.

He said, "Leave. Get out!"

I was at that state where that was all I could do. I called Warhol and got a hold of Ondine to come and take care of her. Andy wouldn't do it. He just couldn't handle it. But Ondine was enough of a monster to handle Edie, who was another monster. One speed freak knows a lot about another. So he got on the phone and he screamed at her and she screamed at him, but they were having a great game: she was finally being handled by somebody who knew exactly what she was up to.

Then three minor Warhol people came up to the room, but not Ondine. They got all the dope she had in the room and laid it out on the bed. They had a funny way of handling it . . . opening up the capsules on the bed and tasting the stuff and saying how great it was, really good speed, and chiding her for not letting them know that she had all this stuff. They were packing it up to use—right? They said to me, "Okay, we'll take care of her. Go ahead and leave." Edie was delighted, because she thought she was among friends; I guess she'd gotten tired of pushing me around and playing tricks on me.

So I left. I got on a plane and went back to Texas and went to sleep for a couple of days. Three or four days later the police came to the house in Texas and said they'd gotten a call from the manager of the Warwick Hotel in New York saying that my wife was in Bellevue Hospital.

New York *Post*, May 2, 1968

EDIE SEDGWICK: WHERE THE ROAD LED
by Helen Dudar

It's hard to keep track of the leading ladies on the pop scene—they come and go so fast that nobody ever stops to wonder what happened to last year's girl. Or even last week's girl.

Like, who has lately thought "Whatever happened to Edie Sedgwick?" Edie Sedgwick, the 1965 girl. After Baby Jane Holzer and before Viva. Youthquaker! Superstar! The girl Andy Warhol was never without. The one with great brown liquid eyes, who silvered her hair to match his and flickered through half his movies and went to all the good parties with him.

It was Viva, this moment's Warhol superstar who mentioned in a *New York* magazine interview that Edie was "in the hospital," and had been for a long time. Viva said she had visited her there.

Later, on the telephone, Viva identified "there" as Gracie Square Hospital, a small, private, discreet establishment on the Upper East Side, whose patients are usually well-to-do and desir-

ous of private, discreet care. . . .

Gracie Sq. Hospital: The switchboard operator reports "She's not here." Will not say whether she had ever been there.

Chelsea Hotel: . . . She left nine months ago. No forwarding address.

Viva: The 11 a.m. call awakened her, and her voice is a suffering whisper. "None of us know where she is now."

Andy Warhol: "I don't really know where she is. We really were never that close. She left us a long time ago."

The caller, remembering pictures of Andy and Edie at this, that and the other thing, persists, "But there was a time when she was with you a lot."

"Yeah, but then she went on her own and we never saw her any more."

"Do you know of any friends who might know where she is?"

"Well, she went with Albert Grossman, you know, Dylan's manager. That's a whole different crowd. But I never really knew her very well."

Manhattan State Hospital

EDIE SEDGWICK (from tapes for the movie *Ciao! Manhattan*)
*"The Siege of the Warwick Hotel." I was left alone with a substantial
supply of speed. I started having strange, convulsive behavior. I was
shooting up every half-hour . . . thinking that with each fresh shot I'd
knock this nonsense out of my system. I'd entertain myself hanging on
to the bathroom sink with my hind feet stopped up against the door,
trying to hold myself steady enough so I wouldn't crack my stupid
skull open. I entertained myself by making a tape . . . a really fabulous
tape in which I made up five different personalities. I realized that I
had to get barbiturates in order to stop the convulsions, which lasted
eight hours.*

*Something was spinning in my head. . . . I just kept thinking that
if I could pop enough speed I'd knock the daylights out of my system
and none of this nonsense would go on. None of this flailing around
and moaning, sweating like a pig, and whew! It was a heavy scene.
When I finally cooled down to what I thought was pretty good shape,
I slipped on a little muu-muu, ran down the stairs of the Warwick,
barefoot, to the lobby. My eye caught a mailman's jacket and a sack of
mail hanging across the back of a chair in the hallway entrance, and
before I knew what I was doing, I whipped on the jacket, flipped the
bag over my shoulder, and flew out the door, whistling a happy tune.
Suddenly I thought: "My God! This is a federal offense. Fooling around
with the mail." So I turned around and rushed back and* BAM! *the
manager was waiting for me. He ordered me into the back office. They
telephoned an ambulance from Bellevue and packed me into it. Five
policemen. I was back into convulsions again, which was really a
drag, and I tried to tell the doctors and the nurses and the student
interns that I'd run out of barbiturates and overshot speed. . . . I could
speak sanely, but all my motor nerves were going crazy wild. It looked
like I was out of my mind. If you had seen me, you wouldn't have
bothered to listen, and none of them did.*

*Oh, God, it was a nightmare. Finally six big spade attendants came
and held me down on a stretcher. They terrified me . . . their force
against mine. I got twice as bad. I just flipped. I told them if they'd
just let go of me, I would calm down and stop kicking and fighting.
But they wouldn't listen and they started to tell each other what stages
of hallucinations I was in . . . how I imagined myself an animal. All
these things totally unreal to my mind and just guesses on their part.
Oh, it was insane. Then they plunged a great needle into my butt and*
BAM! *out I went for two whole days.*

When I woke up, wow! Rats all over the floor, wailing and scream-

ing. We ate potatoes with spoons. The doctors at Bellevue finally con-
tacted my private physician, and after five days he came and got me
out. They sent me back to Gracie Square, a private mental hospital
that cost a thousand dollars a week. I was there for five months. Then
I ran away with a patient and we went to an apartment in the
Seventies somewhere which belonged to another patient in the hospital,
who gave us the keys. The guy I ran away with was twenty, but he'd
been a junkie since the age of nine, so he was pretty emotionally re-
tarded and something of a drag. I didn't have any pills, so, kind of
ravaging around, I went to see a gynecologist and a pretty well-off one.
He asked me if I would like to shoot up some acid with him. I hadn't
much experience with acid, but I wasn't afraid. He closed his office at
five, and we took off in his Aston Martin and drove up the coast . . . no,
what's the name of that river? The Hudson.

We stopped at a motel and he gave me three ampules of liquid
Sandoz acid, intravenously, mainlining, and he gave himself the same
amount and he completely flipped, I was hallucinating and trying to
tell him what I was seeing. I'd say, "I see rich, embroidered curtains,
and I see people moving in the background. It's the Middle Ages and
I am a princess," and I told him he was some sort of royalty.

We made love from eight in the evening until seven in the morn-
ing with ecstatic climax after climax, just going insane with it, until
he realized it was seven and he had to get back to his office to open
it at eight-thirty.

He gave me a shot to calm me down, and because I couldn't come
down, I took about fourteen Placidyls. On the way back something very
strange happened. I didn't realize I was going to say it, but I said out
loud, "I wish I was dead" . . . the love and the beauty and the ecstasy
of the whole experience I'd just gone through were really so alien. I
didn't even know the man . . . it had been a one-night jag . . . he was
married and had children . . . and I just felt lost. It hardly seemed
worth living any more because once again I was alone.

He dropped me off at the apartment where I was staying with the
runaway patient. I had a little Bloody Mary when I got there, and
dropped a few more Placidyls. With my tolerance, nothing should have
happened, but I suddenly went into a coma. My eyes rolled back in my
head.

It was lucky . . . I had called an aide, Jimmy, at the hospital—he
had been a good friend—I had called him anonymously and asked him
to come and visit us. He happened to turn up just as I went into the
coma. He and the heroin addict tried to wake me up. They slapped me

and pumped my chest and they put me in a bathtub full of really cold water. Jimmy began to call hospitals—not psychiatric but medical—and one of them actually told them to let me sleep it off.

But Jimmy just flipped. He knew I was dying, and he was right. He called Lenox Hill Hospital, and the police finally came. Jimmy and the heroin addict were taken into custody, and I was rushed to the hospital. I was actually declared dead. My mother was called . . . and then BAM! I started breathing again.

I was pretty shaken up by what happened because I didn't understand how I could have almost gone out on just fifteen Placidyls when I used to live on thirty-five three-grain Tuinals a day, plus alcohol.

They released Jimmy and the junkie, but of course I was still in the trap. I thought I was fine and that I could leave. But a psychiatrist came to interview me and I was put in the New York State Psychiatric Institute at Columbia Presbyterian Hospital—committed on the grounds of unintentional, unconscious suicide. It was a pretty devastating experience. They put me on eight hundred milligrams of Thorazine four times a day plus six hundred milligrams at bedtime—an ugly-tasting liquid, but it took quick effect and you couldn't hide the pills or spit them out later. I had all kinds of bad reactions from it— I'd get bad tremors and all itchy and wormy. I said I wasn't going to take the stuff any more, no matter what, so they finally took me off it one day. I had a seizure, vomited all over the floor, and I couldn't get up and walk straight. I was going through withdrawal from those tremendous dosages of Thorazine, but they accused me of importing drugs and taking them there in the hospital. My doctor was young . . . a resident . . . and I just told him, "You think I've taken drugs. There's no point in even reasoning with you. I'll just go to some other hospital." I expected to go to some plush, tolerable hospital, but I was not accepted in any private hospital with the record they gave me. They committed me to Manhattan State on Ward's Island, in the middle of the East River, next to the prison.

It was one of the most unpleasant experiences I've ever been through. Really terrifying. I lived in a big dormitory on a ward with about sixty to eighty women. We did all the mopping, cleaning, making beds, scrubbing toilets. And the people there were just so awful. Really pathetic. Some of them were mean. The staff completely ignored you except to administer medication. I thought it was never going to end.

In Manhattan State, even in there, there were pushers. One girl who lived in a smaller dormitory—there were two with about ten beds in them—was pushing speed and heroin. And because I'd been warned *that if ever you were caught using drugs in a state hospital you'd be criminally punished, I didn't touch any drugs during the three months I was there.*

SUSAN WRIGHT BURDEN Her psychiatrist was a foreigner I could hardly understand and who didn't understand her at all. Edie and I always met in the reception room. The first time I went there to see her she seemed very freaked, at loose ends, as if they weren't doing her any good at all. But the next time she seemed totally aglow; I couldn't believe how she could look so beautiful in that horrible place. She looked like she'd spent all day dressing and getting made up, and she just sort of floated in . . . as if she was receiving you at her grand estate. But I heard that by the time she left Manhattan State she could hardly function because of all the medication she was given.

HUDDLER BISBY I can remember going to visit Edie in the Manhattan State Nuthouse. I was nuts myself at the time. I had come to New York after spending a week in the desert on . . . I forget what was the name for the Red Hot Psychedelic of that moment. I think it was called MDA, or DMZ, or DDP. Being an acid casualty myself, I naturally can't remember which one it was, but it was a strong one, and somebody gave me fifty of them. It was like melting into the desert. Living in a state of complete and total hallucination. I've only driven a car in my adult life maybe three times and that was one of those times. I drove it because I couldn't see anything. I figured, "It's safe. We're driving in a neon tunnel, no problem." I survived.

I flew back to New York on an airplane out of my mind. Totally out to lunch. I was singing. Speaking in rhyme. Dancing. Dancing wherever I would go. *Very* far out.

I got off the plane. I went right to Susie Burden's house and there's this friend of Edie's, Casey the Crip. He's got chrome-plated aluminum crutches. He's got shrunken legs and an Alpine Sunbeam convertible he drives by using auxiliary mechanisms. He drove us out to this loony bin where Edie was. On the way I took two more pills.

We got inside the hospital (me and Susie and the Crip) by saying we were Sedgwicks, part of the family. They let us in. You give the names, they lead you through doors and doors and doors. Fantastic place. Everybody looked very poor, extremely retarded, and mostly middle-aged. Grown-up fat ladies in blue-gray hospital outfits. Edie was surrounded by these Fat Black Welfare Pussycats, drooling and pissing in their chairs. Very public.

Finally we were able to sit down with her at this long table with some soft drinks we'd brought up from the machines. Seven-up.

By this time I was so wrapped up in Edie that I began to forget where we were. I was looking at her, and she at me, and we started to "Go Up."

To "Go Up" is a time on drugs when you expand in size, become very *large* in context to the size of whatever other loonies are sitting around.

We started to do this, but it was upsetting because she began to look at me as if she was saying, "How the fuck do you qualify to be walking free on the outside while I'm in here? You're no more or less crazy than I am!" I agreed completely. I agreed just in toto.

It freaked me out. All I remember is that when we left, on the way out, we discovered the controls to the public-address system of the hospital (in a little unattended broom-closet of a room). We went in and I tuned the dials to a rock station . . . *Up Full Volume!* As we ran out of the hospital, with our chauffeur in tow on his chrome-plated crutches, we could hear all the inmates freaking out because of the music being blasted at them. The whole hospital went nuts for a few minutes.

JONATHAN SEDGWICK   My mother finally took Edie out of Manhattan State Hospital and brought her back to the ranch in the late fall of 1968. She couldn't walk. She'd just fall over . . . like she had no motor control left at all. The doctor did a dye test of some sort and it showed the blood wasn't reaching certain parts of the brain; they said that in the X-ray pictures it looked like a Swiss cheese. She couldn't talk! "kk . . . kk . . . ggg . . . ddd . . . wowo . . . well, uh, well, no, well . . . sa-ay." It was really strange, man, *awful*. Once in a while three or four words would come out in a rush. Slowly she began to come back. She knew she could do it, but she needed people to have faith in her. I always believed she would make it. I'd say, "Edie, goddam it, get your head together. Man, you have the head to do it. Let it come out." She'd say, "I . . . I . . . I . . . know . . . know . . . know . . . I . . . I . . . can . . . but it's ha . . . ha . . . ha . . . hard."

She was working at it: she apparently reworked or rebuilt other parts of her brain. Every day it would be a little better. You could see how desperate it was when you looked into her eyes and you could see how hard she was trying to reach you. She couldn't even move her arms right to *indicate* what she wanted to tell you. She rarely left the house. Inside she was grabbing something to keep from falling over. When it was dinnertime, she'd wobble in and wobble out and fall down a lot. My mother was uptight about it, trying to be cool about it, saying that Edie would get well.

It was quite a while before Edie was considered well enough to get out on her own and live in town. She ended up in Isla Vista, which is where the street people hung out near the campus of the University of California at Santa Barbara. I heard she was much better. She'd been away from the ranch for a few weeks when I ran into her on the street. She yelled out, "Jonathan!" I turned around and there was Edie running toward me. We hugged on the street. I was going into the coffee shop, Borsodi's. She was wearing sandals that barely stayed on, and her blue jeans were hanging down almost below her butt. She was wearing a see-through T-shirt and a purse slung over her shoulder, looking very disheveled.

We went into Borsodi's and talked. I had a lot of things to tell her I had been through, and we started talking about flying saucers and extraterrestrial beings that talked to us, and she agreed they talked to her, too.

We talked about California falling into the ocean. Do you know that you can take a submarine *under* California . . . eighty to a hundred and twenty miles straight in under Long Beach in those chasms? So California is going to dunk in there and cause a tidal wave that'll be a couple of thousand feet tall. The coastal cities will go. I'd tell these things to Edie and she'd simply say, "Yeah, I know. We shouldn't tell people about it. I mean, *I* know it, and *you* know it, Jonathan, but don't talk about it."

She told me she'd ended up in Bellevue Hospital because she was riding a motorcycle with Bob Dylan and they'd had an accident. I don't know if this is true. She really loved Bob Dylan. Edie—they didn't know who she was—got thrown into Bellevue. She told me she was bearing a baby and they made her abort in the hospital because in her condition she shouldn't give birth to a child. And that killed her. She cried and said, "They made me give up my baby . . . and it was the one thing I really loved and lived for." I don't know whether that was the truth or not.

One night Edie and I were sitting there. She was drinking coffee to speed herself up some more—God!—when out of the blue she said, "Hey, Jonathan! I think you should make love with me!"

I said, "No, Edie, no. I'm not into that!"

"I really think you should do it, Jonathan. *I'd* like to." She reminded me of the time when she went to London with Suky and my mother, and I came over from Germany, from the Army; Edie wanted to make love with me, and I didn't do it then either.

She said, "Everybody always wanted me. My father wanted me. He tried to make love to me. All the men on the ranch wanted me. Even *you* wanted me, Jonathan."

I said, "Yeah, I did. For sure."

So in the coffee shop she kept saying, "I think it's something you should do. Jonathan, I . . . I really think you ought to make love with me now."

She was very high on speed. Her head was shaking up and down. "Jonathan, I think we ought to do it now." I felt maybe we *should* find out what our love was for each other. She was beautiful; I liked her. I knew she'd teach me something . . . but I didn't do it.

Edie had this other trick of being able to talk your sentences as you said them. . . . Did it blow my mind! I couldn't get my words out fast enough. I couldn't beat her! She had me. Edie was right on, it was a lesson . . . and I wanted to learn it . . . to be in the *now*, like Christ in the Mount Olive speech, and then to be able to go to England and do it and just blow their minds because there they've got to feel, and then think, and then talk. With Edie there was no time between feeling and thought. But then finally I disliked it and I got up and left the coffee house. I just didn't like being read that closely.

JOHN GRABLE   I was called Mad John from a song on a Donovan album about a guy named Mad John who escapes from an insane asylum and drifts around the countryside and gets girls to buy him breakfast and all these neat things. I'd heard the song and needed a good street name. My name is John and I was a little bit loony, so I thought Mad John sounded fine. Not any more. I haven't gone under that name for years. I've changed totally. I work, I bathe, I have a roof over my head. About all that's left are the tattoos . . . two big spiders that are on the back of my hands . . . biggest mistake I ever made, since you can't hide them. The rest of my tattoos I can hide with a long-sleeved shirt, but not the spiders.

I was hanging out on the streets of Isla Vista. I met Edie and we just kind of clicked . . . both Aries, and we got off on each other— getting really spaced, just partying and having a good time. The first time I met her she wasn't dressed like the others, who were wearing East Indian tablecloths for dresses and raggedy Levi's. She wore high heels, short skirts, big earrings, and a hat like out of a fashion magazine. But then she started wearing what the others wore. She had a real pretty, innocent face, out of character there . . . like a debutante wearing biker clothes . . . Levi jackets. I fell in love with her at first sight. Man, look at this person—she's perfect! She was

The entrance to Rancho La Laguna

so friendly. Ready for anything. Unreal. In the mornings she'd watch the soap operas on TV and I'd watch *her*.

People on the street weren't too much into staying clean or healthy. Drugs were the first thing. A lot of people liked to drink. And then the eating would be jelly doughnuts. The streets were basically a bunch of people who couldn't make it anywhere else and ended up there getting spaced.

She was always doing just what she wanted. We'd walk into the Sun and Earth together, over to the juice counter, and she'd ask: "I wonder what this tastes like?" She'd open up a bottle and take a drink—"Eeeech!"—put it back, and walk out. Things like that just shocked me. Very presumptuous.

She was flighty like . . . she'd just run off with some other guy. Once in the mountains we went to a party where everybody got real drunk on wine. Edie kept running off with this other dude, and I'd get real pissed. She'd try to tell me, "Hey, it's cool, man." "It's not cool!" "It's cool." It really blew my mind. There was this guy Bob Brown, a musician, big guy who wore clogs and blond hair down to here—a one-man-band type of musician who played all these things at the same time and sang—who came along this night when Edie and I were hanging out, both tripping our brains out on acid, and he said, "Edie, why don't you come away with me and I'll straighten you out." She said, "Okay," and they were gone. Shit, I was really bugged. I couldn't argue. The guy was about three times my size. Not that he would have fought me. But I was so stoned I couldn't even talk. Too much of that sunshine and you can't say anything.

We'd party in people's apartments—square and white and ugly, mattresses on the floor, lots of loud music, Led Zeppelin, things like that, and Edie right in the middle of it and loving every minute. Everyone getting loud and freaky and loose. Yet Edie was different. She could be kind of polished and cultured when she wanted to be— we heard she was born with millions.

JONATHAN SEDGWICK   I came in on her once when she was in a typical Isla Vista apartment—two sliding doors, no furniture because it must've been wrecked, a bed on the floor, with Edie lying on it, retching. Around her were all these nice groveling drug addicts trying to help her . . . it was sort of like a Hieronymus Bosch feeling.

Only once did I help Edie through an overdose of speed. She was vibrating so much I started shaking like a thousand tons of coffee in me. Finally I said, "Edie, I just don't have the power to stop what's inside you right now."

Finally she got into this trip of deciding she had to be stopped; since she couldn't stop herself and her drug-freak friends couldn't either, she decided she was going to be busted by the cops. I talked with her and said, "Hey, you don't want to do it that way, man. It's going to be a bummer for everybody." She said, "No, I'm going to do it."

About a week later people came running up. "Hey, did you hear what happened to Edie? She got busted. Edie got busted, man!"

How? Well, this is the way three people told me, so I believe it. While she was walking along the street, she dropped her purse and a whole bunch of reds and things fell out, right? A cop car pulled up. "What ya doing?" And then the cops get the idea that she was carrying drugs on her. So they got out and threw her up against the car, her hands up over the hood, at which point her purse spilled open again and there're whites, there're reds falling everywhere! The cop who had pushed her against the car turned around and began picking up the stuff, so she wheeled around and gave him a kick in the ass, man, with all the energy and hate she could, and that sent him flying over the hood of the car. She said, "You fucker, man! Don't you touch my purse!" Everybody standing along the street was blown out when they saw that. They cheered and clapped. Edie smiled. The cops were really uptight. They grabbed Edie. The cop who'd been kicked was really hurting. Oh, she just blew out a lot of people. She had a lot of energy, man. She only weighed about eighty pounds and he weighed about two hundred pounds, that cop.

It may not have been like that, but that's what I heard.

39

HENRY PETERS   The court put Edie on probation for five years. After the drug bust she became a patient at the Cottage Hospital in Santa Barbara. It was ironic in a way. She was born there. Her father died there. Now she was twenty-six—it was August 1969—and she had been placed in the Cottage Hospital on her psychiatrist, Dr. Mercer's, recommendation. She had privileges of sorts—which meant that occasionally she could leave when she wanted to.

EILEEN BENSON   Edie was happy in the hospital, but she wanted to get out every day. I was doing social work in Isla Vista and would come and pick her up. She was usually careful about getting back on time—which was ten p.m. in the psychiatric ward. She loved to eat oysters. Once a week we'd go down to the Reindeer Room in Santa Barbara. She'd survive on chocolate milk and candy bars, especially if she'd been speeding. Visitors brought her drugs and she used to save her sleeping pills so she had extra.

She was good company. She told me about a lot of her troubles. She was very frank. I found her easy to be with. She'd get dressed up and wear her wigs. She had wigs hidden about the ward. She spent her week's allowance of eighty dollars on padded bras—twenty of them, black and white, that she'd bought at Robinson's. She hid them because she thought someone might steal them. She told me she was a kleptomaniac and she'd show me things she'd stolen from the hospital gift shop—little pieces of jewelry, planters without plants, cigarette lighters, little figurines.

HENRY PETERS   She'd sometimes talk about the past. Warhol! She was trying to get him out of her system. She hated the Factory because of the dope. "I hate them. I hate them!" She said he got people screwed up until they were automatons, robots, doing what he wanted them to do, and discarded them. She said: "The *way* those sons-of-bitches took advantage of me. Warhol is a sadistic faggot." Big black boots and a motorcycle jacket and a whip . . . which is what she said he was like.

PETER DWORKIN   Everybody in Cottage had a kind of ambivalence about Edie . . . an angel in a lot of ways, and it was difficult not to love her. When you come upon an extraordinary person, you allow them a lot more latitude than you do an ordinary person. Edie was very elusive . . . trying hard not to let anybody ever get close to her in any real sense; she would throw up these giant clouds of camouflage. I don't think she knew that people realized what she was doing. She would have been devastated if she knew people weren't falling for it. It was poignant to see that people loved Edie for being Edie but that she couldn't accept that: she always had to feed them something else —that she was "Edie the Model," "Edie the Movie Star."

She had a looseleaf notebook with photographs of herself . . . newspaper clippings and cut-outs, mostly from fashion magazines. I remember being saddened by that. She'd show it to the patients so that they could be made sure that she'd been a model and been in movies, and that she was *Edie Sedgwick*. She talked about that stupid horse sculpture that the state bought from her father and then gave to the Earl Warren Showgrounds. She was putting him down but at the same time letting people know that she was somebody.

She insisted on being the center of attention. She'd make noise if people weren't paying attention to her: she'd shriek and laugh and joke and do outrageous things like eat seven meals at one sitting. She would eat all the food of the patients who weren't there. It was almost a ward joke: "Edie's eating!" She'd really shovel the food in. It was frightening because there seemed to be so much anger involved—just forcing this food down herself.

I was very fat then. I weighed about three hundred pounds. I was very unhappy and felt very unattractive. Edie, of course, was exactly

Edie, 1969

the opposite. She made jokes about how skinny she was—that she was a concentration-camp victim. I used to give her back rubs sometimes—in her room or mine. I remember being really fascinated by her body—she didn't have any breasts, and it was strange to look at her. We had a sexual experience, but it was minimal. It was not such a big deal. We just kind of goofed around. It was exploratory on a lot of different levels. We were caught at it. Somebody walked in and out, and then we put on clothes. It was talked about: "Why don't you *not* do that . . ."

MICHAEL POST I'd just gotten in. The first day. The nurse said, "This is your room and this is your roommate, blah, blah, blah." It was about ten-thirty in the morning. I lay down on the bed, put my hands behind my head, and was just about to take a deep breath and go *Ahhhh,* when Edie came in. She was wearing one of those white cloth things that they make you wear for X-rays. She came in smoking a cigarette—this horrible, raspy cough—and she looked as light as a feather . . . like she was walking on air . . . and she sort of came down and lighted on one side of the bed. She held my wrist. I thought, "Oh, wow, this chick really looks like she's been through the war! The *war.*" She said, "I'm Edie Sedgwick." "My goodness," I thought, "this sure is a friendly hospital." I said I'd read something about her in the paper not too long before . . . about her father being a sculptor. We went on like that . . . just kind of small talk, really. Down the hall she was in a private room, alone. She walked me down there. Two beds. She had so much junk strewn over the other bed—shoeboxes full of photographs, letters, stuffed animals, drawings, cosmetics, clothing, cigarettes, comic books. ZAP comic books. Have you ever read ZAP comic books? Oh, God! And *Mr. Natural.*

That's how I met her. There wasn't anything sexual between us while I was in the hospital. I didn't want to be another statistic on the boards. I saw her go through a number of guys. I totally divorced myself from any sort of sexual association with her because I thought it was a total drunken rip-off. Like once a guy named Preacher came in—filthy jeans, black leather jacket, Hell's Angels–type guy—and I thought, "What is she doing with *him?*" Before that, it was somebody who'd just gotten out of prison—notorious as the Santa Barbara cat burglar. He would steal people blind while they were right in bed sleeping . . . take the rings and watches off their fingers. He was with her. I didn't want that. Besides, I had made a vow to myself that

I would not make love to anyone before I was twenty-one. But I thought Edie was fascinating.

I was in Cottage Hospital to quit the drug world. To get away from it. But even in the hospital I couldn't. People in the corridors kept coming at me to ask, "Can you get me this? Can you get me that?" I would say, "But I'm a patient here. How in the world am I going to get that?" They wanted me to get, like, hundreds of thousands of pills. I'd tell them: "That sort of thing put me in here, and I'm here to come down from it as slowly as possible so that it won't rip my brains apart. I don't want to have anything to do with it any more."

Speed pills I took very rarely. Just on a Friday or Saturday night. Then we'd watch television, smoke cigarettes, and make speed doodles. Everyone was into that, just getting wired on these speed tablets . . . drawing pictures . . . just intricate nothings.

It was a real circus. They were all very concerned about the moral decay of the ward. "There's just rampant sex on this floor." They must have been bored with their daily routines, so this big black staff lady got it into her head that Edie and I were screwing. She reported it, and all hell broke loose. There was this *huge* meeting: the director of the hospital, the head psychiatrist on the floor, all the patients had this big powwow. Terrible. It reduced Edie to tears. Cornball absurdities. It wasn't based on anything!

I got out before Edie. But I came back to see her. I wanted to get to know her better. We would go up into the mountains, to the hot springs. A couple of times we went up there at night. We looked at the stars and watched an eclipse. We brought up a cake and opened some presents. It was Vietnam Moratorium Day. We were driving by the Draft Board and everyone was out picketing. It was funny, because my own records had been burned up when they'd set fire to the Selective Service Building and the new ones designated me 4-F by mistake, so I never served.

We used to go up in the mountains and sit around and drink wine and beer. We'd sit in the hot springs and then run down to the creek and splash around in the cold creek, then run back up and get in the hot, then the cold. Kind of like shock treatment, I guess.

40

PREACHER EWING   One night I took Edie out from the Cottage Hospital. She'd been taking uppers in there and she was really having a bad time . . . shaking and stuff, and saying that she had some kind of allergy. It was a weird trip when she came down off amphetamines, she had to score on downers to help her through. So we trundled on out to Isla Vista, and when we couldn't score on reds anywhere, she scored a balloon of junk from some guys up in their room . . . that's a rubber balloon with the bottom of it filled with heroin and then tied up . . . about sixty dollars' worth she bought. These two junkies shot her up right there on the bed. Then they had some . . . I mean, they'd got it for her, so they deserved some, right? One guy did up a dime, which is ten dollars' worth, see, and the other guy did a nickel, worth five dollars. That was enough for them. They did Edie with a dime and it fazed her for about thirty seconds, right? Then they did her up with another nickel and *that* didn't even faze her. The whole scene . . . really strange. I don't like being around junkies anyway. I took her home. She had the rest of the balloon in dime papers, one right after another. She snorted one and ate all the rest, right? It was past the time she was supposed to be back to the hospital and she was going through all these trips. She really began freaking out. Her arms flailing, her head knocking back and forth. I held her all night long in a headlock to keep her from doing herself damage.

Preacher Ewing at T Talley's funeral

So I got to know her. She decided she didn't want to go back to the hospital. She wanted to stay with me. Of course, I was living with my club brother T Talley and Sandee, his old lady. Me and T were in the Vikings motorcycle club. The three of us lived in a little shack off Mason Street. It was okay with them. We went to see Edie's psychiatrist, Dr. Mercer, and it just blew his mind. He had this whole therapeutic program and it didn't include living with a bunch of outlaws.

SANDEE TALLEY   The first time I met Edie was through Preacher up at Cruiser's house on Chino Street. I wasn't impressed with her. From what everybody said, I imagined some super-queen. But pretty soon she and Preacher were getting it on and she came to live with us. She still thought she was a movie star or somebody. She'd walk around with no clothes on in front of everybody. She tried to be a biker chick. She used to borrow my clothes, which made me laugh because she had a whole wardrobe. But she wanted to wear my tummy blouses and get a pair of Levi's like mine. She really wanted to ride.

You know why I think you were attracted to her, Preach? Because you and Hank Loible, who worked with you in the Crank Shop, had a thing going about rivalry. Edie was Hank's girl friend—"Oh, Edie! My superstar" type thing—and so, Preach, you says, "Well, fuck you, I can get her if I want."

PREACHER EWING   She was with Hank and she was pretty foxy-looking. Hank was a Viking. I met Edie at his parents' house. His folks really dug on her because they liked having a lady in the house.

T TALLEY   Edie didn't belong with the bikers. Like, she was a rich hippie. The rich hippies, their mommy buys them a chopper—a four-thousand-dollar chopper—and they drive it until the weather gets cold and they get themselves a nice, warm car. Your true biker takes his bike out whatever the weather because he loves it. When a rich hippie gets in an accident, he sells his bike, what's left of it. "Oh, I got hurt. I don't want this." The good biker fixes his. I've been lucky. I've been down quite a few times . . . tasted the pavement quite a bit. You live by a bike; you die by a bike. That's what I believe.

The bike club we took Edie to was called the Vikings—an old outlaw club. We took Edie to the meetings at this bar called the Spigot—so she could meet the bike people and see how they dressed and acted and what they thought about life in general. She walked around giving these bikers Hollywood kisses. You can't go around kissing bikers on both cheeks like she was kissing them. Ordinarily, they'd "turn her out" right on the spot. I guess you know what "turning out" is. Rapin' her. Edie figured, I guess, it couldn't happen to her because she was different.

I think Edie saw it as a great new world to enter into. She dug the bike scene. Most people do, you know.

It's a trip looking at all these old pictures. You can see how I used to look. I'm not working now. I just got out of the hospital. Right now I've got a fifty-fifty chance of living. When someone says, "Well, you're sure taking it good," I says, "That's not bad if you're a biker."

I got the worst cancer you can have—melanoma. The doctor kept me pretty happy there in the hospital. He said, "Don't worry, T, if it does go the worst, I'll give you something so you can go out on your bike and do it your way." He knew that I don't want to be laid up in a hospital slowly dying. That just wouldn't be no class at all. I told him, "I want to die on my bike . . . I want to do a role involving nobody else except for myself." He'll probably give me a big old needle which will give me enough time to get on my bike and go over a cliff.

I've seen death so many times on my bike . . . I've been inches from death. Because when you're on a bike, you have no protection. But the feeling . . . it's just so beautiful. When you're on a bike, you get to know every inch; you know when your nuts are going to work loose; you know how much your engine's going to take; you can smell things you can't smell in a car; you can see things on a bike which you can't in a car because you're all cooped up and boxed in. When a biker goes from one place to another, he's having a good time every second . . . especially when you have forty or fifty bikes and everybody's in formation, side by side, and you're passing the old wine bottle or smoking a joint or whatever you're doing. You look at each other's bike, making sure everything's working good. Usually you have a road captain; he'll make sure that everyone's in formation . . . and it's really beautiful when fifty bikes are coming up the road. When we're going around a curvy road, everybody breaks down the formation and we go into a single file around corners because it's a lot safer. Then we regroup. Those fifty bikes must seem like two hundred. The people just freak.

Back in the old days a bike herd would make the people tremble. They used to chase the cops all over the valley. The cops didn't have radios then . . . so it was one-to-one. The bikers drove their bikes right through the grocery store and just terrorized the citizens. Two hundred guys'd go through, picking up the groceries on the fly, and one guy'd pull the telephone wires in the back so the guy couldn't make a phone call. That's how the bikers got a bad name. But basically they want to be left alone—go up in the mountains and party for three or four days non-crash, you know, popping pills, drinking, getting women.

There's the German flag. It's a strong symbol. It does blow out citizens. Your regular person on the streets, when they see somebody wearing a swastika, relates to the Nazi thing. But it isn't so much a Nazi thing; it's to blow people out.

Here's two of my brothers shooting tongue. Otherwise, kissing. That's quite common with bikers. It's not because we're fags. Like, if I haven't seen a brother in a long time, I'll go up there and, instead of shaking hands, I'll go up and shoot some tongue because I love him so much.

PREACHER EWING I'm a Universal Light Church minister. That's a mail-order minister, you understand. I wrote my name on the dotted line. I didn't particularly want to be a minister, but . . . why not? Somebody was signing people up. So after I married one dude and his old lady, they started calling me Preacher.

SANDEE TALLEY When T said, "Would you like to have a biker's wedding?" I said, "Well . . . okay. Why not?" You know. Good party. Big. Lots of food at the wedding. We had chicken and potato salad. And venison. Jocko shot a deer and the cops were looking for him because he'd done it out of season. We had three or four cooks. We had a cake, but the tiers fell down.

PREACHER EWING When I married Sandee and T, I forgot the Harley Davidson manual which I was going to read from at the wedding. That was going to be my sermon. I was going to substitute Sandee for all the parts, like I was going to read from the General Maintenance section and say, "Oil her regularly," "Lubricate her annually," and whatever. When I realized I'd lost the manual, I started looking for a Bible. This other dude, Dick Howell, rode around on a scooter looking for a minister. We finally found this old black Baptist minister that lent me a book with the ceremony in it. So I read the straight ceremony, but when I got to the part, "Do you swear before God and these witnesses?" I looked around at these "witnesses" and I started cracking up.

SANDEE TALLEY   When I was walking down the aisle everybody was saying, "Don't do it."

T TALLEY   It was on the radio and in the newspapers. This boy was selling papers: "Read all about it! At 7:30, the bikers will be coming down Main Street." The people were up on the rooftops.

PREACHER EWING   They had the National Guard out at the intersections outside of town. There were over two hundred bikers in town, many of them one-percenters . . . the outlaw clubs.

SANDEE TALLEY   T's mother came to our wedding. She is so beautiful. She doesn't preach to you, but she is religious—a Seventh Day Adventist. She had told her friends that she was going to a bikers' wedding. They told her, "Don't go. Be careful." So she came and really enjoyed herself. One of the Slaves went up to her—he was pretty stoned—and he said, "You're a pretty far-out lady. Would you mind if I kissed you?" He did, and she went back and told all those people at the Seventh Day Adventist church that she'd never met such a nice group of young people in her whole life. Well-balanced, nice, young people.

T TALLEY   See this picture of Sandee at the wedding with her pants laced up to here? We showed it to Edie and she liked the pants so much she wanted some. Edie was trying to be like Sandee.

SANDEE TALLEY   But she was so skinny that she'd blow away on a bike.

Me and Preacher knew Edie's problem. We were trying to keep her away from the drugs. It was difficult. We couldn't very well say, "Look, Edie, we can smoke, but you can't."

I feel bad about the way I treated her, because at first I was willing to help. But after a while I didn't want to be a nursemaid to anybody. That's what it came to.

PREACHER EWING   Edie was a little larger than life in her capacity to hit the depths. But she always had a sort of purity that came through. I really felt good around her sometimes. I used to call her Princess, because that's what she thought she was. That was the role she played. She knew she was in bad shape, as low as any street urchin can get, but it was part of her underpinnings that she wasn't really one of them. She'd say her parents were so fantastically upper-class that she wasn't even allowed to play with any children from Montecito, which is the old-money enclave of Santa Barbara. They didn't have enough class. They were below her, or she would say that she was too intelligent even to communicate, or that nobody else was capable of feeling on the level that she felt. It was part of her leverage out there in Isla Vista that she wasn't their kind; she was condescending. It was really ludicrous, because she'd ball half the dudes in town for a snort of junk. That's how hurting she was. But she was always very ladylike about the whole thing.

SANDEE TALLEY   We mostly kept Edie at home. You couldn't take her out in public because she'd walk around with a spaced-out look in her face.

PREACHER EWING   After a couple of weeks T and Sandee were just righteously blowing: "God, get her out of here."

I'd say, "We're going . . . but she'll be cool. Give her a few days more."

One night Edie and I were staying with friends and I went out on a bicycle they had there at the house looking for something to score and I couldn't find nothing. So I came back to the house to tell her. She was gone . . . and I remember the radio was playing "Just Like a Woman." Right? I was completely blown out to find she'd split. I rode that bike all over town looking for her and I couldn't find her anywhere.

The next morning I went up to Hank's apartment out in Isla Vista. On impulse. We weren't on good terms at all. I had kicked him out of the Crank Shop. Then we got in a fight a few weeks later and he had broken a pool cue over my head. He had always been saying that he was going to get Edie, that they were going to get married, right? Hank was going to be rich. He was always rapping about that. So when I went up to this apartment of Hank's, I asked him if Edie was there. I don't remember what he answered. But I looked in the door and she was laying out on his bed, junked out. I jammed. I just decided to leave the scene.

41

DAVID WEISMAN   Edie was back in Cottage Hospital the summer
of 1970 when I made my first attempt to recontact her and finish
Ciao! Manhattan. Actually, at this point she seemed like she had really
gotten a new grip on her life. That was one of her tricks: "I've really
been to the depths, but now I want to start a new life. A normal,
simple life." That was the image that Edie was projecting at that time,
and I got very caught up in it. "Okay, Edie, we're going to finish *Ciao!
Manhattan;* we're all going to do it together; it's our project; we
believe in it."

What had happened with *Ciao! Manhattan* was that there were too
many parts undone to make it cohesive: some were agonizingly interesting; a lot of it was just drivel. A labyrinth. So we had to start afresh
and shoot some more material into which to fit the original.

We decided to shoot the rest of the film in Santa Barbara and Los
Angeles in color. We wanted to create a whole different dimension—
more garish, cartoonish, plastic—to contrast with the New York part.

The plan for the film was to concentrate on Edie. We were going to
focus very strongly on the relationship between her and the kids in
California . . . that's what *Ciao! Manhattan* was going to be all about.
There's a long-haired kid who's rejected his sense of helplessness and
is looking for a new route . . . and hitchhiking down Old Malibu Road
at four in the morning he meets this girl with her jacket open who tells

him who she is. But he has *no* idea that his own life-style, his independence, his self-awareness, his whole generation has been created by her, by Edie Sedgwick . . . that the freak-out she did in the Sixties helped create the life-style that this boy now lives. He has absolutely no idea what she's talking about; he cannot relate to it in the least.

She finally got authorization from Dr. Mercer to finish *Ciao!* She was very anxious to complete it. So she got a little apartment on West Padre Street, a block from the hospital and a block from Dr. Mercer. Two professional nurses, Sherry and Maxie, were lined up by the Sedgwick family to keep an eye on her, along with John and Janet Palmer, while we got everything ready to start on her film.

EDUARDO LOPEZ DE ROMAÑA   The two nurses used to drive this big Cadillac. When Edie would begin crying, having an emotional breakdown, one of the nurses would pick her up and throw her against the other nurse, who would catch her and embrace her. "What are you doing, Edie?" BOOM . . . back to the other nurse! Some pair!

DAVID WEISMAN   Sherry was a fat lady. She was tiny but enormous. She used to eat and eat and go to the Roller Derby all the time. Maxie was thin and hyperthyroid. An amusing pair.

MICHAEL POST   There was always total anxiety about the film. That was Edie's life; it was film, film, film, film, film, and how she was to look in the film. She even got her breasts done. Edie saw an ad in the Bikini Factory . . . a little shop in Santa Barbara—a flyer eight and a half by eleven inches taped in the window. She asked the nurses whether they thought she should get the silicone operation for her breasts, and one of them said, "Why not?"

I went over to her apartment one day and I could see that she couldn't bend over because of a brace. "What's all that about?" She said, "Oh, I've had an operation. Surprise! Surprise!"

PREACHER EWING   They looked like somebody had pumped her up . . . like softballs, with scars under them. Her father had always made fun of her flat chest. She was so happy when she got those silicone breasts because now her father was wrong; she'd made a liar out of him.

JOHN PALMER   She'd tell people she'd had the breasts done and then she'd pull up her shirt and show them to everybody. In *Ciao! Manhattan* we had to explain those breasts. In the black-and-white footage she had these small breasts. Since Edie didn't want the public to know she'd had the silicone injections, we had one of the actors say this line: "Goddam, your tits sure did get bigger since then." And Edie says, "Yeah, I eat better now and I do my exercises."

MICHAEL POST   Dr. Mercer was in charge overall. Edie went to him once a day. She called him "the egg-and-walrus man." That's from a song by the Beatles that she thought fitted Dr. Mercer. He was a kind of a round man with a little bristly mustache—a kind of Humpty Dumpty figure with a walrus head. She called him Big Daddy.

JOHN PALMER   I always felt Dr. Mercer was an obstacle to the film. He would say, "Well, I don't think Edie should do the filming. She's not well enough."

One of the climactic scenes of the film was Edie having shock therapy. It was a completely fictionalized idea. Edie felt very strongly that it should be used in the movie because it was real. Dr. Mercer was against it.

JANET PALMER   Mrs. Grace let us use her clinic for the shock-treatment scene. They tried to keep the poor old loons who were the patients out of the way. There was one girl wandering around saying that she was going home; apparently she'd been doing that for three months; she was all dressed up, carrying her suitcase. She said her aunt was coming to collect her. It was awfully sad—these poor old ladies strapped down to their beds, singing to their dolls.

MARLENA GRACE   Edie did a beautiful job telling the crew how these electric shock treatments worked. I told Dr. Mercer, "Doctor, you would have thought she'd been jumping for years, the way she's got it down what happened." She showed them how the airway goes in— that's the little round rubber thing that goes in the patients' throats after they're asleep from the pentothal. She did the convulsions over and over again.

Edie on the *Ciao! Manhattan* set, at the bottom of a swimming pool, Los Angeles

Edie with David Weisman

JOHN PALMER   She got completely into it—the authenticity of the shock treatment. "No, no," she'd say. "The gag doesn't go in the mouth until after that's been done." When it came time for the injection of sodium pentothal, she would say, "Oh, can't it be real pentothal?" A steady stream of advice.

It was a funny sight to see Edie with her rainbow dress, the gag in her mouth, and those electrodes attached to her head, sort of half asleep, waiting maybe forty-five minutes on the table while we set everything up. She wore that dress because she thought it had dramatic value, and another thing, she had to have this cross. And she had to have her mirror there. She hid it tucked in underneath her bottom so, between convulsions, she could check her make-up. Just as we'd be ready to go, Edie would say that she had to check, so Janet would come in with the lip gloss and the eyeliner and the mascara, and she'd glue her lashes down and comb the fall out. Edie adored it. It was like main-lining for her. She'd suddenly say the cross should be somewhere else and she'd move it; we'd get into this big argument with her. There'd be hundreds of little games like that to prolong things. We had a big hassle with Dr. Mercer and Mrs. Grace over the twitching. We dramatized the twitching just a shade. Edie was all for that. She ate it up.

At the coffee breaks she'd go out into the corridors and talk to the patients. She knew half of them. She'd giggle with them and put that big smile on, flash those pearly whites and seduce some mad, insane freak, you know. The patients liked her. Everybody liked Edie the first time.

We thought it was only going to take four hours to do the whole thing; we stayed there for two days. There was always the pressure of getting out of this mental institution with everyone drugged to the gills . . . with a sort of cloud descending on everything . . . a night-hospital kind of tranquility which we had to escape. We got Michael Post to play a mad person in the corridor, standing there painting the wall.

After the shock-treatment scene we moved to Los Angeles and shot the rest of the picture around there. One of the main locations was in the bottom of an empty swimming pool where we built the set for Edie's place. It was the coldest winter they'd had in years in California. Edie was playing her role—especially down there in the swimming pool—without any top on, to show off those new silicone breasts of hers. She used to put a heating pad on them to warm the silicone, which, you know, gets cold.

WESLEY HAYES David Weisman had me working on the script of *Ciao! Manhattan*—because I was nineteen and off the streets and he felt I could help with the accuracy of the dialogue. He'd be typing away. He'd ask me: "Wes, look, like, there's this scene when a boy meets a girl. What would you say? How do you think it would go?" I'd say, "Well, it'd be like this . . ." and I'd tell him. He'd go, "Fantastic!" and write it down.

I met Edie at night—the whole scene with the lights, and she came in all dressed in white . . . long hair, and a fan. Everyone was buzzing around her . . . and when you got close to her, there was this warmth you could feel, like a heat. She was sparkling. When she arrived, it was, like, the hum. "The one" is coming. There she was. She was so fine and clean and pure. I never saw anything like her. I was excited. Dave said, "Now, if you play your cards right, Wes, you'll get a date with her." So I said, "Okay," and I went and took a shower.

She came to me that night. In a cubicle, a little bitty closet where I slept with this other guy that worked with me. There she was. The queen comes down to the stable . . . to the stable boy. It was bizarre. I was experiencing something very beautiful because she could have had . . . whatever. We had a little night. She knew a lot of things, but not like jaded: very gentle and young. I mean, she was, like, tops. Little crummy mattress. Everything was perfect . . . just like it should be in a storybook. You just say: "Wow, that was fine." You're just there for a moment. And then she goes away and you don't feel lost.

But after that, any time I'd see her, she was like a monster. I would hear Dave and John Palmer whispering: "She's too much; she's too demanding. She's just outrageous." All this time they were taping her . . . so they could use the stuff in *Ciao! Manhattan* . . . fantastic stories. She would go out and get pissed: she was on Seconal and vodka. She became totally different. She didn't know where she was. "Is Paul America here?" she'd say. "Let's go somewhere" . . . and we'd have to tell her, "Edie, we're in California, not New York."

She'd sneak out. Coerce somebody, which was very easy for her because her charm was always still there, always, into getting her booze so she could get totally blasted out of her mind and do these weird things. She'd go naked. Hitchhiking with her shirt open so her breasts would show. Sometimes she wouldn't go to sleep until somebody came and slept with her. She said she wanted to have more silicone. Pop her breasts out some more. She'd say, "David, I want a shock treatment

Edie in *Ciao! Manhattan*

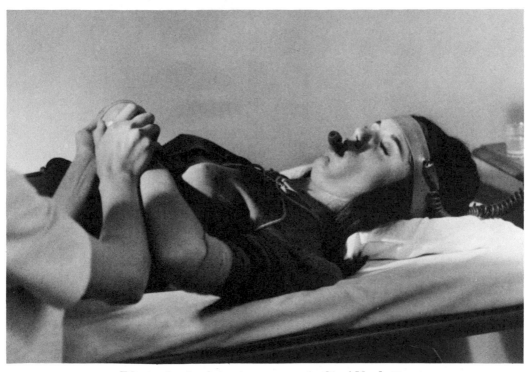

Edie in the shock treatment scene in *Ciao! Manhattan*

today." She loved the sodium pentothal. She could be calm for a couple of days, but then, *psssht,* she'd be right back up, hyper-city, back on the booze and stuff, responding to the stimulus and being outrageous. "Where's Edie?" "I don't know." "Oh, goddammit, now we've got to find her. How'd you let her get away? Go out, search and search." I tried to maintain my respect for her. But sometimes things became just too gross. One night Dave said, "You've got to come through for me. Edie's got to have sex. You've got to go up there. It's up to you, Wes."

I went upstairs to her. I felt sorry, not because I was offering myself as a sacrifice but because she was doing all these things. Her room was in total disarray. Like a bad porno film. But she'd respond! That's what made me mad. I kept asking, "Edie, what are you doing to yourself? We *know* you're pulling this number. Why won't you come through?"

"Nuh, nuh, nuh." She would never give an inch.

JEFFREY BRIGGS   Everybody was pissed at Edie. They were getting toward the end of *Ciao! Manhattan.* To get one damn line out of her would take hours . . . hours! Her longest marathon—which we all remember and joke about—was the last line of her role in the film. The line was: "Oh, God. That's what I hate about California. They roll up the fucking sidewalks at midnight." Right? Tough line, right? But, man, she got a hold of that sucker and we were *forever* trying to get it out of her right. She'd find more ways to fuck it up. She'd say almost the whole line: "Oh, God! That's what I hate about California. They roll up the fucking sidewalks . . ." and then she'd stop and try to figure out what came next. Or she'd say "two a.m." or "noon," something like that just to screw it up. It must have gone on for three hours. She'd say: "Oh, fucking God! That's what California . . ." Then, blah, blah, she'd say, "Oh, I screwed it up, I'm sorry." "Cut!" "Beep." "Sound whatever, scene whatever, take eighteen," or "thirty-five," some outrageous number. She was just lying there on the water bed half naked, with her corduroy pants on, and that one line to say.

DAVID WEISMAN   I carried on like a Gestapo inquisitioner. I screamed in her ear so that I became so hoarse that in an hour I couldn't talk. It was a locking of the horns. She was stronger than me; she broke me. I was determined, but she won.

Somehow she got the notion that we were finished with her and that with the film almost done we were going to throw her away like a dishrag. So she did a song-and-dance those last nights. So that we'd have to keep on shooting the film forever . . . trying to get it right . . . so we wouldn't abandon her.

MICHAEL POST   They sent Roger Vadim, the French film director, upstairs to talk to her. We had used him as an actor in the film. Edie was interested in him. "When is Vadim coming? When is Vadim coming?" she had been saying all day. He told her that once she was finished with *Ciao! Manhattan* he wanted her to star in his film *Pretty Maids All in a Row*. Vadim had this big thing about how we were too strict with her and that what she needed was love. He would sit there for hours and tell her how she was going to be the biggest star the world had ever known.

Minutes later Edie came down and started to finish the filming. She was sick, with this bad cough, and she was going through the DTs, and was just so wanting of Vadim's love and what he had promised her.

After a couple of minutes the film ran out . . . and everyone took off on their little trip. I went to sleep. Edie went off with Vadim to Malibu. Maxie, the thin nurse, was just violent. She put her foot down. "You're not going with him. You're coming back with us to Santa Barbara." Edie shrugged them off. She had these thoughts of Vadim coming in and sweeping her off her feet and taking her to some movie Camelot . . . she'd be the next Brigitte Bardot or Jane Fonda. She went with him.

The next morning I woke up at Dave Weisman's place. He came in early in the morning: "Michael! Michael! Can you go out and get Edie at Malibu?"

So I went up to Malibu. All right, as *usual,* I'd go out and pick her up . . . drive her to and fro. I drove her back to Santa Barbara. She was very sick. Vomiting all the way back. We went right to Dr. Mercer's place and he gave her a shot. We went back to the apartment, where she kept writhing in pain. She finally said, "Well, I guess maybe going into the hospital is all right."

It was so ironical. Here she went off to Mrs. Grace's and did this whole bizarre film gig of shock treatments—off there to Hollywood, off to stardom—and then BOOM, back into Mrs. Grace's to go through *real* shock treatments. Exactly what she had acted out. It was really a quirk . . . a weird twist of fate.

NAN O'BYRNE   She'd call me from the clinic and ask me to come over and sew a button on for her. "Bring a needle and thread," and she'd carefully describe what color I should bring. Pink. One of Edie's favorites. So I'd go over there and say, "Now, Edie, I think it's time that you learned to sew a button on yourself." We sat down on the bed and she said, "You know . . . I just don't know how." That afternoon she was fairly close to remembering me . . . though I don't think she remembered what we'd done together in New York. She just knew I was a friend. She told me, "The only thing about these shock treatments . . . though they say they're good for me . . . is that I can't remember anything. It really makes me mad."

I said, "Don't take any more."

"I have to," she said. "My doctor says I have to."

So she began sewing the button on. Every now and then she'd stop and ask, "Is this right?"

I'd say, "Of course it's right, look at it!"

"I don't know how to tie a knot."

I said, "Edie, tie a knot, man. You know how to tie a knot."

She'd do it . . . very proud . . . very proud of that button.

MICHAEL POST   She was in the clinic from January 17 to June 4, 1971. She had shock treatments—I don't know how many—maybe twenty or more. Dr. Mercer told me that she'd had some shock treatments in the East. He authorized the new ones because he thought Edie could be close to suicidal. Really an ugly scene. But a couple of days after she was up there . . . she just looked out of this world again. Just really fabulous.

JANET PALMER   Michael Post was the only person who ever stuck to Edie. He was always there, he was really marvelous. One of the charms of Michael Post, which was sweet for Edie, was that he was the only person she couldn't get into bed. Michael was determined to stay a virgin until he was twenty-one. Then it was all to happen on a flat rock up on a mountain with the sun shining.

MICHAEL POST   We had a big argument. She said I reminded her so much of her brothers. I didn't want to be thought of as reminding her of someone who had died. I didn't want to be a living death. So I said, "This is going a bit too far."

the story of Edie Sedgwick Superstar of New York's Silver Sixties

CIAO! MANHATTAN
1965-1972

with music by
John Phillips
Richie Havens
Kim Milford
Skip Battin
Kim Fowley

But I couldn't forget her. I always knew from the start that she was the girl I was going to marry. She and I would never really split apart. On Valentine's Day I sent her the world's largest valentine. Then I went to see her at Mrs. Grace's on her birthday. It was a foggy day in the city and as soon as I got halfway up into the mountains it was all sunny. I went to give her some yellow flowers. She came to the door in a satin pink-and-white bathrobe and pink ostrich feathers. She had on a tall wig. It looked horrible. It was one of those funky mail-order wigs that you buy one and you get the other for free. As soon as the door opened, she kind of zoomed out. She was really tired of the hospital routine. She said, "I wish you'd come and see me more often."

When she got out, she wanted me to move into her two-bedroom apartment with her. She said, "Michael, I've got to be living with someone when I get out. Otherwise I'll have Sherry and Maxie there, and I don't want that. Here I am, twenty-eight years old, and how do you think it makes me feel when someone says, 'Oh, so you have to have nurses living with you'? It makes me feel like I'll never get well."

I really was in love with her, but I was firmly resolved. Edie put me to the test. It really came right down to her actually raping me, it really did. It happened in her apartment one night. Edie delivered an ultimatum: "Let's do it, or else. I need someone who's got guts. If you're not him, then let's not see each other any more."

Edie's ultimatum came one month after I was twenty, and I thought, "Here I am, only eleven months from my goal." But I really felt she was serious. She felt rejected, and as a way of defending herself, she came back at me with, "Listen, if we're just going to have a hi-and-goodbye relationship, I don't need it. You've got this fucking fantasy about how everything's going to be flowers, violins, and all this bullshit when you're twenty-one. You're screwed up!"

So I did it. It sort of destroyed the fairy-tale idea of when I'd do it— but I was scared of losing her if I didn't. And then, I suppose, I realized the game I was playing with myself about procrastinating was pretty foolish. I had always kissed with her and petted until there was only one thing left to do and I would say, "Well, it's time for me to go and hit the books again." She always seemed kind of disgusted. So this time, even though I was planning on leaving, I ended up staying.

42

MICHAEL POST   I dreamt Edie in my dreams every night. I couldn't control my dreams. Wilderness dreams, city dreams, beaches. High dreams, heavy dreams: masquerade balls, not gay or frivolous, but eerier and grotesquely bizarre. There was this one dream when Edie had on Indian buckskins. She had a big brown bag of Seconals. I was just totally wrapped up. I'd read half a paragraph and the next thing on my mind was Edie. I used to fantasize that I would even be making love to her on the night she died. It would be like a great send-off.

I thought, "God! This is driving me insane." I thought I could turn her into a person who could function in society without the use of drugs and alcohol, but I always had the feeling that once I did that, then I would lose her. I was so mad about her that I had to take the chance. We'd been together on practically a twenty-four-hour daily basis. I asked, "Would you like to get engaged?" She just looked at me. I said, "Well, you know, I've never asked anyone else." She said, "Yes." I said, "Well . . . you know I have no income right now. It's going to be a while before I can finish school and afford to support us." She said, "Screw the support thing."

After we'd been engaged for two weeks, she said, "I don't want to wait any longer. Either we get married or just forget it." I was really wondering about getting married. I had fantasies right up until the last moment that exactly as the minister would say, "And do you, Michael,

Edie and Michael on their wedding day, Rancho La Laguna, July 24, 1971

take Edith . . ." I would say, "No, I'm going to leave," and I *would* . . . leave her standing there at the altar. I always told myself, "You can always get out and retain your freedom right up until the very last instant." All those things I'd heard for twenty years: "Get me to the church on time." I always felt I could turn around and keep on walking, just walk until I was just completely dead exhausted tired. But I couldn't do it. I mean, I was *so* in love with her.

Then we went for lunch to the Sedgwick ranch. Coming from a middle-class home, it was impressive to me. The living room seemed very weighty, and for someone to have all these books and to have done as many things as Mr. and Mrs. Sedgwick had done. . . . I thought, "Oh, boy, this is going to be a real challenge." I was a bit long-haired and whiskered at the time, and I thought that was probably not something Mrs. Sedgwick was going to enjoy, but she was very polite. We had been down there a number of times. Edie would put me on a big white horse. Really a spirited horse. Crazy. Edie was always for running flat out. She was born on a horse. Well, this time we came in for lunch—Edie, my brother Jeff, Suky, and myself. All of a sudden Edie said out of the blue, "One moment, Mummy," saying it in such a way that I looked at her and felt, "Oh-oh, this is going to be pretty interesting . . . whatever she's going to say." She announced, "Michael and I want to get married." I flushed, and I looked at Mrs. Sedgwick. She said, "Well, that's very good news. I couldn't be more happy." She sounded really sincere.

SUKY SEDGWICK   Mummy was very generous to Edie when she offered the ranch for that clowning that went on at the wedding. Mummy provided the background . . . and that's beautiful that Edie was married at the ranch, *against* the ranch. There is a unity, and her life with Michael was like going back to the beginning. Except that she didn't have much left.

MICHAEL POST   Our wedding was on the 24th of July, 1971. The ranch gets scorching hot in the summertime, but on that day there was a nice, cool breeze. Edie wanted a formal wedding. I objected to a certain degree, but I thought, "Well, might as well go through with it."

JEFFREY POST   We had morning coats and cutaways. Edie's wedding dress was white satin, and the bridesmaids wore yellow picture hats. The ceremony was held in the back of the house—an aisle made of agapanthus and white ribbon up to an altar, and all around it there were cattle eating in the Sudan grass, grazing there. You'd hear them. The grass was maybe four or five feet high.

MICHAEL POST   They played Mendelssohn on the phonograph from Mrs. Sedgwick's bedroom or bathroom when it was time.

JONATHAN SEDGWICK   I wasn't invited to the wedding. In fact, I was told not to come. I represented a life-style that they didn't want to see. Then Edie called me up and begged me to come. I said my wife, Krista, and I would sneak in at the last moment. We did, and we blew everybody out. Everybody was *shocked!* My sister Pamela and her husband, Jerry, and Mummy were all thinking how awful it was that I was there with my long hair and the way I was dressed. But others came up and they told Mummy, "God! Doesn't Jonathan look good" . . . they were saying I was so beautiful and fine and Krista was lovely . . . and my mother didn't know what to say, it was blowing her out.

I was wearing a velvet top with a series of buttons down the front, a Robin Hood tie . . . a leather jerkin is what it looked like, with big full sleeves, blue jeans, and these boots. That was it. And long hair. I wore an earring then, but it was out, I think, for the wedding.

They didn't want Edie and me together. There's one picture of us kneeling down, telling each other how happy we are for each other, but I've never been able to get it.

I brought a man with me called Paco—an English Yogi. Edie loved him. He was reading this girl's hand in the hallway just before Edie came through to be married. Paco grabbed Edie's hand, looked at it, and then looked at her. And Edie said, "Yes, I know."

Still, the feeling at the wedding was radiance. Afterwards we all went swimming naked in the pool. A lot of older wedding guests came down and watched, and they really dug it; the wedding photographer came down, too, and he started taking pictures. Then my mother found out about it and she sent word to the pool via one of the older people that she wanted us to get out. She was ordering us. But we didn't get out. We got out when we felt like it . . . which was when Edie and Michael were getting ready to leave, late in the afternoon. We went up to the front of the house and threw the rice. Someone in the family picked up gravel and threw it over everyone, Edie, too, and it didn't feel too nice. That woman was laughing . . . just this weird laugh. It was like a vengeance or something. Really weird.

Edie and Michael's apartment, Santa Barbara

WESLEY HAYES   The *Ciao! Manhattan* people wanted to film it. The Sedgwick family—who all looked like Kennedys—didn't want us to. It was bizarre. Everybody there was separate, scattered. It was like a bunch of people invading a ghost town. What was anybody doing? Nobody knew and nobody cared. "Hey, Edie's married! Maybe she's making a recovery of some sort. She's not going to embarrass us any more." One sensed: "What am I doing here? Why bother? Let her go. Who needs it?" They were solemn. They didn't want to talk to anyone. I was dressed in a purple outfit, with a little goatee. I had a hat and everything. Everybody went through the motions. Once again I saw Edie totally sane. Fine. Little bouquet. "Let's throw flowers." What a beautiful area she was brought up in—that Sedgwick ranch. I'm thinking, "God, she's got all this! She's got all this beautiful land. She could have had such fun. She could have gone out there and done something. But no."

It came time to throw flowers: "Okay, everybody, let's throw the flowers . . . and send them off." Edie and her new husband drove down the road a bit and they almost ran into a pole. The car spun around a couple of times. Edie got out of the car. She was pissed off. Her veil fell off. She's cussing, "Shit!"—everybody went down there. "Okay, let's throw the flowers again!" They started pushing the car. So here it was again—it wasn't smooth sailing.

MICHAEL POST   After we got married she wanted to get pregnant. She had tests. But she found out she wasn't. I got her to stop drinking, and off the pills, and things were just beautiful. We spent August on the beach, a nude beach in Santa Barbara, where we just lay around in the sun. We'd go out and rock 'n' roll dance. To the Yankee Clipper. It's got big aquariums with these Day-Glo painted fish that show up under black lights. Little clipper-ship models. Small discotheque. Bit too dark. Edie was just a fabulous dancer. Always on air . . . except when there was too much booze in her, and then I'd have to sort of hold her up. But she'd always insist on it . . . even if she couldn't dance under her own power. It was always dance, dance, dance. She'd say, "Well, I've got to dance some things out." But then it was time for me to go back into school. She got a bad ear infection in October and they gave her antibiotics to cure it. She turned out to be allergic and came down with serum sickness, which is in your bones and makes you ache twenty-four hours a day. So she was on pain medication for that . . . and then the pills started coming back. She stayed in bed a lot of the time and I read children's books to her—*Winnie-the-Pooh*.

JOHN PALMER   Edie still had fantasies about making more films. Michael was going to be her agent. She was waiting to see what was going to happen to *Ciao! Manhattan*.

MAUDE CARO   She also talked about going to art school. She went with Michael and sat in on his classes. I was reminded of Charles Dickens, about how when he first got married, his little bride would sit there and hold the pencils for him. Dickens' bride finally falls asleep. She thinks she's being such a help.

MICHAEL POST   She continued to be really dependent on Dr. Mercer. Once a day on weekdays, and then on weekends Mrs. Sedgwick was on the phone to him. He controlled the pills, and also the strings to the purse. So he was checks, pills, and Mummy. He didn't like that much authority. But he took it. He'd get a phone call from Edie saying, "Well, Michael lost the pills," or "They were in my pocket and got soaked in the washing machine." She'd go into deep thought as to how she was going to get a couple of pills out of him. She'd pace back and forth in the apartment. "Hmmmmmm, no, that won't work, I've used that one too many times." If he said no (and he would once or twice), it was pretty miserable there for the night. She'd drink herself to sleep with vodka, or she'd get a couple of bottles of wine and just blast out.

After a while I found myself in charge of giving her medication. I wasn't officially put in charge. I mean, I didn't have a title or a badge that announced "Mr. Post—the Doler-Outer." But at nighttime I'd dole them out. She told me she was ready to marry anyone as long as he could keep her in enough sleeping pills so that she could sleep. Let me see . . . I think it was two tablets of three-hundred-milligram Quaalude and also two capsules of three grain Tuinal—really a lethal kind of dose—and that, given to her at ten or eleven, would, after an hour or so, put her out. But often at three a.m. she'd be up again, just buzzing, just ZOOM. Sometimes I'd wake up and find the lights on and she'd be in bed writing letters. She had dreams—one that someone was shooting broken glass into her hands. She said, "My dreams are really trippy." Her sisters were conspiring against her in many of them.

She called me Daddy . . . always did. If I didn't give in, it was, "Daddy, you're always on me. I'm always wrong. It's me that's causing the trouble." And she'd break into tears. So I'd say: "Really, what d'ya want? D'ya want to continue this screwed-up life of sleeping pills to bed, pills for this, pills for that, just pills, pills, pills? I've had my fill of pills. It's ruining both of us. This *game* about pills. The drugged-out mornings. It's Dr. Mercer in the afternoon. Then I get home from school and by that time you want to do something: 'Let's go dancing' . . . party, party, party." "Daddy," she'd say, "I've been to so many hospitals so many of these past years that I've got a lot of time I've got to make up."

43

TOM GOODWIN I knew Edie well in the Cambridge days and at her apartment on Sixty-third Street in Manhattan, so when I got a job working on the television program "An American Family," I tried to call her. I didn't know her married name so I just called the ranch and they said she wasn't there. They were really nasty. I figured I was going to be in Santa Barbara for a long time working on the program, and that I'd just run into her. We were going to film Lance Loud at this fashion show at the Santa Barbara Museum—a big event for the Santa Barbarians. Edie was there with her brother-in-law. She had on a simple low-cut dress—flowers on the front. Her neck bones were very gaunt . . . thin, really. She looked very clean and beautiful; her smile when she turned it on was just beautiful Edie. I went up to her and said, "Hey Edie. It's Tom Goodwin." Somehow her recognition process was very slow. It took about ten minutes. She finally remembered. "Tomkin, how are you? Where have you been?"

JACK BAKER In the lobby of the museum I met Lance Loud and his girl friend, the cameraman, and the producer of "An American Family." The museum wouldn't let them through the door to the fashion show because of the way they were dressed. Lance always dresses eccentrically, and Jackie Horner was divine-looking, with black dots around her eyes, her body surrounded with a sort of feathered boa, and she looked like some gorgeous black bird. I managed to get them through. The museum director wanted me to guarantee that they would behave. The museum is quite stuffy, and he was terrified that they were going to *do* something.

LANCE LOUD   It was quite a struggle at the door. I don't want to label myself as "counterculture" because I was totally brought up on Post Toasties, but I was dressed in elegant "opposite class." I was with Jackie Horner, and when you come in with her, it's like coming with the Hope Diamond. She blinds everybody. And the Santa Barbara matrons didn't like it at all. They thought we were monsters. That scared me. I was in shock after we got in, and that entire evening when they were shooting "An American Family" I was freaked out. But Edie came up . . . drawn by those cameras. She said, "I haven't seen you for eons!" I asked her where she'd been, and she said, "I've been put away for a while," and she giggled. She introduced herself to someone standing there as "Edie Sedgwick Post . . . temporarily."

I knew all about her. One Sunday some years back my father was reading *Time* magazine. He was chuckling, he always thought *Time* was very funny. He had opened it up to the art section and said, "Look at this crazy, crazy, crazy guy" . . . and he showed me this picture of Andy Warhol and Edie. I said, "Well, what's wrong with him?" My father said, "Well, this guy has dyed his hair silver and his girl friend has dyed *her* hair silver, and she wears these big ball earrings." He read me the article.

I immediately fell in love with them. They were so non-vocal, and yet it seemed, from what I could tell, they were getting their way . . . really just riding, riding, riding the wild surf of New York society. My eyes were big as saucers. I just fell in love with that idea.

So they became the only hobby I ever had. I went to the library; I read up on Pop Art. I read *everything* I could about Andy Warhol, about his underground Factory, and all that jazz. I went *crazy* for it. As for Edie . . . I thought she was just like the fairy princess of the whole thing. How lucky she had to be . . . and how dynamic to be alive and her and to go to parties all the time. I got really bubbly when I thought about it!

So time went by and I started writing these letters. I'd write Andy and ask . . . oh . . . what does he think about, who's he going around with? I heard that Edie was being phased out. I didn't know why. But since I was indebted to Andy more or less, and Edie was just part

An American Family from the public television series

Edie (with bare arm) in *An American Family*, filmed on the last night of her life

of his art, I assumed that if Andy moved on to someone else, it was obviously for the better.

He *finally* wrote me a letter. It was a crinkled piece of paper inside a big envelope, just a little wadded piece of paper on which was typed: "My number is . . ." and then his phone number. That was all. My eyes . . . oh, God! . . . my heart, my soul, my toenails started blooming. I was just going *crazy* for him.

Before I called him, I got six girls to phone him up and I had them say: "Oh, hi, I really like your stuff. Oh, by the way, I live in Santa Barbara . . ." just to see if he might say, "Oh, do you know Lance Loud?"

I finally called him myself, and we talked. I would call him collect every weekend, Friday and Saturday night, three or four in the morning my time, six his time, and he'd still be awake to tell me what he'd done that night and how exciting it was. In Santa Barbara it was quite a chore to find something to do until *eleven*, even on a weekend night. So I'd get a girl and we'd drive around up and down the streets until it was time to call Andy. I'd stop at gas-station phones and call and call until he got home. He would talk to me about my parents and how I owed it to them to be a good boy, and stuff like that. He'd get angry at me because I told him how much I hated my parents. I told him I was going to run away to New York, and I asked him if he'd please let me be in a movie. He said, "Sure . . . but you can't stay at my house because . . . well, no one stays at my house because I have a thing about that. But I'll find you a place to stay." I was all set to go. I was so excited. There was *nothing* that kept me from going except my own laziness.

Oh, he was really great. I believed it when he told me to be good to my parents. I believed *anything* he told me. Then he'd say, "Oh, tell me you love me." I'd say, "I love you, Andy." He'd say, "Oh, say it like you *mean* it. Oh, tell me again." He wanted a nude picture of me. So I sent him one without a shirt on. I sent him a big package full of clothes —some underwear which I spray-painted fluorescent pink, and a spray-painted T-shirt, and all this jazz—and I poured all my mother's perfume in the box . . . all of it . . . and all my father's after-shave lotion. I sent it to him, and over the gas-station phone one night I asked him, "Did you get my package?"

Andy drew his breath in like this, "Uhhhh," and he said yes, they had received all the clothing, but they'd given it to people they didn't like so they'd be able to smell them coming.

After he got shot, he changed his number and I never spoke to him again. The whole relationship fell down. I tried to write him, but the letters came back. He suddenly became very, very private. He got very scared after that for a long time. So I never met him.

One day I was up in Isla Vista to look at all the sexy college boys at the beach . . . they're so stupid you feel like you could talk them into anything if you really wanted to . . . and while I was sitting there looking around, this big German Shepherd ran down the dusty road onto the beach, followed by this girl with brown hair with flowers stuck in it, and a sort of pixie dress, brown and very short. She was carrying a bouquet of lilies, it looked like, and weeds and these old dandelions. She and the dog ran together, just beautifully, right into the water, and she ran right up until the water touched the hem of her dress, and stood there with the dog swimming around her.

It was so neat, because she had just flown down the beach on this Indian Summer day and everyone stopped everything: all those big men playing football, and those crazy, crazy biceps flying all over the place, you know, like fireworks . . . and everyone's eyes bugged out.

Well, it *was* Edie Sedgwick. And I, you know, just died. I knew who it was even though I had never seen photos of her with brown hair, and hadn't really heard anything about her except maybe some mumblings that she was a drug addict and all that jazz. Well, I have a roped-off pew in the church of my heart for the obsessed.

I walked up to her, and the closer I got, I thought, "Oh, it has to be" . . . because those eyes were so sad and so descriptive. I walked up to her and said, "I've wanted to meet you for the longest time." She said, "Oh, thank you," in this little baby voice. We kissed and all that. She said, "You aren't a fag, are you?" and I said, "Well . . ." but before I got a chance to give her my bit, she said, "I'm so tired of fags. That's all I ever knew in New York. Fags. Fags. Fags." I said, "Really?" and she said, "Yeah. I don't ever went to meet another one in my life. All the boys were so pretty, but they all liked other boys."

Well, if that was so, she certainly was making up for lost time there in Santa Barbara. I had a friend who went to visit her in the Cottage Hospital—he's one of those blond surfer types . . . so sexy that you think they can't *have* sex; they have to stand around on the beach all day—and he said she had boys in there all the time for sex; she'd lock the door so the doctor couldn't get in . . . "Oh, come on, come on! Let's do it right now!" Really frantic.

I never visited her. She asked me to down there on the beach. I went home and died a million deaths. I was going to go and visit her, but I was very shy, and, besides, I thought our meeting on the beach was the tops. I don't want to bother popular people. I'd rather idolize them.

It was such a surprise to see her at the fashion show. Edie came up, drawn like a moth to flames by those cameras. I was frightened. I thought suddenly it would appear that I was standing there with a ghost of myself in the future. It would seem like "Oh, look, there's Lance, and there's what's going to happen to him." I didn't know what to do. She seemed to be grasping that ray from the camera. She just stole the scene. It was a natural thing . . . as though the need for it was great.

MICHAEL NOVARESE My clothes were the ones being shown that night. I had six models and the girls had sixty changes. We showed day clothes, suits, coats, cocktail clothes, evening clothes, fur trims, and also beaded clothes. It lasted for about an hour—quite an elaborate show. I sat on a stool, center stage, and talked about the dresses. Edie was sitting in the third row center of the audience, and throughout the entire show she didn't take her eyes off me . . . as if I were hypnotizing her. She would follow the model, but as soon as the model would leave her area of vision, her eyes would come directly back to me. It was a weird, very eerie feeling, because we had not met. She seemed almost transfixed. I was not offended that she was staring at me. When someone's staring at you, you receive it: it's pleasant. But then you become curious as to why.

After the show was over, she came backstage and introduced herself and said she had never known such moments of happiness as she had watching the clothes; the clothes were so beautiful; the models were like gazelles. She said she'd had the greatest impulse to get up on the runway and model herself—to model what she was wearing. When I asked why she hadn't, she said her husband would not think it was a good idea. She wanted to see some of the dresses up close; there was a particular red chiffon which she adored. She tried it on. She said, "I haven't seen clothes like this in so many years. I have been away."

She went up to a few of the models and told them how beautiful they were, and what poise, and how steady they'd been on the runway, which had not been an easy one to work.

Just before Edie left, she went and stood in front of the standing mirror; it was a natural pose, the champagne glass in her hand, and she stood there staring, no change of emotion, very quiet, intense . . . the mid-morning stare that one has at times. You know? You've had

a bad night the night before; it's ten in the morning, and you look
in the mirror wondering, "Why did I drink so much last night?" with
that almost disgusted, hard-edged stare. . . .

JACK BAKER   After the show was over, Lance and Edie ended up
dancing down a long corridor of the museum arm in arm singing that
Fifties song "Young Blood"—"Looka there, Looka there, Young Blood
. . . I can't get you outta my mind." I had been invited to a number of
parties; Lance, Edie, Jeffrey Post, and Jackie Horner wanted to go
with me. They talked me into taking them, which is one of the biggest
social mistakes I ever made.

An awful evening! I got absolutely loaded, but I spent a lot of time
talking to Edie. She was talking about the future, oddly enough, with
a childlike kind of enthusiasm. It was a very touching kind of performance, because she seemed terribly weak—like a fluttering, fading
moth. She wasn't strong enough: when she would walk from room to
room, she would always be leaning against her brother-in-law, Jeffrey
Post. I felt I should help her. Yet there was an incredible kind of radiance, a smiling . . . an inner glowing quality about her which I felt
was so unique. But there was something very ancient about her. She
reminded me of Isak Dinesen, a magnificent old lady, despite the fact
that she was still a youthful and beautiful girl . . . some of that aged
quality that turns up in some of the photographs of Dinesen—the gold
hat, the turbans, terribly wrinkled, but with that same birdlike quality.
There was something Japanese about her whole performance that
night. The mothlike quality, the slight fluttering, the terribly feminine
fragile quality that you find in Kabuki theater. I almost remember her
as having Japanese white rice powder on her face.

MICHAEL POST   I'd just gotten home from night class when Edie
phoned me up and said, "I'm at a really neat party, won't you come on
out?" I told her that I had a French test at eight in the morning and I
had to study. She said, "Daddy, I really need you out here."

So I said, "Well, all right. I'll be right out."

JEFFREY POST   One group there was talking about dope . . . going
on about speed and pot and how great it was. That's what made me
so proud of Edie. She told them, "I've had it, I've had the whole thing,
and let me tell you it's not worth it. Don't do it. *Don't.*" To hear her
say it to a gathering of people, most of them strangers, not to just
Michael and me, was really fantastic. Of course, they were being

pseudo-sophisticated and saying things like, "You have to take it to survive."

That was why it was ironic later when Veronica Janeway got so vicious. She was saying to Edie, "You're sick! You're an addict, a dope addict. You're a heroin addict." Edie was wearing a sleeveless dress. She had two cats which had scratched her arms. Veronica was pointing at the marks. "Look at that! Look at that! I do volunteer work in a hospital and I know all about this stuff."

I said, "Those aren't heroin marks; that's from a cat."

Edie was just thrown back. Veronica was very loud. Then she began on how ugly Edie was—a jealousy in her about beautiful women. On and on she went. She must have been drunk. When Michael arrived, right away she lit into him: "Who do you think you are—looking like Jesus Christ? What are you doing here?"

Edie whispered to me, "This woman hates me."

I said, "Don't worry about it. Everything's going to be all right."

MICHAEL POST　She had a drink in her hand when I got there. It was vodka. She'd definitely had a couple of drinks before . . . she had this look . . . a sort of sad look, as if she were feeling an overall physical and mental ache of some sort.

Veronica Janeway was dragging Edie down. They were talking about hospitals. She was saying, "Listen, dearie. I'm sorry, but you're doomed and your marriage is doomed and everyone's doomed." Edie was trying to tell her that you can learn something by going through the hospitals . . . and that it's not a completely dark, dismal, dead-end road. She was saying, "Look . . . I've been through all that. I'm getting out of it now. I've just gotten married. We're trying to build this whole marriage-type ideal plan. . . ."

Veronica Janeway said, "Oh, God! You'll only stay with him a few hours or a few days."

I looked at her and I felt like saying, "Well, listen, Toots, who the hell do you think you are!" I squatted down next to Edie and I said, "Let's leave right now." She said, "No, I can't. I've got to make her see this."

It was at this point the host asked Veronica Janeway to leave. "Split! . . . Take her away."

JOHN PIERCE　I was sitting with a grand old lady in her mid-eighties—Mrs. Peter Cooper Bryce—and this girl came up and threw her arms around Mrs. Bryce. It was Edie. I had never seen her before.

I said, "That's a splendid, friendly way to meet people." She turned and threw her arms around me. I thought that was very pleasant. We spent part of the evening together after that. She was very frank. She told me that she had an incompatible marriage with her husband and had only married him because—as she said—"He came to see me in the hospital."

She said she wanted to talk to me the next day. "I like to fuck first. I have to before talking; it relaxes me." I said that certainly there were other ways of relaxing. "Not for me," she said. So I said, "Go ahead and take care of that with somebody else and then we can have our talk." She said she guessed that would be all right.

She was sitting on my lap. People sort of stared. Her eyes were lovely. I said that no one with her face and eyes could be anywhere as bad as she said some people thought she was. Sort of trying to build her up. That seemed to please her, though I don't know how deep it penetrated.

MICHAEL POST   On the way home from the party she told me she'd met this guy John Pierce from New York and she'd told him she was married but she didn't know how long it would last. I don't know if she was testing me or trying to run or trying to hurt.

I guess I knew she was going to leave me one day. I honestly felt that she was in love with me, but that I was beneath her. She wanted me really to manage her money, her career, be her agent. But I couldn't feel comfortable doing that. I couldn't ride on her coat-tails. I had to find my own way. Because with her I couldn't really speak up. I wasn't refined. I hadn't experienced or seen society the way she had. I wasn't literate in the arts or music or literature. At parties it was Edie always talking, not me. I felt like a sore thumb walking around.

It was one o'clock when we got home. She said how troubled she was about the woman who attacked her. I told her that the woman was so far gone that she didn't even know what she was saying. I tried to get her to forget it. She said, "But, dammit, I just wanted to get through to her."

Something then happened that was really strange. A lot of psychic things happen to me. I asked her to come over. "You know," I said, "I want to hold you."

It seemed such a really nice thing. I thought to myself, "I'll close my eyes right now and in my mind go shooting through space holding Edie." For some reason I really wanted to imprint that scene for eternity in my mind.

But then I said to myself: "No, I won't close my mind and do that. I'm growing out of that stage of living on past thoughts and daydreaming. I'm married now, with school to finish, and getting some sort of job, and then making it on my own and with Edie." I gave her the "meds," and she started falling to sleep really fast. Her breathing was bad—it sounded like there was a big hole in her lungs . . . this sort of flopping, rough noise. She was such a cigarette fiend. It was a fixation with Edie to feel the heaviness of smoke in her lungs. She wanted to stop when she was thirty. That night it sounded so bad that I thought of waking her up and telling her that if she didn't stop tomorrow I was going to give her a spanking or something. After all, it was our first anniversary, November 15, 1971 . . . six months exactly from the first night that we had sex.

44

MICHAEL POST The alarm went off. It was seven-thirty. I opened my eyes, closed them, and then opened them again . . . started to get up and move around. I looked over and I noticed Edie was still in that exact same position . . . on her right side with her head facing down on the corner of the pillow. It was odd because usually she would flop the pillow on the floor and lay flat on the bed. Well, I thought . . . well, I had done that once or twice in my life . . . woken up in the same position I'd gone to sleep in.

But that morning I touched her on the shoulder . . . and she was just . . . just cold. I sort of freaked out. My whole body lifted off the bed. I fiddled with the phone and started screaming and yelling, "I think my wife's dead! Get someone over! Haul ass!" Then I rolled her over and tried resuscitation. Her jaw was locked . . . cold and stiff. I kept at the mouth-to-mouth resuscitation until I heard the doorbell ring and a policeman came in.

The policeman touched her wrist to see if there was a pulse; he was not doing *any*thing, you know. So I started yelling at him, "Do something, do something! I believe in miracles. Get her up! Resuscitate her!" Same thing when the guys from the ambulance came in. They said, "You know, there's nothing we can do," before they'd even tried to do anything. It was like they were all telling me, "Just forget it. Forget it." All those school years I'd heard that even if someone's completely blue in the face, resuscitation works. But no one did anything. I was running around . . . no clothes on . . . tears streaming down my face.

They were rude. I just got furious. Edie didn't have any clothes on. They wanted to take her body away. I said, "Well, not without any clothes on." They kept asking about drugs. Dr. Mercer arrived. He talked about the medications. She just looked so helpless.

JONATHAN SEDGWICK   I immediately said on the phone: "Don't let them get to her! She's not dead yet, man!" I felt she'd simply astro-projected, which means that you've separated your consciousness from your body and you're still connected by some sort of energy: some call it a silver thread, or a silver cord. Jimi Hendrix went out on it and never came back. Edie did, too.

I tried to see if we could stop it, but they'd already taken the blood out of her, and once that's done, you're dead.

JANET PALMER   Michael was carrying on. "My baby is dead! Last night she was all right and today she's dead. I killed my baby. . . ." All I could think of was how awful it would be to wake up and find someone dead lying next to me. For ages I used to poke John at night. I was afraid he would die in the night.

BRUCE WILLIAMSON   I went to see Brigid Berlin about an article I was planning on Edie Sedgwick. Anyway, Brigid played a tape for me on which she phoned Andy Warhol to tell him about Edie's death. A rather strange, cryptic tape, vague, though it went something like this—

Brigid told Andy that Edie had suffocated, and Andy asked *when?*, not sounding particularly surprised or shaken. But then, that's Andy. Brigid pointed out to him that Edie hadn't died of drugs, she had suffocated in her sleep. And Andy asked *how* she could do a thing like that. Brigid didn't know. Then Andy asked whether *he* would inherit all the money? (I took the *he* as a reference to Edie's young husband at the time of Edie's death.) Brigid said that Edie didn't have any money. Then, after a pause, Andy continued with something like, Well, what have *you* been doing? Then Brigid started talking about going to the dentist.

CORONER'S REGISTER

SANTA BARBARA COUNTY
State of California

JOHN W. CARPENTER
~~JAMES W. WEBSTER~~
Sheriff-Coroner

Coroner's File No.__C-3945_____

PERSONAL DATA ON DECEASED

Name(s)_____POST, Edith Sedgwick_____
Sex___Female_____ Race__Caucasian__ Age__28_____ Date of Birth_____April 30, 1943_____
Birthplace_____California_____ Citizen of___USA_____
Marital status___Married_____ Occupation___Actress_____
Last usual residence____2515 De la Vina Street, #11 - Santa Barbara, California_____
Soc. Sec. # 568-72-8030_____ Other_____ Fingerprinted___Yes__

INJURY

Date of Injury__November 16, 1971_____ Time_____Unknown_____ At Work___No___
Place of Injury__Residence_____

DATA ON DEATH

Date of Death__November 16, 1971_____ Time__9:20 A.M.__
Place of Death___(same above)_____

Death classified as: Natural_____ Accidental_____
Suicidal_____ Motor Vehicle Accident_____
Homicidal_____ Undetermined__/Accident/Suicide_____

Type or means of Accident, Suicide or Homicide_____Barbiturate over-dose_____

Death Certificate signed by ~~James W. Webster, Coroner~~ Joseph RISTAGNO - Deputy Coroner

MEDICAL

Cause of Death was determined by:
Autopsy__X___ Investigation_____ Examination_____
By___Lawrence L. McALPINE, MD - Pathologist_____ Date__November 16, 1971_____

Death was caused by:
Immediate Cause_____ ~~Probable~~ Acute barbiturate intoxication_____
Due to _Potentiated by_ ~~Rule out~~ ethanol intoxication_____
Due to _____ (Affid. dated 1-11-72)
Other significant conditions_____

Blood Sample Results:
Alcohol _0.17%_____ Carbon Monoxide_____ Other _Barbiturates - 0.48 mg%_____
Drawn by_____ Date_____ Time_____
Tested by._____ Date_____ Time_____

INQUEST

Place_____ Date_____ Time_____
Jurors' Verdict_____

(Over)

PATTI SMITH   I remember the day I heard the news. It was a nice day out. In this thrift shop I saw an ermine jacket . . . little ermine tails all over it. Though it was falling apart, I said, "I'll take a look at that." It reminded me of Edie—of Edie's hair. I don't want to make it seem like all I thought about was Edie Sedgwick night and day. But she was one of the many things that moved me . . . Bob Dylan, Jackson Pollock. Anyway I put some money down for the jacket and kept saving. It was eighteen dollars. I finally got it. It had a cotton flowered lining that had been sewed into it. It looked cheap, but it was really a cool cut. That night I put it on my pillow and slept on it because it was really soft. The next day I went down to get the New York *Post* and opened it up. There was that picture of her. It was such a shock, really. I didn't usually think about her too much. Perhaps it was because I had bought that jacket. It really killed me. God, it was weird.

Then that day Bob Neuwirth called me. He said, "Well, the lady's dead" . . . just this little sentence. The same thing he said when Janis Joplin died. Then we went on with this whole other conversation—as though he had to get that bit of news out of the way. But then he said that I should write a poem for her because he couldn't deal with it. Bobby was the one who really got me to write, really pushed me. I hung up the phone. I felt really bad. I feel a real responsibility to the images I get attached to. I had the phone in my hand, just putting it down, and I just got this thing . . . dah, dah, dah, dah, and I thought, "Oh, oh, I'm going to write a poem." The rhythm persisted and the poem, "Oh it isn't fair, oh it isn't fair, how her ermine hair turned men around." It was like it was not even my own voice. I was alone at the Chelsea Hotel holding the phone and babbling this poem. I just copied it down. It was like tracing a face. It came in perfect rhythm without any effort from someplace. It had to be written. If I would have held my mouth, it probably would have come out of my ears. I always think these kinds of poems are important . . . I don't mean important to art or to anything except maybe to some lost soul that needed some classification or some peace. When I finished it, it was like somebody could go to sleep.

EDIE SEDGWICK (1943–1971)

'I don't know how she did it. Fire
She was shaking all over. It took
her hours to put her make-up on.
But she did it. Even the false eyelashes. She ordered gin with triple
limes. Then a limosine. Everyone
knew she was the real heroine of
Blonde on Blonde.'
oh it isnt fair
oh it isnt fair
how her ermine hair
turned men around
she was white on white
so blonde on blonde
and her long long legs
how I used to beg
to dance with her
but I never had
a chance with her
oh it isnt fair
how her ermine hair
used to swing so nice
used to cut the air
how all the men
used to dance with her
I never got a chance with her
though I really asked her
down deep
where you do
really dream
in the mind
reading love
I'd get
inside
her move
and we'd
turn around
and she'd
turn around
and turn the head
of everyone in town
her shaking shaking
glittering bones

second blonde child
after brian jones
oh it isnt fair
how I dreamed of her
and she slept
and she slept
forever
and I'll never dance
with her no never
she broke down
like a baby
she suffocated
like a baby
like a baby girl
like a lady
with ermine hair
oh it isnt fair
and I'd like to see
her rise again
her white white bones
with baby brian jones
baby brian jones
like blushing
baby dolls

45

JEFFREY POST   The funeral itself was very small. Michael took
care of every detail—the ceremony, what was to be read at the church
and at the grave site. There was no organ music, no singing. The
casket was covered with magnolias. Edie's wedding bouquet had been
done up with magnolias.

The casket was in the church. My eyes were focused on it the entire
time because I knew that within an hour it was going to the burial site
and that was it. I was twenty-two and Michael was twenty-one. The
flowers, the casket . . . all of those are objects . . . but when you
go to the cemetery itself, where you've seen your brother select a plot
for Edie and also buy one for himself right next to it, that rips you.

JEFFREY BRIGGS   I went to the funeral, but that was because I
don't think I had anything better to do. I wasn't working at the time.
But anyway it would have been bad if she'd had her funeral and no
one from her *Ciao! Manhattan* situation had shown up. I ordered up a
bunch of flowers. David Weisman had called up from New York and
said to get them . . . and to get Margouleff to pay for them. So I
called up a Santa Barbara florist and ordered three floral pieces and
charged them to him. Seventy dollars. Nice flowers. No corny posies.
Margouleff and I drove to the church. We didn't intrude on the family scene. We sort of made our appearance so the family would know

that we were represented. It's a very pretty church—light, polished wood. Nice morning light coming through the windows. We stood outside until everyone else had filed in. Some real old geezer was up in the pulpit talking. There were maybe a hundred and fifty people there. Tops. Michael and Jeff Post, of course, and the Sedgwicks. You could spot those Sedgwicks from a mile away—black eyebrows like straight lines, same cheekbones and facial structure, same complexion. I didn't introduce myself to any of them.

JONATHAN SEDGWICK   The funeral was a drag, man. Everybody was feeling sorry for themselves. Michael was feeling sorry for himself. Mummy was feeling sorry for herself. Krista and I were the only people there who felt sorry for everybody else.

I cried. I hurt a lot about Edie, and I hurt a lot about Minty, and I hurt a lot about Bobby, and I hurt a lot about Fuzzy. Sometimes I wonder how many people a family can destroy with their stupidity.

SAUCIE SEDGWICK   Edie was buried in the Oak Hill Cemetery in Ballard, up over the San Marcos Pass. It used to be a dingy village so small that if you went through it at fifty miles per hour you'd miss it. It's in the Valley, but it's nothing. A few live-oak trees. No one would ever go there except to see the veterinarian.

JEAN STEIN   On the day I drove into the Santa Ynez Valley to see Edie's grave, the big sprinkler systems worked across the alfalfa fields. That evening the deer would come out of the hills for the water.

The main street in Ballard is called Baseline Avenue—just a couple of blocks long. A sign by the Presbyterian Church was advertising a variety of funeral services . . . a white "limosine," an organist, humanist services, and even burial at sea.

Edie's grave is a simple slab of polished red granite that reflects the trees. The inscription reads EDITH SEDGWICK POST, WIFE OF MICHAEL BRETT POST, 1943–1971. In the lower right-hand corner I noticed the words ROCK OF AGES, which turned out to be the quarry's trademark.

JOHN ANTHONY WALKER   Living in Auroville, India—twenty thousand miles from anywhere—is a very attractive person called Mike Brady from Boston. He's Irish, a fireman and a very high being . . . and a beautiful drunk. We were sitting one night in Pondichery in an Indian drinking place. For some reason Edie was very strongly

on me that night so I decided to have Myers's daiquiris because it was Myers's daiquiris that Edie and I had in the Casablanca, where the whole Cambridge scene between us took place. They had never heard of a daiquiri in South India so we had to make them ourselves. They got the lemons out from behind the bar and we bought a bottle of dark rum. When they finally brought out a jug . . . I think it was a metal can . . . we took the lemons and we squeezed them, and then they brought out the sugar little by little to add to the mixture. India is a very poor country and there's never enough sugar. We set up a glass for Edie, which is an Indian thing . . . a way of honoring some spirit that was killed. So there was a glass for Edie sitting on the other side of the table from my friend Mike and I. I remembered that Edie smoked, so I put a cigarette in the ashtray there. The cigarette wasn't lit and it just sat there. And the drink sat there. And I talked about Edie.

For years and years I had this whole Edie imago that I would play out, this sort of fantasy . . . this set piece. All these things I knew better another day, another time, but I faded out on Edie when I moved to India. The truth had been drained out of me by telling her story over and over again, and it is difficult to be truthful about things. My memory is very bad and my recollections are really not that clear for being fantasized. But I tried to tell Mike all about her. One has to try.

I used to have many ready-made statements about Edie. I can tell you the first time I met her was one of those flashes one has that stays fixed as years go by. There she was, and everything else fell away. It's recognition . . . we were like children coming together on the sand. Edie had just come to Cambridge from Silver Hill. She was beautiful, she looked like an Italian roadside madonna. She was very central to me then; there was something expressing itself through Edith which I could respond to, but it was larger than humans could handle at that point. Edie was a star who by mistake got incarnated into a human body, and never could figure it out and wanted to get back up there.

I remember spending one whole night with Edie drinking coffee in Cambridge . . . this was sort of splendid because she didn't have the seventh party to go to. As cup of coffee after cup of coffee kept mounting, she described her sense of the big dimensions, of multitudes . . . the mass and the multitude. Edie disliked rules; she disliked boxes; she disliked the door locking behind her in Silver Hill; she disliked going to sleep. She had to try for the biggest stage possible, and that's why she moved to New York.

I really don't know what Edie was. If she could have chosen a family, Edie would have chosen *her* family . . . nothing less would have suited her. But I don't know why she couldn't pull it together. There was something that was non-destructive in her—echoes of other planets, other worlds that would shine through. The last time I saw her was in New York at the Dom, and her head was shaven and blond. She was with a friend who was a bum off the street called Teddy or something. She kept saying, "I want you to meet my friend," and he was a down-and-outer, a panhandler. I spent time with them, and that was all he was. But she wanted to have that aspect of her life accepted along with everything else about her.

There was no end to the vortex that swung around Edie. If one got too close one could whirl out and hit one's little head against a fire hydrant or sewer line. I kept my distance; I wasn't going to do that. Edie could devour anything and I was survival-oriented and would never commit myself to saving her. But it would have been a delectable death.

You want to know how I feel about Edie. That night in Pondichery I think I spilled it all out, which is maybe why I can't come back with it . . . she might not still be in close enough to evoke her presence. I don't have the same capacity to be at a table at the Casablanca with Edie that I could have then. But that night at the bar in Pondichery I told Mike Brady all about her, and the drink sat there and the cigarette sat there. It was really weird, she came down so solidly. Twenty minutes later, I looked across the table and the cigarette was lit and smoking. Edie was there.

Addenda

Genealogy of
Principal Characters

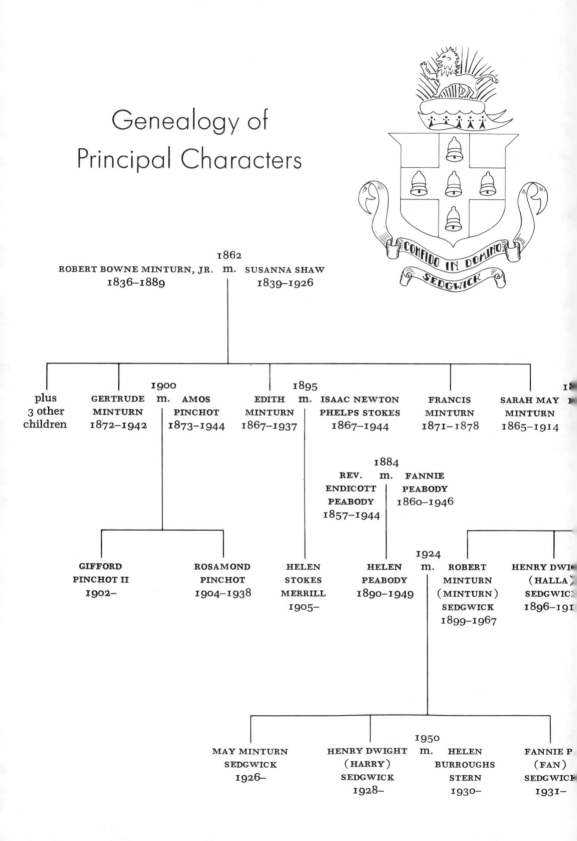

CONFIDO IN DOMINO

SEDGWICK

1862
ROBERT BOWNE MINTURN, JR. m. SUSANNA SHAW
1836–1889   1839–1926

plus   1900   1895
3 other   GERTRUDE m. AMOS   EDITH   m. ISAAC NEWTON   FRANCIS   SARAH MAY
children   MINTURN   PINCHOT   MINTURN   PHELPS STOKES   MINTURN   MINTURN
            1872–1942   1873–1944   1867–1937   1867–1944   1871–1878   1865–1914

                                                1884
                                        REV.   m. FANNIE
                                        ENDICOTT   PEABODY
                                        PEABODY   1860–1946
                                        1857–1944

                                                            1924
GIFFORD   ROSAMOND   HELEN   HELEN   m. ROBERT   HENRY DWI
PINCHOT II   PINCHOT   STOKES   PEABODY   MINTURN   (HALLA
1902–   1904–1938   MERRILL   1890–1949   (MINTURN)   SEDGWIC
                                1905–   SEDGWICK   1896–191
                                                          1899–1967

                                                1950
            MAY MINTURN   HENRY DWIGHT   m. HELEN   FANNIE P
            SEDGWICK   (HARRY)   BURROUGHS   (FAN)
            1926–   SEDGWICK   STERN   SEDGWICK
                             1928–   1930–   1931–

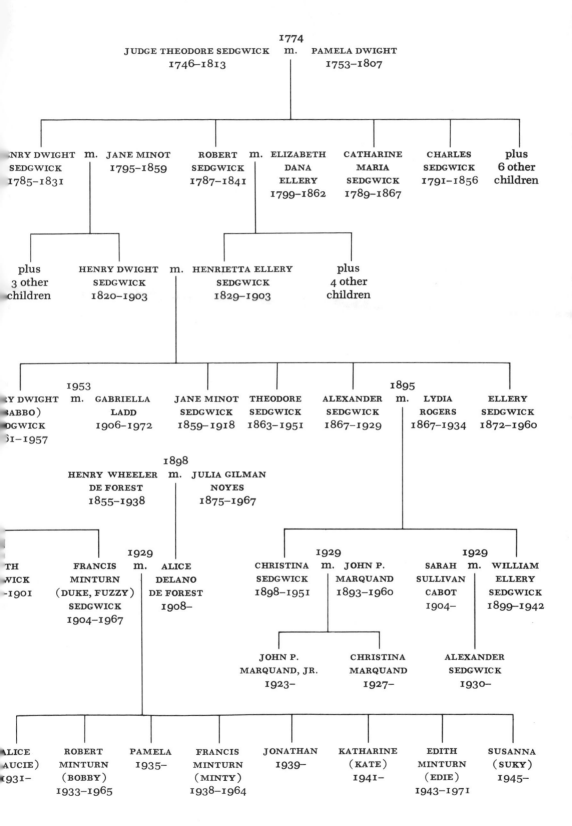

1774
JUDGE THEODORE SEDGWICK   m.   PAMELA DWIGHT
1746–1813   1753–1807

 NRY DWIGHT   m.   JANE MINOT   ROBERT   m.   ELIZABETH   CATHARINE   CHARLES   plus
SEDGWICK   1795–1859   SEDGWICK   DANA   MARIA   SEDGWICK   6 other
1785–1831   1787–1841   ELLERY   SEDGWICK   1791–1856   children
                                                    1799–1862   1789–1867

plus   HENRY DWIGHT   m.   HENRIETTA ELLERY   plus
3 other   SEDGWICK   SEDGWICK   4 other
children   1820–1903   1829–1903   children

1953
RY DWIGHT   m.   GABRIELLA   JANE MINOT   THEODORE   ALEXANDER   m.   LYDIA   ELLERY
ABBO)   LADD   SEDGWICK   SEDGWICK   SEDGWICK   ROGERS   SEDGWICK
DGWICK   1906–1972   1859–1918   1863–1951   1867–1929   1867–1934   1872–1960
1–1957

1898
HENRY WHEELER   m.   JULIA GILMAN
DE FOREST   NOYES
1855–1938   1875–1967

1929   1929   1929
TH   FRANCIS   m.   ALICE   CHRISTINA   m.   JOHN P.   SARAH   m.   WILLIAM
WICK   MINTURN   DELANO   SEDGWICK   MARQUAND   SULLIVAN   ELLERY
1901   (DUKE, FUZZY) DE FOREST   1898–1951   1893–1960   CABOT   SEDGWICK
          SEDGWICK   1908–   1904–   1899–1942
          1904–1967

                                      JOHN P.   CHRISTINA   ALEXANDER
                                      MARQUAND, JR.   MARQUAND   SEDGWICK
                                      1923–   1927–   1930–

ALICE   ROBERT   PAMELA   FRANCIS   JONATHAN   KATHARINE   EDITH   SUSANNA
AUCIE)   MINTURN   1935–   MINTURN   1939–   (KATE)   MINTURN   (SUKY)
1931–   (BOBBY)   (MINTY)   1941–   (EDIE)   1945–
             1933–1965   1938–1964   1943–1971

Afterword

When I began working on this book, in 1972, a close friend of Edie Sedgwick pointed out that Edie kept us all in different compartments. He warned me that learning about her other friends would take ten years. He was right.

I started by interviewing members of Edie's family whom I had known over the years. Some of her relatives did not wish to be interviewed, but those who did, tried, often painfully, to tell what they felt was true. Some of the people interviewed had never met Edie, but knew about the times in which she lived. Before the book was completed, I had interviewed about two hundred fifty people. In 1977, George Plimpton started the herculean task of editing thousands of pages of transcripts. Then we worked together to give the book its present form. After the initial editing process, I found that there were still many unanswered questions, so I continued to edit and to interview people. I am particularly grateful to those individuals who spoke with me again and again.

Every effort has been made to retain each individual's unique conversational style, excerpting entire passages verbatim from the interviews whenever possible, although sometimes it was necessary to combine segments from several conversations to form a single passage. In some cases, names and places have been changed to preserve the anonymity of certain individuals. Naturally, any similarity between their fictitious names and those of persons living or dead is purely coincidental.

JEAN STEIN

433

Biographical Notes

The following notes are about the people who speak in the book. Not everybody is mentioned here; the people not included being those who wished to remain anonymous (their interviews are published under pseudonyms) and those we could not locate.

WILLIAM ALFRED was born in New York City on August 16, 1922, received his B.A. from Brooklyn College and his M.A. and Ph.D. from Harvard University. Since 1954 he has been a member of the faculty at Harvard University, where he is a professor of English. William Alfred's published plays include *Agamemnon, Hogan's Goat, Cry for Us All, To Your Heart's Desire*, and *Nothing Doing*.

MARIO AMAYA was born in New York City in 1933. He received his B.A. in Art and English Literature from Brooklyn College and did his postgraduate studies at London University. Mr. Amaya is an art critic who founded *Art and Artists* magazine in London and contributes to *Connoisseur* magazine and *Architectural Digest*. His books include *Pop as Art, Art Nouveau*, and *Tiffany Glass* as well as numerous exhibition catalogs. He has organized a number of exhibits and has held the following positions: chief curator of the Art Gallery of Toronto; director of the New York Cultural Center, Farleigh Dickinson University; and director of the Chrysler Museum. He is currently the director of Development at the National Academy of Design in New York City.

BOBBY ANDERSEN: "I was hired to be Edie's nurse but quickly became her friend and companion. During the Sixties I was as a rule overdressed, over-drugged, and always on the hustle for a new way to keep a roof over my head without holding a job. Since then I've spent my time trying to recover some

435

semblance of a normal life-style—lots of wasted time looking for a stable relationship and definitely too much time spent getting laid by swines with hoses."

EMILE DE ANTONIO: "I was an acquaintance of Edie's during the Warhol days.
In the Sixties I directed several films—*Point of Order*; *Rush to Judgment*; *In the
Year of the Pig*, etc. I am now working on more films, writing for journals and
writing a screenplay."

JACK BAKER: "I knew Edie's father well but did not meet Edie until the last
night of her life. I was forty in the mid-Sixties, not part of the revolution but very
aware of it through teaching art in Santa Barbara and through my children. I
am a painter and have traveled with exhibitions in Europe, Africa, and India.
Now I travel less professionally and live a quiet, laid-back existence on the beach
south of Santa Barbara and spend part of the year in Hawaii."

GORDON BALDWIN: "I was Edie's friend and a very early accomplice—willing
or not. In the Sixties I attended Harvard, then moved to California, where I ran
a community center, edited friends' books, and drew pictures. Since then I've
received a Rome Prize fellowship and run an out-of-print book business. I draw,
edit, and befriend poets."

G. J. BARKER-BENFIELD: "After growing up in England and taking a B.A. at
Trinity College, Cambridge, I came to America in 1963 to do graduate work in
history at UCLA, where I completed a Ph.D. in 1968. I was appalled at the war
and protested it throughout. I have been unceasingly opposed to prejudice. I am
now writing and am an associate professor of American Social History at SUNY,
Albany."

EILEEN BENSON: "I met Edie in Santa Barbara at the Cottage Hospital whilst
working as a drug abuse counselor. I was born and raised in England and received my R.N. at a hospital in Bolton, Lancashire, before moving to America in
1956 at the age of twenty-three. In the Sixties I was essentially a homemaker
raising three delightful children—Susan, Shawn, and Mark. I was remarried in
1972 to a man who also befriended Edie, and moved to Westlake Village in
1979. My husband is regional manager for an optical company."

RICHIE BERLIN: "Edie was my friend—in the Sixties I was a friend of many,
going from house to house . . . a relentless pursuit of drugs and thinness. I
was an original. A retarded genius. Now I have been sober and drug free for
almost two years. A day at a time—I'm making it. I run—I ski—I go to the
woods—I have a few friends and from time to time I have some fun. I haven't
been back to New York and try not to go back into the past—know what I mean?"

DAVID BOURDON: "I hardly knew Edie, whom I saw only a few times and always
in the company of our mutual friend, Andy Warhol. I began my career as an
art critic by writing a weekly column for the *Village Voice* from 1964 to 1966,
when I became art editor of *Life*. I wore a tie and jacket and kept my hair short

throughout the Sixties. I guess the look could be called Early Ordinary. I've been a freelance writer since 1974 and produce a monthly art column for *Vogue* and contribute frequently to *Architectural Digest*. I've written books on Christo, Carl Andre, and Alexander Calder."

HELEN BRANSFORD: "As a child I knew Edie from visiting Santa Barbara (our families were friends) and rather idolized her as she was several years older than me. After college, I spent several years in England studying silversmithing. I am currently living in Soho designing and selling jewelry privately."

JEFFREY BRIGGS was one of the principals in the film *Ciao! Manhattan*.

ANDREAS BROWN: "I was born and raised in California and am the owner of New York City's Gotham Book Mart. I organized and wrote the catalog for the landmark 1971 exhibit, "Andy Warhol: His Early Works, 1947–1959.""

BARTLE BULL: "I was a friend of Edie's in Cambridge. During the Sixties I was extremely busy trying to combine professional careers in law and publishing with involvement in civil rights issues and politics. I attended Harvard Law School, worked as a Wall Street lawyer with Cadwalader, Wickersham and Taft, and was a civil rights lawyer in Mississippi. In 1969 I purchased the *Village Voice* with Carter Burden and was its president/publisher from 1970 to 1976. In 1980 I became the director of *World Business Weekly* magazine."

SUSAN WRIGHT BURDEN: "Edie and I were pals. In the early Sixties I organized and managed the Paraphernalia boutique. I then went into photography and worked in the light show at the Electric Circus in St. Mark's Place. Throughout the Sixties I studied nutrition and have since been doing nutrition consulting, and in 1978 specialized in widology. I took two to three hours to dress in the Sixties and was always one and a half hours late. Now I have a Casio watch and am punctual to the second."

JOHN CAGE was born in 1912 in Los Angeles and is the composer of numerous works for piano and harpsichord, voice, percussion and electronic devices, audio-visual effects, and orchestra. One of the most influential and innovative artists of the twentieth century (he invented the prepared piano), John Cage is also the author of *Silence*; *A Year from Monday*; *M*, and *Empty Words*. He is a member of the National Academy and Institute of Arts and Letters.

TRUMAN CAPOTE was born in New Orleans and educated in New York City and Greenwich, Connecticut. After leaving school at seventeen, he worked briefly as a fortune-teller's assistant before landing a job at *The New Yorker*. He is the author of numerous books, among them *The Grass Harp*; *The Muses Are Heard*; *Breakfast at Tiffany's*; *In Cold Blood*; *A Christmas Memory*; *The Thanksgiving Visitor*; *Other Voices, Other Rooms*; *The Dogs Bark*, and *Music for Chameleons*. Many of his works have been adapted to television and the theater. He himself has written screenplays—*Beat the Devil* and *The Innocents*.

L. M. KIT CARSON: "Like a lot of North Americans coming of age in the Sixties, I thought of myself as an outlaw. The fact that Edie pushed the edge was part of what attracted me to her. I worked as a freelance journalist; my first article was published in *Esquire* in 1966. At the end of the Sixties, I made a mock documentary feature, *David Holzman's Diary* (which Jim McBride directed) that won awards at Cannes, Venice, New York, Mannheim, etc. In the Seventies I founded and ran a film festival and became a kind of wandering film-speaker. In 1975 I married an actress, Karen Black, and we have a son, Hunter. Now I write film scripts (*Short People*; *The Last Work*) and am starting to produce films."

LEO CASTELLI is recognized internationally as a major art dealer. Born in Trieste, he speaks five languages and holds a law degree from the University of Milan. In 1932 he worked for an insurance company in Bucharest, then moved to Paris, where he became a partner in the Gallerie Rene Drouin. In 1942 he moved to New York, where he continued to be involved in the avant-garde art world, but it wasn't until 1957 that he opened a gallery in their home on Seventy-seventh Street. He has since opened two new galleries in SoHo and continues to represent major American artists, including Robert Rauschenberg, Jasper Johns, Andy Warhol, Roy Lichtenstein, Larry Poons, Frank Stella, Robert Morris, and Donald Judd.

GREGORY CORSO, one of the major figures of the Beat Generation, is the author of many volumes of poetry, including *The Vestal Lady on Brattle*; *The Happy Birthday of Death*; *The Mutation of the Spirit*, and *Elegiac Feelings American*.

DIANA DAVIS: "The person called Diana Davis is living in the East and never refers to California as 'the Coast.'"

LAINE DICKERMAN: "I was Edie's roommate at St. Timothy's boarding school in 1958–59. In 1964 I married John Gifford, a fellow student at Rhode Island School of Design. In the Sixties I lived mostly in buildings under construction . . . consciously rejecting stuff we'd grown up with: traditional trappings of comfort, financial security, etc.—pseudohip. After living on a farm commune in Pennsylvania with RISD friends, we moved back to Cambridge in 1972 and I worked as an artist. In 1976 I started Straight Wharf Restaurant in Nantucket with my husband and friends, which has become successful. I am currently working on banners, taking courses at Harvard Divinity School, working at the restaurant in the summer and am a part-time tennis pro."

PETER DWORKIN: "In the Sixties I was an overweight precocious hippie, always rather younger than my friends and associates (having been born in 1949). I talked a better game than I played. I worked jobs and bummed it till 1971, when I spent a year at the Corcoran Art Gallery in Washington, D.C., with Walter Hopps, and subsequently five years at the Museum of Modern Art in New York. Since 1977, I have owned and operated a small gallery and shop, Equator, down in SoHo, specializing in American folk art."

ISABEL EBERSTADT: I live in New York City and have two children.

PREACHER EWING: "My name is David Sawyer Ewing and for a brief time I was the Princess's consort. Together we exhausted the scenery from quixoticism to bathos. I opened the Seventies in a motorcycle repair shop and closed them in a film editing room, where I still spend an inordinate amount of time."

JUDY FEIFFER: "I was a close friend of Edie's and spent the Sixties going crazy. I was a wife, a mother, and finally pulled the act together and went out and got a job. Since then, I've spent my time keeping sane."

DANNY FIELDS is the editor of *Country Rhythms*, a magazine about country music and its personalities. He is writing the book and songs for a musical. He is also the publicity director of The Ritz, a nightclub in New York City.

SYDNEY J. FREEDBERG is the Arthur Kingsley Porter Professor of Fine Arts at Harvard.

GEOFFREY GATES: "I was Edie's puzzled but intrigued neighbor and casual friend. During the Sixties, I was working on Wall Street, becoming involved in some work with the Indians in the Southwest and generally trying to be a little too hip. After leaving Wall Street for some ventures in films, oil, and real estate, I am now back in the securities business managing investments for several people who probably appear in this book, among others. More importantly, I am the father of two boys and married to the writer Wende Devlin."

HENRY GELDZAHLER: "I was a friend and counselor of Edie's. During the Sixties I was the curator of Twentieth Century Art at the Metropolitan Museum of Art. I remained a curator and, in 1978, became Commissioner of Cultural Affairs for the City of New York."

ALLEN GINSBERG, one of the principal poets of the Beat literary movement, is the author of *Howl*; *Kaddish*; *Planet News*; *The Fall of America: Poems of These States*; *Mind Breaths*, and *Plutonian Ode*. A member of the National Institute of Arts and Letters to which he was elected in 1973, he won the National Book Award in 1974, and is co-director of the Poetics School at Naropa Institute, Boulder.

THOMAS C. GOODWIN: "I was a good friend of Edie's and a professional associate (chauffeur and companion when her leg was broken). In the Sixties my life-style evolved from psychedelic preppy pop to Marin County country hip. I worked as a hospital E.W. orderly, New York bartender, West Indies charter boat mate and skipper before graduating from Harvard. After work as assistant camera and assistant editor on *Ciao! Manhattan*, I moved to California and have worked in film and television since, now in Washington, D.C."

JOHN P. GRABLE: "As I don't wish to divulge my life history to the public, just tell 'em, 'Mad John is alive and well in Isla Vista.' God Bless Edie!!!"

SAM GREEN: "I was Edie's audience, accomplice, and friend. As director of the Institute of Contemporary Art in Philadelphia during the Sixties, I spent every waking moment there aching to be in New York, and when I got there I spent every moment not missing anything. I'm still living in New York—not missing anything."

HELEN HARRINGTON: "My relationship to Edie was men and bars. During the Sixties I was occupied with men, water, and painting; silver, velvet, and cold lofts, cold, very cold lofts with some tropical release sailing across the Atlantic. Since then continuing the plot and adding babies. I like bats—mostly fruit bats, also Victorian diamond bats."

EDMUND HENNESSY: "I think it was in 1963, at the beginning of my senior year at Harvard that I met Edie in Cambridge. I was living in Paris the next year, when Edie arrived with Andy Warhol and her two white mink coats. I liked Edie's acquisitive new friends, and later in New York I became a 'Factory person' for a while and acted in a few of Andy's and Paul's movies. In the late Sixties I started working in a rare book shop and spent ten quiet and industrious years there. During that time I assembled the best Max Beerbohm collection in private hands. Tiring of dirty and dangerous New York, I moved to San Francisco a few years ago. Tiring of clean and safe San Francisco, I have recently moved back East and plan to return to New York, which I miss terribly—dirt, muggings, porno shops, sales tax, Moonies, and all."

MARY BETH HOFFMAN: "I lived in Paris from 1967 to 1979. A son was born to me in '75 and a daughter in '79. Am presently living in Aspen, Colorado, with my husband, Robert E. Fulton, and two children. We make films (experimental) on perception and fly bush planes—needless to say, we hike and ski."

CHARLES HOLLISTER was a childhood friend of the Sedgwick children. He is currently the dean of Graduate Studies at Woods Hole Oceanographic Institute and a senior scientist there in Geology and Geophysics. He is working on "high energy benthic boundary layer experiments—the effects of chepsal cements and radioactive waste disposal on the deep sea floor."

JASPER JOHNS was born in Augusta, Georgia, and lived in South Carolina during his childhood with his grandparents and other relatives. After studying at the University of South Carolina, he went to New York in 1949 and attended art school for a short time before being drafted into the Army. He then lived in downtown New York, supporting himself by working in a bookstore and making displays for stores, including Tiffany & Co. His work has been exhibited in museums and galleries in the Americas, Europe, and Japan, including the Museum of Modern Art, the Smithsonian, the Whitney Museum of American Art, and the Tate Gallery. Jasper Johns is a member of the National Institute of Arts and Letters. At present he lives in the country outside New York City and in St. Martin, French West Indies.

BETSEY JOHNSON: "Edie was my first fitting model in 1965 when I designed clothes for Paraphernalia. I did lots of 'silvers' (jerseys and plastics) for Edie and did her clothes for *Ciao! Manhattan*. Now I'm designing velvet and satin collar cuffs for dresses!!"

IVAN KARP: "I was a wincing acquaintance of Edie's. During the Sixties I was observing in wonderment, as always."

ALEXANDRA (SANDY) KIRKLAND: "I was Edie's friend. In the Sixties, I was going to school. Now I am a housewife."

GEORGE KLAUBER: "I am president of Klauber/Roberts, a graphic design firm and adjunct professor of Graphic Design at Pratt Institute. The rest of the time I spend pursuing multifarious interests and avoiding as much as possible the invidious responsibilities of landlording my brownstone in Brooklyn Heights."

KENNETH JAY LANE: "I was Edie's friend and a friend of her family, as well as an old friend of the Andy Warhol set (particularly Andy). In 1963 I invented costume jewelry for the beautiful people—was lionized by them and became one of the most splendidly beautiful of them—a genuine Sixties character! Handsome, tall, thin . . . sitting in the back of my vintage Rolls (and matching driver) wearing either my floor-length leopard—or monkey—or unicorn, coat— all of which have disappeared. Today I am the same—only less lionized—less beautiful and less splendid. I am now a genuine Eighties character."

WENDY LARSEN: "My family—also a large one of seven children—lived on a ranch in Santa Ynez, a few canyons over from the Sedgwicks as the crow flies. We were all friends with the younger Sedgwicks—Edie, Kate, Minty, and Jonathan."

RICKY LEACOCK: "My relationship to Edie was worshipful. In the Sixties I was discovering and delighting in the new *cinéma-vérité* film technique as well as making film projections for Sarah Caldwell's Opera Company of Boston. I am now teaching and making films at MIT."

ROY LICHTENSTEIN was born in New York City in 1923. He gained international prominence in the early 1960s with his comic-strip paintings. He has had numerous one-man shows, including retrospectives at the Whitney Museum of American Art in New York and the Tate Gallery in London.

LANCE LOUD is living in New York and goes to a school for video art with the intention of becoming a television producer. "I do a hundred jumping jacks a day and juice two pounds of spinach and two pounds of carrots daily. I don't do windows."

MOLLY MCGREEVY: "It is so weird to look back on what I now perceive as a trendy life of Caligulan excess. What was I doing in the Sixties? Entertaining. Playing can-you-top-this. Being stoned. Wearing the shortest minis. Owning the Popest Art. Producing tasteful but unsuccessful movies. Acting in tasteless but successful plays in Kansas City. Having a formal sit-down dinner for twelve in Halls store window to promote something or other. And laying the ground for divorce, near-breakdown, conversion. I thought the Vietnamese War was a miniseries on TV! How did I manage to remain eighteen for so long? I now think I'm being granted a brief period of adulthood before I lapse into senility. I have gone back to school and am getting my master's in theology at General Seminary. Some of my friends are waiting for this activity to pass, sending me get well cards in the meantime."

THOMAS JAMES MC GREEVY: "I was a friend of Edie's brother, Bob. In the Sixties I was collecting kinetic art in New York. Now I'm eating enchiladas in Santa Fe."

NORMAN MAILER, author, playwright, filmmaker, mayoral candidate, actor, has twice won the Pulitzer Prize—in 1969 for *The Armies of the Night* (for which he also won the National Book Award) and in 1980 for *The Executioner's Song.*

GERARD MALANGA: "I was a close friend and confidant of Edie and associate to Andy Warhol in silk screening and filmmaking. In the Sixties, I also was writing and publishing poems and producing my own films. I continue to publish books of poems with Black Sparrow Press; travel extensively giving poetry readings at universities and colleges; using the photography medium to meet people and create works of art. I like to think of myself as having escaped from the Dionysius, which had long claws, articulated hands, and may have been warm-blooded. I see myself as a life-long anti-establishment man. I divide my time between New York City and Millbrook, in upper New York State."

JEAN MARGOULEFF: "I served as Mayor of Great Neck Estates from 1969 to 1973."

ROBERT MARGOULEFF is a record producer and recording engineer whose records include four platinum albums, eight gold albums, ten gold singles, three Grammy nominations, and a Grammy Award for engineering Stevie Wonder's *Innervisions.* As an engineer specializing in acoustic construction, he has built or improved world-class recording facilities and nightclubs. He is also a musician and pioneer in synthesizers who has performed on many albums for other artists and also performs his own work with Malcolm Cecil under the name Tonto's Expanding Headband.

JOHN P. MARQUAND, JR.: "Edie's grandfather and my grandfather were brothers. In the Sixties, I had my shoulder to the wheel and I lived on West Fifty-seventh Street in Manhattan. Now I live on West Fifty-fourth Street, three blocks farther downtown, with my shoulder closer to the wheel."

TAYLOR MEAD: "I was an acquaintance of Edie's and made numerous films with Andy Warhol, including *Lonesome Cowboys*; *Nude Restaurant,* and *Imitation of Christ.* Other films include *The Red Robbins* with Kenneth Koch; John Schlesinger's *Midnight Cowboy,* and more recently Eric Mitchell's *Underground USA.* I have been working on films with Michel Auder, Gary Indiana, and John Chamberlain; giving poetry readings and writing."

HELEN STOKES MERRILL is a first cousin of Francis Sedgwick and lives in New York and Bedford Hills.

DUANE STEVEN MICHALS was born in McKeesport, Pennsylvania, in 1932 and received his B.A. from the University of Denver. Mr. Michals is a photographer whose work has appeared in *Vogue, Esquire,* the *New York Times,* and other periodicals. He is also represented in the permanent collection of the Museum of Modern Art in New York City, Chicago Art Institute, and the George Eastman House. He is the author of the following books of photography: *Sequences; The Journey of the Spirit After Death; Things are Queer; Take One and See Mt. Fujiyama,* and *Real Dreams.*

DR. JOHN MILLET worked as a physician for the Austen Riggs Foundation in Stockbridge, Massachusetts, when he met Francis Sedgwick. He was a founder and the medical director of the Silver Hill Foundation in the Thirties. In the early 1940s, Dr. Millet was affiliated with the Association for Psychoanalytic Medicine and was one of the founders of the Columbia University Center for Psychoanalytic Training and Research—the first psychoanalytic institute in this country affiliated with a university. Dr. Millet contributed to research on allergic disturbances, peripheral vascular disorders, and psychosomatic medicine. In the Sixties he was the assistant dean at the New York School of Psychiatry. He was a chairman of the executive committee of the World Federation for Mental Health and a fellow of the New York Academy of Medicine and the American Psychiatric Association. Dr. Millet died February 18, 1976, at the age of eighty-seven in Nyack, New York.

PAUL MORRISSEY was born in New York City and received his college education at Fordham University. After serving in the Army, Mr. Morrissey worked for an insurance company and the Department of Public Welfare. He was involved in independent film production for four years prior to working with Andy Warhol on such films as *Chelsea Girls; Four Stars; Bike Boy; Nude Restaurant; Lonesome Cowboys; Blue Movie; L'Amour; Women in Revolt.* His pictures include *Flesh; Trash; Heat; Andy Warhol's Frankenstein,* and *Andy Warhol's Dracula.*

BILLY NAME: "Edie and I were amico. In the Sixties I was a lighting designer and photographer. . . . I lived like a comet, and since the Sixties have been doing the planetary canon."

VICTOR S. NAVASKY is a graduate of the Yale Law School and a journalist whose work has appeared in many forums, from the celebrated *Monocle,* which he helped to found, to the *New York Times,* where he worked as an editor. His book *Kennedy Justice* was nominated for the National Book Award. Mr. Navasky published *Naming Names,* a book about Hollywood blacklisting. Since 1978 he has been the editor of *The Nation* magazine. He lives in New York City with his wife and three children.

BOB NEUWIRTH: "I'm well and I continue to make art."

NICO: "Edie and I were co-stars and friends. In the Sixties I was modeling and acting and singing. Since then I have been the author of songs and a singer of 'dirgelike songs themselves full of girlish Gothic imagery and a spacey romanticism' (John Rockwell, *New York Times*, 1979). I have a new album coming out."

MICHAEL NOVARESE: "I met Edie once at the Santa Barbara Museum when I was doing an evening fashion show. My career has since expanded into men's wear. I have been making personal appearances across the country in specialty shops for men's wear and also as a fashion consultant. My dress is a very classic manner. Hair always being closely cut, a well-trimmed mustache, and always sporting a bow tie. I am told that I have a very pleasant outgoing personality. This possibly is one of the reasons making personal appearances and giving personalized fashion shows have always been easy for me."

NAN O'BYRNE: "Maybe the reason Edie and I cared for each other and became friends had to do with some very basic agreement that I can't quite put my finger on. . . . She had a much harder job than I with so many people to please and satisfy. I flunked out of the University of Texas in 1961 and moved to Berkeley. Most of the Sixties I spent out of the country in Italy, Asia, and Mexico—the rest of time I spent in New York, Berkeley, or Austin. In the late Sixties I worked at Capra Press in Santa Barbara, then moved to Los Angeles in 1975. I worked in graphics and book design until the middle of 1980 when I started writing music and that's what I'm doing now."

PATRICK O'HIGGINS was an editor at the old *Flair* magazine when he first met Helena Rubinstein in 1950. He was her confidant and personal secretary for fifteen years until her death in 1965 at the age of ninety-three. He detailed the story of their association in *Madame: An Intimate Biography of Helena Rubinstein*. Mr. O'Higgins was published in *Town and Country, New York*, and *Harper's Bazaar* before his death on June 21, 1980.

ONDINE: "I am living quietly cultivating friendships and relatives, and creating things in a more relaxed way. I'm through with drugs, the Sixties, and most aspects of the film and theater scene of New York . . . but I'm not ruling anything out. I remember Edie fondly and feel no remorse at her death or anyone else's either. To describe me now I would say that I'm overweight, graying, and have the air of a rather important actor who's kind of gone to seed around the edges. It's quite obvious I eat and drink very well and I carry my weight like a dancer. I am knowledgeable in almost everything; but cooking, religion, *Maria Callas*, and guilt feelings are my specialties."

JANET PALMER is currently living in England.

JOHN PALMER distributed *Ciao! Manhattan* in Europe, with David Weisman. He is now involved in sailing and photography in the South Pacific.

PHILIP PEARLSTEIN was born in Pittsburgh, Pennsylvania, in 1924, received his B.FA. from Carnegie Institute of Technology and his M.A. from New York University. He has had numerous one-man shows at galleries in the United States, Europe, and Canada, as well as group shows and retrospective exhibits.

Mr. Pearlstein received a Fulbright fellowship, a Guggenheim fellowship and was a National Endowment for the Arts grantee in 1968.

LESTER PERSKY was Edie's friend, confidant, and admirer. Since the Sixties he has produced *Equus*; *Hair*, and *Yanks*. He is now producing *Handcarved Coffins*, by Truman Capote, directed by Hal Ashby; and *Lone Star*, directed by Robert Altman, among other projects.

MICHAEL POLLARD acted in *Melvin and Howard*.

JEFFREY POST lives in California.

MICHAEL B. POST lives in California.

SHARON PREMOLI: "I knew Edie when she first moved to Cambridge. It was her gray Mercedes period—we lived in her car. I never wanted to get out, but I finally did and moved to New York for a while before moving to Rome. I had trouble leaving there as well. After several years and an ex-Italian husband, I have returned to New York where I live with my daughter Sasha. She goes to school, and I am involved in real-estate investments and try to return to Italy as often as possible."

RICHARD RAND: "I am a New York–based scholar and writer."

ROBERT RAUSCHENBERG was born in Port Arthur, Texas, in 1925 and was educated at the Kansas City Art Institute, the Academie Julien in Paris, the Art Students League in New York (where he studied with Rytlacil and Kantor), and Black Mountain College in North Carolina, where he worked with Josef Albers. His work has been shown in the United States and Europe since 1951. He has received many prizes and awards, including the grand prize at the Venice Biennale. Rauschenberg is active in the politics of art, having founded Change, Inc., a foundation aiding artists in coping with financial emergencies, and lobbying in favor of tax-exempt status for works donated by artists to nonprofit institutions.

RANDY REDFIELD: "I am now the Comtesse Charles-Constantin de Toulouse-Lautrec, and I was a friend of Bobby Sedgwick, Edie's brother. Widowed in the early Sixties, I spent several years on the road (Europe studying Japanese and the Far East putting it to use) with my infant daughter, then married a Frenchman and lived a provincial housewife's life for the rest of the decade. In 1970, I bought a farm and started learning how to raise sheep and horses. I'm still farming and still learning. Through it all, I fit right in with the scenery at hand."

JACK REILLY was the bartender at the Casablanca when Edie lived in Cambridge. He now owns Ryles Bar in Cambridge, Massachusetts.

RENÉ RICARD was seventeen when he hitchhiked to New York from Boston and ended up appearing in the Warhol film *Kitchen* with Edie Sedgwick. He has traveled extensively since 1965. He is an art critic, publishing essays in

Art Forum and *Art in America,* and has done catalogues for galleries in the Netherlands and France. He is also a poet whose work has appeared in anthologies. The Dia Art Foundation published a book of his poetry, *René Ricard: 1979–80.*

DOMENIQUE ROBERTSON: "I was a good friend of Edie's and a freelance journalist for French-Canadian newspapers and magazines during the Sixties. I am now writing poetry and raising three children, keeping a sense of humor."

EDUARDO AGUSTO LOPEZ DE ROMAÑA: "After dropping out from mathematics in 1969, I received my M.S. in electrical engineering from the University of Southern California. I worked for Sierra Audio before joining Disco Vision Associates in 1980. Today I work at managing video disc mastering equipment at their Watson plant. I am still not married."

BARBARA ROSE is a writer and art critic. She received a B.A. from Barnard, and studied at the Sorbonne before receiving an M.A. from Columbia University. Ms. Rose has taught at Sarah Lawrence and Yale, and has worked as a contributing editor for *Art International*; *Art in America and Artforum*, and *Arts Magazine.* She is the author of *Claes Oldenberg*; *Pavilion—Experiments in Art and Technology* (co-author); *American Art since 1900 and Readings in American Art*; *American Painting*, and *Patrick Henry Bruce.*

PAUL ROTHCHILD: "During the early and mid-Sixties I was involved in the folk movement. Produced sixty albums, including albums by Phil Ochs, Tom Paxton, and the Paul Butterfield Blues Band.

"During the rock years produced fifty albums, including all of the Doors except their last album; Janis Joplin's last album, *Pearl*; two by Bonnie Raitt, *Sweet Forgiveness* and *Home Plate*; and the first two albums by The Outlaws. Most recently musical director on *The Rose*, which was nominated for a Grammy Award and an Academy Award."

LILIAN SAARINEN, born in New York in 1912, studied art with Alexander Archipenko while she was still a teenager. Her sculpture is in the collection of the Fogg Art Museum, Cambridge, and the Addison Museum Gallery, Andover, Massachusetts.

GLORIA SCHIFF was the fashion editor, *Harper's Bazaar*, senior editor, *Vogue* magazine, and she says she is "now passionately interested in Chinese studies and tennis."

JOEL SCHUMACHER has lived in Los Angeles since 1972. He writes and directs movies: *Sparkle*; *Car Wash*; *The Wiz*; *Amateur Night at the Dixie Bar and Grill*; *The Incredible Shrinking Woman.*

ETHEL SCULL: "I have studied art since I was nine years old. I went to Parsons and the Art Students League. Painted privately in Larry River's class in Great Neck. Good talent but no genius, so I collected. In the Sixties I was one of the foremost art collectors, especially of Pop Art. It was hectic . . . stimulating . . . effervescent. Meeting the artists in their studios and galleries, I discovered the major artists of the Sixties: Johns, Rauschenberg, Rosenquist, and Segal, etc. My life had all the glamor and glitter of a Hollywood starlet's. I broke my back in 1971 and art life ceased until 1980 when I began lecturing on art at the Museum of Modern Art, the Guggenheim, universities, and for private tours."

ALEXANDER SEDGWICK: "I am Edie's second cousin. I was a college teacher in the Sixties and am still the same."

FANNIE P. SEDGWICK (FAN): "Youngest child of Helen and Minturn Sedgwick. Having completed a happy earlier career at three levels of government in Washington, D.C., and in New York, I am now savoring the rewards of entrepreneurism, recruiting computer professionals. I am presently living in San Francisco."

HARRY SEDGWICK: "I am Edie's first cousin. I was heavily involved in New York City politics and in my business world of new ventures during the Sixties. My life was on a very conventional track: family, business, civic affairs. Then, prodded by intense and successful psychoanalysis, I began to look in and move out. The late Sixties and Seventies were a random walk—growing up with my kids and exploring or, rather, groping through a series of relationships with women who were important to me. Looking back on it, I suppose I was still conventional . . . only the rules had changed. Life gets better and better. My children are flying. My businesses flourish as I do. So beginneth the Eighties!!!"

JONATHAN SEDGWICK is living in California.

ROBERT MINTURN SEDGWICK was graduated from Harvard in 1921, where he had played on the football team that won the Rose Bowl in 1920. After teaching at Groton, Mr. Sedgwick became an investment counselor with Scudder, Stevens and Clark from 1927 to 1963, when he formed his own concern, Sedgwick Financial Services, Inc. He was a member of the Porcellian Club; trustee of Groton School; chairman of the board, Garland School, Boston; board of directors of the State Street Trust Company of Boston; board of directors of Riggs Foundation, and chairman of the board of the Massachusetts Society of Prevention of Cruelty to Children. Mr. Sedgwick died January 5, 1976, at the age of seventy-six.

SAUCIE SEDGWICK is married and mother of one son. She lives in New England, where she works for a scholarly publication.

SUKY SEDGWICK is living in California.

GEORGE SEGAL is a native New Yorker, born in 1924. He was graduated from New York University and earned a master's degree at Rutgers. He was a member of Hansa Gallery and first showed his paintings in 1955. Mr. Segal made his first sculpture in 1958, and has become famous for his tableaux of white figures, done from live models, in real-object environments.

PATTI SMITH moved to New York from Pitman, New Jersey, in 1967 when she was nineteen. Although she was initially interested in drawing, she soon began writing poetry and gave readings accompanied by musicians. She is a published poet (books include *Seventh Heaven*; *Kodak*, and *Witt*), playwright and a rock musician. Her albums include *Horses*; *Easter*; *Radio Ethiopia*, and *Wave*.

PETER SOURIAN: "I knew Edie through her brother Bob, who was my roommate at Harvard, Eliot House, 1952–55. I was in the U.S. Army—finished in late Fifties and began publishing novels in the Sixties (*The Gate*; *The Best and Worst of Times*; *Miri*). I have taught college English, especially at Bard College, since 1965. Since 1970, I have been TV critic for *The Nation*."

TERRY SOUTHERN: "His relationship to Edie has perhaps best been described as biblical. Born in Alvarado, Texas, he received his B.A. from Northwestern University in 1948, and then studied at the Sorbonne in France until 1950. His novels include *Flesh and Filigree*; *The Magic Christian*; *Candy*, and *Blue Movie*. Screenplays include *Dr. Strangelove*; *The Loved One*; *The Cincinnati Kid*; *The Magic Christian*; *Barbarella*; *Easy Rider*, and *End of the Road*. Mr. Southern has written many short stories and critical essays, an anthology of which appeared under the title *Red Dirt Marijuana And Other Tastes*. He is currently completing a novel, *Youngblood*."

HELEN BURROUGHS STERN: "After six years of playing house, Harry Sedgwick and I were divorced in 1956. . . . By the time I was twenty-four years old, I had given birth to three Sedgwick children. In 1957 I married Philip Stern, or he married me, however one sees it. Philip and I set up house in Washington, where we had two more offspring. I then spent most of the Sixties attempting to erase forever all memory of the Fifties. No purge was ever more unsuccessful . . . life was chaotic as Fibber McGee's closet, into which I kept stuffing more and more awful mistakes. Gradually, things are sorting out. I am now a sculptor, artist, and songwriter and received an undergraduate degree in anthropology at the top of my class from George Washington University. Since 1978 I've been a teacher of Mexican orphaned children and recently I've organized a cottage industry: we are making beautiful greeting cards from designs that the orphans themselves make, which earned $15,000 this Christmas for the orphans."

PATRICIA SULLIVAN: "I knew Edie through Gillian and John Anthony Walker. Despite the Sixties I wore a lot of basic black and pearls, led a frivolous life by night in New York and purported to have a serious bank job by day. I still live in New York and now work for an environmental organization."

SANDY TALLEY's husband T died in 1973. She has since remarried and now works for the Department of Motor Vehicles in California.

JONATHAN T. TAPLIN: "I only met Edie twice. In the Sixties I was going to college and working as a road manager for Judy Collins, Bob Dylan, and The Band on the side. Moved to Woodstock, New York, in 1969 where Dylan and The Band were living. Now I am producing films: *Mean Streets*; *The Last Waltz*; *Carny*, and am president of Lion's Gate Films."

RONALD TAVEL: "As Andy Warhol's scenarist from December 1964 through the summer of 1966, I wrote the first sound films in which Edie appeared: *Vinyl, Kitchen, Space.* I wrote mostly plays during the Sixties and named and founded the Theatre of the Ridiculous movement, July 29, 1965. I also published a novel (Olympia Press) and wrote some commercial screenplays and treatments. Published a number of cinematic essays and some poetry. Since 1975, when I taught at the Yale University Divinity School, I have been on and off connected with Ivy League universities. I have also been involved in regional theater in New England, central New York State, Washington, D.C., etc."

VIRGIL THOMSON, composer, music critic, and conductor, was born in Kansas City, Missouri, in 1896. His works include *Four Saints in Three Acts* and *The Mother of Us All* (operas with Gertrude Stein); *Lord Byron* (with Jack Larson); *Fantasy in Homage to an Earlier England; Ode to the Wonders of Nature; The Plow that Broke the Plains* and *The River* (films with Pare Lorentz); *Louisiana Story* (with Robert Flaherty), and many works of orchestral and chamber music. In addition to serving as chief music critic for the New York *Herald-Tribune* from 1940 to 54, his writings have appeared in *Vanity Fair* and the *New York Review of Books.* There are also eight books, including *Virgil Thomson by Virgil Thomson* and *A Virgil Thomson Reader.*

WENDY VANDEN HEUVEL: "I am Jean Stein's daughter and I've grown up with most of the people in this book. I am now a student at the New York University Experimental Theater School."

CHERRY VANILLA: "My relationship to Edie was cosmically casual. In the Sixties my life-style was psychedelic, but I am now poetry in motion. Ah, the mystery of what makes history!"

"GORE VIDAL wrote his first novel, at nineteen, *Williwaw,* aboard an Army freight-supply ship in the Aleutian Islands during World War II. Among his novels are *The City and the Pillar; Washington, D.C.; Myra Breckinridge; Burr,* and *Creation.* Among his plays are *Visit to a Small Planet* and *The Best Man.* Politically, he is active—to say the least."

VIVA: "I've had two daughters, published two books, *Superstar* and *The Baby,* and a political novel is nearly completed. I've made roughly four hundred videotapes in collaboration with my ex-husband, done several video shows, and acted in seven or eight movies—in the last one, a film by Wim Wenders, my eldest daughter played my daughter. I've done a lot of TV and presently am obsessed by politics and economics, in particular the so-called Third World. I'm rather belatedly exploring Marxism but have come to realize that probably stripping the male sex of most of the privileges that have stealthily crept up on them may be necessary before we move on to the equally important installation of a world Marxist economy. I know all you readers will say I'm entrapped by an outmoded nineteenth-century idea; nevertheless, I stick ferociously to my guns."

DIANA VREELAND: "I was a friend of the family and, as editor of *Vogue,* where Edie posed for us—which she did beautifully—I was her employer. I am now special consultant to the Costume Institute of the Metropolitan Museum of Art."

"GILLIAN WALKER is a family therapist at the Ackerman Institute for Family Therapy in New York City."

JOHN ANTHONY WALKER lives in Auroville, Southern India.

ANDY WARHOL—artist, filmmaker, author, magazine publisher—attended Carnegie Institute of Technology before moving to New York City to pursue a career as an illustrator. One of the most famous of the Pop artists, Mr. Warhol has had one-man exhibitions at the Leo Castelli Gallery, Ferus Gallery, Stable Gallery, Morris Gallery, and the Sonnabend Gallery, as well as being exhibited in major museums around the world. Mr. Warhol has also directed and produced numerous films and has received the Film Culture Award and the Los Angeles Film Festival Award for his work. He produced the rock group Velvet Underground, and continues to publish *Interview* magazine. His books include *Andy Warhol's Index*; *Andy Warhol's Philosophy from A to B and Back Again*; *Popism: The Warhol 60's*, and *Andy Warhol's Exposures*.

CHUCK WEIN: "Edie and I were mock elitists in fellowship based upon how fucked-up everyone else was. I was her roommate, shrink, astrologer, and Tarot instructor. I spent the Sixties adventuring in the Far East, managing bizarre nightclub acts like Rosita the python lady, a French drag queen and two over-the-hill Australian strippers. I spent '62 in Copenhagen stoned on absinthe. In '63 I sat at the Café de Paris in Tangier long enough to be asked to cover the Algerian/Moroccan border war for the English papers. I attended Harvard in the Leary acid-experiment days. Now I am too busy receiving ancient friends to describe my present trans-Amazon discoveries . . . besides, I'm sure to attract the most prurient of interest. Name of next film, *Lunar Cross*, about Nazis on the moon in 1946."

DAVID WEISMAN: "I returned to California from Europe in 1974 and spent several years recovering from *Ciao! Manhattan*. I subsequently became involved with film advertising and marketing as well as developing new screen properties. In addition to co-producing *Shogun Assassin* in 1980, I worked on the production and worldwide marketing of the docudrama, *The Killing of America*."

BRUCE WILLIAMSON: "Before joining *Time* magazine as a staff writer and film critic (1963–1966), then *Playboy* as movie critic-contributing editor (since 1967), I was writing freelance, clever sketches and songs for Julius Monk's Upstairs-Downstairs and Plaza 9 revues—going straight after my early post-Columbia University years as a Beatnik, actor, usher (CBS-TV) and social misfit. I don't remember how I looked in the Sixties. . . . I have bought up and destroyed the negatives of all photos known to exist."

JANE WYATT's husband, Edgar B. Ward, went to Cate School and Harvard College with Edie's father. The Wards and the Sedgwicks have been close friends ever since. Jane Wyatt worked in TV and the theater, and her husband has been involved in investment management.

Acknowledgments

The listing of acknowledgments does not begin to suggest the support, the advice, and the many hours that thoughtful people gave George Plimpton and me for this book.

A profound appreciation to the following members of Edie's family who gave generously of their time: John P. Marquand, Jr., Helen Stokes Merrill, Alexander Sedgwick, Fan Sedgwick, Harry Sedgwick, Jonathan Sedgwick, Saucie Sedgwick, Suky Sedgwick. I sadly regret that Minturn Sedgwick is not here to see the final form of the work which he encouraged and to which he contributed so much.

I would especially like to thank Edie Sedgwick's husband, Michael Post, for the many hours he generously gave me.

I am deeply grateful to the following individuals: to Gillian Walker for her invaluable critiques, her assistance, and encouragement since the book's inception; to Christina Spilsbury, who for the past two years has worked with the greatest dedication and spirit on every aspect of the book from editing to typing the manuscript in its many incarnations; to Walter Hopps who has worked tirelessly and with great sensitivity on editing the photographs for the book; to Dorothy Schmiderer for her fine work in designing the book; and to Guy Fery who created the book's jacket.

I also wish to thank Robert Gottlieb, the publisher and editor, and Martha Kaplan, for their editorial advice and for their persistence and faith in this book.

I am deeply indebted to the following: Richard Avedon, Rainer Crone, Katrina vanden Heuvel, Wendy vanden Heuvel, William vanden Heuvel, Robert Margouleff, Jane Nisselson, John Palmer, Freddy Plimpton, Michael Post, Doris Stein, Dr. Torsten Wiesel, Chuck Wein, David Weisman, and Bruce Williamson.

I am sorry that the following individuals are no longer alive to be thanked for their important contributions to the book: Roger Baldwin, Stanley Levison, Dr. John Millet, and my father, Dr. Jules Stein.

I am also extremely grateful to the few who gave invaluable critiques, but who wish to remain anonymous.

The following I would also like to thank for their generous contributions to the book: Bobby Andersen, Joyce Baronio, Eve Babitz, Richie Berlin, William vanden Bossche, Susan Wright Burden, Leo Castelli, Joseph Chaikin, Langdon Clay, Maude Schuyler Clay, Nita Colgate, Lady Diana Cooper, John Coplans, Sarah Cross, Johanna Mankiewicz Davis, Dorothy Dean, Adrian DeWind, Patty Dryden, Dennis Dwyer, Isabel Eberstadt, Robert A. Edwards, Poly Eustis, Preacher Ewing, Jane Friedman, Dr. James Gaston, Dr. Willard Gaylin, Henry Geldzahler, James Goodale, Richard Goodwin, John Gossage, Stephen Graham, Lily Guest, Ann Gyory, Shirley Haizlip, Amy Harrison, Randolph Harrison, Wesley Hayes, Melinda vanden Heuvel, Pamela Hill, Fayette Hickox, Debra Hodgson, Dr. Anne Houdek, Barbara Warner Howard, Cy Howard, Robert Hughes, Jay Iselin, Deborah Kahn, Doris Kearns, Adrienne Kennedy, Stephen Koch, Lesley Krauss, A. Fredric Leopold, Ellis Levine, Bea Levison, Sterling Lord, Rupert Lowenstein, John McCormick, Judith McNally, Gerard Malanga, Dr. Judd Marmor, Rebekah Maysles, Jessica Mitford, Joan de Mouchy, Lynn Nesbit, Ondine, Robert Oropall, Susan Pearce, Pauline Pierce, Donald Pennebaker, Eileen Prescott, Elaine Prince, Joe Pula, Irving Rudd, Charlotte Salisbury, Larry Schiller, Richard Schoolman, Alan Schwartz, Guillermina Seguel, Timothy Seldes, Betty Sheinbaum, Stanley Sheinbaum, John Silberman, Terry Southern, Paul Spike, Bert Stern, Dr. Daniel Stern, Elizabeth Stille, Sandee Talley, Marietta Tree, Myra Tweti, Viva, Charles De Vries, Lew Wasserman, Anthony West, Lally Weymouth, Tom Wicker, and Terry Young.

For assistance in research, transcribing, and typing, day and night, I am especially grateful to Barbara Shalvey, who worked tirelessly and with great dedication since the beginning of this book as a transcriber. Then I would like to thank the following for the hard work and energy which they gave to this book: Carol Atkinson, Cynthia Babak, Abbe Bates, Joe Babine, Kathy Babine, Robert Becker, Paul Bloom, James Collins, Wendy D'Lugin, Philip Heckscher, Alice Knick, Nancy Looker, Richard Macsherry, Luke Mattheissen, Ester Nordin, Susan Otte, Janine Robbins, Mary Louise Rubacky, Amy Schewel, Allison Silver, Kathy Slobogin, Shirley Sulat, and Hallie Gay Walden.

For reasons of structure, the following people who were interviewed do not appear in the book, but their influence on it was not small: Pamela Wilder Barnes, Peter Barnes, Stanley Bard, Toddy Callaway Belknapp, Nina Bernstein, Rosie Blake, Alan Blank, Franziska Boas, Susan Bottomly, Amanda Burden, John Cale, Christopher Cerf, Patrick Tilden Close, Rhett Dennis, Timothy Dickenson, Jim Dickson, Luiji Facciuto, Charles Henri Ford, Suzy Frankfurt, Ashton Hawkins, Brooke Hayward, Dr. Clinton Hollister, Jane Holzer, Dennis Hopper, Jackie Horner, Robert Hughes, Sophie Klarer, Billy Kluver, Greg Knell, Stefan Krayk, Ron Kuchta, Sique Kuchta, John Larsen, Dorothy Lichtenstein, Sy Litvinoff, S. Lockwood, Donald Lyons, Earl McGrath, Gene Moore, Christina Paolozzi, Francis Plimpton, Oakes Plimpton, Marcia Pressman, John Richardson, Larry Rivers, Robbie Robertson, Mickey Ruskin, Stephen Shore, Mort Sills, Steven Soles, Saul Steinberg, Bert Stern, Gloria Steinem, Dr. Ian Story, Dr. John

Talbott, Katrina Toland, Dennis Vaughn, Edgar B. Ward, Gwen Warner, Tennessee Williams, Bud Wirtschafter.

I would like to thank the following organizations for their cooperation: The Harvard Club, The Massachussetts Historical Society, The New York Genealogical & Biographical Society, The New-York Historical Society, The New York Society Library, the *New York Times*, the Performing Arts Research Center of the New York Public Library, and the Historical Room of the Stockbridge Library Association.

Picture Credits

Finkelstein, Black Star. PAGE 186: Courtesy of Ranier Crone. PAGE 190: Mrs. Warhola and Andy Warhol high school portrait—Collection of John Richardson. PAGE 191: Andy and his mother—Duane Michals. Shoe—Collection of Truman Capote. PAGES 210–211: Gino Piserchio. PAGE 227: Collection of Viva. PAGE 241: Bob Adelman. PAGE 244: Photo by Enzo Selerio, Condé Nast Publications. PAGE 248: Photos by *New York Times,* Fred Eberstadt, *Life* magazine. PAGE 251: Photo by Fred Eberstadt, *Life* magazine. PAGE 253: Mick Jagger—Richard Marx. Philadelphia—Collection of Sam Green. PAGE 258: Andy—Alfred Statler. PAGES 272 AND 277: Raenne Rubinstein. PAGE 291: Richard Avedon. PAGE 297: Collection of David Weisman. PAGE 300: Photo by Gianni Penati, Condé Nast Publications. PAGE 304: Langdon Clay. PAGE 312: Maude Schuyler Clay. PAGE 344: David Chaimers Marks. PAGES 350–351: Donald Macsorley, Courtesy of Richard Leacock. PAGE 364: John Gossage. PAGE 373: Preacher Ewing. PAGE 378: Eduardo Romaña. PAGE 382: Collection of Sandee Talley-Hanline. PAGE 391: Richard Davis, Collection of David Weisman. PAGE 392: Eduardo Romaña. PAGE 395; Top—Richard Davis, Collection of David Weisman. Bottom—Collection of David Weisman. PAGE 399: Richard David, Collection of David Weisman. PAGE 402: Hal Boucher. PAGE 405: Joseph Babine. PAGE 411: Production of WNET/ Thirteen, Title Design by Eli Bunin/Photo by Don Perdue. Beverly Jackson. PAGE 426: John M. Fox.

Special thanks to Billy Name/Factory Foto, whose photographs appear on pages 210–211, 233, and 281. To Stephen Shore for photographs on pages 181, 202–203, 207, 210–211, 215, 219, and 231. To Terry Stevenson for the frontis, and pages 262, 320 from the David Weisman Collection, 324, and 330. And to Gerard Malanga for pages 210–211, 244, and 227 from *Screen Tests/A Diary* by Gerard Malanga and Andy Warhol—Collection Malanga; page 236: Factory Foto/Collection Malanga; page 293: Photo by Gerard Malanga.

A NOTE ON THE TYPE

The text of this book was set on the Linotype in a
face called Primer, designed by Rudolph Ruzicka,
who was earlier responsible for the design of Fairfield and Fairfield Medium, Linotype faces whose
virtues have for some time now been accorded wide
recognition.

The complete range of sizes of Primer was first
made available in 1954, although the pilot size of
12-point was ready as early as 1951. The design of
the face makes general reference to Linotype Century—long a serviceable type, totally lacking in manner or frills of any kind—but brilliantly corrects its
characterless quality.

This book was composed by Maryland Linotype
Composition Co., Inc., Baltimore, Maryland. It was
printed and bound by The Haddon Craftsmen, Inc.,
Scranton, Pennsylvania.

Typography and binding design by
Dorothy Schmiderer